OWN YOUR OWN FRANCHISE

Everything You Need to Know about the Best Opportunities in America

Ray Bard and Sheila Henderson

A Stonesong
Press Book

ADDISON-WESLEY PUBLISHING COMPANY, INC.
Reading, Massachusetts   Menlo Park, California   New York
Don Mills, Ontario   Wokingham, England   Amsterdam   Bonn
Sydney   Singapore   Tokyo   Madrid   Bogotá
Santiago   San Juan

Many of the designations used by manufacturers and sellers to distinguish their products are claimed as trademarks. Where those designations appear in this book and Addison-Wesley was aware of a trademark claim, the designations have been printed in inital capital letters (i.e., Dunkin' Donuts).

Although every effort has been made to insure that all information is accurate and up-to-date, the authors or publisher cannot be held responsible for any errors that may appear, nor for any liability or loss incurred as a direct or indirect consequence of the use and application of any information contained in this book.

Library of Congress Cataloging-in-Publication Data

Bard, Ray.
   Own your own franchise.

   "A Stonesong Press book."
   1. Franchises (Retail trade)—United States.
I. Henderson, Sheila, 1950–   . II. Title.
HF5429.235.U5B37   1987   658.8'708   87-14389
ISBN 0–201–11439–9

A STONESONG PRESS BOOK

Cover design by Copenhaver Cumpston
Text design by Joyce C. Weston
Set in 10-point Times Roman by Compset, Inc., Beverly, MA

ABCDEFGHIJ-DO-8987

First printing, August 1987

ACKNOWLEDGMENTS

A book of this scope involves the cooperation and efforts of many people. We appreciate the willingness of the selected franchise companies to work with us. They took the time to complete our detailed questionnaire and respond to our telephone queries. Many others made valuable contributions. Mr. Neil Blickman of the Federal Trade Commission and Mr. Andrew Kostecka of the Department of Commerce were particuarly helpful. The timely work of our contributing writers, Susan Elliott, Ruth Kent, Bonnie Skaar George, Jeanette Brown, Barbara Johnston, Eric Von Jares, Susan Kettler, and Teri Nelms, made it possible to meet our publication deadline. Linda Webster did her usual good work with the geographical directory. Sherry Bykofsky, managing editor of The Stonesong Press, was instrumental in the early development of the book plan and in the editing of the manuscript. George Gibson and Cyrisse Jaffee, our editors at Addison-Wesley, made many useful suggestions and provided encouragement throughout the process.

Ray Bard
Sheila Henderson

CONTENTS

INTRODUCTION

HUNDREDS of thousands of people have started new businesses in the last decade—aptly labeled the age of the entrepreneur. Many of them have purchased a franchise and, as a result, franchising has boomed and is now the fastest-growing segment of American business, accounting for more than $550 billion in goods and services in 1986. The Department of Commerce recently estimated that U.S. franchises have more than 478,000 outlets and over 6 million employees. In the last fifteen years the number of companies offering franchises has more than doubled to over two thousand. John Naisbitt, the author of *Megatrends,* predicts that between now and the year 2000 the percentage of national retail sales that come from franchises will increase from the present one-third to over one-half. He also has projected that franchise sales will top $1.3 trillion by 2010.

Franchising is a system used by a company (franchisor) that grants to others (franchisees) the right and license (franchise) to market a product or service and engage in a business developed under the franchisor's trade names, trademarks, service marks, and methods of doing business. The International Franchise Association (IFA) defines franchising as "a continuing relationship in which the franchisor provides a licensed privilege to do business, plus assistance in organizing, training, merchandising, and management in return for a consideration from the franchisee."

Franchising is now successful and popular for several reasons. Potential investors and owners find it attractive because franchising companies offer tried and true business models as well as start-up assistance and follow-up support. And although the start-up funds required for a franchise are often more than the cost of starting up alone, the failure rate of franchises is significantly less than for other types of individually owned businesses. In 1987, Andrew Kostecka, the Department of Commerce franchise specialist and author of the department's annual publication *Franchising in the Economy,* stated that "for the last ten years, the failure rate for franchises has been less than 4%." Various sources indicate that the independent-business failure rate is far higher. Kostecka thinks it is at least 50%; others estimate it even higher.

1

Our purpose in writing this book is to provide readers with information about some of the top franchise companies operating in the country. There are a number of sources available that attempt to list all or most franchise companies, but such references can do little more than list the company name, address, and type of business. By offering depth instead of breadth this book is unique and invaluable among franchise guides. We have selected, according to the criteria described below, those franchises that offer the best opportunities. In addition, we have gone far beyond the usual brief listings by providing franchisor profiles that describe in detail the business and industry of which they are part; what it takes to buy in and get started; the ongoing assistance and support the parent company provides, as well as what is required to make it work; and other valuable information about the company and the industry. These profiles will enable you not only to compare opportunities among several franchise companies but also to become more knowledgeable about franchise opportunities in general.

The research for this book started with a detailed survey and questionnaire mailed to hundreds of companies. This was followed up with further research and telephone contact with many responders. Before making our final choice of which companies to include in this book, we decided on four selection criteria. The companies profiled here

- are actively seeking franchisees in several states;
- have been franchising this business for a minimum of three years;
- have at least twenty units operating;
- and during the last three years have shown growth or remained relatively stable in the number of units operating.

We were looking for only those franchisors that have sustained a certain level of growth and success. If a company wants to expand in only one or two states or, for whatever reasons, is not seeking new franchisees, we did not include it in the book. For indicators of longevity and size we assumed that a company would have its business concept tested and most of the bugs worked out after three years and with at least twenty units in operation. If a company had not maintained some level of growth or stability in its number of units during the last three years, we took that as an indication of problems within the company or the industry in general. Additionally, we took care to include franchise companies that represent a wide variety of industries and investment levels.

We mailed a detailed four-page questionnaire to the 455 companies that met our criteria. Almost 200 companies responded, and from those we chose our final 160. We carefully followed up the questionnaires whenever necessary with personal telephone calls and analyzed all the information received, so the entries are more than a recapitulation of the company promotional packets we advise you to write for. Some companies did not respond to the questionnaire, so we have doubtless omitted companies worthy of inclusion. But we are confident *Own Your Own Franchise* contains a splendid mix of in-depth profiles that will inspire anyone who has ever had entrepreneurial dreams.

How to Use This Book

Each entry contains the following categories of information.

STATISTICS

The *Statistics* section, presented in table form, shows both the year the company began and the year it began franchising its particular business. The number of units the company had in operation in 1985 and 1986, broken down into several categories according to ownership and location, are then projected for a two-year period. A few companies declined to provide us with projections. In those cases a N/A (not available) appears in place of the data. The start-up investment required, including the franchise fee, is also given in dollars. Some companies such as Chem-Dry Carpet Cleaning have a standard start-up investment ($8,400). Other companies, such as National Video, have a range of investment alternatives ($39,000 to $250,000), depending on the type of store and the initial inventory. A review of this numerical profile will give you a sense of the growth the company has been experiencing, the mix of company and franchisee units, the mix between units in the United States and in other countries, the number of states represented, and the company's short-term plans.

The numbers indicate where the company has been and where it plans to go, but they don't tell the whole story. Use the information in this first section to get a partial picture of the company's trends and formulate questions to search out more information. If a company is growing slowly, it may be either undergoing a prudent, well-planned expansion or instead facing a lack of working capital. On the other hand, a rapid expansion could be either the result of a successful concept or product with all the necessary support personnel and resources or an indication that the company is stretched thin and won't be able to support your operation adequately. Because of the nature of their service, some franchise companies can expand much faster than others.

THE BUSINESS

The *Business* section provides basic information about the industry and the company. It includes yearly company sales, average franchisee gross sales, and average franchisee net revenue. (Some companies would not provide us with the average franchisee gross sales and average net revenue.) The section also provides a description of the nature of each company's service or product.

When planning to invest in a franchise, you will have much better odds of success and of achieving a good return on your investment if the industry trends are favorable. For example, franchises such as restaurants and maid services look good now because of the growing number of women who enter the labor force creating a problem of less household time available for food preparation and home maintenance. However, do take the time to investigate beyond the first level of the trend. All restaurants are not growing at the same rate. What tastes are changing and how rapidly? Pizza's popularity may remain steady; beef consumption may slow down. Look also at the competition. In maid services, for instance, many companies are jumping on the bandwagon to take advantage of the working-woman trend, and some are better than others. Also, when looking for a franchise, keep in mind that a unique and desirable product or service can give you a competitive edge in the marketplace.

The financial numbers provide an indication of the volume of business, but *when you review the average franchise's gross sales and net income figures, remember that those numbers are only averages and are in no way meant to be a guarantee.* If you are interested enough to seriously discuss investing in a specific franchise, closely examine any earnings claim documents the company provides. Such claims are not required, and many companies do not offer them. If the claims are available, ask for detailed supportive information on how the estimated income was determined. See the Franchise Checklist at the end of the Introduction for specific questions to ask before buying a franchise.

WHAT IT TAKES

This section covers the financial requirements (at the time of our research) for investing in the franchise and other specific qualifications that you as a franchise owner may need. Investment information includes the initial franchise fee, the range of the total initial investment, the amount required in cash, and the availability of financial assistance. Information is also provided about the way each territory (if any) is determined, the length of the franchise agreement and any renewals, the cost of additional units, the availability of master franchises, the acceptability of passive ownership, and the nature of royalties and other ongoing fees or payments. Some franchisors require specific industry experience or education, but most feel that their training programs and support systems—along with your commitment and hard work—are sufficient for a successful operation.

Among many details, you should consider the following carefully.

- The financial aspects of the franchise arrangement should be clearly spelled out. Closely check the information provided by the company and request further information on any requirements not entirely clear.
- Check one company's fees and royalty rates against others' in the same industry and then compare the services the companies provide.
- If it is important that you have a specific territory, are there provisions for it to be protected adequately? Negotiating an exclusive territory can be the most important aspect of buying a franchise.

GETTING STARTED

This section takes you from the time you sign an agreement to the grand opening. It covers whether and how the company will help you choose a site and help plan, construct, decorate, equip, and furnish your operation. It also indicates how long it will take you to get started after you have signed the franchise agreement. Information is provided about size and location of facilities; any special requirements regarding the facility design, product purchases, or company working relationships; the type and number of personnel you will initially need to hire; what is covered and who is included in the initial training program; and company assistance for your grand opening.

Although we have provided as much information as possible, some information (i.e., qualifications of the company staff) you will need to ascertain when you talk to the company representative and other franchisees. Try to pin down details on

- the length and nature of the ongoing assistance promised by the company;

- any charges beyond the franchise fee for the start-up assistance provided, particularly any hidden costs, such as transportation and lodging during training;
- the extent and nature of involvement by company personnel who will help prepare your facility for business;
- the length of the training program and the topics covered, as well as what supportive materials, such as manuals, will be provided to help get you started;
- the kind of advertising program available for your grand opening and the portion of the cost that will be shared by the company.

The amount and quality of company assistance provided during this phase can represent considerable savings in time and money for you. An excellent source for more detail on the questions just cited is someone who already owns one of the company's franchises in the geographic area you are considering. Don't hesitate to ask questions about any concern you may have.

MAKING IT WORK

This section explains the ongoing support that is provided by each franchisor to make your business achieve its profit potential. This continuing assistance may include advertising, public-relations, and marketing support; regular meetings, conventions, and training programs; office supplies, business forms, or management systems; product manufacturing or distribution systems; research and development of new products or services; and special financial arrangements, such as accounts-receivable financing and group insurance programs.

The information in the book provides a base for you to sort out what services are covered by the ongoing fees you will be paying. Use the information in the company profiles and discussions with the company representative and franchisees to compare the amount you will be paying on a monthly basis with the services that will be provided by the company. Are there services or materials that will require you to pay an additional fee? How available are company personnel after you get started? Can they be easily reached when you need technical assistance?

Although effective franchisor support is essential to your success, *you* are still the key to making your franchise fly. Be prepared to spend even more time than you may anticipate on the day-to-day running of your franchise and on the crucial task of keeping good relations with the parent company.

COMMENTS

This section includes miscellaneous pertinent information about the company—rankings from the 1986 *Venture* magazine and 1987 *Entrepreneur* magazine (if applicable); information regarding membership in the International Franchise Association (IFA); the availability of an earnings claim document; locations where franchisees are being sought; and any special additional information about company ownership, industrial honors, or community service.

The rankings from *Venture* and *Entrepreneur* are included to indicate how other sources have rated the company. Any ranking of companies is complex and depends on the criteria chosen for comparison, so use the rankings only as additional information rather than the final word. *Venture*'s "Franchisor 100"-list is based on ROI (return on investment). It is based on a relatively small sample (an average of three franchises per franchise company) and by admission "is far from an exact science." *Entrepreneur*'s "Franchise 500"-ranking formula includes several factors, such as years in business, number of operating units, start-up costs, and growth rate. Nevertheless, the magazine warns that "comparing franchise companies is like comparing apples and oranges."

The IFA is a trade association formed in 1960 to serve the interests of firms involved in franchising. It has become the spokesperson for responsible franchising and encourages high standards of business conduct. New members are screened carefully and must pledge to adhere to a comprehensive code of business ethics and an ethical advertising code. The IFA has developed a good reputation because of its efforts in promoting fair business practices and disclosure of information. Its Code of Ethics is printed at the end of the Resources section (see p. 409). If a company is a member of the IFA, this means that the company has met the requirements of conduct for membership. As with all organizations, however, membership does not absolutely guarantee ethical and honest dealings. Nor does nonmembership mean a company uses shady business practices. When you are requesting information from a company that does not belong to the IFA, you might ask why it doesn't.

Whether or not a company provides an earnings claim document, it is important for you to obtain information about what revenue, expenses, and income you can generally expect from your investment in the franchise. As much as possible, this information should be obtained from the company. There is confusion in the industry about the Federal Trade Commission (FTC) disclosure rule whereby companies must provide certain information to potential franchisees. The FTC does not restrain companies from making claims of possible earnings, but it does require that franchisors provide information regarding the basis and assumptions for any earnings claims, including the percentage of existing franchises that have actually achieved the results claimed.

**GETTING MORE
INFORMATION**

This section describes the kinds of materials you will receive when you request franchise information from the company. Many companies have packets that are comprehensive; others are more limited. The names, addresses, and phone numbers of each company contact are listed for your convenience.

CHOOSING A FRANCHISE

You may browse through the book looking for names and businesses that catch your eye, or you may institute a more systematic search. The three indexes that appear at the end of the book are structured to facilitate your franchise shopping. The first index lists the 160 franchises according to business type, industry category. The second is organized by the amount of investment required. And the final index provides a geographical listing of the companies that are seeking to open new franchises in each of the states and in foreign countries at the time of this writing.

If you prefer to purchase a franchise in the state in which you live, the best way to begin the search is by using the geographical index to see what companies want to expand in your state. A few companies, such as McDonald's, ask that candidates for franchises be willing to relocate, but most will evaluate the opportunity for their business in your location. When you have narrowed your interest to one or several franchises that are available in your state, you will want to read profiles of similar companies to get as much information as possible about how franchising works for that particular business. And, as we have discussed, you will want to contact current franchisees.

The industry index allows you to locate easily all of the franchises included within a certain industry. For example, if you are interested in the growing automotive aftermarket, you could use the index to locate all of the oil and lube, muffler, and rustproofing franchises included in the book by checking the Automotive section.

If you have a specific amount of money available to purchase a franchise, you may want to use the investment index. It breaks the working capital needed into categories, beginning with under $10,000 and ending with more than $500,000. Many companies provide financing directly or have made arrangements to assist you in acquiring financing from other sources; if so, you may find you can afford a higher start-up level.

After you have identified the type of business you are interested in purchasing and have read the profiles of various companies, you may want to extend your search beyond this book, using what you have learned to seek information more knowledgeably about franchises not covered here. Make a trip to the library for a search of magazine articles published in the last two or three years about the industry and the franchise companies you have identified as potentially right for you.

After you have done some research and narrowed your interest to a few companies, you can request that they send their information packet. If the packet does not include a disclosure statement, request that they send you one. The Federal Trade Commission requires that all franchisors provide disclosure statements to prospective buyers at least ten business days before money is accepted or an agreement is signed. The FTC also requires that prospective franchisees receive the disclosure statement at the time of or before their first personal meeting with the franchisor. Franchisors are not required to register their offering with the FTC, and the disclosure rule does not regulate the terms of the agreement between you and the franchisor; but the disclosure statement does provide you with some good information. It should include information on the following twenty-two subjects; and if it does not, you should get the missing information from the franchisor or from independent research.

1. Information identifying the franchisor and its affiliates and describing their business experience.
2. Information identifying and describing the business experience of each of the franchisor's officers, directors, and management personnel responsible for franchise services, training, and other aspects of the franchise program.
3. A description of the lawsuits in which the franchisor and its officers, directors, and management personnel have been involved.
4. Information about any previous bankruptcies in which the franchisor and its officers, directors, and management personnel have been involved.

5. Information about the initial franchise fee and other initial payments that are required to obtain the franchise.

6. A description of recurring or isolated fees or payments franchisees are required to make after the franchise opens.

7. A description and itemization of the franchisee's initial investment, including an accounting of all expenditures (which may be specific or estimated by a low-high range) that the franchisee will be required to make in setting up the franchised business.

8. Information about any restrictions requiring purchase or lease of goods and services used in the franchise from the franchisor, its affiliates, or other designated sources.

9. Information about any restrictions on the quality of goods and services used in the franchise, including any requirements that the franchisee purchase such goods and services, in accordance with specifications provided by the franchisor, from designated sources.

10. A description of any assistance available from the franchisor or its affiliates in financing the purchase of the franchise.

11. A description of all supervision, assistance and other services which the franchisor will provide to the franchisee, including any training programs provided to franchisees and any assistance in selecting a site for the franchise that will be provided by the franchisor.

12. A description of any territorial protection that will be granted to the franchisee.

13. A description of the trademarks, service marks, trade names, logo types and other commerical symbols owned by the franchisor that will be licensed for use by the franchisee.

14. A description of any patents or copyrights owned by the franchisor, whether the franchisee may use them, and the terms and conditions under which the franchisee may use them.

15. A description of the extent to which franchisees must personally participate in the operation of the franchise.

16. A description of any restrictions on the kinds of goods and services the franchisee may sell, and whether the franchisee is restricted as to the customers to whom he may sell goods and services.

17. A description of the conditions under which the franchisee may repurchase, renew, or transfer ownership of the franchise, as well as conditions under which the agreement may be terminated or modified by either the franchisee or the franchisor.

18. A description of the involvement of any celebrities or public figures in the franchise.
19. A complete statement of the basis for any earnings claims made to the franchisee, including the percentage of existing franchises that have actually achieved the results that are claimed.
20. Statistical information about the present number of franchises; the number of franchises projected for the future; the number of franchises terminated, the number the franchisor has decided not to renew, and the number repurchased in the past; and a list of the names and addresses of other franchisees.
21. The financial statements of the franchisor.
22. A copy of the Franchise Agreement and other contracts or agreements which the franchisee must sign.

We can't stress often enough how important it is to collect information from people who have already been running a franchise you are considering. Other people who have made the decision to purchase and operate the franchise will often tell you firsthand about the financial arrangements, the start-up and ongoing assistance provided by the company, and how much profit can realistically be expected. Although it is required by law to give you only a partial list, the company should provide you with a complete list of its franchises. If it offers only a partial list, ask for a complete one, at least for the franchisees in your state or geographic area. Don't talk to just one or two franchisees; contact several. The time you spend talking to others by phone or in person can be one of your best investments. They are the best sources to get a feel for the hands-on experience of day-to-day operation. Before you make telephone calls or onsite visits, organize your notes to make sure you cover all the important points.

Part of your research about a franchisor should include a check with the Federal Trade Commission (FTC). The Washington, D.C. office keeps a file of complaints about franchisors, and its address and telephone number are in the resource list following the franchise profiles.

Before making a final decision about a franchise investment, you should also seek the assistance of an attorney who is familiar with franchise law. Federal and state franchise laws as well as the particular franchise agreement will need to be reviewed and interpreted. The American Bar Association's Forum Committee on Franchising lists over fourteen hundred member lawyers. Contact your local or state bar association for the names of attorneys in your area who are familiar with franchising. As with other legal specialties, it is important that you find someone who knows the area. Don't be afraid to ask what franchise experience and training an attorney has had.

To help you evaluate the financial aspects of the arrangement, you should also seek the assistance of a good accountant, who can help you examine the franchisor's financial information, assist you in determining the merits and potential of the financial opportunity, and help you make your financial plans and projections.

After all this preparation, you should be ready to make a decision and sign your name on the dotted line. A final reminder: Just because franchises have a much lower failure rate than other businesses doesn't mean that they are an easy street to riches. Although most franchisors will make every effort to help you succeed, your success will ultimately depend on your commitment and long hours of hard work. If you make the decision to own your own franchise, we wish you good franchising and much success.

Making the Decision: A Checklist for Evaluating Your Choice

There are five elements critical to your success as a franchise owner: you, the product or service, the market, the franchise company, and the franchise agreement. When you begin to investigate seriously whether or not franchising is for you, these five areas should be carefully evaluated. All five are critical to your success.

YOU

Before you spend the time investigating specific opportunities, you should start with yourself. It will be your efforts that turn any business opportunity into well-earned profits. You need to feel positive about franchising and what you have to offer before you proceed with your investigation. The Small Business Administration and the International Franchise Association are good sources of materials to help you learn more about franchising. Here are some questions you should consider before proceeding:

1. Are you ready to risk your time and money?
2. Are you willing to put in long hours for several years to make the business a success?
3. Do you like managing on your own?
4. Do you work well with people?
5. Are you a self-starter?
6. Do you consider yourself ambitious, enthusiastic, and positive?

7. Can you manage lots of little pieces at the same time?
8. Can you take care of details, monotonous tasks, and other routine items?
9. Can you listen to and accept assistance from others?
10. Do you have or can you acquire enough working capital to buy a franchise?
11. Are you willing to give up some independence to obtain the advantages offered by franchising?
12. Are you in good physical and mental health?
13. Do you have a record of stability and good character?
14. Do you have a good credit rating?
15. Do you have the support of your family?
16. Do you have experience and education that would be helpful in operating a business?
17. Do you understand the various legal structures you can create for the business (proprietorship, partnership, or corporation)?

PRODUCT OR SERVICE

When you are ready to investigate seriously franchise opportunities, it is important to find a product or service you want to represent. Checking with customers and competitors as well as the company can give you information about the product or service. Here are some appropriate questions in this regard:

1. Can you be enthusiastic about working with the product or service?
2. Is there something about the product or service that gives it a competitive advantage?
3. Is it a high-quality, reputable product or service?
4. Has the product or service been market tested?
5. Is the source of the product or service reliable?
6. Is the product or service priced competitively?
7. Does it have patent or trademark protection?
8. Is it covered by any guarantees or warranties?
9. Does it meet safety, health, or any other federal or state standards?
10. Is the product or service well known because of national advertising?
11. Are there new products or services in development by the franchise company?

MARKET

Regardless of how hard you might work and how good your product or service might be, you need enough of a market to make you successful. Time spent in a library researching industry trends would certainly pay off. The periodical index will guide you to recent articles about specific businesses. Consider these questions about the market:

1. Is the overall industry growing, remaining steady, or declining?
2. What is the demand for the product or service in your area?
3. Are there competitive products or services in your area?
4. How does the franchised product or service compare in price and quality with those existing in your local market?
5. Is there a year-round or only a seasonal demand for the product or service?
6. Is there a long-term demand for the product or service, or is it likely to be more faddish?
7. Has there ever been a franchise awarded in your territory? What happened?
8. Is the population in your territory projected to grow, remain stable, or decrease in the next few years?

THE FRANCHISE COMPANY

It is important that you learn as much as possible about the company. You and the company will become partners for the length of the franchise agreement. You need to feel good about working with the company's personnel. Information about the company can be obtained from the company itself; from back issues of the business publications such as the *Wall Street Journal, Business Week, Forbes,* and so forth; from credit-rating services such as Dun & Bradstreet; if publicly owned, from stock-rating services such as Moody's and Standard & Poor's and from stockbrokers; from Better Business Bureaus in cities where franchises are operating; from the Federal Trade Commission; from state agencies that deal with franchise laws; from bank and supplier references; and from present owners of the franchise. Here are some key questions for you to answer about the company.

1. What are the company's reputation, financial stability, and quality of management leadership?
2. Is there a parent company? If so, what role does your prospective franchise play in the overall company? What are the parent company's reputation, financial stability, and quality of management leadership?
3. Who are the key officers, directors, partners, and managers? What experience do they have in the industry and in franchising?

4. Is the company a member of the International Franchise Association?

5. How strong is the company's balance sheet? How do financial ratios (such as debt to net worth, current assets to current liabilities, and liquid assets to current liabilities) compare to other companies in the same industry?

6. What is the company's credit rating with local and national credit-rating services such as Dun & Bradstreet?

7. Has the company or any of its key officers filed for protection under any of the bankruptcy laws?

8. Have any of the company's officers ever been convicted of fraud or embezzlement or been involved in any civil or criminal litigation?

9. What are the company's short-term and long-term goals?

10. How many people are on the home-office staff? What are their jobs?

11. When was this business started? When was it first franchised?

12. What were total sales for franchise operations last year? The year before? Planned for next year?

13. What is the average gross revenue per franchise? Average net revenue?

14. How many franchisees are now in operation? How many are company owned and operated? How many were added last year? Planned for this year?

15. How many states have operating franchisees? Plans for expansion?

16. How does the company plan to deal with the competition?

17. Has the company franchised other businesses? What is the track record?

18. Has the company been penalized for the violation of franchise law?

19. Has the company been sued by a franchisee? What was the issue? How was it resolved? What has been done to correct the situation?

20. Is there any pending legal action against the company? If so, what is it and what is the likely result?

21. How much does the company spend in research and development annually? As a percentage of revenue?

22. How many franchisees have failed in the last three years? What were the primary reasons?

23. How many franchisees sold their business to someone else in the last three years? What were the primary reasons?

24. How many franchises have been terminated in the last two years? Why?

THE FRANCHISE

When you get to this stage, you need to take time to investigate carefully the details of the agreement. The services of a good CPA and attorney are an essential investment when reviewing the profit potential and the agreement. Be sure to obtain legal and accounting input *before* signing any agreement or paying out any fees. Be sure also to contact people who have already been operating the franchise. They can offer information that can only be gained through experience. Here are the questions:

1. Is the franchise exclusive or nonexclusive? Do you get a specific protected territory?
2. What is the length of the agreement? The renewal period? Terms under which the agreement can be canceled, terminated, or renewed by the company or you?
3. What is the arrangement if you sell the business? Does the company have the right of first refusal? Does the company have the right to approve the buyer?
4. Are you required to manage the business?
5. What is the reasonable profit potential of the franchise? Are company projections based on franchisees' experiences in similar territories? How does the company information match with what owners of the franchise tell you?
6. How much is required to get started? How much in cash?
7. What is the franchise fee? What will you need to spend for land, facility, equipment, materials and supplies, merchandise, staffing, advertising and marketing, and so forth?
8. What services are provided by the company to help you get started (site selection, lease or purchase negotiation, facility layout and decoration, grand-opening plans, service or maintenance contracts, etc.)? Is there a charge for any of these services?
9. Does the company finance any of the initial costs? If so, for how many years and at what interest rate?
10. How much working capital will you need for operating and staff costs until the business reaches a cash-flow break-even point? Are the sales and revenue projections based on other franchisees' experience in a territory similar to yours?
11. Can the company help you with financing (arrangements with banks and other institutions, referrals, etc.)?

12. Who is responsible for finding the location? Does the location have to meet the company's site specifications? If you must find the location, is there enough time (five to six months) for you to do the necessary work?

13. Do you purchase the land or the building or lease either from the company? How long is the lease? Is the lease term for the same time as the franchise agreement?

14. Is there an ongoing royalty fee? If so, how much? When and how is it paid? How does it compare with others in the same industry?

15. Are there requirements on what you must sell? Are there restrictions on what you can sell?

16. Is there a centralized purchasing system? Are you required to use it? Are the prices competitive?

17. Are there special requirements (uniform facility layout, use of company logo, company uniforms for employees, purchase of company products, insurance etc.)?

18. From the time you sign the agreement how long will it take you to start the business?

19. How many employees will you need to staff the business? Full-time? Part-time? What is the salary structure?

20. What kind of initial training program does the company offer? How long does it last? Who pays? Is training for the manager only or for employees too? What subjects are covered?

21. Is there follow-up training? Who is included? How often? What subjects are covered? Who pays?

22. Are there regular regional or national conferences where you can meet and exchange ideas with other franchisees?

23. Is there an ongoing advertising fee? If so, how much is it? How is it paid?

24. Does the company provide advertising, public-relations, or marketing support (newspaper and magazine ads, telephone-book ads, brochures, catalogs, TV and radio commercials, national media coverage, point-of-purchase displays, press-release packets, etc.)? Who pays? Is there a co-op plan where the company shares the costs?

25. What is the company's national advertising budget?

26. Does the company offer customer accounts-receivable financing? What is the cost?

27. What kind of ongoing information does the company provide (company newsletter or magazine, product or service updates, industry or market updates, etc.)?

28. What kind of administrative or managerial support is provided (headquarters or regional resource staff; toll-free hotline; regular onsite visits; policy management-procedure and customer-service manuals; business or accounting forms; accounting, inventory, personnel, and computerized billing systems; computerized operations information; etc.)?

29. How experienced are the members of the company support staff? Do they seem knowledgeable and helpful? How many other franchises does the person assigned to you cover?

30. Is there a company-sponsored insurance program? If yes, what does it cover (general liability, property, auto, life, major medical, dental, disability, worker's compensation)?

31. Does the company sponsor recognition or award programs for franchisees?

32. What information (such as financial statements, audited balance sheets, etc.) are you required to provide the company? How often?

FRANCHISE PROFILES

American International Rent A Car

BUSINESS: car rental
  FOUNDED: 1969
  FRANCHISED: 1969
START-UP
  INVESTMENT:
  $30,000–$500,000

		AS OF		PROJECTED BY	
		1/1/85	1/1/86	1/1/87	1/1/88
NO. OF UNITS					
OWNED BY:	COMPANY	0	0	0	0
	FRANCHISEES	1,300	1,300	1,500	1,650
LOCATED:	IN U.S.	240	240	300	350
	OUTSIDE U.S.	1,060	1,060	1,200	1,300
TOTAL:		1,300	1,300	1,500	1,650
NO. OF STATES W/ UNITS		40	40	48	50

THE BUSINESS

The car-rental industry's expansion over the last thirty-five years has been closely tied to the increase in airline travel. In 1984-85, almost 235 million passengers flew to domestic destinations, compared to 169 million in 1970. This increase affected car-rental revenues: in 1984, industry receipts amounted to over $4.4 billion, up 12 percent over the previous 5 years. They are expected to almost double by 1990 to approximately $7 billion. Although airports generate around 75 percent of car-rental revenues, the suburban market is growing because people are keeping their cars longer and renting for out-of-town business or pleasure trips.

American International Rent A Car has captured a large percentage of the off-airport market with sites located less than two miles from airport terminals. During 1985, several locations were opened in Amtrak stations. AI boasts 30,000 vehicles in 240 domestic locations. Worldwide, the company has 1,300 locations in 33 countries throughout North America, Europe, the Middle East, the Pacific, and Latin America. Revenues for 1985 are estimated at $200 million.

WHAT IT TAKES

Your initial franchise fee will range from $5,000 to $400,000, depending on the size of your rental fleet. Accordingly, your exclusive territory will vary from a five-mile radius from the airport to an entire county. Depending upon your site and fleet, your total initial investment—and the amount you will need in cash—can vary considerably. The term of your agreement will be five years with a five-year renewal. Your royalty fee will be 7 percent of annual gross sales. The company requires no previous knowledge about the car-rental industry. Absentee ownership is discouraged.

GETTING STARTED

You will need an office of about 500 square feet on a sufficiently sized lot. You can locate in a business center near the airport, in a hotel or motel, or in some other appropriate site. The company will help you select the site, design the layout, decorate, purchase or lease your fleet, and plan your staffing. The number of your employees will depend on the size of your operation—about five for a 75-car fleet and twelve for a 200-car fleet. A staff representative will come to your site for one to two weeks to assist with personnel training, accounting methods, fleet planning, general operations, and analysis of your local market and competition. You can open one to six months after you sign the agreement. AI will help with your grand opening.

MAKING IT WORK

AI offers a twenty-four hour toll-free reservation service with an immediate confirmation number that is linked to major airline reservation systems. The 1–800–I AM HERE telephone number eliminates long waiting lines at airport car-rental counters. The customer calls the number upon arrival at the airport, tells the operator his or her location, and is picked up by a courtesy van.

AI's central billing program provides corporate accounts with individual charge cards for authorized frequent travelers, and the corporation receives one monthly statement summarizing rental activity. These services and AI's low rental rates are marketed through an extensive national advertising campaign in airline inflight magazines and travel-industry trade publications. You'll pay no advertising royalty for this media coverage, but newspaper ads, magazine ads, mailers, and brochures are available on a co-op basis.

American International's corporate sales force generates group sales through volume commercial and travel-industry accounts, including major travel-agency consortiums and various branches of the government. AI also participates in conventions and trade shows for commercial accounts, travel agents, tour operators, and wholesalers and sponsors airline-reservation center promotions.

You'll meet with headquarters staff and other franchise holders at the national conference and at two regional conferences each year. Staff will visit your site on a regular basis to help your operation run smoothly, and you'll receive a weekly newsletter and periodic bulletins about new services, the car-rental industry, and company news, such as reports from the research department on fleet programs and new marketing directions.

Your policy, management, and customer-service manuals will be handy reference guides for running your operation. The company also supplies forms for inventory, personnel, ordering, and accounting plus systems for inventory control, bookkeeping, expense analysis, and computerized billing. Finally, the company offers accounts-receivable financing to minimize cash-flow problems.

COMMENTS

In 1987 *Entrepreneur* magazine ranked American International twenty-ninth among its "Franchise 500," and the 1986 *Venture* magazine ranked it eighty-eighth among its "Franchise 100." A member of the IFA, the company is seeking franchisees throughout the United States and in Canada and the Caribbean.

GETTING MORE
INFORMATION

The franchise packet includes four-color marketing brochures, a booklet containing article reprints and AI ads, and a licensee application. For more information, call or write:
Marge Wavernek
Vice-President, Franchise Development
American International Rent A Car Corporation
4801 Spring Valley, Suite 120B
Dallas, TX   75244
(214)   233–6530

American Speedy Printing Centers

BUSINESS: printing
and copying
FOUNDED: 1977
FRANCHISED: 1977
START-UP
INVESTMENT:
$110,000

		AS OF		PROJECTED BY	
NO. OF UNITS		1/1/85	1/1/86	1/1/87	1/1/88
OWNED BY:	COMPANY	0	0	0	0
	FRANCHISEES	284	234	424	524
LOCATED:	IN U.S.	284	234	424	524
	OUTSIDE U.S.	0	0	0	0
TOTAL:		284	234	424	524
NO. OF STATES W/ UNITS		30	32	36	39

THE BUSINESS

Americans currently spend more than $24 billion for printing each year. Although the majority of such printing is for traditional business purposes—annual reports, forms, sales tools, etc.—the demand for printing has increased because of personal and organizational needs, like theater programs, bake-sale posters, and neighborhood association newsletters. American Speedy Printing Centers represent a crossover between the quick-print shops (which have a 13 percent share of the printing business) and large, conventional printing companies. In addition to quick copying, the Speedy Centers handle large, sophisticated projects as well as services such as word processing and computerized mailing lists. In 1985 the total annual volume for Speedy Printing franchises was $50 million.

WHAT IT TAKES

Your Speedy Printing franchise fee will be $37,500, $20,000 of which must be paid in cash. Your total initial investment of $110,000 will include not only the franchise fee but also $34,500 for equipment, $7,500 for leasehold improvements, $20,000 for working capital, and $10,500 for contingency funds. The company can arrange a loan, secured by your personal assets, to supply funds for start-up costs, training costs, and a portion of your initial fees. Normally, equipment is financed on a lease or loan basis. If you are qualified, the company can either provide direct equipment financing or assist you in making application for financing at your bank.

The term of your agreement will be twenty years, and your franchise agreement will guarantee you an exclusive territory determined by zip code. Your royalty fee of 5 percent of your monthly cash receipts (money you have actually collected) will be used to underwrite the cost of ongoing services. You'll also pay an additional 2 percent of cash receipts as an advertising fee. Master franchises are available. If you prefer, you can employ a manager to operate your center on a day-to-day basis.

GETTING STARTED

Your Speedy Printing Center will probably be about 1,200 square feet in a shopping center, office building, or commercial park. A site-selection specialist will use a sophisticated set of criteria to evaluate possible locations for your center. When your site is determined, the company will negotiate the lease and provide you with a custom floor plan that conforms to company specifications for organization and efficiency. You'll also receive advice about equipment and supplies.

The company will help you hire your staff of one part-time and two full-time employees. You will go to the company's education center in Birmingham, Michigan, for two weeks of management and technical training. The curriculum features intensive classroom and laboratory sessions on printing technology, production techniques, marketing, and management. You can attend an optional third week of on-the-job training at an existing center.

You can reasonably expect to open thirty to forty-five days after you sign the agreement. A technical representative will install your equipment, and a franchise consultant will be on hand for the first week to help with organization, administration, pricing, and advertising. The consultant will also assist you in making direct sales calls to get your business off to a good start. In conjunction with your opening week and throughout the first ninety days, the company will initiate a professionally prepared direct-mail campaign to businesses in your area. It will also provide funds for your initial inventory and supplies and for advertising and marketing materials. For the first ninety days after your opening, the home office will check with you weekly.

MAKING IT WORK

Your franchise consultant will conduct ongoing onsite evaluations of your center's appearance, organization, and performance. You'll also receive a quarterly advertising planner, which serves as the foundation for your sales-promotion program. The company coordinates all advertising, promotion, and public relations. One-half of your advertising fee will be allocated for developing and implementing national advertising programs, the other half for local advertising. If there are other Speedy Printing Centers in your area, you can form advertising co-ops to pool local advertising funds to purchase media time and space. In addition to your 2-percent monthly advertising fee, you are required to purchase an ad in your local telephone-book directory.

Your training will continue with regularly scheduled seminars and workshops covering technical, financial, and marketing topics. National conventions and regional conferences are held in alternate years. You can request on-site visits and ask technical, management, or marketing questions on a toll-free hotline. You'll get the company newsletter every six weeks, a monthly company report, and quarterly updates about the printing industry. The company sponsors a variety of franchise achievement awards.

You'll benefit from the company's continual testing of new equipment, services and supplies. Any activities and programs not covered by the royalty fee are often offered at significant discounts due to the company's purchasing power. Your insurance package will cover property, liability, auto, life, dental, worker's compensation, and major-medical insurance needs.

COMMENTS

Speedy Printing was ranked 79th in *Venture* magazine's 1986 "Franchise 100" and 106th in *Entrepreneur* magazine's 1987 "Franchise 500." A member of the IFA since 1977, the company is seeking franchises throughout the United States.

GETTING MORE INFORMATION

The franchise information packet includes a four-color booklet; a question-and-answer brochure; a sheet outlining the procedures, costs, and payment plan; and a personal profile questionnaire. For more information, write or call:
Robert S. Phillips
Executive Vice-President
American Speedy Printing Centers
32100 Telegraph Road
Birmingham, MI   48010
(800)   521–4002 or (313)   645–6333

Athletic Attic

BUSINESS: retail
  sporting goods
FOUNDED: 1973
FRANCHISED: 1974
START-UP
  INVESTMENT:
  $99,500–$232,500

NO. OF UNITS		AS OF		PROJECTED BY	
		1/1/85	1/1/86	1/1/87	1/1/88
OWNED BY: COMPANY		15	16	19	25
FRANCHISEES		170	158	173	188
LOCATED: IN U.S.		170	154	172	193
OUTSIDE U.S.		15	20	20	20
TOTAL:		185	174	192	213
NO. OF STATES W/ UNITS		40	41	43	46

THE BUSINESS

The fitness revolution is a way of life for millions of people—young and old—who make sports-related activities part of their daily lives. They want good equipment, the finest athletic footwear, and the latest fashion activewear. Catering to this market, Athletic Attic franchises grossed $35 million in 1985, with individual units grossing $295,000 and netting a profit of approximately 12 percent of sales. Athletic Attic stores are retail sporting-goods operations specializing in the sale of activewear, apparel, athletic footwear, and related sporting goods (racquetball, tennis, soccer and others). Athletic Attic offers a new concept in women's athletic fashions and footwear. More than ninety of the Athletic Attic stores belong to multiple store owners.

WHAT IT TAKES

Your initial franchise fee will be $7,500, guaranteeing you an exclusive territory negotiated between you and Athletic Attic. The term of the original agreement varies. Your total investment will be $99,500 to $232,500, depending on how much you spend for remodeling or leasehold improvements ($5,000 to $70,000), initial advertising ($1,000 to $3,000), inventory ($70,000 to $125,000), and fixtures and working capital ($16,000 to $27,000). You must invest at least $45,000 in cash and have a net worth of $120,000. The company can assist you in locating potential partners. Additional franchise units sell for $5,000 each, and master franchises are available. You will be expected to manage the business yourself. Your ongoing royalty fee will be 3 percent of gross sales. Prior experience is not required.

GETTING STARTED

Athletic Attic will assist you with site selection; lease-and-purchase negotiation; construction; facility layout and decoration; lease or purchase of furniture, fixtures, and equipment; and acquisition of supplies and merchandise. The typical Athletic Attic is 1,500 to 2,000 square feet, located in a local mall or shopping center or regional mall. You will need three full-time and five part-time employees; the company will help with hiring. Training for all employees will be held at company headquarters in Gainesville, Florida, covering all areas of store operations, including preopening setup, buying, merchandising, open-to-buy, advertising, promotions, and salesmanship. Hands-on training continues for five days, followed by five days of videotape instruction. The company will help with your grand opening, which should be three to four months after buying your franchise.

MAKING IT WORK   As part of your .5 percent monthly advertising fee, you will receive an advertising kit containing newspaper and black-and-white magazine ads, telephone-book ads, presentation books, national media coverage, in-house media packages (slides, videotapes), point-of-purchase displays, signs, banners, contest outlines, seasonal promotional displays, press releases, and a public-relations/marketing manual. Television and radio commercials are also available at nominal cost. The company sponsors a national track club, generating publicity for the Athletic Attic name. Once a year Athletic Attic franchise owners meet for a national convention, supplemented by biannual regional conferences and annual one-day seminars. You'll receive publications from the home office that include company news; management how-to articles; notices of manufacturers' close-outs, special buys, and overstocked items from other stores; business-meeting schedules, and other information to assist you in day-to-day management. Surveys are conducted six times a year. Two awards honor achievement. Backup services include headquarters resource persons; regular onsite visits; manuals for policy, management procedure, and customer service; all types of forms; and systems for bookkeeping, inventory, personnel, expense analysis, and computerized billing. Athletic Attic has a central purchasing program offering volume discounts and company labels on products. You will not be required to sell company products only. However, you must carry insurance against all types of public liability, with personal-injury coverage of a minimum of $200,000 per person, $500,000 per accident, and property damage of not less than $50,000 (cost for the insurance ranges from $1,000 to $2,000 annually).

COMMENTS   *Entrepreneur* magazine ranked Athletic Attic 227th in its 1987 "Franchise 500." A respected track coach, Jimmy Carnes, and world-class distance runner Marty Liquori conceived the idea for this company and are actively involved. Athletic Attic Marketing, Inc., is the parent company. Athletic Attic provides an earnings claim document. The company wants to increase its operations across the United States and in several foreign countries.

GETTING MORE
INFORMATION

The franchise information packet contains brochures on the company's operations and a four-page application form. For details, contact:

Wayne Lindsey
Director of Franchise Sales
Athletic Attic
P.O. Box 14503
Gainesville, FL   32604
(904)   377–5289

Baskin-Robbins Ice Cream Company

BUSINESS: ice cream
  parlor
  FOUNDED: 1946
  FRANCHISED: 1949
START-UP
  INVESTMENT:
  $60,000–$125,000

		AS OF		PROJECTED BY	
NO. OF UNITS		1/1/85	1/1/86	1/1/87	1/1/88
OWNED BY: COMPANY		40	40	40	40
	FRANCHISEES	3050	3185	3285	3385
LOCATED: IN U.S.		2297	2542	2617	2692
	OUTSIDE U.S.	793*	683	708	733
TOTAL:		3090	3225	3325	3425
NO. OF STATES W/ UNITS		49	49	50	50

*Figure includes units on military bases, which have been accounted for in U.S. total since 1986

THE BUSINESS

More than 1.3 billion gallons of ice cream and related products are produced annually in the United States—that's more than fifteen quarts per person each year! Eighteen percent of American households visit an ice cream parlor at least weekly. Baskin-Robbins has established itself as the world's major ice cream company, with more than 3,300 stores in thirty-seven countries and every state except Vermont. It all began when Irv Robbins opened his Snowbird Store in Glendale, California, featuring twenty-one exotic ice cream flavors. In 1946 Robbins entered into a partnership with his brother-in-law Burton Baskin to form the company that has developed over 500 flavors of ice cream and continues to introduce a new flavor each month.

WHAT IT TAKES

Depending on the amount of construction and equipment needed to meet Baskin-Robbins's specifications, the average start-up cost is between $60,000 and $125,000. The company does not provide financing. The term of the initial agreement is for five years with a renewal period of another five years. The ongoing royalty fee is one-half of 1 percent of gross sales. There is also an ongoing advertising fee of 3 percent.

    Experience in the ice cream business is not required to qualify for a franchise, but some business experience is certainly a help. You can purchase a franchise and have someone else manage it, but the company prefers that the owner manage the operation.

GETTING STARTED

After you sign a franchise agreement, Baskin-Robbins will assist you every step of the way—from finding the best location to planning grand-opening details. Store sites are selected by Baskin-Robbins and usually require 600 to 800 square feet of space. The company will help you line up freezer cases and other equipment, as well as the distinctively colored furniture and fixtures and the Baskin-Robbins store signs.

To help you get off to a good start, two weeks of training are provided for you or your manager at Baskin-Robbins's national training center in Burbank, California. The program covers the essentials of operating a Baskin-Robbins franchise—how to handle, prepare, sell, and serve products; recruit, train, and manage employees; and build and maintain customer relations. About ten part-time employees will be needed to staff your store. The district manager will assist you in selecting and training your employees and preparing for your store opening.

MAKING IT WORK

The company holds regional conferences, one- or two-day seminars two or three times a year, and district meetings two or three times a year. Other important information is provided through a twenty-four-page quarterly company magazine and through product updates and market research. Your advertising fee will help support national advertising that includes television, radio, and newspaper ads; in-store displays; and the Baskin-Robbins Rose Bowl Tournament Parade float on New Year's Day. Camera-ready promotional pieces —such as newspaper ads, magazine ads, direct-mail pieces, telephone-book ads, and brochures—are made available for your local advertising.

To help insure your success, the corporate office is available to help with a toll-free hotline, onsite visits from district and headquarters staff, policy and customer-service manuals, an inventory system, and various business forms. The company has regional suppliers from which you can buy the basic thirty-one flavors and other Baskin-Robbins products—or you can make your purchases from other approved suppliers. Baskin-Robbins's national, regional, and local research will provide you with timely information about customer reactions to company products and services.

COMMENTS

The company was selected America's favorite fast-food chain by *Restaurants & Institutions* magazine. It was ranked thirteenth in *Entrepreneur* magazine's 1987 "Franchise 500" and first among ice cream franchises. In 1986 *Venture* magazine ranked Baskin-Robbins thirtieth among its "Franchise 100." A member of the IFA since 1985, the company is looking for new franchisees in all states and several foreign countries.

GETTING MORE INFORMATION

The Baskin-Robbins franchise packet includes several press releases, a brochure describing its operations, a copy of the company magazine, a *Restaurants & Institutions* magazine reprint, a listing of Baskin-Robbins stores throughout the world, and a five-page business application. For more information, write or call:

Mr. James Earnhardt
President
Baskin-Robbins Ice Cream Company U.S.A.
31 Baskin-Robbins Place
Glendale, CA   91201
(818)   956–0031

Bath Genie

BUSINESS		AS OF		PROJECTED BY	
		1/1/85	1/1/86	1/1/87	1/1/88
NO. OF UNITS					
OWNED BY: COMPANY		1	1	1	1
FRANCHISEES		33	48	64	90
LOCATED: IN U.S.		34	49	65	91
OUTSIDE U.S.		0	0	0	0
TOTAL:		34	49	65	91
NO. OF STATES W/ UNITS		10	15	17	20

BUSINESS: porcelain bathroom fixture resurfacing service
FOUNDED: 1976
FRANCHISED: 1983
START-UP INVESTMENT: $19,500 plus supplies

THE BUSINESS

Bath Genie has patented a porcelain repair process called Diamondcote bathtub resurfacing. With Diamondcote, stained, chipped, or worn tubs, sinks, and ceramic wall tiles can look as good as new, and even change color. Bath Genie guarantees its Diamondcote finish against flaking, peeling, and sagging for a full year, but the finish has a life expectancy of ten years.

Although refinishing a bathtub can cost between $200 and $300, that may be cheaper than buying a new bathtub when the additional costs of delivery, plumbing, and removal of the old tub are factored in. Furthermore, the quality of an existing tub made of porcelain-covered cast iron can never be matched by a low-priced new fixture. And refinishing is a quick, convenient process. The work is done onsite with no fixtures removed or plumbing readjusted.

WHAT IT TAKES

Your franchise fee will be $19,500, with $500 due when you sign the agreement and the remainder when you begin your training. There is no limit to the term of your franchise agreement, which grants an exclusive territory based on population and potential market. Additional franchise units are available for the same fee, but Bath Genie discourages passive ownership. Bath Genie does not charge an ongoing royalty or advertising fee.

The range of investment is very flexible. Because most of your work will be done onsite, you can do business out of your house. It is also possible to open a shop where a homeowner can bring fixtures to be resurfaced.

GETTING STARTED

A typical Bath Genie refinishing shop is 700 to 1,000 square feet in a freestanding building or an industrial center. You must locate a shop site, but the company will help you with leasing and purchasing equipment, including vehicles, and with buying supplies and merchandise. If you open a shop, you will need one full-time and one part-time employee, whom Bath Genie will help you hire. You and one of your employees will receive training at the Bath Genie national headquarters in Marlboro, Massachusetts, and at one of the company-owned stores in the Boston area. The four- to five-day program includes all aspects of operations and management under actual working conditions. Topics include the resurfacing process, marketing, sales procedures, advertising, hiring procedures, customer service, and bookkeeping. You can be in business within a few weeks after signing the agreement. Home-office personnel will assist you on a consultant basis during your grand opening.

MAKING IT WORK

Bath Genie offers a complete range of support services and charges no ongoing fees. The comprehensive advertising program includes newspaper and telephone-book ads, brochures, presentation books, seasonal promotional materials, and a lead-referral system.

The operations manual, which is constantly updated, outlines the systems, procedures, forms, and policies needed on a day-to-day basis. Bath Genie will also provide you with various forms you'll need plus accounting, inventory, and expense-analysis systems. You'll stay informed about both the company and the resurfacing industry, through an annual national convention, a newsletter, and regular technical and company updates. Bath Genie has a centralized merchandising system for its products, which are the only ones that can be used.

COMMENTS

In 1987 Bath Genie was ranked 396th in *Entrepreneur* magazine's "Franchise 500". The company is seeking franchises in every state.

GETTING MORE INFORMATION

The franchise packet includes a list of franchise investment benefits, a list of potential costs and profits, and a promotional question-and-answer page describing the resurfacing process. The two-page financial and personal questionnaire asks for business experience and business references. For more information, write or call:

John Foley
President
Bath Genie, Inc.
109 East Main Street
Marlboro, MA   01752
(800)   ALL–TUBS

Blimpie

BUSINESS: fast-food
  submarine-sandwich
  restaurant
FOUNDED: 1964
FRANCHISED: 1971
START-UP
  INVESTMENT:
  $70,000–$110,000

		AS OF		PROJECTED BY	
NO. OF UNITS		1/1/85	1/1/86	1/1/87	1/1/88
OWNED BY:	COMPANY	2	1	1	1
	FRANCHISEES	230	250	325	450
LOCATED:	IN U.S.	232	251	326	451
	OUTSIDE U.S.	0	0	0	0
TOTAL:		232	251	326	451
NO. OF STATES W/ UNITS		16	16	18	25

THE BUSINESS

Blimpie successfully established a foothold in the fast-food market by showing that the formula of no cooking plus a limited menu equals success. A Blimpie is simplicity: freshly cut ham, salami, cappacola, prosciuttini, and provolone spread out on twelve-inch-long French or Italian bread. Sliced tomatoes, shredded lettuce, and finely chopped onions are piled on top; and oil, vinegar, salt, pepper, and oregano are sprinkled on for a finishing touch.

The chain has maintained virtually the same menu since it began but in recent years has added chili, hot microwaved sandwiches, and breakfast sandwiches. Overstuffed fresh sandwiches are 80 percent of Blimpie's sales, with beverages accounting for 17 percent and desserts and other items 3 percent. The ratio of take-out to eat-in food is approximately 35 percent to 65 percent in urban locations and 50 percent to 50 percent in suburban locations, with take-out higher in new units that have drive-up windows.

From a modest beginning in Hoboken, New Jersey, in 1964, Blimpie has expanded to systemwide sales of around $80 million. In 1985 the average gross sales per franchise unit were $400,000 to $500,000 with an average net income of 15 to 20 percent per franchise unit.

WHAT IT TAKES

You'll need $15,000 for the initial franchise fee, which will purchase an exclusive area determined by population for a term of twenty years. Your total investment, including the franchise fee, will range from $70,000 to $110,000, and $40,000 of that must be paid in cash.

If you need financial assistance, you'll have to seek it from your own sources. The fee for additional franchise units is the same as the original, and master franchises are available. Although the company allows passive ownership of the initial unit, this practice is discouraged. You'll pay an ongoing royalty fee of 6 percent of gross sales, with an additional 3 percent fee for advertising.

You don't need restaurant experience to own a Blimpie franchise, although management experience is a plus. The company will teach you everything you need to know to run your operation profitably, including operational and administrative methods, advertising strategies, and public-relations approaches.

GETTING STARTED

The first step in opening your new Blimpie franchise is locating an appropriate facility. Typically, you'll need approximately 2,000 square feet of space, enough to seat about seventy customers. The company will do an initial location analysis of your area and consult with local realtors on selected sites. Construction is usually not required, since most Blimpies are in existing freestanding buildings, malls, and shopping centers. They can be in business districts and suburban communities, near sports centers and large industries, and on college campuses. When the perfect location for your restaurant has been found, the company will negotiate to secure the best lease possible. The lease will actually be between the landlord and Blimpie; then Blimpie will sublease the facility to you.

The next step will be to renovate and fully equip your restaurant. The company architect will design your unit to meet Blimpie's standards of uniformity and reflect your particular locale. The exterior will feature the new Blimpie logo—the Blimpie name in the shape of a streamlined hero sandwich in bright red, green, and yellow. The interior layout will provide for a two-register service area, similar to most fast-food restaurants, plus a comfortable seating area. Your decor will be simple, bright, and contemporary. Your total design package will also include fixtures, equipment, uniforms, and packaging.

For two weeks you'll attend Blimpie University in New York City, where your formal classroom instruction will include hands-on training sessions. The company also has a program of advanced management training that includes onsite visits by training personnel. The company will help you hire the two to three full-time and seven to eight part-time personnel you'll need and then will provide in-store training for them.

You'll need about six months from the time you purchase your franchise to make your Blimpie restaurant operational. When it's time to launch your new business, the company will send staff to assist you with the grand opening.

MAKING IT WORK

Your 3 percent advertising fee will cover all press and public-relations materials. In addition, Blimpie supplies professionally prepared advertising and promotion programs in a cooperative arrangement with individual stores nationwide. You can get newspaper and magazine ads, telephone-book ads, brochures, menus, billboard posters, seasonal displays, and radio and television commercials. The chain's new advertising theme, "America's Best-Dressed Sandwich," has been incorporated into a radio jingle.

The company insists upon standardization of the foods used in all Blimpie sandwiches. The company will assist you in working with local and regional purveyors to purchase food and paper supplies at the best prices possible. You may use independent suppliers if they meet the company's quality standards. Blimpie will also help you guard your profits with special equipment—a precise scale and a quality slicer—that will insure portion and waste control.

You'll receive Blimpie's monthly company newsletter plus periodic company-information updates and product or service updates. The company provides a variety of easy-to-use business forms plus policy and procedural manuals. Onsite visits are arranged as needed. Regional offices have been opened around the country to help speed up communication between the home office in New York and the individual franchisees. A newly instituted company-sponsored recognition program provides performance awards. The company-owned store in Atlanta is used to conduct ongoing research and development.

COMMENTS

Ranked 114th in *Entrepreneur* magazine's "Franchise 500" for 1987, the company is seeking to expand throughout the United States and in Canada and Europe.

GETTING MORE INFORMATION

The information packet contains an eight-page description of the company's operation, several press releases, a color picture of a store exterior and interior, and a sample menu. For more information, write or call:
Stephen Sloane
Franchise Consultant
Blimpie
740 Broadway, 6th Floor
New York, NY   10003
(212)   673–5900

Bojangles'

		AS OF		PROJECTED BY	
BUSINESS: fast-food chicken and biscuit restaurants	NO. OF UNITS	1/1/85	1/1/86	1/1/87	1/1/88
	OWNED BY: COMPANY	160	158	135	135
FOUNDED: 1977	FRANCHISEES	144	151	180	230
FRANCHISED: 1979	LOCATED: IN U.S.	304	309	315	365
START-UP	OUTSIDE U.S.	0	0	0	0
INVESTMENT:	TOTAL:	304	309	315	365
$595,000–$792,000	NO. OF STATES W/ UNITS	20	18	17	17

THE BUSINESS

Tapping into the demand for nutritious, made-from-scratch meals in the convenience of a fast-food environment, Bojangles' opened its first restaurant in Charlotte, North Carolina, in 1977. The Bojangles' menu features spicy Cajun-style fried chicken with Cajun gravy, rice, and pinto beans, as well as more than thirty varieties of breakfast biscuits. The restaurants feature a distinctive design with uniquely styled wallpaper and carpeting along with accessory items such as ceiling fans, globe lights, and hanging plants. Unlike most fast-food chains, Bojangles' prefers to build on the side of the street which will be on the drivers' right as they head to work, since breakfast draws the largest percentage of a unit's daily customer traffic.

WHAT IT TAKES

Your initial franchise fee will be $35,000 for an exclusive territory, valid for twenty years and renewable for two ten-year options. Your total initial investment, including the franchise fee, will range from $595,000 to $792,000, with $75,000 to $100,000 required in cash. Bojangles' provides indirect assistance with financing. Additional franchise units sell for $25,000 each; master franchises are not available. You must be a participating manager, although partners are allowed. Ongoing royalty fees are 4 percent of gross sales after sales taxes and other required taxes. Prior food-service experience is not required.

GETTING STARTED

Bojangles' will provide you with a set of preliminary plans designed to fit your site along with a complete set of building specifications. The company also provides help with lease negotiation; site selection; purchase negotiation; facility layout and decoration; lease or purchase of furniture and fixtures; acquisition of equipment, materials, supplies, and merchandise; and staffing and hiring. The typical Bojangles' restaurant is 2,900 square feet in a freestanding building. Including yourself, you will need twenty full-time and twenty-five part-time employees. All management employees receive four weeks of training at a Bojangles' restaurant in Charlotte, followed by two weeks of classroom instruction. Topics covered include training for various restaurant jobs, basic shift supervision, administrative control of a unit, equipment training, and interpersonal skills. Normally, you'll need a year after purchasing your franchise to prepare for your opening, and Bojangles' will provide assistance with your grand opening.

MAKING IT WORK

As part of your ongoing 4 percent advertising fee, you will receive newspaper ads, black-and-white and four-color magazine ads, mailers, telephone-book ads, brochures, television and radio commercials, point-of-purchase displays, billboard posters, signs, banners, contests, seasonal promotional materials, incentives, press releases, and a public-relations/marketing manual. National conventions are held every two years and regional conferences semiannually, with ongoing assistance from operational consultants available to you. Bojangles' issues monthly and quarterly newsletters and updates on product, company, and market information as needed. Areawide franchise meetings and regular surveys are part of Bojangles' program.

Recognition programs honor those with top sales. Backup systems include headquarters and regional resource persons; a toll-free hotline; regular onsite visits; manuals on policy, management procedure, and customer service; all necessary forms; and systems for inventory, personnel, and computerized management information. Bojangles' maintains an ongoing product and menu research-and-development department. The company has divisions to produce and/or distribute merchandise and a central purchasing program offering volume discounts. You must use only company products.

COMMENTS

A division of Horn & Hardart since 1982 and a member of the IFA since 1984, Bojangles' makes an earnings claim document available to potential franchisees prior to or during a personal interview. The company is seeking to increase franchise operations in the Northeast, South, and Midwest.

GETTING MORE INFORMATION

The franchise packet contains a four-color brochure on the company's history and operations, a breakdown of capital requirements, a summary of the franchise and lease program, and an application form. For more information, write or call:

William E. Thelen
Bojangles'
Vice-President, Franchise Development
P. O. Box 240239
4421 Stuart Andrew Boulevard, Suite 400
Charlotte, NC   28224
(704)   527–2675

Boston Pizza

BUSINESS: pizza and		AS OF		PROJECTED BY	
	NO. OF UNITS	1/1/85	1/1/86	1/1/87	1/1/88
pasta family restaurant	OWNED BY: COMPANY	1	1	1	1
FOUNDED: 1963	FRANCHISEES	58	60	70	80
FRANCHISED: 1968	LOCATED: IN U.S.	0	0	0	3
START-UP	OUTSIDE U.S.	59	61	71	78
INVESTMENT:	TOTAL:	59	61	71	81
$125,000–$600,000	NO. OF STATES W/ UNITS	0	0	0	2

THE BUSINESS

Eaten by the slice in a mall or in a sit-down restaurant, pizza is a favorite food not only in the United States but also in Canada, where sixty Boston Pizza franchises currently operate and another twenty are expected by 1988. In 1985 fifty-eight Boston Pizza franchises earned $37.5 million, with each unit grossing an average of $650,000.

Boston Pizza is known for its unique pizza sauce and special pizza dough. Although pizza is the foundation of the business, Boston Pizza restaurants also offer barbecued ribs, Greek salad, sandwiches, nachos, soup, Boston cream pie, and Italian lasagna, linguini, fettucine, and tortellini. A separate menu appeals to children, and special lunchtime combinations attract the business crowd. Beer and wine are also served.

WHAT IT TAKES

Your financial investment in a typical Boston Pizza restaurant of 4,000 to 5,200 square feet will be $400,000 to $600,000, including the initial franchise fee of $25,000. A smaller mall unit will cost $125,000 to $160,000. You will also pay an ongoing royalty fee of 7 percent of sales, excluding alcohol sales, and an extra 4 percent fee for advertising. Additional franchise units are $25,000 each, or you can purchase a master franchise, depending upon your area. Your original franchise agreement will last ten years, with subsequent five-year renewal periods, and will guarantee you a minimum protected territory of one square mile. The company will assist you with financing, but 40 percent of the total initial investment must be in cash.

GETTING STARTED

You'll complete five weeks of hands-on training at an existing Boston Pizza restaurant, a week of classroom training at the head office, and a week of on-the-job training at your facility after its opening. The training program covers all aspects of food-service operation and company procedures as well as general restaurant accounting. Most Boston Pizza restaurants are in operation six to eight months after purchase of the franchise.

During those months, the company will help you with site selection, lease or purchase negotiations, and design of the layout. Boston Pizza will also oversee the construction or renovation of the building. If you're interested in a small, pizza-by-the-slice unit, you'll most likely set up in a shopping mall. A full-scale Boston Pizza restaurant of 4,000 to 5,200 square feet can be located in a shopping center or in a freestanding building.

As work on your facility progresses, company personnel will advise you on decorating; acquiring furniture and fixtures; setting up service and maintenance contracts; and obtaining materials, supplies, and merchandise. The company requires corporate approval of all plans, layouts, furnishings, equipment, uniforms, smallwares, menus, packaging materials, and foodstuffs used in Boston Pizza restaurants. To help you meet quality standards, the company has established a central purchasing program and identified both required and preferred suppliers. The company's volume discounts will help you lower your operating expenses. Boston Pizza personnel will help coordinate the initial hiring and training of your employees, the number of which will depend on the size of your operation.

MAKING IT WORK

Of your 4 percent advertising fee, 2.5 percent purchases cooperative advertising materials, including billboard posters; newspaper, magazine, and telephone-book ads; and miscellaneous promotional supplies like banners, flags, and balloons. The balance of your fee covers local television and radio commercials, press packages, and the public-relations/marketing manual.

The company will update your comprehensive operations and procedures manual periodically and send you a quarterly company newsletter and regular bulletins. Twice a year, senior management personnel will visit to review your business. Corporate staff specialists will help you solve problems in marketing, purchasing, accounting and finance, operational procedures, sales training, and staff development.

Other administrative and managerial resources include various business forms and inventory, personnel, and expense-analysis systems. The company also sponsors an insurance package with property and general-liability insurance for your restaurant, and life, major-medical, dental, and worker's compensation coverage for you and your employees.

Boston Pizza's product manager conducts research and development on foods and menus. Management promotes a team concept with franchisees, seeking information and ideas through regular meetings of an advisory council representing all regions. The company also convenes annual regional conferences and a national conference, where the franchisee of the year is recognized.

COMMENTS

Boston Pizza was ranked 220th in *Entrepreneur* magazine's 1987 "Franchise 500." The company was an official supplier to Expo 86. A member of the IFA, it is selling additional franchises in the western and northwestern United States as well as in Australia, Canada, Europe, and Japan.

GETTING MORE INFORMATION

The franchise information packet includes a four-color brochure that gives an overview of the company, a menu from a Boston Pizza restaurant, sample interior drawings, a list of current Boston Pizza locations, and a very brief confidential profile sheet. For more information, write or call:

R. W. Meister
Director of Franchising
Boston Pizza International Inc.
#212–6011 Westminster Highway
Richmond, B.C.   V7C 4V4
Canada
(604)   270–1108 (call collect)

Brownies Fried Chicken

BUSINESS: take-out
and eat-in fast food
FOUNDED: 1967
FRANCHISED: 1968
START-UP
INVESTMENT:
$75,000–$150,000
(Canadian dollars)

		AS OF		PROJECTED BY	
NO. OF UNITS		1/1/85	1/1/86	1/1/87	1/1/88
OWNED BY: COMPANY		0	1	2	2
FRANCHISEES		60	65	75	85
LOCATED: IN U.S.		0	0	2	5
OUTSIDE U.S.		60	66	75	82
TOTAL:		60	66	77	87
NO. OF STATES W/ UNITS		0	0	1	2

THE BUSINESS

Because of low cost, fast service, and consistent recipes, customers eat at fast-food establishments more often than at conventional restaurants. According to Brownies, the fast-food services that specialize in a few products attract the most business. Their menu consists primarily of fried chicken and side orders, although at food-fair locations in shopping centers, fish-and-chip dinners and hamburgers are also on the menu. Brownies offers both take-out and eat-in service; their food-fair locations only offer take-out.

Brownies franchises in Canada, Taiwan, and the Philippines totaled $16 million (Canadian) in gross sales in 1985. Average annual gross sales per unit come to about $267,000 (Canadian), and net averages $50,000 (Canadian) before management salary and depreciation.

WHAT IT TAKES

A one-time franchise fee of $25,000 (about $15,000 in U.S. dollars) will buy you a ten-year agreement with a five-year renewal period. Your territory will be determined by population and natural boundaries. A 4-percent royalty fee and a 3-percent advertising fee are charged on gross monthly sales. Including your franchise fee, your estimated cost of start-up is $75,000 to $150,000 (Canadian), of which 30 percent must be paid in cash. The company will provide you with a specific cost breakdown based on your location and help you to find financing—from government-backed small-business loans—for the other 70 percent. Your start-up expenses will include an equipment package, working-capital requirements, and the costs of leasehold improvements or building renovation. If you want to buy an additional franchise, the fees will be the same. Brownies will allow you to hire a manager, but the company prefers that the franchisee be involved in day-to-day operations.

GETTING STARTED

You can choose to operate either a small facility (only 375 to 425 square feet) in the food-fair section of a shopping center; a medium-sized restaurant (1,000 to 1,300 square feet) with limited seating for 20 to 40 people; or the largest restaurant (1,600 to 2,500 square feet) with seating for 60 to 150 people.

The two larger stores can be located along shopping strips, in downtown retail areas, or in freestanding buildings. You'll want a site with plenty of available parking, lots of windows, sufficient exterior lighting, and a well-displayed sign space. Brownies will help you pick the best location, one that can tap a market of at least 5,000 people. Also, the storefront should be prominent within an established business center. If there's nearby competition, Brownies prefers that the store be on a main traffic artery.

Brownies will both supply a standard set of drawings and specifications for your new or existing building and recommend a construction supervisor. The company's design accommodates equipment, storage spaces, seating, and lobby area and is adaptable to your location. The company also has a standard design package for decor and layout. All Brownies restaurants have standard uniforms, packaging, and signs.

You don't need any previous experience to qualify for a Brownies franchise. A seven-hour classroom training program at Brownies headquarters in Vancouver is provided, with twenty-four more hours of hands-on training at your franchise location. Your employees get three hours of classroom training and twenty-four hours of hands-on training at the restaurant. You'll also receive a comprehensive operator's manual, plus policy and management-procedure manuals. The length of time from purchase to grand opening will vary depending on your size and location, but it usually takes one to six months. Brownies will provide a special package for your grand opening.

MAKING IT WORK

The company does market research and regional and national advertising. The ongoing advertising fee of 3 percent of gross sales covers newspaper, magazine, and telephone-book advertising; mailers; billboard posters; balloons; contests; and displays.

You can get all your supplies at reduced costs since the company buys in bulk. Brownies reserves the right to specify approved brands. The company's operations department tests new products regularly. Brownies holds an annual national convention every two years and conducts quarterly seminars and onsite training. You'll receive a monthly newsletter and yearly surveys. Each year the company sponsors a recognition program that awards the franchise with the highest percentage increase in sales.

COMMENTS

The company has made contributions to handicapped children and handicapped sports. Brownies will send you an earnings claim document if requested. It plans to make a major expansion into the United States.

GETTING MORE INFORMATION

The franchise information packet includes a sample menu and a questionnaire for you to complete. For details, write to:
Peter Atlay
Franchising Manager
Brownies Franchises, Ltd.
#406, 4190 Longheed Highway
Burnaby, B.C.   V5C 6A8
Canada
(604)   291–6060

Budget Tapes & Records

BUSINESS: retail
music store
FOUNDED: 1970
FRANCHISED: 1970
START-UP
INVESTMENT:
$59,000–$98,500

		AS OF		PROJECTED BY	
NO. OF UNITS		1/1/85	1/1/86	1/1/87	1/1/88
OWNED BY:	COMPANY	6	4	4	4
	FRANCHISEES	71	82	85	95
LOCATED:	IN U.S.	77	86	89	99
	OUTSIDE U.S.	0	0	0	0
TOTAL:		77	86	89	99
NO. OF STATES W/ UNITS		14	16	17	20

THE BUSINESS

Budget Tapes & Records prides itself on having inviting stores with friendly, knowledgeable staff members. The company makes every effort to offer the newest technology, such as digital laser-read products. In 1985, Budget franchises grossed $25 million.

WHAT IT TAKES

You will pay $10,000 for the initial franchise fee. The agreement, which is valid for ten years and renewable for a negotiable period, establishes an exclusive territory determined by mileage. You will need an additional $49,500 to $88,000 to set up your store. Your investment will cover prepaid rent ($1,500 to $3,000); inventory ($30,000 to $60,000); fixtures, furnishings, leasehold improvements, materials, and supplies ($7,500 to $15,000); fees and deposits ($500); and $10,000 for operating capital. The company does not provide financing. The franchise fee for additional units is negotiable. You may be an investor-owner, but the company prefers that you be active in the business. You will pay an ongoing royalty of 2 percent gross sales. No prior experience in the music industry is required.

GETTING STARTED

Budget Tapes & Records will assist you with site selection, lease or purchase negotiation, and facility layout. The company charges for construction, facility decoration, lease or purchase of furniture and fixtures, service and maintenance contracts, and supplying merchandise and materials. The typical store is 1,500 square feet, located in a shopping center or freestanding building. Besides yourself, you will need one part-time employee. You will be trained in all aspects of retail business—inventory selection, ordering, personnel, store layout and construction, bookkeeping, preopening, management techniques, in-store merchandising and advertising, and warehouse operations. The first half of your training will be held either at corporate headquarters in Denver or at the company's Seattle branch. Additional training is conducted in existing franchise stores. All costs of training, transportation, and lodging are paid for by the company. (Meals are your responsibility.) You can be open for business twelve weeks after buying the franchise, and the company will help with your grand opening.

MAKING IT WORK

The company offers co-op advertising for newspaper ads, black-and-white and four-color magazine ads, mailers, telephone-book ads, brochures, presentation books, and catalogs. Budget sponsors biannual national conventions for franchise owners plus periodic areawide franchise meetings. The company also conducts onsite training as needed. You will receive a regular newsletter and updates on products, company information, and market trends. The company conducts surveys as needed. To ease your tasks as a manager, Budget provides headquarters-based and regional resource persons, a toll-free hotline, regular onsite visits, onsite troubleshooting, policy manuals, all types of forms, and systems for bookkeeping and inventory. Budget distributes merchandise through a centralized system, making it possible for you to stock a full range of products not available to all independent music stores. You may purchase from other suppliers if you wish. Budget sponsors award programs to recognize top sales performance.

COMMENTS

Budget Tapes & Records was ranked 233rd in *Entrepreneur* magazine's 1987 "Franchise 500." A division of Danjay Music & Video, Budget has won several advertising awards at both national and regional levels. The company wants to add new franchises in twenty-one states.

GETTING MORE INFORMATION

The franchise information packet contains question-and-answer sheets describing the company's operations. For details, contact:
Evan Lasky
President
Budget Tapes & Records
10625 East 47th Avenue
Denver, CO   80239
(303)   373–1760

Century 21

BUSINESS: real estate
  sales
  FOUNDED: 1971
  FRANCHISED: 1971
START-UP
  INVESTMENT:
  Variable

	AS OF		PROJECTED BY	
NO. OF UNITS	1/1/85	1/1/86	1/1/87	1/1/88
		(15 regions)		
OWNED BY: COMPANY				
FRANCHISEES	6,422	6,520	6,720	7,120
LOCATED: IN U.S.	6,076	6,144	6,270	6,570
OUTSIDE U.S.	346	376	450	600
TOTAL:	6,422	6,520	6,720	7,120
NO. OF STATES W/ UNITS	50	50	50	50

THE BUSINESS

As the largest real estate company in the United States, Century 21 claims to have the most offices, most sales associates, greatest sales volume, and highest market share among real estate firms. The company's four-tiered system is made up of International Headquarters, Regions (27—15 company-owned, 12 franchised), Brokers (6520 franchised as of January, 1986), and Sales Associates. Century 21 offices were involved in approximately 11 percent of all residential brokerage activity in the United States during 1985. Taking into account all Century 21 offices, the company participated in more than 620,000 transactions in 1985, earning more than $1.6 billion in commissions on total sales of $40 billion. The average office sold $6.5 million in property. The company offers a preferred client club to help increase repeat business. Related services include the Century 21 Securities Corporation, Mortgage Corporation, and CENGUARD insurance. A national accounts center acts as a resource for companies who seek residential, commercial, industrial, and management expertise for corporate relocations, investments, acquisitions and divestments, and other real estate–related activities.

WHAT IT TAKES

You need $9,500 to $14,000 for the franchise fee, depending on the state in which you locate. You will have a nonexclusive territory, valid for five years and renewable for five more years. Total investment, including the amount of cash required varies widely from area to area. Master franchises are available in foreign countries. You must manage your Century 21 franchise yourself and you must have on staff a responsible broker duly licensed by the state. Expect to pay an ongoing royalty fee of 6 percent of gross revenues.

GETTING STARTED

Century 21 does not provide assistance with establishing your office since most new franchises convert an existing operation. The typical office is located in an office building, mall, shopping center, freestanding building, or commercial industrial park. You must follow a policy and procedures manual that requires, among other things, adherence to certain logo usage. A three-and-a-half-day orientation seminar is held at the International Management Academy in Irvine, California, covering mass media advertising, support services, Century 21 referral programs, orientation, the Century 21 system, and training and sales management. Training continues at regional offices, covering all aspects of real estate sales—listing, selling, financing, business planning, referrals, and more. If you convert an existing office, the length of time to grand opening is usually six weeks to two months after purchase of the franchise.

MAKING IT WORK

As part of your advertising fee of 2 percent of gross revenues, Century 21 provides newspaper ads, black-and-white and four-color magazine ads, mailers, telephone-book ads, television and radio commercials, national media coverage, and a lead-referral system. An annual supply catalog identifies approved suppliers and their products and services, such as presentation books, catalogs, in-house media packages (slides, videotapes), point-of-purchase displays, billboard posters, signs, banners, contests, seasonal promotional materials, and incentives. However, you will not be required to buy from these sources. You will also receive press releases and a public-relations/marketing manual. Public relations for special promotions is free. In 1985 the company spent more than $31 million on national and local advertising.

Century 21 holds an annual national convention, annual regional conferences, periodic seminars, and onsite sales training as needed. A company newsletter is published every other month, along with a customer-oriented magazine. Broker councils exist in most regions and meet monthly. Surveys are conducted at least four times a year, and biannual meetings of broker, region, and corporate representatives are held to discuss issues relating to the marketplace and the Century 21 system. Award programs honor production and gross closed commissions. Administrative resources include headquarters and regional resource persons, regular onsite visits, all types of forms, and systems for bookkeeping and inventory. Most of these items are available for purchase from the company or from approved suppliers. A research division conducts industry-trends research and oversees projects such as surveys. An insurance package is currently being arranged.

COMMENTS

Century 21 was ranked eleventh in *Entrepreneur* magazine's 1987 "Franchise 500" and fortieth in *Venture* magazine's 1986 "Franchise 100." A division of Metropolitan Life Insurance, Century 21 is a member of the IFA. The largest corporate donor to Easter Seals, the company has donated $10 million over the last eight years. Century 21 wants to expand its franchise operations throughout the world.

**GETTING MORE
INFORMATION**

The franchise information packet contains a full-color brochure on the company's operations, a history of Century 21's growth, and copies of recent articles on the company. For further details, contact:

Monte Helme *or* Diane Gaynor
Public Relations/Publications
Century 21 Real Estate Corporation
18872 MacArthur Boulevard
Irvine, CA   92715
(714)   752–7521 (call collect)

Chem-Dry

BUSINESS: carpet and
upholstery cleaning
FOUNDED: 1977
FRANCHISED: 1978
START-UP
INVESTMENT:
$8,400

		AS OF		PROJECTED BY	
NO. OF UNITS		1/1/85	1/1/86	1/1/87	1/1/88
OWNED BY: COMPANY		0	0	0	0
	FRANCHISEES	685	746	1,000	1,500
LOCATED: IN U.S.		674	736	975	1,400
	OUTSIDE U.S.	11	10	25	100
TOTAL:		685	746	1,000	1,500
NO. OF STATES W/ UNITS		42	45	50	50

THE BUSINESS

Before 1977 there were three basic methods of carpet cleaning—shampooing, steaming, and dry cleaning. Each had its disadvantages, ranging from rapid resoiling and toxicity to overwetting and shrinking. Then Robert and Rebecca Harris developed a new cleaning method, a combination of special cleaning formula and carbon dioxide. They founded Harris Research Inc., patented their discovery, and began marketing it under the Chem-Dry name. The company has expanded its product and service line to include upholstery and drapery cleaning as well as specialized stain removal, deodorizing (particularly pet odors), and mold and mildew prevention. All Chem-Dry services are unconditionally guaranteed. The number of Chem-Dry units grew to 685 in 1985 by word of mouth alone; the company did not solicit franchises until 1985.

WHAT IT TAKES

The Chem-Dry Carpet Cleaning franchise fee is $4,900, which must be paid in cash, plus an additional $3,500 for equipment, supplies, training, and an initial advertising package. Harris Research will finance the $3,500 for a term of thirty months, interest free, which amounts to $116.67 per month. After you pay off the financed amount, you begin paying a standard royalty fee of $100 per month.

Your franchise agreement is for a five-year term, with an additional five-year renewal period, and gives you exclusive rights to a population area of 60,000 people. Additional franchise areas are available under the same terms and conditions.

GETTING STARTED

With a Chem-Dry franchise you won't need any special facility or location. You can operate out of your home or simply put an additional phone line into an existing office. Also, you needn't buy a company truck or van, since the cleaning equipment fits easily into a compact station wagon or hatchback. With your franchise you'll receive a complete equipment package including two high-powered industrial cleaning machines with attachments, a carbonation unit and sprayer, and enough Chem-Dry solution to clean 64,000 square feet of carpeting.

You will have two training options. You (and your employees, if you like) can attend the two-day training and management program at Harris Research's offices in Cameron Park, California, and gain hands-on practice in cleaning methods and equipment maintenance. (You may attend this training program again at no charge if you ever feel the need for a refresher.) Or, instead, you and your employees can complete your training by using the company's videotaped training package. Either way, you'll learn proper phone and sales techniques (including a system for getting referrals) business-promotion techniques, and business-management skills. You'll receive the company's bookkeeping system, complete with invoices, accounts-receivable ledgers, accounts-payable sheets, expense forms, and so forth. To supplement your training, Harris Research will provide you with policy, management-procedure and public-relations/marketing manuals. The start-up package also includes a radio jingle, four-color brochures, discount certificates, and slicks for newspaper and telephone-book ads. In addition, you'll receive letterhead stationery, business cards, vehicle signs, and uniforms. The time between your franchise purchase and your grand-opening promotions will be three weeks.

Chem-Dry franchises have been set up to accommodate a variety of business goals and strategies. You can run the business part-time or full-time, work alone or with several crews, and provide the full array of services or only basic carpet cleaning. You even set your own prices. Harris Research's sole restriction is that you operate out of only one location and under only one company name.

MAKING IT WORK

The company's official registered trademark, the Chem-Dry Charlie character, appears on all advertising, promotional, and company- or product-identification materials (from uniforms to bottle labels).

Harris Research produces a wide variety of these materials and sells them to franchisees at low costs. You can get brochures, mailers, door hangers, catalogs, point-of-purchase displays, seasonal materials and displays, billboard posters, signs and banners—all with Chem-Dry Charlie prominently featured. For special events you can use costumed "Charlies" to hand out balloons and promotional literature, and there's a Charlie hot-air balloon that's a real attention getter. The company has also produced an animated television commercial and a videotaped sales presentation.

Every year Harris Research sponsors a national convention plus five or six regional conferences for franchisees from the United States and Canada. Also, every other month there are two-day seminars covering every aspect of your business. A monthly newsletter passes along new motivational and practical ideas, notices, product-research developments, and advertisements. The company periodically sends not only information updates of company news but also questionnaires about your opinions, needs, and interests. Yearly and monthly company-sponsored contests and awards recognize achievements in sales and service.

You can use Harris Research's toll-free orderline to maintain your equipment and supply inventories, and most orders can be shipped within twenty-four hours. When you buy your franchise, you'll be given an open line of credit allowing you to pay for supplies on a thirty-day basis. You are not restricted to using only Chem-Dry products; however, other products must be of comparable or better quality and be approved by the company.

The company's group insurance program especially for Chem-Dry owners includes two types of coverage: business coverage for property, equipment, supplies, and general liability insurance; and family coverage for life, accident, and medical insurance for you and your family. You can also select optional coverage for disability-income insurance, dental insurance, or additional life insurance.

COMMENTS

In 1986 Chem-Dry was ranked 69th in *Venture* magazine's "Franchise 100" and 133rd in *Entrepreneur* magazine's 1987 "Franchise 500." The company is seeking franchisees throughout the United States and in other countries.

GETTING MORE INFORMATION

The franchise information packet contains a color brochure; a copy of the company newsletter; photocopied letters from satisfied Chem-Dry franchisees and customers; information about the Chem-Dry product, the franchise agreement, and company support; sample flyers and brochures; a pamphlet detailing the company group

insurance program; and a mail-back form requesting further information. For details, write to:
Steven M. Oldfield
Executive Vice-President of Sales
Chem-Dry Carpet Cleaning Company
3330 Cameron Park Drive, Suite 700
Cameron Park, CA 95682
(800) 841–6583 (national) or (800) 821–3240 (California)

Coast to Coast Total Hardware

			AS OF		PROJECTED BY	
BUSINESS: retail hardware store	NO. OF UNITS		1/1/85	1/1/86	1/1/87	1/1/88
FOUNDED: 1928	OWNED BY: COMPANY		0	0	0	0
FRANCHISED: 1928		FRANCHISEES	1,047	1,058	1,065	1,100
START-UP	LOCATED: IN U.S.		1,047	1,058	1,065	1,100
INVESTMENT:		OUTSIDE U.S.	0	0	0	0
$167,000–$270,000	TOTAL:		1,047	1,058	1,065	1,100
	NO. OF STATES W/ UNITS		31	32	33	36

THE BUSINESS

In 1928 the Melamed brothers started a hardware business that actually profited and grew through the Great Depression. Today, Coast to Coast Total Hardware has nearly 1,100 franchises nationwide. Annual gross sales for all franchises in 1985 were over $500 million, and average gross sales for each franchise were $490,000. In addition to standard hardware items, the stores feature small appliances, materials for the do-it-yourselfer, and sporting-goods, garden, and hobby supplies.

WHAT IT TAKES

You'll pay an initial franchise fee of $3,000 for a five-year agreement. At the end of the five years, you'll automatically have an option to renew your agreement for another five years. The company doesn't charge any royalty fees. Your total investment will depend on the size of store—usually 4,000 to 8,000 square feet. Among your start-up costs will be approximately $110,000 to $175,000 for inventory, $15,000 to $29,000 for fixtures, $20,000 to $31,000 for equipment and site improvement, and $22,000 to $35,000 for working capital. You'll need to pay half of the total start-up investment in cash, but Coast to Coast will help you secure a loan for the remainder from traditional sources. If you want to buy more franchises, the same terms apply. The company allows but discourages passive ownership.

GETTING STARTED

Coast to Coast can help you with site selection. Typical locations are shopping centers and strips, downtown retail districts, and free-standing buildings. The company evaluates sites based on traffic patterns, existing competition, and projected population growth. Once you've chosen a site, the company will negotiate a lease or purchase and assist with facility layout, equipment lease or purchase, employee hiring, and grand-opening plans. All stores use the same logos and signs and follow a uniform merchandise layout. Coast to Coast provides displays for seasonal specials, sales, and grand openings.

Coast to Coast will send you or your manager to a four-day new-owner training seminar at the Central Organization offices just outside of Minneapolis, Minnesota. You'll learn about personnel management, inventory control, display building, and computer ordering. You'll then attend a one-day systems orientation at one of the three divisional offices. Your Coast to Coast district manager will assist you with more specific training. It will take about six weeks from purchase of your franchise to your grand opening.

MAKING IT WORK

The company's buyers conduct market research and analyses, collect trade-show information, and recommend to franchisees which merchandise to stock and how much to order. The company's central purchasing program, centralized merchandising system, and Coast to Coast–brand products will save you money. The company selects preferred vendors but allows you to buy from any wholesaler. Coast to Coast holds merchandise shows twice yearly in each region.

Coast to Coast will share advertising costs with you, including telephone-book and direct-mail ads, radio and television commercials, co-op billboards, and newspaper ads. They'll also send you photographs of newly developed display prototypes. If you need any special materials, banners, or price cards to duplicate the displays, you can order them from the company. The buyer you'll work with specializes in your locale, so he or she can design advertising programs tailored to your specific market.

You and your employees can stay up-to-date through the company's quarterly magazine, semiannual newsletter, and weekly updates on products and company information; semiannual advisory board meetings; conventions; and research reports. You and your staff can participate in periodic training sessions, product seminars, and clinics. You'll also have access to a videotape library, a toll-free hotline, and policy-and-procedure manuals. You're encouraged to call on your district manager anytime you have a problem.

Your store will have a computer terminal linked directly to a main computer at the central office. As a result, you'll be able to order merchandise weekly for same-week delivery; balance your inventory to maintain proper stock levels; get weekly, monthly, and quarterly financial statements; and get automatic notification of payroll taxes due. The central office provides all quarterly and annual payroll reports plus other accounting services and free advice on taxes and finance.

With Coast to Coast's group insurance, you and your employees can have life, hospital, and major-medical insurance. Long-term disability, worker's compensation, and third-party-bonding coverage and Individual Retirement Accounts also come with the benefits package.

COMMENTS

A charter member of the IFA, Coast to Coast was rated forty-eighth in *Entrepreneur* magazine's 1987 "Franchise 500." An earnings claim document is provided prior to or during a potential franchisee's personal interview. The company is looking for new franchises in most states.

GETTING MORE INFORMATION

A full-color franchise information packet comes with a confidential questionnaire to assess your potential. To order an information packet, write to:
W. P. Lindstrom
National Sales Manager
Coast to Coast Total Hardware Stores, Inc.
10801 Red Circle Drive
Minnetonka, MN   55343
(612)   935–1711

ColorTyme

BUSINESS: rent-to-own TV, video and audio equipment, and appliances
FOUNDED: 1979
FRANCHISED: 1982
START-UP INVESTMENT: $36,000–$75,000

		AS OF		PROJECTED BY	
NO. OF UNITS		1/1/85	1/1/86	1/1/87	1/1/88
OWNED BY:	COMPANY	0	0	0	0
	FRANCHISEES	397	462	500	550
LOCATED:	IN U.S.	397	462	500	550
	OUTSIDE U.S.	0	0	0	0
TOTAL:		397	462	500	550
NO. OF STATES W/ UNITS		42	42	42	43

THE BUSINESS

Rent-to-own as a philosophy appeals to a young and mobile society that wants to own high-quality video and audio equipment, televisions and appliances without the high cost of buying such items outright. By renting to own, consumers may enjoy the latest products, trading them back to the store periodically for state-of-the-art merchandise. Rent-to-own began in 1959 in Wichita, Kansas, when a TV and appliance retail store, Mr. T's, offered units for rent and got a strong response. Willie Talley was a prime developer of the rent-to-own business in Wichita. Talley later joined the Curtis Mathes Corporation where, in fifteen years, he developed 500 rental locations for the company. In 1979 he started ColorTyme Distributing Company as a division of Curtis Mathes and a few years later purchased the whole company, changing its name to ColorTyme, Inc. The company's purpose was to provide services such as store identification, personnel training, and consumer advertising to rental accounts. In 1985, ColorTyme franchises grossed an average of $600,000 for each store, with average net income of $120,000.

WHAT IT TAKES

You will need $10,000 for the initial franchise fee, establishing an exclusive territory in your market for a renewable five-year period. Your total investment will range from $36,000 to $75,000, with $50,000 required in cash. The company will help you arrange financing for the remainder. Additional units also sell for $10,000; master franchises are not available. You will pay an ongoing royalty fee of 3 percent of gross sales. You may be a nonoperating manager of the business, but the company prefers that you have a hand in day-to-day operations. No prior experience in a rent-to-own business is necessary.

GETTING STARTED

ColorTyme will help with setup tasks such as site selection; lease or purchase negotiation; construction; facility layout and decoration; the lease or purchase of furniture, fixtures, equipment, and vehicles; and acquisition of supplies and merchandise. The typical facility is 2,500 square feet, located in a shopping center or strip mall. Besides yourself, you will need two full-time employees, and ColorTyme will advise you in hiring procedures. The company will provide five weeks of training in all operational areas for you and/or your manager. You can be open for business within ninety days of buying the franchise, and ColorTyme will help with the grand opening.

MAKING IT WORK

For your 1 percent advertising fee, you will receive mailers, brochures, television and radio commercials, national media coverage, in-house media packages (slides, videotapes), point-of-purchase displays, billboard posters, signs, banners, contests, seasonal promotional materials, incentives, press releases, and a public-relations/marketing manual. You can meet other ColorTyme franchise owners at an annual national convention, regional conferences held once or twice a year, and periodic areawide franchise meetings. Also, you'll learn more about the industry through periodic seminars and quarterly on-site training sessions.

You will receive a company newsletter and regular updates on products, service, company information, and market trends. Award programs recognize excellence in performance. To ease your administrative tasks, the company offers headquarters and regional resource persons; onsite visits; policy, management-procedure, and customer-service manuals; all types of forms; and systems for bookkeeping, inventory, expense analysis, and computerized billing and information management. Research-and-development departments study methods and products to improve your business, particularly in the area of advertising effectiveness. ColorTyme offers a central purchasing program for volume discounts, a centralized merchandising system, and private-label merchandise designed especially for the rental customer. You may sell noncompany products.

COMMENTS

In 1987 ColorTyme was ranked 108th in *Entrepreneur* magazine's "Franchise 500" and fifty-eighth in *Venture* magazine's 1986 "Franchise 100." A member of the IFA, the company wants to increase operations in seven states.

GETTING MORE INFORMATION

The franchise information packet contains a brochure describing the company's operations. For details, contact:
Wayne Atchison
Vice-President, Franchising
ColorTyme, Inc.
P.O. Box 1781
Athens, TX   75751
(214)   675–9291

Command Performance

BUSINESS:			AS OF		PROJECTED BY	
			1/1/85	1/1/86	1/1/87	1/1/88
specialized hair	NO. OF UNITS					
salons	OWNED BY: COMPANY		0	2	4	10
FOUNDED: 1976		FRANCHISEES	320	325	340	400
FRANCHISED: 1976	LOCATED: IN U.S.		314	319	328	385
START-UP		OUTSIDE U.S.	6	8	16	25
INVESTMENT:	TOTAL:		320	327	344	410
$25,500–$121,500	NO. OF STATES W/ UNITS		40	40	41	46

THE BUSINESS

The demand is always high for hair-cutting and -styling services. In fact, Americans spend $13 billion on haircare products and services each year, and that figure is expected to grow to $20 billion by 1990. Command Performance, a widely recognized name in haircare services, has established itself in forty states. The company's innovative system of cutting and styling hair, launched in 1976, took advantage of the then revolutionary trend of offering both men and women haircare at one location. Command Performance's reputation rests on its client-oriented philosophy, sophisticated styling programs, high-tech interiors, and carefully chosen locations. Franchise operations in 1985 grossed nearly $80 million from over 300 locations nationwide.

WHAT IT TAKES

Your minimum cash investment required will be $25,500 to $35,500, which includes a one-time $21,500 franchise fee plus $5,000 for lease deposit, $5,000 for real estate rental, $3,000 for working capital, and $1,000 for opening supplies. Construction costs could run an additional $14,000 to $86,000, which includes $60,000 for any leasehold improvements and $14,000 to $26,000 for equipment and trade fixtures. At the low end, your total investment could be $25,500; at the high end, $121,500.

Your franchise territory will depend on the results of demographic studies, and your contract will apply for fifteen years, renewable for the same period. Owning additional franchises is practical because you do not personally have to operate each franchise. (Over 70 percent of Command Performance shops are owned by multiple-unit franchisees.) Each additional franchise involves the same estimated costs just described, including the franchise fee. For each operation you would be responsible for a royalty fee of 6 percent of gross sales.

GETTING STARTED

You can expect free start-up assistance from Command Performance in these areas: site selection, construction, facility layout and decoration, furniture and equipment leasing, merchandise and supplies acquisition, staffing, and grand opening. For a fee you can receive assistance in negotiating service contracts and purchasing real estate. A typical facility is 1,200 to 1,500 square feet located either in a mall, strip shopping center, commercial center, or a freestanding building. Depending on facility preparation, you can open your shop anywhere from one week to six months after signing your franchise agreement.

The company recommends that besides yourself you have ten full-time and six part-time employees, all of whom will receive a four-day training session at corporate headquarters near Boston in Wilmington, Massachusetts. You'll be shown innovative programs for attracting and retaining clients, creative hair design, stylist productivity, administration, and effective salon-management practices. You or your manager will attend a three-day basic management seminar covering staff motivation, inventory maintenance, and record keeping. Your stylists will receive technical training in "hair art" at the Command Performance Institute in Cincinnati, Ohio, or at one of the regional training centers. In a four-day program they'll learn how to precision cut, color, and apply permanents. The person you appoint as senior stylist will attend the institute for another six days of extensive training.

MAKING IT WORK

Virtually all aspects of salon operations are discussed in a series of manuals for you, your manager, your stylists, and even the receptionist. Further personnel assistance is offered through a series of national, regional, and local seminars on new haircare developments and business procedures. An awards banquet is held each year to recognize top franchisees and their employees; employees are also recognized in the company newsletter.

Each year the company conducts research on its customers' desires, habits, and needs. Provided to all the owners, the results are the basis for Command Performance's product-development efforts and promotional campaigns. There's no charge for newspaper ads, brochures, seasonal promotional materials, radio commercials, press releases, and the company public-relations manual. However, you pay a fee for television commercials, billboard posters, and four-color magazine ads.

Command Performance has its own line of haircare products which you can sell for additional revenue. Although you may stock noncompany products of equal quality, you are eligible for generous volume discounts by selling company-brand products.

COMMENTS

Command Performance was ranked eighty-sixth in *Entrepreneur* magazine's 1987 "Franchise 500." A member of IFA since 1982, the company is a corporate sponsor of the Children's Miracle Network Telethon. It is seeking franchisees throughout the United States and in Europe and in Japan.

GETTING MORE INFORMATION

The franchise information packet contains a collection of glossy, color brochures and pamphlets describing the Command Performance concept and illustrating hairstyles and company haircare products. Also included are a monthly newsletter, an annual-meeting review, and a seven-page confidential qualifications report (application) with detailed instructions. Write or call:

Carl M. Youngman
Chairperson
Command Performance
355 Middlesex Avenue
Wilmington, MA 01887
(800) USA–HAIR or (617) 658–6586

Comprehensive Accounting Corporation

BUSINESS:
accounting services
FOUNDED: 1949
FRANCHISED: 1965
START-UP
INVESTMENT:
$73,000–$83,000

NO. OF UNITS		AS OF		PROJECTED BY	
		1/1/85	1/1/86	1/1/87	1/1/88
OWNED BY:	COMPANY	0	0	0	0
	FRANCHISEES	455	391	400	460
LOCATED:	IN U.S.	454	390	399	459
	OUTSIDE U.S.	1	1	1	1
TOTAL:		455	391	400	460
NO. OF STATES W/ UNITS		40	41	43	45

THE BUSINESS

According to the Small Business Administration, approximately 92 percent of the 17.3 million businesses in the United States can be classified as small. These businesses are the potential client base of Comprehensive Accounting Corporation franchisees, who provide business clients with accounting services ranging from monthly operating statements, detail general ledgers, bank reconciliations, and payroll registers to business planning and consultation, tax-record maintenance and preparation, accounts receivable, and various specialized operating statements. Typically, only large companies with specialized accounting departments have such financial-management tools.

WHAT IT TAKES

A CAC franchise costs $20,000, which gives you use of the nationally recognized company trade names and trademarks and guarantees you a protected market location for fifteen years, renewable for an additional fifteen years. Beyond your initial fee, you'll need about $53,000 to $63,000 more to get your practice going. If you qualify, CAC can provide you with financing for all or part of this additional capital. After your office is open, you will pay an ongoing royalty fee to the company based on a percentage of your gross billings.

To be considered as a franchisee, you must have a degree in accounting, or its equivalent in work experience plus college credits (certification as a CPA is not necessary). This is a hands-on operation; the company expects you to take an active role in running your franchise unit. No franchise fee is charged for any additional units you may want to open within your protected territory. However, if you are interested, you can purchase a master franchise and subfranchise additional CAC offices for a percentage of the franchise and royalty fees.

In addition to its standard Affiliate arrangement, CAC offers a Sponsorship program. Under the terms of this alternative agreement, you can work as a salaried employee of a CAC franchisee for one year, enjoying the benefits of extensive on-the-job training. During your year of sponsorship you will acquire and develop your own clientele, which you can then purchase from your sponsor when you go out on your own.

GETTING STARTED

Typically, it takes three months from your franchise purchase to your opening. During that time, CAC will help you select a site for your office, which will require about 500 square feet and can be located almost anywhere—in an office building, a freestanding building, or a shopping strip or mall. CAC doesn't assist in lease negotiation, but the company will help out if you want to purchase and/or construct your facility, and provide facility-layout assistance. While you'll probably work alone initially, when your client list has grown sufficiently, you'll need to hire additional staff, and CAC will help you do so.

You won't need any special equipment at first, because the bulk of your communication with the centralized data-processing computer system at CAC's corporate headquarters will take place by mail. However, when you have about forty clients, you'll probably need to invest in an in-office data-entry terminal linking you directly to the mainframe computer. Later, as you continue to expand your client base, you'll expand your in-office capabilities as well, adding a printer system and then finally a self-contained computer system. The company can provide the appropriate equipment to you at a substantial savings over retail purchase.

If you are accepted into CAC's franchise program, you (along with your staff—manager, accountant, and bookkeeper—if applicable) must attend five weeks of intensive training at corporate headquarters in Aurora, Illinois. There, through classroom, videotape, and hands-on instruction, you will learn CAC's exclusive and proven accounting processing methods. You'll also spend a large portion of your time learning how to market your operation, with special emphasis on client acquisition. When you complete the training, you'll receive a six-volume management procedures manual; a marketing procedures manual, an audiovisual bookkeeper training manual, a marketing audiocassette series, pamphlets, forms, and other support materials. Within six months to a year, you'll return for a week of postgraduate training.

If you are joining CAC under the sponsor program, you won't attend the standard affiliate training program. However, you will receive two weeks of corporate training in the CAC marketing system.

MAKING IT WORK

Of your ongoing royalty fee, up to 3.5 percent will be channeled into the National Awareness Fund, which is managed by a special committee that decides how best to use these monies. An aggressive public-relations effort has resulted in numerous articles about the company appearing in many leading, business, trade, and professional publications. The company can provide you with mailers, brochures, billboard posters, and signs. In addition, the company has developed an award-winning videotaped sales presentation program designed for use with both groups and individual prospects. CAC offers consultations on the screening and selection of sales personnel and conducts sales training programs—both introductory and refresher courses—at cost.

CAC sponsors an annual national conference, biannual regional conferences, quarterly three-day seminars, annual onsite training programs for every franchise operation, an annual regional training program specifically designed for bookkeepers, and monthly area-wide or city franchisee meetings. You will receive a bimonthly company newsletter, plus periodic company-information and technical updates. CAC also presents national and regional seminars to CAC clients on topics ranging from tax planning/strategy to business financing. Also, clients receive a monthly newsletter and an annual questionnaire about the CAC services they've used.

Each franchisee is assigned to a corporate consultant, who provides ongoing counseling, assistance, and advice. Your consultant will have access to all the computerized information regarding your practice and will be able to help you anticipate and solve problems. You can reach your consultant, or data processing personnel, on the company toll-free hotline. If needed, your consultant will provide onsite assistance, at cost. A further support structure you will benefit from is the Franchise Owner Advisory Council, which meets four times a year and serves as a sounding board for franchisees' ideas, opinions, and recommendations. An additional group, the Forms and Procedures Council, is made up of representative franchise owners who help update and improve procedures, and methods.

As a CAC Affiliate, you will manage your own accounts with company-provided bookkeeping, expense-analysis, billing, and management-information systems. The company will also furnish you with monthly statistical reports regarding your client acquisition, billings and collections, and more. You can get discounted equipment and supplies through the company's centralized purchasing program. Further, you can take advantage of group life and general-liability insurance plans. CAC sponsors various achievement awards for franchisees.

COMMENTS

CAC was ranked 102d in *Entrepreneur* magazine's 1987 "Franchise 500." A member of the IFA since 1983, the company makes an earnings claim document available to potential franchisees prior to or during a personal interview. CAC has served as the official tabulator for the National Easter Seals Telethon. The company is seeking affiliates in the forty-eight continental states and Puerto Rico.

**GETTING MORE
INFORMATION**

The franchise information packet includes a brochure on both corporate and affiliate offices and personnel, reprints of articles about CAC in national magazines, a flyer on CAC's computer graphics capability, an information sheet about the sponsorship program, and a sample financial statement (the type CAC affiliates give their clients). Finally, a confidential resume requests detailed information regarding your personal, educational, professional, and financial history. For details, write to:

> Edward D. Muse
> President
> Comprehensive Accounting Corporation
> 2111 Comprehensive Drive
> Aurora, IL   60507
> (800)   323–9000 or (312)   898–6868

Corporate Finance Associates

BUSINESS: mergers,
  acquisitions, and
  financial consulting
FOUNDED: 1956
FRANCHISED: 1960
START-UP
  INVESTMENT:
  $40,000–$50,000

		AS OF		PROJECTED BY	
NO. OF UNITS		1/1/85	1/1/86	1/1/87	1/1/88
OWNED BY:	COMPANY	0	0	0	0
	FRANCHISEES	60	65	75	85
LOCATED:	IN U.S.	59	63	70	80
	OUTSIDE U.S.	1	2	5	5
TOTAL:		60	65	75	85
NO. OF STATES W/ UNITS		20	22	32	32

THE BUSINESS

In 1985, total U.S. industry-wide sales of $179.6 billion were reported for mergers and acquisitions, a 47 percent increase from 1984. Corporate Finance Associates is an organization of business deal makers with expertise in mergers, acquisition searches, business and product-line divestitures, financing, and general business consulting. The company's specialty is intermediating in the sale and acquisition of midsized companies in the $500,000 to $20,000,000 range. CFA's largest single sale in 1985 was $40 million; however, most sales were in the $2 million to $15 million range.

Because of the highly confidential nature of mergers and acquisitions, CFA's work is rarely publicized. The company primarily serves smaller, individually owned businesses or corporations, who otherwise would have turned to real estate agents or attorneys to help them with sales, mergers, and financing—although these professionals are rarely experts in such matters.

By joining CFA, a franchisee gains the credibility of a large organization, the access to a virtual clearinghouse of buyers and sellers, and the support of a network of associates and resources. A call to CFA from a client launches a national and international search for an appropriate buyer or seller. Consulting is an increasingly important service in CFA and is expected to grow. Founded in 1956, CFA now has more than sixty offices throughout the world and a record of service to over 2,350 clients in the last ten years.

WHAT IT TAKES

Rather than charging a franchising fee, the company collects a one-time performance fee of $10,000. No territory is involved because you'll work in cooperation with the CFA network. Your agreement will be for one year, with one-year renewal options. Your other start-up costs will range from $30,000 to $40,000. All start-up expenses, including the $10,000 fee, must be paid in cash. It may take about a year for you to generate any income, so you'll need sufficient resources for your personal expenses until you complete your first transaction. You'll pay CFA 7 percent on all sales and mergers and 4 percent on financing fees.

Of the sixty-five inquiries per month CFA receives about franchising opportunities, only about six or seven people are selected for an interview. CFA encourages only knowledgeable, financially stable businesspeople with entrepreneurial instincts. CFA representatives will interview you by telephone to decide whether you are qualified. If they believe you are, CFA will pay half of your round-trip transportation costs to the Atlanta administrative offices, where you can get details about all aspects of CFA's operations.

GETTING STARTED

The company recommends that you staff your office with one other full-time employee. CFA offices are usually 600 to 1,000 square feet and are located in office buildings and commercial centers. CFA representatives will help you with site selection, lease negotiations, and lease or purchase of office equipment. You'll be provided with an inventory of over 130 screened companies for sale and a large file of prequalified buyers. CFA will provide literature, contracts, and various forms to help expedite and finalize your business deals.

Before opening, you'll attend school for two days in the Atlanta, Georgia, office. In one-on-one training sessions you'll learn how to run a CFA office, find clients, structure deals, handle financing, and use effective marketing techniques. You should be ready for business within two months from the time you join CFA, and the company will assist with your grand opening.

MAKING IT WORK

You can participate in a cooperative advertising program to get newspaper and telephone-book ads, brochures, mailers, and press releases. You'll also use a lead-referral system to access national and international listings that are updated daily. You can also access a listing of prequalified buyers and lenders for financing. The CFA buyers' file is probably the most comprehensive one of its kind in the country. If you're qualified as a consultant, you may be added to the company's roster of available consultants. (You may sell the services of other consultants on the roster for a portion of the consulting fee.) Members with buyer clients may solicit the help of members in other territories in acquisition searches. Older members will help you get direct-contact exposure for your offerings and guide you through your first deals.

CFA holds an annual international conference, several regional meetings each year, and periodic two-day educational seminars. You'll receive weekly company and technical updates, a company newsletter, and a quarterly magazine geared to your clients' interests. Administrative office personnel can offer case-by-case guidance and coaching, and for help in areas outside your expertise (including international affairs) you can consult with qualified CFA members. Your operating manual answers many questions and offers tested selling and soliciting techniques. You'll use the company's inventory, bookkeeping, and expense-analysis systems, and CFA will provide you with the necessary forms for ordering stationery, contracts, and business forms. Each year CFA rewards outstanding performance by franchisees in several categories.

COMMENTS

A division of Bonneville Financial Corporation, the company is seeking new franchisees in most states and in Asia, Australia, Europe, Japan, Mexico, and South America.

FOR MORE INFORMATION

The franchise information packet contains a brochure with the story of CFA and an introduction to its concepts, a sales brochure, a list of members you can contact for references, and a background profile form for you to fill out and return. For more information, contact:

Michael M. Rothberg
Membership Selection Chairman
Corporate Finance Associates
6600 Peachtree–Dunwoody Road
300 Embassy Row, Suite 670
Atlanta, GA   30328
(404)   399–5633

Corporate Investment Business Brokers

BUSINESS: business
  brokerage firm
  FOUNDED: 1979
  FRANCHISED: 1982
START-UP
  INVESTMENT:
  $60,000

NO. OF UNITS		AS OF		PROJECTED BY	
		1/1/85	1/1/86	1/1/87	1/1/88
OWNED BY:	COMPANY	0	0	0	0
	FRANCHISEES	105	167	210	260
LOCATED:	IN U.S.	103	164	200	245
	OUTSIDE U.S.	2	3	10	15
TOTAL:		105	167	210	260
NO. OF STATES W/ UNITS		35	36	45	50

THE BUSINESS

More than 2.5 million businesses changed hands last year, involving one company out of five. That amounts to a potential $250 billion market that Corporate Investment Business Brokers are working to capture. The cumulative value of the 12,000 businesses currently listed for sale through the CIBB national information network is in excess of $1 billion, and growing. These businesses entrusted to CIBB for sale include every imaginable industry—wholesale and retail, light and heavy manufacturing, restaurants, service companies, and so forth.

Average gross sales per franchise represent $4 million, yielding an average annual net income of $123,000 for the franchisee. Nationally, 50 percent of all business sales placed in escrow do not close; but when CIBB is involved in a sale, more than 93 percent of the business sales placed in escrow do close—earning CIBB brokers regular, substantial commissions. Another CIBB benefit is that competition for clients is considered low since there are less than 2,000 business brokers nationwide, many with only local connections.

WHAT IT TAKES

The initial cost for a CIBB franchised affiliate is about $60,000, of which $35,000 is the franchise fee. Each franchise agreement will entitle you to exclusive territory rights for ten years, with a renewal period of another ten years. After your initial investment you'll pay an ongoing royalty fee of 6 percent of gross sales, plus an advertising fee of 2 percent of annual gross sales.

Although $25,000 of your initial investment must be in cash, loans are available from CIBB for venture capital, equipment and inventory financing, accounts-receivable financing, and mortgage arrangements. You can hire a manager, but the company would prefer that you oversee operations. As a business broker, you'll receive a commission of 12 percent of any sale, and you'll earn a 10 percent referral fee in some cases. CIBB does not require that potential franchisees have any previous experience in the field.

GETTING STARTED   CIBB will assist you in site selection, facility layout and decoration, staffing, and lease negotiations. The typical operating facility is 1,400 square feet, usually located in an office building. In the executive management training program at corporate offices in Phoenix, Arizona, you'll be trained in making appraisals, procuring a buyer and seller, preparing contracts, evaluating financial statements, hiring and training staff, advertising, and more. Your ten full-time employees, primarily sales agents, will receive onsite training from CIBB executives assigned to your territory. These CIBB staffers can help you open your office, often within sixty days after you become a CIBB franchised affiliate.

MAKING IT WORK   The company will keep you abreast of developments in the field through a quarterly newsletter, monthly company updates, regular memos, industry and market updates, and seminars. You'll also have access to a toll-free hotline, procedure-and-policy manuals, and a computerized management-information system. Headquarters resource persons will help you with administrative problem solving and onsite troubleshooting. In addition, the company offers free assistance in handling particular sales and in planning franchise expansion. Onsite training can take the form of on-the-job instruction, face-to-face consultation, or videotaped instruction as frequently as every five to six weeks.

Cooperative advertising is available to the franchisee in the form of newspaper and telephone-book ads. For the ongoing advertising fee you'll receive brochures, presentation books, national media coverage, and all press and public-relations materials. CIBB will provide you with listings of businesses for sale from each office in the United States and will enable you to list your clients. CIBB also has international relationships with firms based in Europe, Asia, South America, and the Middle East. The company annually sponsors a national or regional conference plus areawide franchise meetings. CIBB offers extensive life, major-medical, and disability insurance coverage.

COMMENTS   The company was ranked 62nd in *Venture* magazine's 1986 "Franchise 100" and 157th in *Entrepreneur* magazine's 1987 "Franchise 500." The company is currently seeking franchisees in most states and overseas.

GETTING MORE
INFORMATION   The franchise information packet includes several national-magazine reprints, two brochures describing CIBB's operations and career opportunities, a pamphlet on buying and selling a business,

and a two-page business application and personal financial statement.

For more information, contact:

Arthur A. Madden
Director of Franchise Marketing
Corporate Investment Business Brokers, Inc.
1515 East Missouri Avenue, Suite 100
Phoenix, AZ 85014
(800) 382–8240

Create-A-Book

BUSINESS:		AS OF		PROJECTED BY	
personalized book	NO. OF UNITS	1/1/85	1/1/86	1/1/87	1/1/88
printing	OWNED BY: COMPANY	0	0	0	0
FOUNDED: 1980	FRANCHISEES	90	125	175	250
FRANCHISED: 1982	LOCATED: IN U.S.	90	124	170	240
START-UP	OUTSIDE U.S.	0	1	5	10
INVESTMENT:	TOTAL:	90	125	175	250
$4,395–$5,000	NO. OF STATES W/ UNITS	10	25	35	45

THE BUSINESS

The Create-A-Book company prints and sells personalized children's books. "Reading is exciting when the story is about you!" is a company slogan. Any child can have his or her name printed throughout colorful storybooks along with the names of friends, relatives, pets, age, hometown, and so forth. Create-A-Book can be operated out of your home on a part-time basis. Sample titles include *A Birthday Surprise, My School Fun Book, My Space Adventure, The Big Parade,* and *My Christmas Wish.* Personalized Santa, Hanukkah, and Easter letters are also available. Franchisees have the complete equipment to print and bind the books. It takes less than five minutes from start to finish to print, bind, and place a book in a hard cover. There are many ways to sell and market Create-A-Books—on location in malls and stores or through fund-raising drives, mail-order operations, sponsors paying for books given to schools, or representatives selling books part-time. Franchisees set their own prices, generally charging $8 to $9 per book, with materials for each book currently costing $2.15.

WHAT IT TAKES

You will need $2,995 for the franchise fee, establishing an exclusive territory based on population figures. The franchise is a lifetime agreement. Your total investment will be $4,395 to $5,000 to cover the franchise fee and equipment, which includes an Apple Computer, a printer, a disc drive, and a monitor. All of the investment must be in cash. Fees for additional units will be based on your history with the company. Master franchises are available. You may be a franchise owner without being the manager of sales. Create-A-Book charges no ongoing royalty fees, and no prior bookselling experience is necessary.

GETTING STARTED

The company will help you with site selection; decoration; lease or purchase of furniture, fixtures, and equipment; service-maintenance contracts; and merchandise acquisition. The average Create-A-Book operation is 60 to 100 square feet, located in a mall, shopping center, or freestanding building. One part-time employee can run the business. Classroom training will be held in Cincinnati for you and any employees for one to two days to explain marketing techniques, sales, use of equipment, printing, binding, and placing books in covers. You'll also receive a videotape for a one-day onsite session for you and your employees. The company emphasizes that its book-making process is simple and can even be learned by your children. You can be selling your first books within one to two weeks after buying the franchise, and the company will help with your grand opening.

MAKING IT WORK

The company offers co-op advertising funding for newspaper ads, black-and-white and four-color magazine ads, mailers, brochures, radio commercials, in-house media packages (slides, videotapes), point-of-purchase displays, signs, and seasonal promotional displays. Create-A-Book sponsors an annual convention and regional conference for franchise owners. Top sellers are recognized at the annual convention. A monthly newsletter covers selling tips and marketing ideas; surveys are conducted once a year. The company provides headquarters and regional resource persons, policy and management-procedure manuals, and order forms. Create-A-Book places a priority on developing new marketing and sales techniques, as well as new books. The company's central purchasing program offers volume discounts, and there is a centralized merchandising system. Company divisions produce and distribute materials, which are sent out via United Parcel Service from Cincinnati the same day that orders are received. You may develop your own products if you wish.

COMMENTS

Create-A-Book has won various civic awards and has been recognized for outstanding contributions to local communities. The company wants to add new franchises in twenty-eight states and Canada.

GETTING MORE INFORMATION

The franchise information packet consists of a sample brochure and order form, a description of the company's concept, and a testimonial from a Florida school superintendent. For more information contact:

Robert Young
Director
Create-A-Book
6380 Euclid Road
Cincinnati, OH   45236
(513)   793–5151 or 793–9789 (call collect)

Dairy Queen

BUSINESS: fast-food restaurant specializing in soft-serve ice cream
FOUNDED: 1940
FRANCHISED: 1944
START-UP INVESTMENT: $275,000–$700,000

		AS OF		PROJECTED BY	
NO. OF UNITS		1/1/85	1/1/86	1/1/87	1/1/88
OWNED BY:	COMPANY	7	7	N/A	N/A
	FRANCHISEES	4,774	4,779	N/A	N/A
LOCATED:	IN U.S.	4,204	4,229	N/A	N/A
	OUTSIDE U.S.	577	577	N/A	N/A
TOTAL:		4,781	4,786	N/A	N/A
NO. OF STATES W/ UNITS		50	50	N/A	N/A

THE BUSINESS

The first Dairy Queen served just one product: a soft-serve cone with a distinctive curl on top. That little cone was the start of the largest dessert franchise in the world. Dairy Queen's "soft serve" contains the same basic ingredients as ice cream, but with less milk fat. Dairy Queen products include sundaes, shakes, parfaits, banana splits, cones, and a line of hard-frozen novelties and soft-serve dairy products packed in convenient sizes for home use. In 1944, Dairy Queen was one of the first companies to franchise. By 1985, Dairy Queen franchises were grossing $1.7 billion, with average gross sales per unit of $200,000 to $700,000.

WHAT IT TAKES

Your initial franchise fee of $30,000 will grant you a perpetual license to operate but not an exclusive territory. Two types of stores are available. The Dairy Queen/Brazier (Plan A) is a total food-service program with soft-serve dairy products and the Brazier line of fast foods (hamburgers, hot dogs, chili dogs, cheese dogs, fish sandwiches, french fries, etc.). The Dairy Queen/Limited Brazier (Plan B) serves primarily soft-serve products plus a small line of fast-food items. Your total investment will range from $275,00 to $700,000, depending on your choice of Plan A or B and the cost of your land. Construction costs for Plan A range from $140,000 to $165,000 plus the cost of land and site improvements, and equipment costs range from $130,000 to $160,000. Plan B's construction costs range from $60,000 to $70,000 plus the cost of land and site improvements, and equipment costs from $55,000 to $80,000. An optional equipment-installation fee of $2,200 and an optional construction-coordination fee of $3,000 is also available. The company requires that $85,000 of the total cost be in cash, and the only financial assistance available from the company is for half of the franchise fee. You should have a minimum net worth of $150,000 (excluding homestead and personal property). There is no franchise fee for additional units; master franchises are available. You may be an owner-investor rather than an active manager of the business. You will pay an ongoing royalty fee of 4 percent of gross sales, plus a 3 to 5 percent sales-promotion fee per month, with the rate determined annually by the American Dairy Queen Corporation. Prior restaurant-management experience is helpful but not necessary.

GETTING STARTED

Dairy Queen's franchise-development managers will provide you with site criteria, counseling and assistance in site selection, and a site-feasibility study examining population trends, traffic counts, proximity of shopping areas, visibility, and accessibility. The company's engineering department provides a standard equipment-layout plan and equipment list, and a list of sources for equipment, products, and supplies. Dairy Queen helps with facility decoration for a fee. The typical Dairy Queen store is 2,500 square feet. When parking space is a consideration, the store typically is located on a 23,000 square-foot lot with a minimum 130 to 150-foot frontage. Malls and freestanding buildings are common locations. The building and/or equipment layouts must be approved if one of the company's standard designs is not used. Your staff will consist of eight full-time and thirty-five part-time employees. At your own expense you will travel to Dairy Queen's national training center in Minneapolis for two weeks of education on proper preparation and serving of all products, counter etiquette, suggestive selling, financial management, personnel management, marketing, merchandising, and equipment operation and maintenance. For thirty-five days before you open your store, a visiting team will help you train employees, contact suppliers, and order initial inventory. After your opening, the visiting team will supervise the first week of operations, and the company will later provide three weeks of training for you and your employees in your store. You can be open for business within six months after buying the franchise.

MAKING IT WORK

Your advertising fee will cover newspaper ads, mailers, brochures, point-of-purchase displays, signs, banners, seasonal promotional displays, incentives, press releases, and a public-relations/marketing manual. Additional marketing devices such as radio or television commercials, billboard posters, and contests are available either as part of your fee or with co-op funding. Dairy Queen holds a national convention every two years and regional conferences once or twice a year. Four to six times a year the company conducts on-site training on financial management and cleanliness. You will receive a magazine issued eight times a year, a monthly newsletter, updates on products and market information as needed, and occasional surveys. Dairy Queen also provides headquarters and regional resource persons; on-site advising; policy, management-procedure, and customer-service manuals; all types of forms; and bookkeeping, inventory, personnel, and computerized-billing systems. Dairy Queen sells equipment to licensees, and its central purchasing program provides volume discounts for company brands, although you may buy approved noncompany products. Dairy Queen sponsors insurance for property, general liability, life, major medical, disability, and worker's compensation coverage.

COMMENTS

Dairy Queen was ranked seventh in *Entrepreneur* magazine's 1987 "Franchise 500". Dairy Queen is a major corporate sponsor of Children's Miracle Network Television. The company wants to add new franchises in thirty-nine states.

GETTING MORE INFORMATION

The franchise information packet contains brochures on the company's operations and a franchise offering circular. For details, contact:

John Hyduke
Vice-President of Franchise Development
Dairy Queen
5701 Green Valley Drive
Minneapolis, MN 55437
(800) 624–6985 or (612) 830–0312

Debit One Mobile Bookkeeping

BUSINESS: mobile
bookkeeping service
FOUNDED: 1983
FRANCHISED: 1983
START-UP
INVESTMENT:
$50,000

		AS OF		PROJECTED BY	
NO. OF UNITS		1/1/85	1/1/86	1/1/87	1/1/88
OWNED BY: COMPANY		0	0	0	0
	FRANCHISEES	35	85	185	360
LOCATED:	IN U.S.	35	85	185	360
	OUTSIDE U.S.	0	0	0	0
TOTAL:		35	85	185	360
NO. OF STATES W/ UNITS		16	29	35	50

THE BUSINESS

Debit One is a unique business designed to fit the mobile lifestyle of modern America. Instead of the owner of a company lugging financial records to an accountant's office, where the paperwork is often tied up for two to three weeks, Debit One brings bookkeeping services to the company. Debit One's mobile bookkeeping vans are designed as offices complete with computers and software, and Debit One personnel can complete a client's books in just a few hours.

Jack Dunn, the president and founder of Debit One, has more than twenty-seven years of accounting experience. Dunn began his mobile bookkeeping service in a bread truck, but today Debit One franchisees operate out of late-model Winnebagos equipped with modern office fixtures.

As a Debit One bookkeeper, you will be free to arrange your work schedule as you prefer, allowing yourself as much free time as you want. You will also have the chance for additional income by doing backwork and personal income taxes for your clients and their employees.

WHAT IT TAKES

A cash fee of $18,000, plus working capital and enough money to lease or finance the fully equipped van, will get you started in as little as two weeks. The range of your total investment may be as high as $50,000. Debit One will provide you with approved sources for leasing or financing, and guidelines for your proposal package. Then you will be in control of a specified, exclusive territory with a population of 100,000 persons. Each franchisee pays a monthly royalty fee of 8 percent of the gross sales.

The term of the original franchise agreement is five years, with renewal periods of five years. You may be either an owner-operator or an owner-investor, but in either case you must have the necessary knowledge and skills in accounting to run the business. Debit One encourages franchisees to own multiple units; in fact, 86 percent of the franchisees own more than one. Additional franchises cost $12,000 for the second and $10,000 for each additional unit.

GETTING STARTED

Because your van will be your office, your start-up costs will be low. You must handle the expense of leasing or purchasing your vehicle, computer, and furniture, but the company can help you order an outfitted van from a new Springfield, Missouri, company that has been formed to provide vehicles for Debit One. Then you'll receive extensive, professional training to augment your previous accounting knowledge. At the company's corporate training center you will receive two days of classroom training in management, three days in computer operations, and three in sales. Your sales staff will join you for the last three days, to be followed by two more days of on-site sales training. A Debit One representative will come to your location to help you develop clients and get your operation off to a running start.

MAKING IT WORK

There is no ongoing advertising fee. The company feels that the vans, with Debit One Mobile Bookkeeping painted in large letters on the side panels, are the best advertising available. In fact, people have been known to stop the vans on the highway and say, "I need you." The monthly royalty fee, however, provides you with newspaper ads, presentation books, an in-house media package (slides, videotapes), and a marketing manual.

You will be paid a percentage of collections, and your sales representatives are paid on commission. You'll have no payroll to contend with. Debit One provides resource people, a toll-free hotline, manuals to cover all your needs, forms, and bookkeeping and personnel systems. Each franchise operator receives the franchise operations manual along with videotapes, upgraded software support as laws change, and the latest marketing techniques.

The company hosts national conventions annually and one-day seminars twice a year. Regular communication between the franchise operator and Debit One is encouraged. You'll get a bimonthly company newsletter with hints for boosting sales, the latest tax news, and reminders about vehicle maintenance.

COMMENTS

Debit One is a member of the Better Business Bureau. The company is seeking franchisees in almost every state, and it is investigating expansion into Canada and Europe.

GETTING MORE INFORMATION

The franchise information packet contains a list of business references, copies of articles explaining the mobile bookkeeping idea, information sheets on Debit One, color pictures of an outfitted mobile van, and a three-page application form. For more information, write or call:

Sharon Rogers
Marketing Assistant
Debit One Mobile Bookkeeping
3433 S. Campbell, Suite S
Springfield, MO   65807
(800)   331–2491 or (417)   887–0715

Deck The Walls

BUSINESS: retail			AS OF		PROJECTED BY	
artwork and frame	NO. OF UNITS		1/1/85	1/1/86	1/1/87	1/1/88
store	OWNED BY: COMPANY		11	31	1	1
FOUNDED: 1979		FRANCHISEES	98	159	264	339
FRANCHISED: 1979	LOCATED: IN U.S.		109	190	265	340
START-UP		OUTSIDE U.S.	0	0	0	0
INVESTMENT:	TOTAL:		109	190	265	340
$150,000–$200,000	NO. OF STATES W/ UNITS		37	37	39	42

THE BUSINESS

Deck The Walls, the largest chain of art/custom-framing stores in the United States, sells open- and limited-edition prints, posters, ready-made frames, and photo frames. Each store also has a custom-framing center with a wide selection of moldings and matts. Deck The Walls is a subsidiary of WNS, Inc., a publicly held corporation founded in 1968. WNS also owns Wicks 'N' Sticks and Wallpapers To Go. The total annual dollar volume for all franchise operations in 1985 was $33,600,000, and each franchise unit grosses an average of $250,488.

WHAT IT TAKES

Your total initial investment will be approximately $184,500. Your expenses will include $27,500 for the franchise fee; $25,000 for display fixtures, equipment, freight, and storage; $87,000 for construction and leasehold improvements; $35,000 for merchandise and supplies; and $10,000 for working capital. The total estimated cost of starting your Deck The Walls store can vary by approximately $25,000, depending on geographic location, store size, and other factors; 25 to 30 percent of the total start-up costs must be in cash. The company can give you an estimate for any site you are considering.

You can get financial assistance both from the company and from the Small Business Association and other financial institutions. Passive ownership is allowed but discouraged. If you buy an additional store, the franchise fee of $27,500 will apply. You'll pay an ongoing royalty fee of 6 percent of gross sales.

GETTING STARTED

A typical Deck The Walls gallery is 1,400 square feet in a regional shopping mall, although a few are in shopping centers or along shopping strips. The company specifies site-selection criteria, and company real estate experts negotiate the lease. Also, the company can provide the construction and installation of fixtures necessary to meet its standards. All units have a uniform layout and decorating scheme, and the company will assist you with the purchase or leasing of furniture, fixtures, and equipment.

Previous experience and knowledge of either art or the retail business are not necessary. You'll need two full-time and five part-time personnel to run your franchise. Before opening your Deck The Walls store, you'll receive nine days of comprehensive classroom training at corporate headquarters in Houston, Texas. For another nine days corporate personnel will train you and your employees in your store.

Before your store opens, the regional franchise director and the new-store coordinator will help you stock your original inventory, which is chosen by corporate merchandising experts. You can open your store within eight to twelve weeks after purchasing the franchise, and Deck The Walls will assist you with your grand opening.

MAKING IT WORK

As part of your initial investment, you will get a public-relations/ marketing manual, press materials, grand-opening materials, and presentation books. You can also buy an optional advertising package that includes newspaper ads, telephone-book ads, brochures, mailers, and catalogs. The company will send you a quarterly newsletter, plus periodic technical updates on products and services and updates on industry and market information. The company annually sponsors one national and two regional conferences, and it regularly conducts city- and areawide franchise meetings and one-day seminars.

For operations and merchandising assistance you can call the company's toll-free hotline, and company experts can come to your store between the regular visits from your regional director and other company support staff. You will receive manuals covering policy, management procedure, customer service, and production presentation, as well as forms for inventory, personnel, orders, and accounting. An outside vendor offers a bookkeeping system, but the company provides inventory, personnel, expense-analysis, and computerized management-information systems. WNS sponsors an insurance package with property, general-liability, major-medical, dental, and worker's compensation coverage.

The corporate office strongly supports ongoing research, development, and testing of products. Merchandise, equipment, and supplies are produced and distributed by the company, and products carrying company brands and labels are exclusive to Deck The

Walls franchises. However, you may buy non-company products from approved vendors with whom the company has negotiated volume discounts. Merchandise from any other vendors must be reviewed and approved by the company.

COMMENTS

Deck The Walls was ranked 71st in *Venture* magazine's 1986 "Franchise 100" and 173rd in *Entrepreneur* magazine's 1987 "Franchise 500." The company is a member of the IFA. Deck The Walls donates products to local and regional charities for fund-raising activities. An earnings claim document will be made available prior to or during your personal interview. The company wants to expand to all states except Alaska.

GETTING MORE INFORMATION

The franchise folder contains a corporate profile, information about Deck The Walls, an overview of support given to franchisees, a list of current store locations and developing locations available for purchase, an overview of estimated costs for purchasing a franchise, photographs of a typical Deck The Walls store, and a confidential personal profile form for potential franchisees to complete. For more information, contact:

Houghton B. Hutcheson
Deck The Walls
7915 FM 1960 West, Suite 300
P. O. Box 4586
Houston, TX   77210–4586
(800) 231–6337 or (713) 890–5900

Dial One

BUSINESS: network of affiliated service and maintenance companies
FOUNDED: 1982
FRANCHISED: 1983
START-UP INVESTMENT: $4,000–$10,000

		AS OF		PROJECTED BY	
NO. OF UNITS		1/1/85	1/1/86	1/1/87	1/1/88
OWNED BY: COMPANY		0	0	0	0
	FRANCHISEES	550	810	1,600	3,500
LOCATED: IN U.S.		460	680	1,300	2,900
	OUTSIDE U.S.	90	130	300	600
TOTAL:		550	810	1,600	3,500
NO. OF STATES W/ UNITS		9	12	18	30

THE BUSINESS

Founded on the principle of banding together service contractors to increase sales and visibility, Dial One affiliates include plumbing firms, landscapers, roofers, television-repair companies, and many other service businesses. In all, fifty trades are represented by the Dial One service network in twenty United States regions, plus cities in Canada, Japan, and Germany.

Researchers have found that 65 percent of consumers do not know whom to call when a property-maintenance problem arises, and they lack confidence in the quality of most maintenance firms. Dial One responded to that need by building local networks of reputable businesses linked by a strict code of ethics. The company slogan, "Dial One of Us to Reach Any of Us," signifies that the consumer can get quality maintenance help by calling any Dial One representative.

Total sales volume for Dial One members was $150,000,000 in 1985.

WHAT IT TAKES

In order to become a Dial One affiliate you must have an established service business and a solid reputation, as confirmed by your customers and by other professionals in your industry. Your franchise fee of $4,000 must be paid in cash, and you may need up to about $6,000 for additional start-up costs. Your franchise agreement will run for four years, with a four-year renewal option. As a Dial One representative, you will have an exclusive assigned district territory. If you purchase an additional franchise territory, the fee will be half of your original investment; master franchises are also available. An ongoing royalty fee for company affiliation is based on a percentage of gross sales with a monthly maximum.

GETTING STARTED

Since you are already an existing enterprise, you won't have to arrange for a special facility. However, the Dial One logo must appear throughout your system—on your business vehicles, uniforms, and advertising signs. The company's internationally approved supplier program will allow you to purchase equipment, vehicles, uniforms, signs, and all types of materials at a significant discount.

If accepted into the Dial One network, you, your co-owners (if any), and your employees will receive on-site continuing education regarding money management, leadership skills, customer satisfaction, equity building, advertising, and marketing. As a district owner or a master franchisee, you will receive, free of charge, five days of classroom and video training plus consultation in Long Beach, California. The training covers all aspects of Dial One operations.

MAKING IT WORK

Dial One conducts national conferences semiannually and regional conventions three times a year. At the local level the company conducts eight-hour seminars and arranges weekly luncheons for Dial One contractors.

To serve franchisees the home office operates a toll-free hotline; arranges both regular and troubleshooting visits by regional resource personnel; and provides manuals on company policy, management procedures, and customer service, as well as systems for bookkeeping, inventory, and computerized information management. Insurance coverage is available for worker's compensation, property, automobile, and general liability for contractors. Credit-union affiliation is available in some locales.

The company distributes a biannual newsletter, monthly product/service updates, and quarterly company updates. Questionnaires and surveys are administered twice a year, and the company sponsors various employee recognition programs.

As a member of the Dial One network, you'll receive direct referrals from other Dial One contractors and sales leads from the regional office, which processes the response cards customers receive from each Dial One contractor who serves them. Dial One also performs research in maintaining good service and product selection.

For a fee of 2 percent of gross sales Dial One franchisees can obtain cooperative advertising in the form of newspaper ads, mailers, brochures, presentation books, catalogs, locally broadcast television and radio commercials, national media exposure, and billboard posters.

COMMENTS

In 1986, *Venture* magazine ranked Dial One eighteenth among its "Franchise 100," and *Entrepreneur* magazine ranked the company fiftieth in its 1987 "Franchise 500." The company won the 1985 Commercial Vehicle Graphics Contest for its truck logo design. A member of IFA since 1980, Dial One is seeking franchisees throughout the United States and in Australia, Canada, Japan, and Europe.

GETTING MORE INFORMATION

The franchise information packet consists of a four-color folder containing many reprints from trade publications, *Entrepreneur* magazine's "Franchise 500" list, and a pamphlet explaining Dial One services. For more information, write or call:

Bill Kroske
President
Dial One International
4100 Long Beach Boulevard
Long Beach, CA   90807
(800)   DIAL–ONE or (213)   595–7075

Diet Center

BUSINESS: weight-
control programs and
products
FOUNDED: 1970
FRANCHISED: 1972
START-UP
INVESTMENT:
$27,000–$49,000

		AS OF		PROJECTED BY	
NO. OF UNITS		1/1/85	1/1/86	1/1/87	1/1/88
OWNED BY:	COMPANY	0	0	0	0
	FRANCHISEES	2,010	2,130	2,250	2,370
LOCATED:	IN U.S.	1,850	1,960	2,060	2,160
	OUTSIDE U.S.	160	170	190	210
TOTAL:		2,010	2,130	2,250	2,370
NO. OF STATES W/ UNITS		50	50	50	50

THE BUSINESS

Sybil Ferguson developed the Diet Center weight-loss plan when she needed surgery but was in such poor health—simultaneously over-weight and malnourished—that her doctor insisted she postpone it until she was in better shape. After the plan restored her health, Ferguson started the franchised Diet Center program in 1972. By 1976 it had expanded to 120 offices, primarily in the western United States. The 1,000th center opened in 1980 and the 2,000th in 1985, making Diet Center the largest franchised weight-loss program in the world. Serving men, women, and children, Diet Center offers a com-prehensive five-phase program for weight loss; private, daily coun-seling; sound nutrition; behavior modification, and lifelong health maintenance. The company also sells vitamins and other products. Diet Center has expanded into Canada and has grown largely on the recommendation of satisfied customers. In 1985 franchise opera-tions grossed $165,750,000, with average gross sales per unit of $82,486.

WHAT IT TAKES

To qualify as a Diet Center owner and/or counselor, you must have lost weight on the program. Depending on the population area of your franchise, the initial fee will be either $12,000 or $24,000. This will be an exclusive territory, valid for ten years and renewable for five. Your total investment, including the franchise fee, will be $27,000 to $49,000, all of which must be paid in cash. Additional units are priced the same, and master franchises are available. You may own a Diet Center without actually managing it. You must pay an ongoing royalty fee of $1.20 per dieter day (each day a dieter spends in the reducing phase of the program).

GETTING STARTED

As part of your franchise fee Diet Center will help you with site selection, purchase negotiation, and facility layout and decoration and will provide the materials, supplies, and equipment necessary to start your business. The typical center is 1,000 to 1,500 square feet, located in an office building, mall, shopping center, freestand-ing building, or medical building. Including yourself, you will need one or two full-time and one or two part-time employees. New franchise operators attend a one-week counselor training seminar at Diet Center headquarters in Rexburg, Idaho, where they learn about all phases of Diet Center operations, counseling, nutrition, accounting, and advertising. You can expect to open your center within forty-five to sixty days after buying a franchise, and the company will help with your grand opening. You must follow the Diet Center guidelines and policies described in the procedures manual.

MAKING IT WORK Your advertising expense is considered part of your continuing license fee. You will receive newspaper ads, black-and-white and four-color magazine ads, mailers, telephone-book ads, brochures, presentation books, catalogs, television and radio commercials, national media coverage, videotapes, point-of-purchase displays, billboard posters, signs, seasonal promotional displays, a lead-referral system, incentives, press releases, and a public-relations/marketing manual. The company has its own video department to produce the films used in behavior modification with clients and its own printing facilities to create literature.

Diet Center sponsors national conventions and regional conferences twice a year and conducts areawide franchise meetings. The company issues monthly magazines and newsletters and periodic updates on nutrition and company news. Customer surveys are conducted regularly and the company sponsors award programs for its franchisees. Backup services include headquarters resource personnel; manuals for policy and management procedure; forms for personnel, orders, and accounting; and systems for computerized information management and billing.

Research and development departments create new products for the company's Ferguson Laboratories, a state-of-the-art facility supplying products to Diet Center outlets. You can benefit from volume discounts on company brands, although you may also sell other types of products. The company has a centralized purchasing program and merchandising system.

COMMENTS Diet Center was ranked fourteenth in *Entrepreneur* magazine's 1987 "Franchise 500" and twenty-fifth in *Venture* magazine's 1986 "Franchise 100." A division of American Health Companies, Inc., Diet Center has been a member of the IFA since 1981. In 1985 the company established the Sybil Ferguson Wellness Institute in Provo, Utah.

GETTING MORE INFORMATION

The franchise information packet contains a four-color brochure on the company's operations, a Federal Trade Commission disclosure, and a two-page application form. For more details, contact:

Ray Lindstrom
Franchise Sales Director
Diet Center Inc.
220 South Second West
Rexburg, ID 83440
(208) 356–9381

Docktor Pet Centers

BUSINESS: retail pet
and pet-supply stores
FOUNDED: 1966
FRANCHISED: 1967
START-UP
INVESTMENT:
$149,800–$192,500

		AS OF		PROJECTED BY	
NO. OF UNITS		1/1/85	1/1/86	1/1/87	1/1/88
OWNED BY:	COMPANY	20	11	10	10
	FRANCHISEES	123	154	190	290
LOCATED:	IN U.S.	140	160	190	280
	OUTSIDE U.S.	3	5	10	20
TOTAL:		143	165	200	300
NO. OF STATES W/ UNITS		29	31	35	40

THE BUSINESS

Household pets and their care represent annually a $4 billion retail industry. Docktor Pet Centers is the largest franchise chain of pet department stores in the United States. The stores sell cats, dogs, birds, and other, more exotic pets, along with a complete range of pet supplies, from vitamins and flea collars to combs and sweaters. In 1985 the total annual dollar volume of business for all franchise operations was $115 million; individual franchise operations averaged gross sales of $515,000.

WHAT IT TAKES

The Docktor Pet Center franchise fee is $15,000. Your other start-up costs will include $85,000 to $115,000 for equipment, fixtures, and/or leasehold improvements; $1,800 to $2,500 for signs; $30,000 to $35,000 for opening inventory; $8,000 to $10,000 for animal inventory; and $10,000 to $15,000 for working capital. Your total initial investment, therefore, will range between $149,800 and $192,500. Usually you'll need to pay about one-third to one-half of this total in cash. The company has arranged indirect financing through Allied Lending Company. Your agreement will run for twenty years and will guarantee an exclusive territory extending to a five-mile radius around your store.

Two-thirds of Docktor Pet Center franchisees own more than one store, but the company expects you to run your first store successfully for a while before you apply for more. The franchise fee for a second store is $5,000, for a third is $4,000, and for a fourth is $2,500. As an alternative, you may take advantage of their master-franchise opportunities. You'll pay an ongoing royalty fee of 4.5 percent of sales.

GETTING STARTED

If you can't tell a cockatiel from a cocker spaniel, don't worry. The company isn't looking for veterinarians—simply business-oriented, hard-working animal lovers. The company will bring you to their headquarters in Wilmington, Massachusetts, for a three-week training program that covers store operations, pet care, accounting management, inventory, personnel selection, merchandising and promotion. Should you decide to hire a manager rather than operate your own store, your manager will attend a similar training program. The company has also prepared various manuals on animal care, handling, and training for your kennel personnel. An on-site advisor will guide you during your first two weeks of operation.

Docktor will help you find a store site and negotiate your lease. Your store will most likely be located in a large regional mall, where customer traffic is always high (which is one of the ingredients of success for Docktor Pet Centers). The company will not only help you find the best location but will also design your store to ensure the most effective store layout and merchandise display. Docktor Pet Centers are set up so that animals and birds are out in the open, where customers can hold and play with them. An open pen is built in the front window for puppies, and all Docktor Pet Centers have a "puppy love room" where customer and canine can have some private get-acquainted time.

MAKING IT WORK

You'll have access to Docktor's merchandise system with over 1,800 items, including over 600 products with the Docktor label. The company will provide you with a bookkeeping system that has computerized inventory tracking and all the necessary accounting forms. Company counselors will visit you regularly to provide any assistance you might need.

Docktor Pet Centers doesn't do much advertising—instead the company will help boost your sales with such promotional materials as point-of-purchase displays, signs, and customer handouts (for example, the "Puppy Care Kit," which tells new dog owners about nutrition, medication, grooming, housebreaking, and more). The company also offers many sales incentives and contests for franchisees.

The monthly company newsletter describes the various contests and recognizes franchisees' performance records and other accomplishments. The company sponsors annual national and regional franchisee conferences and biannual seminars. You'll have access to a regional consultant on an ongoing basis.

COMMENTS

A member of the IFA since 1968, the company is seeking franchisees primarily in the southern and western states.

GETTING MORE INFORMATION

The franchise information packet includes a question-and-answer sheet covering basic information, a sample company newsletter, copies of several magazine and newspaper articles about the company, and a confidential qualification report for potential franchisees. For more information, contact:

Clyde H. Trerfessen
Director of Franchise Development
Docktor Pet Centers, Inc.
355 Middlesex Avenue
Wilmington, MA 01887
(800) 325–6011 or (617) 658–7840

Dr. Vinyl

BUSINESS: mobile
  vinyl-repair service
  FOUNDED: 1972
  FRANCHISED: 1980
START-UP
  INVESTMENT:
  $14,900–$29,900

		AS OF		PROJECTED BY	
NO. OF UNITS		1/1/85	1/1/86	1/1/87	1/1/88
OWNED BY: COMPANY		11	15	16	17
	FRANCHISEES	42	66	80	105
LOCATED:	IN U.S.	53	81	96	122
	OUTSIDE U.S.	0	0	0	0
TOTAL:		53	81	96	122
NO. OF STATES W/ UNITS		17	21	23	25

THE BUSINESS

Dr. Vinyl provides automobile dealers a mobile, wholesale specialty service for new and used vehicles. Besides the basic services of vinyl, leather, and dashboard repair and redyeing, Dr. Vinyl also provides specialty services, such as applying pin striping and side molding and installing rear-window deicers. For repair work the company can match any automotive vinyl color, by trim code, from the year 1975 on. Also, both leather and vinyl can be redyed in either the same color or a completely different color. Dr. Vinyl Field Associates (as franchisees are called) develop a call list of car dealerships that require daily or twice-weekly service. The repair and dye work is done at the dealership. Most Dr. Vinyl services and products are unconditionally guaranteed for one year.

In 1985 the total annual dollar volume for the fifty-three Dr. Vinyl franchises was $1,635,550, and each franchise had average gross sales of $28,199.

WHAT IT TAKES

No experience is required to own a Dr. Vinyl franchise, but this is not the ideal business for anyone who is color blind! The franchise fee will be determined by the size of the operation you want. A Class

C franchise (with one person and one van) is $14,900; a Class B (two people and two vans) is $19,900; and a Class A (three people and three vans) is $29,900. The franchise fee will cover your initial inventory, which includes an assortment of products in various colors, widths, and sizes. The term of the agreement is ten years with a ten-year renewal, and you'll be guaranteed a countywide exclusive territory. You'll pay a monthly fee of 7 percent of gross sales.

Your minimum initial investment will be $14,900, plus the cost of a van to transport your supplies. Of that amount, at least $11,175 must be paid in cash. For Class B and Class A franchises, you will be expected to pay a proportionately higher cash amount. For the balance, Dr. Vinyl may provide financial assistance.

Master franchises are available, but Dr. Vinyl discourages passive ownership. Fees for additional franchises vary, depending on the population and potential market in your county.

GETTING STARTED

Dr. Vinyl's training program has several unique aspects, including a sneak preview. If you are interested but tentative, you can go to Kansas City and spent eight hours in the field with an established Dr. Vinyl technician. Then, if you decide that this is the franchise for you, Dr. Vinyl will reimburse your travel expenses. Once you've signed up, you'll begin the formal, two-week technical and sales training program which covers every aspect of vinyl, leather, and plastic repair, as well as on-the-job business-development procedures. After you are judged proficient in technical and sales ability, you will spend additional time going over office procedures. You may return anytime within the first eight weeks after starting your own franchise for three days of follow-up training. Your travel and other expenses associated with training will be reimbursed up to a predetermined limit.

The home office will help you prepare a dealership call list and, for a fee, will advise you about equipment leasing and purchasing. Since you'll be operating from your van, you can run your office in your home. This is a business you can probably handle by yourself, depending on the size of your territory. However, husband-wife teams also work well. You can be in business within two weeks after signing your agreement.

MAKING IT WORK

For your franchise fee Dr. Vinyl will furnish you with comprehensive dealer-information kits, business cards, logos for your vehicles, newspaper ads, brochures, and customer presentation materials. You'll also receive order and inventory forms, a computerized billing system, and an accounting package with monthly operating statements, balance sheets, and business valuation. If necessary, accounts-receivable financing is available.

The company sponsors special recognition programs for franchisees with the highest gross sales. High-quality service is also emphasized. Product quality is guaranteed by the Dr. Vinyl brand-name line of supplies, which you will be required to use unless you get special permission from the home office. The Dr. Vinyl laboratory can custom match any vinyl color when you supply a sample.

The company will make a special effort to keep your inventory well stocked—orders you send in on a weekday morning will be shipped by the next working day. With the company's centralized merchandising system and volume-purchase discounts, you'll be able to maintain a higher profit margin.

For problems or questions that arise you can rely on a field representative who will come by regularly and a toll-free hotline to the home office. Also, you'll receive information through the company's monthly newsletter and quarterly technical updates. You also can attend the company's annual national conference and annual two-day seminar to sharpen your business skills.

COMMENTS

Dr. Vinyl, which joined the IFA in 1981, was ranked 311th in *Entrepreneur* magazine's 1987 "Franchise 500." The company is seeking franchisees in most states except in New England.

GETTING MORE INFORMATION

The franchise information packet contains a four-color ad; a detailed question-and-answer pamphlet; a brochure explaining training, business procedures, areas of service, and investment; and letters of endorsement from three successful Dr. Vinyl field associates. For more information, write or call:

Thomas E. Rafter, Jr.
President
Dr. Vinyl & Associates, Ltd.
3001 Cherry Street
Kansas City, MO   64108
(800)   531–5600

Duds 'N Suds

BUSINESS: self-
  service laundry
FOUNDED: 1980
FRANCHISED: 1983
START-UP
  INVESTMENT:
  $180,000–$205,000

NO. OF UNITS		AS OF		PROJECTED BY	
		1/1/85	1/1/86	1/1/87	1/1/88
OWNED BY:	COMPANY	2	9	21	71
	FRANCHISEES	8	23	147	252
LOCATED:	IN U.S.	10	32	168	323
	OUTSIDE U.S.	0	0	0	0
TOTAL:		10	32	168	323
NO. OF STATES W/ UNITS		4	12	45	50

THE BUSINESS

There are laundromats, and then there are Duds 'N Suds, combination laundries and entertainment centers. The "suds" in the name comes from the sale of beer, and entertainment comes from pool tables, video games, large-screen TVs, and a lounge area, creating an atmosphere that has Duds 'N Suds washers turning at more than twice the national average. Of the average store's 3,300 square feet, only about 1,300 square feet are used for the washers, dryers, and drop-off area. Beer is sold only to laundry customers and never before noon. To date, no city council has refused to grant a liquor license to a franchise applicant, partly because of a professionally made videotape that Duds 'N Suds supplies to show their high-quality laundries. The company reports a 100 percent survival rate for its franchises.

WHAT IT TAKES

You will need $25,000 for the franchise fee, which guarantees an exclusive territory for ten years, renewable for another ten. Your total investment, including the franchise fee, will range from $180,000 to $205,000, depending on lease arrangements and the cost of improvements. Thirty to 50 percent of the total must be in cash. Fees for additional units vary, depending on the number of units purchased, and master franchises are available. You may own a franchise without being the operating manager, but Duds 'N Suds does not encourage this. Ongoing royalty fees are $425 a month, beginning six months after you begin operations and are adjusted from the Consumer Price Index after your third anniversary. In addition, you will pay 1 percent of your gross revenues, on a quarterly basis for advertising. Previous experience is not required.

GETTING STARTED

A typical facility is 3,300 square feet, located in a shopping center or freestanding building. Duds 'N Suds will help you select a site; negotiate a lease or purchase agreement; plan the facility layout and decoration; and lease or purchase furniture, fixtures, equipment, and merchandise. The company will also help with construction for a fee. You may shop around for the best sources of equipment and merchandise, but all items purchased must be in compliance with company specifications. If you prefer, Duds 'N Suds will provide a complete turnkey operation—a finished, fully equipped facility for your purchase and use. You will need one or two full-time and five part-time employees. You'll attend one week of classroom training at corporate headquarters, followed by on-the-job training and consultation as needed. Your training will cover personnel, daily management, laundry maintenance, service information, snack bar, security, business records, advertising and promotion, graphics and standards, and the grand opening. You can expect to be open within six months after purchasing your franchise.

MAKING IT WORK

As part of your quarterly advertising fee you'll receive newspaper and black-and-white magazine ads, brochures, mailers, presentation books, radio commercials, national media coverage, in-house media packages with slides and videotapes, point-of-purchase displays, signs, contests, seasonal promotional displays, a lead-referral system, incentives, press releases, and a public-relations/marketing manual. Annual conventions are supplemented by quarterly regional conferences and on-site training as needed. The company issues a monthly newsletter with customer-oriented information and holds quarterly areawide franchise meetings. Surveys are also conducted quarterly. Recognition programs honor excellence in operations. Backup systems include headquarters resource persons; a toll-free hotline; regular on-site visits and troubleshooting; policy, management-procedure and customer-service manuals; all types of forms; and systems for bookkeeping, inventory, personnel, and expense analysis. A company think tank and company store to test marketing ideas act as research and development departments. Duds 'N Suds has divisions to conduct research and development activities and to produce and distribute equipment and supplies. Offering volume discounts through a central purchasing system, the company uses established brands such as Sony, Maytag, and Tide, but you may pick your own product lines. Accounts-receivable financing is available, as is company-sponsored insurance for property, general liability, and worker's compensation coverage.

COMMENTS

Duds 'N Suds was ranked 386th in *Entrepreneur* magazine's 1987 "Franchise 500." A member of the IFA, the company is seeking to increase franchise operations in most states as well as internationally.

GETTING MORE INFORMATION

The franchise information packet contains information on all aspects of company operations, reprints of numerous articles on the company, a comparison of Duds 'N Suds laundries with conven-

tional laundromats, and a four-page application form. For more information, write or call:
Bruce Schutz
Director of Franchise Sales and Marketing
Duds 'N Suds
120 Hayward
P. O. Box B, Welch Station
Ames, IA   50010
(800)   222-3837 (national) or (800)   247–0082 (in Iowa)

Dunhill Personnel

BUSINESS: personnel recruitment and placement
FOUNDED: 1952
FRANCHISED: 1961
START-UP INVESTMENT: $16,000–$100,000

NO. OF UNITS		AS OF		PROJECTED BY	
		1/1/85	1/1/86	1/1/87	1/1/88
OWNED BY: COMPANY		2	2	4	6
FRANCHISEES		294	308	324	345
LOCATED: IN U.S.		289	302	318	339
OUTSIDE U.S.		7	8	10	12
TOTAL:		296	310	328	351
NO. OF STATES W/ UNITS		42	44	45	46

THE BUSINESS

According to the U.S. Department of Commerce, temporary help is one of the nation's fastest-growing industries. Currently employing over 600,000 temporary workers daily, the industry generates more than $6 billion annually and is growing about 20 percent every year. Although the majority of all "temps" work on office/clerical, light-industrial, and marketing assignments, the National Association of Temporary Services claims that professional temps represent one of the fastest-growing segments in the temporary-help industry. Professional temps include accountants, engineers, systems analysts— even nuclear plant designers.

Dunhill Personnel System is an international company offering both temporary and permanent personnel placement. It has three different franchises in the personnel-services industry. The full-service franchise recruits permanent management and professional personnel; the office-personnel franchise specializes in permanent high-demand clerical and secretarial workers; and the temporary-service franchise contracts out office or light-industrial staff on short- or long-term assignments. Dunhill offices place workers in more than fifty-five different occupational and industrial categories, including data processing, electronics, health care, banking, accounting and finance, insurance, machinery, food processing, plastics, and chemicals.

In 1985, Dunhill franchises grossed $36 million in permanent and office personnel and $40 million in temporary placements. Average gross sales per unit were $140,000 for permanent placements and $900,000 for temps.

WHAT IT TAKES

You will need the following amounts for Dunhill franchise fees: $30,000 for a full-service agency and $17,500 for an office-personnel franchise or $53,000 to $116,000 for a temporary-service franchise, depending on population and market density. This establishes an exclusive territory (determined by availability) for ten years, renewable for another ten. Your total investment, including the franchise fee, for a full-service agency will be approximately $16,000; approximately $30,000 for an office-personnel agency; and $40,000–$100,000 for a temporary-service agency. Initial operating expenses are built into the financial requirements, giving you a cushion for three to four months until the business begins to establish itself. Dunhill will accept one-half to one-third of the franchise fee in cash (varying for each franchise), and it will finance the remainder. Additional units sell for $15,000 for the full-service franchise and $8,000 to $12,000 for the temporary service; master franchises are not available. You must be the manager of your franchise. Ongoing royalty fees are 7 percent of gross receipts for a full-service agency; 7 percent of gross receipts for an office-personnel agency; and for a temporary-service agency, 2.5 percent of the first $500,000, 2 percent on the next $500,000, and 1.75 percent on everything in excess of $1 million each year. No prior experience in personnel services is required.

GETTING STARTED

Dunhill will assist you with your office layout. The typical facility ranges from 500 to 2,000 square feet and is located in an office building, mall, shopping center, freestanding building, or commercial industrial park. You will need three to four full-time employees for your staff. Training for the full-service and office-personnel franchise owners is offered at Carle Place, New York, for ten days with both classroom and hands-on experience. For the temporary-service franchisee, hands-on training is conducted in the franchisee's office for the salesperson, service coordinator, and owner for up to one week. Training for full-service and office-personnel offices covers marketing, recruiting, management, and bookkeeping. Training for each temporary-service office coordinator covers recruiting, screening, testing, evaluating, interviewing, and general orientation. For the temporary-services sales representative, training covers sales techniques, presentation, and marketing; and for the temporary-service owner it covers administrative functions and managing. You can be open within a month after buying your Dunhill franchise.

MAKING IT WORK

Advertising fees are 1 percent of gross receipts for full-service and office-personnel franchises and .5 percent of gross receipts for the temporary-service operations. As part of the advertising fee Dunhill offers black-and-white magazine ads, mailers, newspaper and telephone-book ads, brochures, presentation books, and a public-relations/marketing manual. Dunhill also offers national media coverage, in-house media packages (e.g., slides, videotapes), contests, seasonal promotional materials, a lead-referral system, sales incentives, and press releases. You must use the Dunhill logo on all materials and supplies. The company has developed a direct-mail program that can be personalized to your area. For full-service franchise owners the company sponsors an annual national convention and ten regional conferences. Temporary-services franchisees attend three-day seminars twice a year. For all Dunhill franchises ongoing training includes basic consultant training and unit-manager training eight times a year, and for temporary-services offices, basic sales-and-service training four times a year. Dunhill publishes a company newsletter twice a month, updates on service and company news as needed, industry/market information monthly, and a customer-oriented newsletter quarterly. The company conducts surveys monthly and sponsors various award programs. Backup services include headquarters and regional resource persons; regular on-site visits and troubleshooting; policy, management-procedure, and customer-service manuals; and systems for expense analysis and computerized management information. The company offers accounts-receivable financing and insurance programs for life, major-medical, dental, and disability coverage, and it is negotiating for property, automobile, and worker's compensation coverage and third-party bonding.

COMMENTS

Dunhill was ranked 135th in *Entrepreneur* magazine's 1987 "Franchise 500." The company has been a member of the IFA since 1970 and has received the IFA service award for twenty-five years in franchising. The company wants to increase franchise operations throughout the United States and in Canada.

GETTING MORE INFORMATION

The franchise information packet contains brochures on each type of franchise, maps showing existing franchises, copies of the company newsletter, and recent four-color ads. For details, contact:
Robert F. Davis
Vice-President of Marketing
Dunhill Personnel Systems, Inc.
One Old Country Road
Carle Place, NY   11514
(516)   741–5081 (call collect)

Dunkin' Donuts

BUSINESS: coffee shops specializing in donuts and bakery products
FOUNDED: 1950
FRANCHISED: 1955
START-UP INVESTMENT: $160,000

NO. OF UNITS	AS OF		PROJECTED BY	
	1/1/85	1/1/86	1/1/87	1/1/88
OWNED BY: COMPANY	73	74	45	35
FRANCHISEES	1,286	1,373	1,471	1,603
LOCATED: IN U.S.	1,260	1,321	1,394	1,471
OUTSIDE U.S.	99	126	122	167
TOTAL:	1,359	1,447	1,516	1,638
NO. OF STATES W/ UNITS	39	39	39	39

THE BUSINESS

Americans of the 1980s, on the move and in a hurry, create a high demand for fast, tasty snack foods. Dunkin' Donuts franchises meet the demand by providing fast-food outlets that sell donuts and other bakery products, soup, and coffee and other beverages. Located to appeal to a clientele of both business people on the go and families, the stores offer quality products and speedy service in clean, compact, attractive surroundings.

The annual dollar volume for all Dunkin' Donuts franchise operations in 1985 totaled $543,637,000. The average annual gross sales per unit were $431,000, with an average annual net profit per unit of $42,500.

WHAT IT TAKES

The total initial investment needed for a Dunkin' Donuts location is approximately $160,000, of which $65,000 must be in cash. Included in that total is your franchise fee of $20,000 to $40,000, depending on the location you select and the type of shop you decide to run. You can get financial assistance from Dunkin' Donuts or through a loan from a local financial institution. The length of your first franchise period will be twenty years, and the company will allow you to take an option to extend. You may purchase additional franchise units for $20,000 to $27,000 each, and master franchises are available. Dunkin' Donuts Incorporated does not assign an exclusive territory. You'll pay the company an ongoing 4.9 percent commission and an additional 5 percent ongoing advertising fee.

GETTING STARTED

You'll need an area of 15,000 square feet (this includes parking space for your Dunkin' Donuts shop). You can locate in either a mall, a shopping center, or a freestanding building. Your shop must comply with the Dunkin' Donuts image and specifications, which are described in guidelines from the company headquarters.

Your initial franchise fee will provide you with assistance from Dunkin' Donuts Incorporated in your selection of a store location;

negotiations for leasing or purchasing the site; construction of your facility; plans for the layout and decoration of the shop; negotiation of the most advantageous service and maintenance contracts; lease or purchase of any vehicles needed; staff selection and hiring; and quantity purchase of materials and supplies with discounts when they are available. For a fee the company will also assist you in leasing or purchasing equipment. Experienced personnel from the company's main office will give you guidance in planning your grand-opening events.

You'll need five full-time and twenty-five part-time employees. Within nine to ten months after signing the initial franchise agreement you can open for business.

Although the company prefers that you have some experience with or knowledge of the donut or food business, such knowledge is not a strict requirement. Dunkin' Donuts maintains a full training program. You, as owner, and your baker will attend a five-week training course at Dunkin' Donuts University in Braintree, Massachusetts, where you will both receive classroom training and hands-on experience in all production techniques. You, as owner, will participate in courses covering all financial and administrative procedures necessary to keep your operation running smoothly.

MAKING IT WORK

The Dunkin' Donuts Incorporated advertising program is designed to help you create and maintain a solid customer base. You'll pay an ongoing advertising fee of 5 percent of retail sales. This fee covers newspaper ads, TV and radio commercials, and national media coverage. In some cases the company will also assist you in co-op advertising.

You'll be able to take advantage of volume discounts for purchase of materials and supplies through a central purchasing program. However, you are not restricted to purchasing only those products carried through this program. You may sell any product you choose, as long as it meets the Dunkin' Donuts quality specifications. In addition, regional food/supplies distribution outlets, owned and controlled by franchise owners, serve certain areas.

Dunkin' Donuts will send you a magazine, a newsletter, and technical updates on products and services. The Dunkin' Donuts bakery development department maintains a program of research into new products. You'll also receive administrative and managerial support through headquarters and regional resource personnel; a toll-free hotline; policy and procedure manuals; and personnel, accounting, inventory, and order forms. The company-sponsored insurance program includes coverage for property, general liability, flood and earthquake damage, and worker's compensation protection.

COMMENTS

Dunkin' Donuts was rated nineteenth in *Entrepreneur* magazine's 1987 "Franchise 500" and sixty-fourth in *Venture* magazine's 1986 "Franchise 100." The company is seeking franchises in most areas of the United States.

GETTING MORE INFORMATION

For more information, contact:
 Robert H. Carvin
 Manager of Financial Planning
 Dunkin' Donuts Incorporated
 Box 317
 Randolph, MA   02368
 (617)   961-4000 (call collect)

Duraclean

BUSINESS:
 on-location cleaning
 and restoration of
 carpeting, upholstery,
 and drapery
FOUNDED: 1930
FRANCHISED: 1945
START-UP
 INVESTMENT:
 $13,900–$26,800

		AS OF		PROJECTED BY	
NO. OF UNITS		1/1/85	1/1/86	1/1/87	1/1/88
OWNED BY:	COMPANY	0	0	0	0
	FRANCHISEES	850	900	950	975
LOCATED:	IN U.S.	830	877	922	945
	OUTSIDE U.S.	20	23	28	30
TOTAL:		850	900	950	975
NO. OF STATES W/ UNITS		50	50	50	50

THE BUSINESS

Founded in 1930, Duraclean has enjoyed a steady, consistent growth by offering a unique, patented foam absorption process unlike any other cleaning method on the market. The patented equipment, secret chemical formulas, and special technology are for the use of Duraclean dealers only—they are not sold or furnished to anyone else. This is your protection as a franchisee, and it is covered by a written contract. In a recent survey dealers reported gross profits on services provided ranging from 49 to 77 percent.

 Your number-one customer base in volume will be the residential market, with carpet and rug cleaning, upholstery cleaning, and on-location drapery cleaning. If you purchase optional equipment, you'll be able to clean smaller rugs, upholstery, and aircraft and automobile fabrics. You can also build high, dependable sales in the commercial cleaning market. Heavy-traffic businesses such as restaurants, hotels, motels, and offices are prime prospects for your services, as are businesses for whom appearance is important, such as professional offices, interior designers, and banks. Contract work provides the advantage of a steady flow of work at a predetermined price.

In the water-damage and fire-restoration market you can offer a total restoration program that will include a thorough analysis of the damage and detailed estimates, then cleaning and deodorizing of carpets, furniture, draperies, and walls. Your contacts with insurance agents and adjusters will be important in developing this market, and your Duraclean training shows you how to cultivate these sources of revenue. The other services you can offer in your business are application of stain and spill protection, customized spot and stain removal, carpet repair, static-electricity control, mothproofing, and hand cleaning of fine rug and upholstery fabrics. You also can sell spot-cleaning products.

WHAT IT TAKES

You have your choice of four franchise types: the Standard, the Standard Plus, and two Duravan dealerships. With the franchise fee for all of these types you can either make a down payment and pay the balance in monthly payments or take a discount for full payment. The Standard dealership is designed primarily for residential and some types of commercial work and has a franchise fee of $13,900. The down payment for this type is $5,900, and the company offers financing for the remainder. The Standard Plus dealership would expand your ability to service the cleaning and restoration markets using added equipment and supplies. The franchise fee for this level is $19,800, with a down payment of $9,800; Duraclean financing is available.

The Durovan "E" dealership includes a cleaning system that is mounted in a van and operates from ordinary household current. The cleaning unit may be removed from the van and moved to any location where cleaning is to be done, an advantage in high-rise buildings where fast, heavy-duty cleaning is required. The Durovan "E" franchise fee is $23,800, with a $12,800 down payment; financing of the remainder is available. The fourth type of dealership, the Durovan "DD," has a cleaning system that is permanently installed in your van, and obtains its power directly from the van's engine. The franchise fee for this type of franchise is $26,800. Because the cleaning system is permanently installed in your vehicle, Duraclean offers no financing but will contact local sources for your financing or leasing of the vehicle and equipment.

Your franchise contract will apply for one year, to be renewed annually, and will assure you of an exclusive territory that is determined by demographic data. Master franchises are also available. In addition to the initial fee, you'll pay an ongoing royalty fee determined by the base price of your franchise and a percentage of your sales.

GETTING STARTED

You won't need to search for a business site or worry about layout, decoration, or stocking because you'll be working out of your home. You can start with evening and weekend work and progress to a full-time operation. Dealers with the biggest gross sales and profits are full-time with salespeople and service crews. Duraclean is a high-profit-margin business. Your material costs will average only about 5 percent of sales. If you employ service people, you'll pay them about 15 to 20 percent of receipts, leaving 75 to 80 percent for advertising, selling, and profits.

You'll attend a five-day training program at the Duraclean training center in suburban Chicago at no cost to you for transportation, room and board, or tuition. As soon as your franchise application is accepted, you'll receive clear, comprehensive instruction manuals covering all phases of your operations.Up to 50 percent of your business eventually will come from satisfied customers' referrals, and at the Duraclean training center you'll learn how to cultivate a profitable referral business from interior designers and carpet, furniture, and drapery retailers. Your classes will also cover the safest and most effective ways to clean carpets, upholstery fabrics, and draperies. In addition, you'll learn how to operate your equipment, manage your business, obtain and follow up on customer leads, recognize different fibers and fabrics, remove spots and stains, repair carpets, and handle water- and fire-damage situations. You'll spend two days with an experienced Duraclean dealer with on-the-job training in actual operating conditions. This resource person will also be available for guidance while you are getting established in your business. In as little as one month from the time you sign your franchise agreement, you will be operating your own fabric-care business.

MAKING IT WORK

Duraclean's cooperative assistance program will provide you with a complete, ongoing support system of advertising and marketing materials including a presentation book, personalized sales letters, direct-mail folders, business cards, sales manuals and kits, quotation sheets, news releases, newspaper and telephone-book ads, radio scripts, a monthly magazine, and bulletins with company and product updates. Professional staff are available for ongoing assistance, and the company sponsors regional and international conventions. Service equipment and replacement parts are available at amounts below market prices, and there is a six-month warranty on all new or rebuilt service machines. A company insurance package includes auto, property, life, general-liability and major-medical coverage.

COMMENTS

Duraclean was ranked forty-second in *Entrepreneur* magazine's 1987 "Franchise 500." Duraclean president Ira Marshall was one of the founders of the IFA and has been the group's chairperson. The company seeks to expand throughout the United States and internationally.

GETTING MORE INFORMATION

The Duraclean franchise packet includes an informative thirty-two page color booklet explaining the products and services, a folder describing the dealerships, and a franchise application form. For details, contact:

Paul Tarman
National Sales Director
Duraclean International, Inc.
2151 Waukegan Road
Deerfield, IL   60015
(800)   251–7070 or (312)   945–2000

Dwight Dental Care

BUSINESS: dental care
 FOUNDED: 1982
 FRANCHISED: 1982
START-UP INVESTMENT: $135,000–$185,000

		AS OF		PROJECTED BY	
NO. OF UNITS		1/1/85	1/1/86	1/1/87	1/1/88
OWNED BY: COMPANY		0	0	0	0
	FRANCHISEES	14	26	38	85
LOCATED: IN U.S.		14	26	38	85
	OUTSIDE U.S.	0	0	0	0
TOTAL:		14	26	38	85
NO. OF STATES W/ UNITS		2	3	4	5

THE BUSINESS

In 1985 the health-care industry was worth $430 billion; dental care was a $25.2 billion piece of the pie. Because of the growth of dental insurance plans, an even bigger share of the market will be coming to dentists.

Dwight Dental Care took advantage of trends of the 1960s and 1970s to bring big chain security and brand-name quality into the dental care field. For example, the company saw that two-income families would require convenience and economy, realized that escalating health-care costs would make industries and the government look for ways to save money, and knew that many new dentists have problems running the business end of their dental operations. So the Dwight Dental Care system decided to offer the services that many dentists cannot. Each center operates seven days a week, as well as during the evenings Monday through Friday. Appointments aren't necessary; customers can walk in and have their dental problems taken care of right away. The Dwight strategy seems to work. Over 100,000 patient visits have been made to Dwight Centers since the company started operations. Dwight Dental Care franchisees recently made an average annual net income of $80,000 per unit on average gross sales of $400,000.

WHAT IT TAKES

The initial one-time licensing fee is $20,000, which will buy you a twenty-year agreement. Including the fee, the range of your total initial investment will be from $135,000 to $165,000. Of that, you'll need $20,000 in cash, but Dwight can provide 100 percent financing for the turnkey package through third-party financial institutions.

You'll pay a 6 percent royalty on gross revenues, which will provide for the continuous management and marketing services you'll receive. You must also pay an advertising fee of $1,250 a month. Eventually, you may qualify as a master area development franchisee and open other units for an additional $10,000 each. While passive ownerships are allowed, you must be a licensed dentist to own a Dwight franchise.

GETTING STARTED

You'll receive a wide range of services for your licensing fee. Dwight's director of real estate handles all real estate selections, leases, and landlord-tenant negotiations. Dwight's wholly owned subsidiary, Ark Construction, Inc., will help you with buying, planning, designing, building, and decorating your dental store.

When you become a member of the Dwight network, you will receive training that helps you avoid mistakes commonly made in running a high-volume mall store. You and your staff of four to six people will receive six days of classroom and hands-on training regarding operating hours, staff recruitment, bulk buying, computer use, sales techniques, accounting, insurance billing, estimates, and instrument disinfection. The Dwight marketing manual contains information about consumer habits, psychology, and public relations, and the management team guides franchisees in all aspects of daily operations. You can open your dental center approximately four months after purchasing your franchise.

MAKING IT WORK

Your advertising fee will pay for billboard posters, mailers, brochures, newspaper coupons, and media coverage, including television ads. The company publishes a quarterly newsletter for Dwight Dental Care licensees and a bimonthly patient newsletter that serves as a public-relations and marketing tool. Dwight's plan is to reach a larger patient base with cluster advertising and to use educational programs for staff training on a large-scale basis.

You can purchase equipment and supplies at a discount, and your computer system will minimize problems with recordkeeping. The company offers DwightCare, a dental HMO insurance plan, and markets it to local employers. Another special marketing feature, DwightCharge, is a dental-work credit card that gives the holder up to $5,000 of credit.

COMMENTS Dwight Health Care is the parent company of Dwight Dental Care, which has been a member of the IFA since 1983. The company is seeking to expand particularly on the East Coast and in the South.

GETTING MORE INFORMATION The franchise information packet contains a four-page description of the network, a brochure on the business aspects of dentistry, a copy of the quarterly newsletter, a number of photocopied newspaper articles, sample ads, and a four-page application. For more information, write:
Myles Sokolof
Vice-President, Sales
Dwight Dental Care
280 Railroad Avenue
Greenwich, CT   06830
(203)   629–4338

Eldorado Stone

BUSINESS: sales and installation of manufactured stone and brick veneers
FOUNDED: 1969
FRANCHISED: 1969
START-UP INVESTMENT: $40,000–$80,000

		AS OF		PROJECTED BY	
NO. OF UNITS		1/1/85	1/1/86	1/1/87	1/1/88
OWNED BY: COMPANY		0	0	0	0
FRANCHISEES		23	25	29	35
LOCATED: IN U.S.		17	18	21	25
OUTSIDE U.S.		6	7	8	10
TOTAL:		23	25	29	35
NO. OF STATES W/ UNITS		16	17	20	24

THE BUSINESS Building with natural stone may seem like an attractive option when you decide to build your home or add a new fireplace, but when you find out how much it costs, you may change your mind. Not only is the cost of natural stone prohibitive to many people, but building with it usually requires special structural support. Fortunately, manufactured stone is an inexpensive alternative and is in great demand by building-supply dealers, contractors, architects, and homeowners. Based in Carnation, Washington, Eldorado Stone Corporation has supplied millions of square feet of stone veneer to buyers all over North America since 1969. In 1985 the company's total sales amounted to about $3,500,000.

Eldorado's unique molding method produces stone shapes, textures, and colors that are nearly indistinguishable from the real thing. The stone is lightweight and can be installed over almost any existing or new surface. And, rather than damaging the stone, weathering actually enhances its appearance. Among the most popular types are (1) white monarch—a pure white sedimentary stone; (2) driftstone—an earthy brown and tan stone with a very rough, irregular texture; (3) mica slate—a mica slate texture in various colors for patios, floors, and hearths; and (4) lava—a boulderlike, black volcanic stone. Eldorado Stone franchisees offer not only their wide variety of stone veneers but also full installation services.

WHAT IT TAKES

You'll pay an initial franchise fee of $25,000 in cash. The ten-year agreement will give you an exclusive territory and can be renewed for another ten years. You're also entitled to use the nationally recognized Eldorado trademark on your products. Your total start-up costs will probably run between $40,000 and $80,000. Besides the franchise fee, this amount includes your purchase of a plant site and lease of Eldorado Stone molds, which cost about $35 each. Eldorado Stone will not sell the molds to their competitors.

Should you want to expand, the fees for additional franchises are negotiable, and the company allows passive ownership. Eldorado Stone gets 9.1 cents per square foot of stone sold, which comes to approximately 4 percent of gross sales per month. You don't have to have previous experience in the industry to be a franchisee.

GETTING STARTED

Eldorado Stone will help you choose a plant location and assist you with designing and laying out the manufacturing area. You'll need four or five full-time employees and 2,500 to 5,000 square feet of building space. Sites are usually located in freestanding buildings, commercial centers, or industrial parks. The company also has a smaller franchise package that requires less building space.

You and/or your manager will receive one week of both on-the-job and consultative training at an existing plant. After your grand opening you'll get another week of training at your plant. In the training sessions you'll learn the details of the stone-manufacturing process and the basics of business and sales. Before your grand opening Eldorado Stone will help you find the necessary equipment to lease or purchase, plus all the materials you'll need. The time from your purchase of the franchise to your grand opening will be approximately ninety days.

MAKING IT WORK

For a fee, Eldorado Stone will send you brochures, catalogs, press packages, newspaper and magazine ads, television and radio commercials, displays, banners, and seasonal promotionals. The company also has a lead-referral system you can use.

The company sponsors a national convention each winter and sends franchisees bimonthly newsletters, periodic technical and company-information updates, and industry/market information and surveys. Eldorado Stone offers company-brand products and other equipment and materials through a central purchasing system that offers volume purchasing discounts. You can buy other equipment and materials locally or from the nearest supplier if the items meet Eldorado's specifications. You may sell other similar brands of stone but, as a result, you'll relinquish the exclusive rights to Eldorado Stone in your area.

The company will keep you informed of prices being charged by other franchisees, but you'll set the prices for your products. Eldorado Stone maintains close contact with their franchisees by offering ongoing technical, production, and marketing consultation, as well as on-site troubleshooting. Company representatives will make regular visits to review your production techniques, quality control, marketing and sales effectiveness, and pricing. You'll have a policy manual and the company handbook for quick daily reference. Eldorado Stone is continually improving its product line, testing new products, and developing more efficient methods of manufacturing top-quality precast stone.

COMMENTS

Ranked 289th in *Entrepreneur* magazine's 1987 "Franchise 500," Eldorado Stone is seeking new franchisees in most areas of the United States and in Canada, Europe, Australia, Mexico, and other countries.

GETTING MORE INFORMATION

The franchise information packet includes six pages of full-color photographs showing stone-veneer fireplaces, homes, hearths, and buildings. You'll also find a questionnaire to be filled out and returned to the company's office. For more information, contact:

John Bennett
President
Eldorado Stone Corporation
P.O. Box 27
Carnation, WA   98014
(206)   883–1991   (call collect)

Endrust

BUSINESS:			AS OF		PROJECTED BY	
			1/1/85	1/1/86	1/1/87	1/1/88
specialized	NO. OF UNITS					
automotive-	OWNED BY: COMPANY		1	1	1	1
preservation service	FRANCHISEES		50	55	65	80
FOUNDED: 1969	LOCATED: IN U.S.		51	56	66	81
FRANCHISED: 1979	OUTSIDE U.S.		0	0	0	0
START-UP	TOTAL:		51	56	66	81
INVESTMENT:	NO. OF STATES W/ UNITS		8	8	18	28
$50,000						

THE BUSINESS

Many automobile manufacturers in recent years have cut costs by gradually reducing the thickness of metal used in their cars. On many cars this has caused paint deterioration and rusting of lower fenders and rocker panels. Each year 7 million vehicles are scrapped due to their age and obsolescence, and 7 million newly purchased vehicles and potential customers take to the road. Endrust car-care centers respond to both the new- and used-car market with rustproofing, sound deadening, undercoating, exterior paint sealing, and automotive-fabric protection. The Endrust system uses an exclusive inner and underbody rustproofing process that has been tested and approved to meet all applicable government regulations. Endrust offers a lifetime warranty on new vehicles and a limited one on used cars.

Endrust customers include fleet owners, car dealers, and individual car and truck owners. Endrust car-care centers can service at least three vehicles per day, sometimes handling as many as fifteen. With only three rustproofing jobs a day you could gross over $150,000 a year, depending on the prices charged (the average is $210 per car). Each franchise averages a net income of $80,000 to $160,000 per year, and total volume for all franchise operations in 1985 amounted to $3 billion.

WHAT IT TAKES

The franchise fee of $30,000 must be paid in cash. You'll also need an additional $20,000 available for operating capital. Your dollar investment will be the same for any additional franchises you might open. The franchise agreement is continual and offers you exclusive territory rights determined on the basis of mileage and population. Endrust encourages franchise owners to manage their operations; however, you may purchase a master franchise, which would allow you to subfranchise other Endrust centers in your territory. Endrust does not charge royalty fees.

GETTING STARTED

The standard Endrust facility is 2,500 square feet, located in a free-standing building. The company will assist you in site selection, facility layout, lease negotiation, staffing decisions, and stocking of merchandise. Although this franchise can be operated as part of an existing automotive shop, the company will require you to stock only Endrust products in the franchise part of your business. You can open for business about one month after purchasing your franchise, and Endrust will assist you with your grand opening.

MAKING IT WORK

You'll need a total of one part-time and three full-time employees. Endrust offers free on-site training to all personnel in sales, service, advertising, and administration. Through its elaborate in-house advertising program Endrust supplies each franchisee with free newspaper and black-and-white magazine ads, brochures, radio commercials, telephone-book ads, and a marketing manual. You can also get magazines on Endrust and company-prepared product questionnaires to distribute to your customers. Optional advertising materials that you can purchase include four-color magazine ads, mailers, presentation books, catalogs, and press packages. The company conducts periodic area-wide franchise meetings and offers additional sales and technical training to your staff on site as needed. Top selling franchises receive recognition awards.

COMMENTS

Endrust is seeking franchisees throughout the United States. The company's earnings claim document is made available prior to or during a potential franchisee's personal interview.

GETTING MORE INFORMATION

The franchise information packet includes a reprint from *Entrepreneur* magazine, a brochure explaining Endrust products, and a booklet that displays several sample advertisements and summarizes sales projections. For details, write or call:

Gary B. Griser
Vice-President
Endrust Industries
1725 Washington Road, Suite 205
Pittsburgh, PA   15241
(412)   831–1255

Entré Computer Centers

BUSINESS: personal-
computer sales
FOUNDED: 1981
FRANCHISED: 1982
START-UP
INVESTMENT:
$285,000–$963,000

NO. OF UNITS	AS OF		PROJECTED BY	
	1/1/85	1/1/86	1/1/87	1/1/88
OWNED BY: COMPANY	7	16	N/A	N/A
FRANCHISEES	202	265	N/A	N/A
LOCATED: IN U.S.	185	252	N/A	N/A
OUTSIDE U.S.	24	29	N/A	N/A
TOTAL:	209	281	N/A	N/A
NO. OF STATES W/ UNITS	46	44	N/A	N/A

THE BUSINESS

Personal-computer retailing—the *New York Times* has called it "the fastest growing industry in the world." Estimates are that in 1986 businesses bought 2.6 million personal computers costing $8.9 billion. In 1987 they are expected to buy 3.5 million at a cost of $12.1 billion—more than the total dollar figure for such purchases for all previous years through 1983. Entré is currently the largest publicly held franchisor of retail computer centers. In 1985, Entré Computer Centers grossed $400 million in total sales. The company, selling primarily to businesses and professionals, emphasizes the use of trained consultants to identify clients' needs before recommending appropriate computer systems. This approach has established Entré as a "problem solver" and has encouraged repeat business.

WHAT IT TAKES

You will need $40,000 in cash for the initial franchise fee and design implementation fee. This amount purchases a nonexclusive territory, valid for ten years and renewable for ten. Your total investment, including the franchise fee, will range from $285,000 to $963,000, depending on your selections of inventory, amount of advertising, variations in cost of leasehold improvements, furniture and fixtures, and amount of working capital. Entré will provide a business plan for any loan applications you make. Additional units will also cost $40,000 for the franchise fee; master franchises are not available. You may be an owner-investor without running the business. You will pay an ongoing royalty fee of 5.5 percent of gross monthly sales on all products and services. Extensive computer knowledge is not required, but Entré is seeking owners with business-management experience and preferably sales and marketing knowledge.

GETTING STARTED

Entré will assist you with site selection, lease negotiation, and facility layout and decoration. For a fee, the company will help you acquire materials, supplies, and merchandise. The typical facility is 3,500 square feet, located in a shopping center, freestanding building, or commercial industrial park. You must follow a uniform lay-out-and-decoration scheme, using the company logo on materials and supplies. Your staff will consist of ten to twelve full-time employees and up to three part-timers. The training, which is held at company headquarters in Vienna, Virginia, for one to three weeks, incorporates both classroom instruction and role playing. Topics covered include management, sales, product, and technical training. Owners and/or managers receive general-management, business-planning, and sales-management training; sales representatives study skills and product training; and support personnel receive technical training. After you purchase your franchise, you can expect to be open within six months. The company will assist with your grand opening by creating an advertising campaign tailored to your market.

MAKING IT WORK

For your advertising fee of 1 percent of monthly gross sales you will receive newspaper ads, black-and-white magazine ads, mailers, telephone-book ads, brochures, presentation books, radio commercials, national media coverage, point-of-purchase displays, signs, banners, a lead-referral system, press releases, and a public-relations/marketing manual. Entré franchisees gather once a year for a national convention and quarterly for regional conferences, and the company sponsors frequent seminars and monthly on-site training sessions. Entré publishes a company newsletter, distributes service and industry updates as needed, and conducts surveys periodically. Outstanding franchises are recognized for sales performance, quality, and community service.

The company's backup systems include regional resource persons; a toll-free hotline; on-site troubleshooting; manuals on policy, management procedure, and customer service; forms for inventory, orders, and accounting; an initial supply of stationery; and systems for bookkeeping, inventory, personnel, and expense analysis. The company maintains market and product-development departments. Entré has subsidiaries that produce and/or distribute merchandise, a central purchasing system offering volume discounts, a centralized merchandising system, and company brands. You may sell non-Entré products as long as they are on the company's approved list.

COMMENTS

Entrepreneur magazine ranked Entré 196th among its 1987 "Franchise 500." A division of Entré Computer Centers, Inc., the company has been a member of the IFA since 1982. The company wants to add new franchises in nineteen states and in various foreign countries.

GETTING MORE INFORMATION

The franchise information packet contains brochures describing the computer market and Entré's operations, an annual report, a breakdown of expenses, a sheet with answers to commonly asked questions, and an application form. For more details, contact:

Ed Arrington
Franchise Development Officer
Entré Computer Centers
1951 Kidwell Drive
Vienna, VA   22180
(703)   749–3365

Fantastic Sam's

BUSINESS: family hair care
FOUNDED: 1974
FRANCHISED: 1976
START-UP INVESTMENT: $45,000–$65,000

		AS OF		PROJECTED BY	
NO. OF UNITS		1/1/85	1/1/86	1/1/87	1/1/88
OWNED BY:	COMPANY	25	3	0	0
	FRANCHISEES	715	721	1,400	1,700
LOCATED:	IN U.S.	730	699	1,368	1,646
	OUTSIDE U.S.	10	25	32	54
TOTAL:		740	724	1,400	1,700
NO. OF STATES W/ UNITS		37	40	46	49

THE BUSINESS

The hair-care business generates $15 billion in revenue annually and is virtually recession-proof. In 1974 Sam Ross concluded that a smartly packaged and promoted family hair-care service was the wave of the future. Teaming up with a hair-care expert and businessman, Ross developed his own patented technique of cutting hair, a line of inexpensive but high-quality hair-care products, and a prototype salon that stresses cleanliness, convenient hours and location, and high-quality service. Fantastic Sam's salons were born.

Today there are Fantastic Sam's salons all over North America, Canada, and Japan. England, Australia, and Brazil are the next targets for expansion. In 1985 total sales for all franchises came to $98,000,000, including $4,500,000 for Fantastic Sam's private-label hair-care products, which 95 percent of the franchises use and sell. The average annual gross sales for the franchises equaled $160,000. Fantastic Sam's rate of repeat business is 37 percent higher than the national hair-care industry average, and the success rate for the franchises is nearly 100 percent.

WHAT IT TAKES

The Fantastic Sam's franchise fee is $20,000, and you'll need to have another $25,000 to $45,000 for working capital. All of your start-up costs must be paid in cash, but the home office can provide financing for your equipment. Your franchise agreement will apply for ten years with a ten-year renewal option. Your territory will cover a radius of half a mile from your operation.

You can buy an unlimited number of additional franchises for a $10,000 franchise fee each, and you can be licensed for regional master franchising within your territory. It's not necessary for you to manage your operation. You don't have to have experience in hair-care services to own a Fantastic Sam's. The company emphasizes, however, that you should enjoy working with people.

The company charges a fixed ongoing fee of $131 per week rather than a percentage of gross sales. The fee is, however, periodically adjusted to the cost-of-living index.

GETTING STARTED

Your franchise fee will cover a demographic study to determine site selection, lease negotiation, design and layout of your store, and an optional equipment package. A company leasing agent will sell or lease the necessary salon equipment to you, or you can follow the company's specifications and standards and get your equipment elsewhere. Stores are usually about 1,200 square feet and are in commercial centers or in shopping centers or strips. All stores are decorated alike and display the Fantastic Sam's logo, but the layout may vary depending on the size and shape of the building.

The company will help you recruit the six full-time and two part-time licensed stylists you'll need. As owner, you'll get one week of preopening and operations training at the international training center in Memphis, Tennessee. Then, you or your manager will get another week of operations training at a regional training center, where your stylists also will complete two weeks of training in styling and customer relations. Your stylists will learn exact methods for achieving each hairstyle so that a customer can get the same haircut in any Fantastic Sam's salon. You should be able to have your grand opening about fifteen weeks after buying your franchise, and the company will support you in every phase of the grand opening.

MAKING IT WORK

The company has an extensive marketing and advertising program for which you'll pay a flat weekly fee of $60.73. In turn, you'll get carefully planned ad campaigns for radio and television, magazines and newspapers, direct mail, billboard posters, and displays. The company will target advertising programs to your area to attract new customers and motivate current ones.

The company sponsors a yearly national convention, quarterly regional conventions, quarterly city or areawide franchise meetings, and periodic two-day seminars. A company monthly newsletter; monthly updates on products, services, and the hair-care industry; and yearly surveys will keep you further informed.

Fantastic Sam's spends more money training their stylists than any other hair-care business in the industry—more than $1 million a year. Your stylists will be required to attend regularly scheduled classes taught by regional teams, shop supervisors, and professional trainers from national beauty-supply manufacturers. These classes will be taught in your store after operating hours. You can also get comprehensive videotaped training programs for your store.

Headquarters and regional resource people are always available to help you manage your store and consult with you by phone. Support people will visit your store routinely to troubleshoot and answer questions. You'll get manuals that cover marketing, management, and accounting plus forms for accounting, inventory, personnel, and supply ordering.

In your store you can use or sell Fantastic Sam's name-brand hair-care products, which have been thoroughly tested by Helene Curtis Industries, or other hair-care products that have been approved by the company. A centralized purchasing system and a company division that distributes equipment and supplies will also save you money.

COMMENTS

Fantastic Sam's was ranked twenty-third in *Entrepreneur* magazine's 1987 "Franchise 500" and fifth in *Venture* magazine's 1986 "Franchise 100." A subsidiary of S.M.R. Enterprises, Fantastic Sam's has contributed to the Muscular Dystrophy Foundation, Easter Seals, St. Jude Children's Hospital, and public television. The company is seeking franchisees throughout the world.

GETTING MORE INFORMATION

The franchise information packet contains a ten-page booklet, an application-for-license form, a comprehensive guide to Fantastic Sam's hair-care product line, four magazine excerpts discussing the company's success, and an international store directory. For details, call or write:

Sam M. Ross
Chairman of the Board
Fantastic Sam's
3180 Old Getwell Road
P.O. Box 18845
Memphis, TN   38181–0845
(800)   621–5307 or (901)   363–8624

First Optometry Eye Care Centers

BUSINESS: eye-care center
FOUNDED: 1980
FRANCHISED: 1981
START-UP INVESTMENT: $10,500–$150,000

NO. OF UNITS	AS OF		PROJECTED BY	
	1/1/85	1/1/86	1/1/87	1/1/88
OWNED BY: COMPANY	4	6	8	10
FRANCHISEES	28	28	32	40
LOCATED: IN U.S.	32	34	40	50
OUTSIDE U.S.	0	0	0	0
TOTAL:	32	34	40	50
NO. OF STATES W/ UNITS	1	1	1	1

THE BUSINESS

The success of First Optometry Eye Care Centers reflects recent dramatic changes in the eye-care industry. Some industry sources indicate that commercial chains have captured as much as 45 percent of the dispensing market and now sell at least one of every five contact lenses. The diminishing position of the independent optometrist obviously is not the result of a dwindling market. Estimates are that today's $4 billion-a-year retail vision-care market will grow at the rate of about 9 percent annually, becoming an $8 billion market by 1990. Over that same period of time sales of soft contact lenses are expected to grow to seven times the present volume. An increase in demand is also expected for fashion glasses, which currently claim an impressive 25 percent of the spectacle market. In 1985, First Optometry franchises grossed $7.5 million, with average annual gross sales per unit of $240,000. The company stresses professional service and quality products at reasonable prices.

WHAT IT TAKES

You will need $6,500 for the franchise fee. The agreement, which establishes an exclusive territory extending in a one-mile radius from your store, is valid for ten years and is renewable for ten years at the then current franchise terms but with no additional franchise-fee charges. Your total investment, including the franchise fee, will range from $10,500 to $150,000, depending on whether you convert an existing location or build a new one. In either case some of your investment will go for signs, awning and/or graphics ($2,500 to $5,000), plus $1,500 for the start-up package of printed materials. Of the total initial investment $10,000 must be in cash, with financing available from banks. Additional franchise units sell for $6,500 each; master franchises are available. You may be an owner-investor. First Optometry charges an ongoing fee of 7 percent of cash receipts; however, a scheduled reduction in royalty fees applies during the first twenty-four months of operation. In addition, each franchisee is required to contribute 5 percent of cash receipts to the company's public-relations and advertising program to promote First Optometry Eye Care Centers regionally and nationally. No prior experience in optometry is required.

GETTING STARTED

First Optometry will help you with site selection; lease or purchase negotiations; construction; facility layout and decoration; lease or purchase of furniture, fixtures, equipment and vehicles; service and maintenance contracts; and acquisition of materials, supplies, and merchandise. The typical First Optometry office is 1,500 square feet, located in a mall, shopping center, or freestanding building. You will need one part-time and three full-time employees, which the company will help you hire. Forty hours of training for you and your staff at the corporate headquarters in Roseville, Michigan, will cover telephone sales, paperwork, insurance claims, inventory control, contact lenses and eyeglasses, and advertising. You can be open within one to three months after buying a First Optometry franchise. The company will help with your grand opening.

MAKING IT WORK

For part of your advertising fee you will receive extensive advertising and marketing support, including newspaper and telephone book ads; television and radio commercials; brochures, signs, banners and other point-of-purchase materials; and contests, incentives, and a lead-referral system. Two-hour seminars will be held weekly at your store to keep you and your staff up-to-date on the latest eye-care techniques. You will also receive a company newsletter, updates on company information, a customer-oriented publication, and periodic surveys to assess your needs. You will meet regularly with other franchise owners at areawide meetings. In handling administrative tasks you can rely on headquarters resource persons who go to the franchises for regular onsite visits and onsite troubleshooting, manuals for policy and management procedure, order and accounting forms, and systems for bookkeeping and information management. First Optometry offers a central purchasing program for volume discounts on merchandise and basic supplies, although you may sell noncompany products.

COMMENTS

Entrepreneur magazine ranked First Optometry 475th among its 1987 "Franchise 500." First Optometry wants to expand its offices in eight states.

GETTING MORE INFORMATION

The franchise information packet contains brochures describing the company operations, a sample customer brochure, a reprint of an article on the company from the *New York Post,* and question-and-answer sheets about the franchise. For details, contact:

D. Borsand
Chief Executive Officer
First Optometry Eye Care Centers, Inc.
18600 Florence
Roseville, MI   48066
(313)   773–3500

Fleet Feet

BUSINESS: retail
sports, fitness, and
triathlete equipment
FOUNDED: 1976
FRANCHISED: 1979
START-UP
INVESTMENT:
$45,000–$90,000

		AS OF		PROJECTED BY	
NO. OF UNITS		1/1/85	1/1/86	1/1/87	1/1/88
OWNED BY:	COMPANY	1	1	2	2
	FRANCHISEES	20	23	31	40
LOCATED:	IN U.S.	21	24	33	42
	OUTSIDE U.S.	0	0	0	0
TOTAL:		21	24	33	42
NO. OF STATES W/ UNITS		3	4	6	10

THE BUSINESS

Sports-equipment stores have blossomed in the United States in the wake of the health-awareness and fitness boom. Designed to serve this growing market with specialty sports merchandise, Fleet Feet stores are characterized by a strong program of customer service, training, and sponsorship of athletic events. Fleet Feet began as Fleet Feet Sports, a series of athletic-shoe centers catering chiefly to runners. Its Fleet Feet Triathlete franchise features a new kind of sports shop, an attempt to service amateur and professional athletes competing in triathlon events, in which participants alternately swim, bicycle, and run to the finish line. Fleet Feet's unique triathlon store is the first such franchise available in the United States. Fleet Feet Kids, the third branch of the company, is a business that both sponsors sports programs and sells brand-name merchandise for the children's sports market, which is growing rapidly. Nike's volume in children's apparel is $20 to $25 million annually, Arena swimwear now offers over 100 different children's styles of competition suits, and bodywear companies are developing lines for the youth market. Purchases of specialized sports equipment in Fleet Feet's twenty franchise outlets totaled $5 million in 1985, with gross sales per unit at $300,000 and a net income per unit of approximately $30,000.

WHAT IT TAKES

You don't need knowledge of or experience in the retail sports field to start a franchise. You'll need $10,000 in cash to purchase your initial franchise. Additional franchises will cost you $5,000 per unit, or you may want to go with a master franchise at the outset. You'll be guaranteed an exclusive territory for fifty years, the territory being negotiable with each individual franchisee. You can buy a franchise and hire a manager to operate it. Total start-up fees depend on such variables as geographic area, store size and improvements, inventory requirements, and loan options. To open each of the three types of Fleet Feet franchises the approximate start-up costs can be estimated as follows:

| | FRANCHISE TYPE | | |
ITEM	SPORTS	KIDS	TRIATHLETE
Opening inventory (at cost) (depends upon size/type of store, location, competition, merchandise mix)	$30,000	$20,000	$50,000*
Leasehold improvements (includes cost for floor coverings, signs, wall covering, electrical needs, and other improvements. Cost varies depending on store location and on whether you perform the improvements or contract it out)	$ 8,000	$ 5,000	$10,000
Franchise fee (a one-time fee to purchase the franchise)	$10,000	$10,000	$10,000
Store fixtures (includes all shelves, seating, displays, counters, registers; varies between low and high depending on who builds the store)	$ 7,000	$ 5,000	$12,000
Working capital and cash reserve (includes all deposits, travel expenses, start-up supplies, grand opening expenses and a reserve in the bank)	$ 9,000	$ 5,000	$ 8,000
Total:	$64,000	$45,000	$90,000*

*Because of the added commitment to inventory of the bicycle section of the triathlon store, the initial investment is higher than for an athletic shoe center.

Fleet Feet does not provide direct financial assistance; however, the company offers help with the preparation of loan requests and Small Business Association loan requirements. You'll pay an ongoing royalty fee of from 1 to 4 percent of gross sales, which will entitle you to a wide range of company support services.

GETTING STARTED Besides a computerized market analysis to help with site selection, Fleet Feet will offer guidance with your lease negotiations, advice regarding franchise and lease contracts, total store-layout and store-fixture blueprints, and use of the Fleet Feet name and logo. You'll participate in a four-week management-training program at company headquarters in Sacramento, California. For your grand opening, which will be two to three months after signing of the franchise agreement, you'll have a complete grand-opening package, and company officials will attend your celebration.

Typically, a Fleet Feet Sports store requires 800 to 1,200 square feet of space, a Fleet Feet Triathlete facility 1,200 to 2,200 square feet, and a Fleet Feet Kids outlet 600 to 900 square feet. You'll need one full-time and three part-time employees in any of the three franchise types.

MAKING IT WORK Your monthly service fee will cover the costs of a wide range of company-supplied services, including a regional and national advertising program, group buying, advertising kits with custom-designed Fleet Feet ad materials, a warehouse of Fleet Feet products, annual and semiannual financial analyses, and in-store visits from home-office personnel. Other benefits include assistance in merchandise purchases and sales, an annual franchise conference, periodic franchise-business seminars, headquarters staff on call during all business hours to answer questions and lend support, access to computerized accounting-systems training, and interstore transfer of merchandise and inventory. You'll also receive a weekly memo, a monthly bulletin and newsletter, and promotion schedules for such local activities as speakers, workshops, and clinics. The company sponsors packaged travel programs to sports events for customers as well as several summer sports camps. A group hospitalization and insurance program will be provided for you and your employees.

COMMENTS Fleet Feet was ranked 421st in *Entrepreneur* magazine's 1987 "Franchise 500." Sally Edwards, holder of a master's degree in exercise physiology and president of the Fleet Feet group, is a four-time top-five finisher in the Ironman triathlon, author of three best-selling triathlon books, an Olympic Marathon trials qualifier, and contributing editor to four national magazines. The company is seeking to open franchise stores on the East and West Coast.

GETTING MORE INFORMATION The franchise information packet contains fact sheets on Fleet Feet, Fleet Feet Triathlete, and Fleet Feet Kids; reproductions of two trade-magazine articles about the company and its growth; and a copy of a tabloid publication by the company featuring information of interest to triathletes. For further information, contact:

Sally Edwards
President
Fleet Feet, Inc.
2410 J Street
Sacramento, CA   95816
(916)   442–7223

Flowerama

BUSINESS: cut-flower
and plant retailer
FOUNDED: 1967
FRANCHISED: 1972
START-UP
  INVESTMENT:
  $50,000–$90,000

NO. OF UNITS		AS OF		PROJECTED BY	
		1/1/85	1/1/86	1/1/87	1/1/88
OWNED BY:	COMPANY	12	12	14	14
	FRANCHISEES	81	86	106	118
LOCATED:	IN U.S.	93	98	120	132
	OUTSIDE U.S.	0	0	0	0
TOTAL:		93	98	120	132
NO. OF STATES W/ UNITS		23	23	23	23

THE BUSINESS

The sale of cut flowers has become a booming industry, and as potted plants have begun to play a larger role in interior decoration, their sales have also risen. The Society of American Florists reports that the number of retail flower shops increased from 780 million in 1963 to nearly 3 billion in 1975, and topped $5 billion in 1985.

Flowerama of America grew out of a successful greenhouse business begun by Maurice and Herbert Frink in Cedar Falls, Iowa, in 1952. The business grew to include three huge greenhouses covering about 110,000 square feet, and the Frinks became suppliers for over 250 retail florists. Fifteen years after opening their first greenhouse, the brothers began using trailers as mobile outlets at outdoor locations. In 1970 the "flowers-on-wheels" marketing concept was moved inside to enclosed shopping malls.

The Flowerama concept is patterned after the flower-cart selling done in Europe, where more flowers are sold than in America by a ratio of eighty to one. The Flowerama shops' open displays of fresh, refrigerated cut flowers at reasonable prices encourages impulse buying. The stores also sell flowering and tropical potted plants, dried and silk flowers, terrariums, fertilizers, vases, and related items.

WHAT IT TAKES

To get started in this virtual turnkey operation, you'll need $17,500 for the franchise fee plus up to an additional $17,500 in cash. Construction costs will vary depending on the type of shop you open and building costs in your area. Indirect financial assistance is available in that the company will help with your preparation of loan applications through banks and the Small Business Association. Your ongoing royalty fee of 6 percent of sales will be discounted to 5 percent if kept current. The fee for additional units is half the original franchise fee, and passive ownership is allowed. Your original franchise agreement will last ten years and will automatically be extended with an extension of your facility lease, with no additional franchise fee required.

GETTING STARTED

You'll have an exclusive territory within your shopping-mall location, and help will be provided with site selection and lease negotiation. If you have a particular site in mind, Flowerama will examine its merits; otherwise, they'll propose a location. You'll face no charge for assistance with purchase negotiation, construction of your 450- to 1,000-square-foot shop, facility layout and decoration, and equipment leasing or purchase. Flowerama will also guide you through all aspects of setting up, including merchandise acquisition, staffing (two full-time and three part-time people), and the grand opening, which will be held about two to three months after your franchise purchase.

There are two kinds of Flowerama stores—the kiosk and the in-line shop. The kiosk is the smaller, open shop in the middle of the mall aisle. It requires a much lower investment because of reduced leasehold construction costs. The in-line store is a traditional shop with more space, more security, and greater flexibility in display. Since the shops are built in a protected interior environment, you can display your flowers in the open to encourage browsing. The characteristics of your location will be of prime importance in determining which kind of shop to build.

You or your manager and other key personnel will receive nine days of extensive classroom and on-the-job training at the home office in Waterloo, Iowa. The classroom training covers cut-flower care and preparation, plant care, product display, salesmanship, floral arranging, product ordering, shop maintenance, and record keeping. Your on-the-job training will be at a company-owned retail outlet in Waterloo. You will participate in stocking the initial inventory in your store, and an experienced Flowerama staff member will come to your store to guide you through your grand opening.

MAKING IT WORK

Experienced management personnel will make periodic visits to your shop, giving you the opportunity to discuss operational problems. Every week you will confer with the home office on the Flowerama WATTS line. You'll also have the opportunity to attend seminars offered on an ongoing basis. You will receive an operating

manual that covers management responsibilities, daily working instructions, financial management, employee relations, selling, shop
appearance, and record keeping. Since all of your business will be
cash and carry, you won't have to deal with opening and approving
accounts or billing and collecting overdue payments.

Flowerama is built around impulse buying in locations that attract
shoppers, so you will avoid high advertising costs and gain quick
recognition for your store. However, experience has shown that se-
lective radio and newspaper advertising will help you promote your
floral-arranging programs and maintain specific product promotions,
so an advertising budget of 1 to 3 percent of sales is recommended.
To supplement your advertising budget, you'll receive newspaper
ads, mailers, catalogs, radio commercials, signs, and seasonal promotional materials from the company at no cost. Flowerama's staff
can also advise you on plans for floral holidays.

Frink's greenhouses in Waterloo provide wholesale plant production and offer a central purchasing program with volume discounts.
It's not unreasonable to expect to sell your entire stock of cut flowers each week and most of the potted plants within two to four
weeks. You should turn over the hard-goods inventory within one
to two months.

COMMENTS

A member of the IFA, Flowerama was ranked 242nd in *Entrepreneur* magazine's "Franchise 500" for 1987. An earnings claim document is provided prior to or during potential franchisees' personal
interviews. The company is seeking franchisees mainly in the southern, central, and midwestern regions.

**GETTING MORE
INFORMATION**

Flowerama's franchise information packet contains an eight-page information booklet, a paper detailing their marketing approach, a roster of shops already open, and a prospect qualification resume. For
more information, contact:

Chuck Nygren
Vice-President
Flowerama of America, Inc.
3165 W. Airline Highway
Waterloo, IA   50701
(319)   291–6004

Foliage Design Systems

BUSINESS: interior
landscaping
FOUNDED: 1971
FRANCHISED: 1980
START-UP
INVESTMENT:
$30,000–$50,000

NO. OF UNITS		AS OF		PROJECTED BY	
		1/1/85	1/1/86	1/1/87	1/1/88
OWNED BY:	COMPANY	4	3	3	2
	FRANCHISEES	23	28	35	40
LOCATED:	IN U.S.	27	31	38	42
	OUTSIDE U.S.	0	0	0	0
TOTAL:		27	31	38	42
NO. OF STATES W/ UNITS		8	10	15	20

THE BUSINESS

The interiorscaping industry is vibrant and growing, just like the plants used to enhance otherwise ordinary environments. Over 3,000 people are working today in an industry that did not exist ten years ago. In the last decade industry growth has been a solid 25 percent. And Foliage Design Systems in Ocala, Florida, was the first interior-landscape franchise company in this growing field.

John and Duke Hagood started FDS in 1971 by leasing live plants. From this, the company expanded into wholesale growing; design of plantscapes; and plant rental, leasing, maintenance, and consultation services. FDS promotes the view that plants help create a pleasant, relaxing atmosphere that makes people happy and smooths business transactions, and many FDS customers apparently agree. In 1986, Foliage Design Systems recorded a gross sales volume of $4.6 million with corporate clients like restaurant and hotel chains, banks, and medical facilities from New York to California. FDS offers entry to such nationally known firms as the Holiday Inns, Marriott, Embassy Suites, and Hilton hotel chains and the Bennigan's restaurant chain.

WHAT IT TAKES

The total investment you'll need to start your FDS franchise ranges from $30,000 to $50,000, which includes the initial franchise fee of $8,000 to $20,000, depending on the market territory you are interested in. You'll have to pay your franchise fee in cash, but the company will help you get financing for the remainder by providing all the necessary information you'll need for loan applications to potential lenders. The amount beyond the fee will cover your office equipment and supplies, opening inventory, storage facilities, working capital, vehicles, and introductory advertising.

The term of your original franchise agreement will be twenty years with renewal periods of five years. This will buy you the authority to operate one or more units in a specific market area. You can buy additional franchise territories under the same terms. Once in operation, you will pay an ongoing royalty fee of 4 percent of gross sales.

GETTING STARTED

After FDS approves your application, the franchise development manager will evaluate your proposed market area. You and up to three members of your staff will have five days of training in general operations at the national headquarters in Florida. The training covers the industry, plant identification and care, and office procedures and forms. In an additional four days of on-site training you'll learn about marketing and account servicing, including contracts and interiorscape design.

FDS personnel will help you obtain suitable office space and holding, growing, and acclimatizing facilities. Free help is given with facility layout, service/maintenance contracts, merchandise acquisition, staffing, and the grand opening.

MAKING IT WORK

Through its wholly owned subsidiary, Foliage Supply Company, FDS owns and manages 234,000 square feet of greenhouses. Foliage Supply Company stocks plants, containers, and mulch so a supply of healthy, hearty greenery is always available, as well as uniforms, marketing tools, and related materials. A franchisee can take as long as sixty days to pay for this stock.

Regular corporate advertising, direct mailings to prospective customers, publicity programs, magazine ads, and other media aids are available. Contacts and leads are regularly exchanged. Legal and accounting help is also provided. The company sends franchisees a monthly newsletter and quarterly updates on products, services, and customer-oriented information. An annual meeting for all franchisees is held each June. Market research, product development, group buying and other marketing services will all help keep down the cost of running your service. In addition, FDS offers a company-sponsored major-medical insurance package.

COMMENTS

In 1979, Foliage Design Systems won the Florida Nurseryman and Growers Association award for outstanding achievement in both residential and commercial interiorscaping, and in 1985 the company won the Highest Honor award from IPA and the Honor award from ALCA. FDS was ranked fifteenth in *Interiorscape* magazine's top twenty-five contractors for 1985, and 448th in *Entrepreneur* magazine's 1987 "Franchise 500." The company is seeking franchisees in about half of the states (although Florida is sold out) as well as in Canada, Europe, and Australia.

GETTING MORE INFORMATION

The franchise information packet includes a brochure explaining the value of the interiorscaping business, photocopies of articles discussing the growth of the industry and of FDS in particular, a step-by-step outline of how to become an FDS franchise operator, and a three-page confidential application form. For more information, write or call:

John S. Hagood
President
Foliage Design Systems Franchise Company
1553 South East Fort King Avenue
Ocala, FL 32671
(800) 354–2030 or (904) 732–8212

Foremost Sales Promotions

BUSINESS: marketing and consulting service for retail liquor stores	NO. OF UNITS		AS OF		PROJECTED BY	
			1/1/85	1/1/86	1/1/87	1/1/88
	OWNED BY: COMPANY		0	0	0	0
		FRANCHISEES	120	123	130	130
FOUNDED: 1949	LOCATED: IN U.S.		120	123	130	130
FRANCHISED: 1949		OUTSIDE U.S.	0	0	0	0
START-UP	TOTAL:		120	123	130	130
INVESTMENT:	NO. OF STATES W/ UNITS		18	21	25	25
$100,000–$150,000						

THE BUSINESS

There are shifts in the popularity of various types of liquor—more demand one year for wine coolers than whiskey, for example—but the overall market continues to grow. Serving the individual liquor-store retailer, Foremost Sales Promotions offers consulting and marketing advice regarding in-store layout, inventory control, accounting methods, advertising, merchandising, sales promotion, and liquor-by-wire service. This consulting takes into account the different laws of the states in which the stores do business. Foremost has been serving the liquor industry for thirty-seven years.

WHAT IT TAKES

You will need $150 to $14,560 for the initial franchise fee, which guarantees an exclusive territory based on population. The franchise fee varies depending on the state and the types of services rendered. The franchise is valid for one year and renewable annually. Your total initial investment, including the franchise fee, will range from $100,000 to $150,000, with a minimum of $100,000 required in cash. The company will help you secure financing through conventional sources. Additional units cost the same as the first; master franchises are not available. You may buy a Foremost franchise without being the operating manager, but the company does not encourage the practice. There are no ongoing royalty fees, and no previous experience in liquor sales is necessary.

GETTING STARTED   Foremost charges for all start-up assistance: site selection; lease or purchase negotiation for the site; construction; facility layout and decoration; lease or purchase of furniture, fixtures, equipment, vehicles, and merchandise; establishment of service and maintenance contracts; and acquisition of materials and supplies. The typical facility is 6,000 square feet and can be located in any type of commercial and office buildings, including malls and shopping centers. You will be required to utilize the company's uniform layout, promote their decorating schemes, and use the Foremost logo on materials and supplies. You will need four full-time and four part-time employees. You'll be fully trained in all areas of package liquor store operation. If you have a liquor license, you can be open for business within one to two months after buying your franchise. Foremost will help with your grand opening.

MAKING IT WORK   For part of your initial fee you will receive mailers, telephone-book ads, brochures, presentation books, catalogs, newspaper and magazine ads, and television commercials. The company offers a cooperative advertising program. You can request on-site training as needed and attend an annual convention for franchisees, an anniversary dinner for suppliers and store owners, quarterly franchise meetings, and periodic seminars. Foremost publishes a weekly newsletter, plus company and industry updates as needed. Surveys are conducted as needed. The company sponsors franchisee-recognition programs and offers back-up services, including headquarters and regional resource persons; a toll-free hotline; regular on-site visits and on-site troubleshooting; policy, management-procedure, and customer-service manuals; all types of forms; and systems for bookkeeping, inventory, personnel, expense analysis, and computerized information management. You will benefit, too, from a central purchasing program offering volume discounts and a centralized merchandising system. One requirement is that alcoholic beverages must be purchased from licensed wholesalers. The company sponsors insurance programs for property, general-liability, life, major-medical, dental, and third-party-bonding coverage.

COMMENTS   Rated 224th in the 1987 *Entrepreneur* magazine "Franchise 500," Foremost has received merchandising awards for retail liquor stores. The company, which provides an earnings claim document upon request, wants to add franchises in twenty-four states.

GETTING MORE
INFORMATION

To learn more about Foremost's franchise program, contact:
Gail P. Zelitzky
President
Foremost Sales Promotions, Inc.
5252 North Broadway
Chicago, IL   60640
(800)   621–5150 or (312)   334–0077

Gelato Classico Italian Ice Cream

BUSINESS: Italian ice
cream retailer
FOUNDED: 1976
FRANCHISED: 1982
START-UP
INVESTMENT:
$100,000–$150,000

		AS OF		PROJECTED BY	
NO. OF UNITS		1/1/85	1/1/86	1/1/87	1/1/88
OWNED BY:	COMPANY	5	5	5	5
	FRANCHISEES	22	27	54	100
LOCATED:	IN U.S.	27	32	39	65
	OUTSIDE U.S.	0	0	20	40
TOTAL:		27	32	59	105
NO. OF STATES W/ UNITS		6	7	20	25

THE BUSINESS

Gelato Classico first introduced "gelato" (also known as "Italian ices") in a tiny shop in San Francisco in 1976. Today, Gelato Classico manufactures and packages gelato, sorbetto, and Italian frozen yogurt for retail distribution through its franchised shops. Gelato products are also sold wholesale to many restaurants through local franchisees.

In addition to gelato, Gelato Classico franchises serve sundaes, banana splits, frappes (milk shakes), and the "yo yo," a speciality ice cream sandwich. The menu is rounded out by a balanced selection of other desserts including fine pastries, coffee drinks, espressos, and various soft drinks. Gelato Classico takes pride in using no artificial colors, flavorings, or preservatives in any of their products.

WHAT IT TAKES

Your total initial investment will range from $100,000 to $150,000, which will cover your equipment, inventory, and $25,000 franchise fee, which is normally paid in cash. Your franchise agreement will apply for ten years, with a renewal option for another ten years. You will have exclusive rights to your territory, which will be determined on the basis of area or population density. Although you won't be responsible for paying a monthly royalty fee, you will pay from 1 percent to 3 percent of gross sales to cover local and national advertising. If you later decide to open an additional unit, the franchise fee of $25,000 will apply again. You may also open a master franchise, which would allow you to subfranchise stores in your territory. If you want to hire a manager, Gelato Classico has no objection. No previous experience is required for potential franchisees.

GETTING STARTED

Gelato shop sizes vary from 300 to 1,200 square feet, with the average facility being 800 square feet. You may locate either in a shopping center, off a busy street, or downtown. Gelato offers intensive personal attention by providing the shop design, assisting you with site selection, and visiting your proposed site for final approval. During the construction phase, Gelato will work with your building contractor to ensure that shop layout and decoration conform to the company's high standards. (Gelato Classico shops have produced some of the highest dollar yields per square foot in the retail industry.) Although the decor differs somewhat in each location, all shops have a distinctive Italian decor and display the design work of Ron Nunn, award-winning company architect.

A typical shop has one full-time and eight part-time employees. Although Gelato doesn't provide staffing assistance, all store personnel receive training in good salesmanship and serving etiquette. You and/or your manager will be sent to the company-owned shop in San Francisco for three to five days of hands-on training before your store opens. The training covers shop management, opening and closing procedures, inventory and cash control, staff hiring, and general accounting principles. You can plan to open within two to three months after purchasing your franchise, and you'll receive company help in planning your grand opening.

MAKING IT WORK

In return for the ongoing advertising fee, you will receive special promotional displays, banners, flags, contest materials, and radio commercials for local airing. In addition, you'll receive a quarterly company newsletter, brochures, and mailers. The corporate staff provides continual marketing and advertising support, product development, and a central purchasing system for items such as spoons, cups, and napkins. All ice cream is produced in the San Francisco plant, and the prepacked products can be shipped to your shop daily. Most of the freight cost is covered in a freight allowance provided to each store.

Because the shops are relatively simple to staff and operate, Gelato offers limited on-site training after you open your shop. The company will determine whether additional hands-on training for your service personnel is needed.

Staff at the San Francisco plant conduct extensive experimentation and testing to develop and perfect new flavors. At any given time, the plant produces twenty to twenty-two of the thirty or more flavors produced annually. High-demand flavors such as Dark Chocolate, Coppa Mista, and Vanilla Bean are always in production, but other flavors are available only when the seasonal ingredients are.

With Gelato's approval you may sell related noncompany products during off-season periods.

COMMENTS

Gelato Classico provides an earnings claim document prior to or during a potential franchisee's personal interview. The company is seeking franchise operations throughout the world.

GETTING MORE INFORMATION

The franchise information packet contains an eight-page brochure with color photographs of company products and displays, a pamphlet on the company's history, and a one-page application form. Write or call:

Jeanne L. Hefferman
Vice-President
Gelato Classico Italian Ice Cream
369 Pine Street, Suite 900
San Francisco, CA   94104
(415)   433–3111

Grand Slam U.S.A.

BUSINESS: automated indoor/outdoor baseball-batting ranges

FOUNDED: 1976

FRANCHISED: 1983

START-UP INVESTMENT: $135,000–$175,000

NO. OF UNITS		AS OF		PROJECTED BY	
		1/1/85	1/1/86	1/1/87	1/1/88
OWNED BY: COMPANY		2	2	2	2
	FRANCHISEES	11	30	51	71
LOCATED: IN U.S.		13	32	53	73
	OUTSIDE U.S.	0	0	0	0
TOTAL:		13	32	53	73
NO. OF STATES W/ UNITS		6	18	24	32

THE BUSINESS

Grand Slam U.S.A. is the only franchisor of indoor automated baseball-batting ranges in the world. Along with the batting ranges, Grand Slam academies use an instructional system designed by the National Baseball Coaches Advisory Board to provide instruction on hitting, fielding, throwing, running, and general body conditioning for baseball players.

The parent company, the Athletic Training Equipment Company (ATEC), markets its line of equipment to schools and professional teams exclusively. Batting ranges can be constructed for either indoor or outdoor use. Each coin-operated automated range has its own pitching machine, netting, and automatic ball-retrieval system. With simple adjustments the user can change the speed and trajectory of each pitch. Overall operation is simple and cost-effective; batting ranges require minimal maintenance and can be supervised by a single employee.

Grand Slam's sales increased from $2.8 million to $4 million during fiscal year 1984–85, and within the next five years, 200 to 300 franchises are expected to be in operation. Each unit averages gross sales over $150,000 per year.

WHAT IT TAKES

Depending on location and the number of batting ranges needed, your initial investment could range between $135,000 and $175,000, which includes the $6,000 franchise fee. Your cash investment of $50,000 will cover your down payments on equipment, installation costs, grand-opening expenses, leasehold improvements, and working-capital reserves. The terms of your franchise agreement will apply for ten years, with a renewal period for another ten years. The franchise rights will entitle you to an exclusive territory based on population. For just a $1,500 fee you can open a second facility, or you may choose to take advantage of the master franchise option by investing in several locations within your territory and collecting your share of the revenues and royalties (6 percent of the total annual gross revenues for each facility).

To open your facility, you can expect these start-up costs:

ITEM	COST
5 Batting Modules: 3 softball, 2 baseball at $18,500 each for a total of	$92,500
Building improvements, including electrical, offices, painting, carpeting, counter storage	10,000
1st/last month's rent	7,000
Franchise fee	6,000
Installation charge	5,200
Signs—outdoor, indoor	5,000
Legal/accounting	3,000
Insurance, prepaid	3,000
Office supplies/equipment including change machines, bulletin boards, etc.	2,500
Spectator necessities, including benches, clocks, PA system	2,500
Freight-in	2,000
Bats and helmets	1,200
Janitorial/health supplies and equipment	1,000
Spare-parts kit	750
Maintenance/repair supplies	750
Licenses/permits	500

ITEM	COST
Master control panel	375
Miscellaneous	2,500
Total:	$151,775

The total figure for an indoor facility could range from $143,000 to $163,000. If you decide to have outdoor ranges, your cost would be less—approximately $124,000.

The total figure for an indoor facility could range from $143,000 to $163,000. If you decide to have outdoor ranges, your cost would be less—approximately $124,000.

GETTING STARTED

Grand Slam will assist you in selecting and developing your site and planning your facility. A typical outdoor complex ranges from 15,000 to 30,000 square feet, usually located near a commercial or industrial park. An indoor facility would most likely be situated in a freestanding warehouse-type building of 8,000 to 10,000 square feet, with a minimum ceiling height of sixteen feet so that batting ranges can fit inside. The main requirements for an indoor site are proper zoning, adequate parking, and location in a neighborhood suitable for young people. Grand Slam can offer you a design service if unusual design situations arise or if you wish to upgrade an existing facility. You will also receive company assistance in facility lease or purchase negotiations, supplies and merchandise acquisition, and equipment leasing.

Grand Slam recommends that you operate your complex with three full-time and two part-time employees. You and your manager, if any, can go to the company's Clackamas, Oregon, facility (at your own expense) for three days of hands-on training. You will be instructed in merchandising, facility operations, equipment maintenance, marketing and promotions, and planning a successful grand opening. In addition, every six to eight weeks you can request on-site follow-up training. Since the operating procedures are fairly simple and no previous experience is required, you can expect to open your business within three to six months after the franchise purchase.

MAKING IT WORK

Grand Slam will supply you with promotions, advertising guidelines, fund-raising ideas, and other marketing programs that are designed to increase traffic. You also will receive newspaper ads and TV and radio commercials prepared and ready for use at your discretion, as well as a specially designed management operations manual which covers both the batting ranges and the academy. Grand Slam constantly develops new ideas and products to help improve your operations, and the company sends you a newsletter and product/service updates. You may also take advantage of Grand Slam's toll-free hotline to reach both headquarters resource persons and regional support personnel.

Grand Slam has regional divisions that distribute its merchandise. Also, the company's central purchasing program will allow you to get volume discounts. You may sell or use any products that you feel will enhance your operation.

COMMENTS

A member of the United States Baseball Federation, Grand Slam U.S.A. joined the IFA in 1984. Grand Slam hosts international baseball tournaments. The company is seeking franchisees in thirty-seven states.

GETTING MORE INFORMATION

The franchise information packet is a very detailed collection of brochures, letters, and cost sheets explaining company equipment, operations, and facilities. One color brochure discusses the baseball-academy concept, batting ranges, and exclusive features offered by owning a franchise. Several information packets describe equipment, batting cages, and overall facility specifications. An itemized breakdown of general start-up expenses is also enclosed. For details, contact:

Jim Bryan
Franchise Coordinator
Grand Slam U.S.A. (ATEC)
9057 South East Jannsen Road
P.O. Box 451
Clackamas, OR   97015–0451
(800)   547–6273

Grease Monkey

BUSINESS:			AS OF		PROJECTED BY	
			1/1/85	1/1/86	1/1/87	1/1/88
Specialized routine	NO. OF UNITS					
car-care service	OWNED BY: COMPANY		0	1	3	10
FOUNDED: 1978	FRANCHISEES		150	220	360	450
FRANCHISED: 1979	LOCATED: IN U.S.		150	221	361	458
START-UP	OUTSIDE U.S.		0	0	2	2
INVESTMENT:	TOTAL:		150	221	363	460
$49,750–$81,550	NO. OF STATES W/ UNITS		12	19	25	35

THE BUSINESS

In 1985, Grease Monkey International franchises sold $10 million worth of car-care services, with an average of $250,000 yearly for each outlet.

The company prides itself on speed, service, and efficiency. In ten minutes they'll change a car's oil and filter, check all the fluid levels, check the air in the tires, wash the windows, and even vacuum the interior—all at a price that attracts even do-it-yourselfers.

WHAT IT TAKES

Grease Monkey will consider your application for a franchise if you have a personal net worth of $150,000 or more and can afford to lease or purchase the land and building for the outlet. The initial franchise fee is $20,000, which entitles you to an exclusive territory for ten years. The agreement is renewable for another ten years at the end of the first term.

Your total investment will be from $40,000 to $80,000, and you'll need to have $40,000–$50,000 of it in cash. If you're established as credit worthy, you may find financing through Grease Monkey suppliers.

The chart below shows a breakdown of initial investment costs for a two-bay center:

	RANGE	
INVESTMENT REQUIREMENTS	LOW	HIGH
Franchise fee	$ 7,500	$20,000
Other costs:		
Leasing of premises (deposit)	5,000	9,000
Initial inventories	6,000	9,000
Outdoor signage (lease deposit)	500	750
Dispensing equipment, installation, and small tools	12,000	15,000
Oil tanks and installation	2,000	4,000
Training program (travel and lodging)	0	800

| | RANGE | |
INVESTMENT REQUIREMENTS	LOW	HIGH
Office equipment and furniture	1,000	2,000
Uniforms and miscellaneous	750	1,500
Prepaid expenses and deposits	1,000	2,000
Initial advertising	1,500	2,500
Initial working capital	12,500	15,000
Subtotal:	42,250	61,550
Total: (including franchise fee)	$49,750	$81,550

The low-range franchise fee applies only to the fourth and subsequent franchises when you buy four or more at the same time. Three-bay centers cost another $4,000–$5,000 for the extra equipment. You can own as many franchises as you want, and you don't have to manage them yourself. If you already own a Grease Monkey franchise, you will be given first consideration on new sites in your operating area. You'll pay a royalty fee of 5 percent of your gross monthly sales (less sales tax) to the company.

GETTING STARTED

Grease Monkey will advise you on where to put your outlet to best take advantage of the competitive fast-lube market. The company has the final say on location, but the staff will work with you through real estate orientation, part of the site selection process. Centers can be located in an existing building, such as a closed service station, but the building has to be situated correctly on the lot. If you can find a property owner or other outside investor to build to suit or remodel, you may lease your site instead of buying it. The company will also help you with construction, decorating, and finding supplies.

You'll have the standard Grease Monkey building designed for efficiency and beauty, displaying the company colors and trademark. Typical freestanding Grease Monkey centers occupy about 10,000 square feet of land. The buildings are usually about 1,475 square feet, with the main floor usually 28 by 50 feet and a basement under the service area.

The company will help you staff your center with three or four full-time and two part-time people. You or your manager will need to have a general knowledge of business principles and some experience; however, the company will give you a training program and operations manuals. Owners and managers will spend six days in Grease Monkey's Denver, Colorado, headquarters learning about marketing, accounting, and comprehensive operations. You or your

manager and crew will get one to three more days of hands-on training at your service center.

MAKING IT WORK

Grease Monkey has an advertising trust account set up for your advertising expenses. You pay 4 percent of your gross monthly sales
(less sales tax) into this account, in addition to the 5 percent royalty
fee. You'll get newpaper, radio, and television advertising, along
with brochures, mailers, press release packages, signs, and displays.
The company will consult with you on market planning and give you
a public relations/marketing manual to use. You'll attend seminars
and yearly conventions and get quarterly on-site training on new
techniques. The company will also keep you informed with newsletters, product and service technical updates, and survey data.

You'll have full support from company resources such as policy
and customer-service manuals, headquarters assistance people, and
regular visits from service representatives. The company will give
you accounting, personnel, and order forms and will supply your
bookkeeping, inventory, and expense-analysis systems. When you
buy supplies for your center, volume discounts and company-brand
products will save you money. Also, you can buy brands other than
the company's from a list of approved suppliers.

COMMENTS

Ranked 315 in the 1986 *Entrepreneur* "Franchise 500," Grease Monkey is an Operating Division of Grease Monkey Holding Corporation and a member of the IFA since 1979. The company has been
recognized by the American Advertising Federation and the Holly-
wood Radio & TV Society for local, regional, national, and international advertising. Grease Monkey is looking for new franchises
worldwide.

**GETTING MORE
INFORMATION**

The Grease Monkey information packet is an aggressively designed,
full-color, two-page brochure. For more information, contact:
D. W. MacDonald
Vice President, Marketing
Grease Monkey International
1660 Wynkoop, Suite 960
Denver, CO 80202
(303)   534–1660

Great Clips

BUSINESS: hair salon
FOUNDED: 1982
FRANCHISED: 1983
START-UP
INVESTMENT:
$69,100

		AS OF		PROJECTED BY	
NO. OF UNITS		1/1/85	1/1/86	1/1/87	1/1/88
OWNED BY:	COMPANY	8	9	7	7
	FRANCHISEES	54	110	163	213
LOCATED:	IN U.S.	62	119	170	220
	OUTSIDE U.S.	0	0	0	0
TOTAL:		62	119	170	220
NO. OF STATES W/ UNITS		10	12	13	15

THE BUSINESS

The transition from independent shops to large franchising opera-tions experienced in fast-food, auto-repair, real estate, and tax-preparation businesses is just beginning in the hair-care industry, with a marked shift toward a national network of independently owned franchises expected over the next ten years. People continue to demand quality hair care regardless of economic conditions; ap-proximately 95 percent of Americans get their hair cut regularly by a licensed professional. Most shopping centers need both an ap-pointments-required full-service salon (25 percent of the market) and a low-cost, no-appointment-necessary hair-care shop (75 per-cent of the market). Offering the latter, Great Clips appeals to all ages, projects a positive family image, and complements any shop-ping center. Total dollar volume for all Great Clip franchise opera-tions in 1985 was $13 million, with average gross sales per unit of $118,180 and average net per unit of $29,500.

WHAT IT TAKES

As a Great Clips franchise investor/owner you can operate either a single shop, a group of shops, or shops throughout a complete ter-ritory. For a single shop you'll need $12,500 for the initial franchise fee, but how much of this you must pay in cash depends on what other assets you have available. Your total start-up investment will involve the following:

ITEM	COST
Initial franchise fee	$12,500
Initial advertising-fund contribution	2,500
Security deposits	2,000
Furniture, fixtures, and equipment	9,000
Leasehold improvements	17,000
Office supplies and paper goods	1,000
Cleaning and shop supplies	800
Opening inventory	3,000

ITEM	COST
Insurance payment	1,600
Licenses	200
Legal fees	1,500
Preopening wages	2,000
Grand-opening advertising	8,000
Working capital	8,000
Total:	$69,100

The term of your franchise agreement will be ten years, renewable for two five-year periods. Your specific territory will be determined by the television area of dominant influence. You'll pay a royalty fee of 6 percent of total sales. Each additional franchise will require the $12,500 franchise fee, but you may choose to purchase a master franchise instead. No previous experience in the hair-care business is required.

GETTING STARTED

You'll receive seven days of training at a Great Clips training center—two days of franchise-orientation training and five days of management training. You'll learn about site selection, lease negotiations, construction, equipment needs, hiring, advertising, accounting, quality control, scheduling, and customer relations. A typical facility will occupy 1,200 to 1,500 square feet, usually in a mall, or a shopping strip or center. The company can help with your site selection, lease negotiations, and construction plans.

Although the usual time from franchise purchase to opening is three to six months, you could be set up and fully operational within a month. The company will help you plan promotions for your grand opening. Once the business is set up, you'll spend only a few hours a week running your store—you'll handle the insurance, taxes, payroll, and bills. The day-to-day operation will be handled by certified managers. You should plan to employ four to six full-time employees and four or five part-time ones, and Great Clips will guide you in hiring your staff.

MAKING IT WORK

To participate in the Great Clips advertising program, you'll pay an ongoing advertising fee of 5 percent of total sales. This covers newspaper advertising, television and radio commercials, billboard posters, and direct-mail brochures. Sent to customers in your local area, the brochures, as well as the newspaper ads, feature discount coupons. In its first year of operation the average Great Clips shop distributes over 200,000 brochures with coupon offers to households in the immediate vicinity of the shop.

You and your customers will benefit from the Great Clips quality-control program. As a participant in this program, you will sell only company-approved products, which you can purchase through a central purchasing program featuring volume discounts. You'll receive ongoing company support through a bimonthly newspaper, periodic mailings of company information, franchise meetings, manuals, business forms, on-site visits, and a bookkeeping and inventory system. The Great Clips insurance program includes life, major-medical, worker's compensation, disability, and Health Maintenance Organization–type health-insurance coverage.

COMMENTS

Great Clips was ranked 66th in *Venture* magazine's 1986 "Franchise 100" and 276th in *Entrepreneur* magazine's 1987 "Franchise 500."

GETTING MORE INFORMATION

The franchise information packet includes a brochure, samples of camera-ready magazine advertising and newspaper layouts, and a preliminary application form that requests a personal and financial statement. To receive this information, contact:

Raymond L. Barton
Executive Vice-President
Great Clips, Inc.
3601 West 77th Street
Minneapolis, MN   55435
(612)   893–9088

The Ground Round

		AS OF		PROJECTED BY	
NO. OF UNITS		1/1/85	1/1/86	1/1/87	1/1/88
OWNED BY: COMPANY		178	170	170	170
	FRANCHISEES	31	51	75	100
LOCATED: IN U.S.		209	219	241	262
	OUTSIDE U.S.	0	2	4	8
TOTAL:		209	221	245	270
NO. OF STATES W/ UNITS		20	20	22	25

BUSINESS: family restaurant
FOUNDED: 1969
FRANCHISED: 1970
START-UP INVESTMENT: $1,100,000– $1,500,000

THE BUSINESS

Although the company's name is The Ground Round, ground beef is only the beginning of the affordable menu this franchise has designed to appeal to a variety of customers throughout the day. Steak and hamburgers are standard fare, but the menu also includes Mexican food, chicken, seafood, pasta, sandwiches, and appetizers. Ground Round restaurants also maintain a full bar, with draft beer, wine, and cocktails. In addition to their lunch and dinner services

Ground Round restaurants offer specially organized birthday parties for children.

With a lively atmosphere, comfortable surroundings, and varied menu, Ground Round restaurants have become a tremendous success. Since 1969, when the first Ground Round restaurant opened, the chain has grown to over 200 locations in twenty states. In 1985 the average gross sales for each unit totaled $1,400,000, and the average net income per franchise unit was $190,000.

WHAT IT TAKES

Ground Round is seeking franchisees who have significant previous restaurant experience and solid financial resources. Many managers have a college degree, but this is not a prerequisite.

The initial franchise fee for a Ground Round restaurant is $30,000, which buys a twenty-year franchise agreement but does not include an exclusive area or territory. After twenty years you can renew your franchise for subsequent five-year periods. Your total initial investment will be $1.1 million to $1.5 million, $100,000 of which must be in cash. In addition to the $30,000 franchise fee, you'll need approximately $200,000 to $350,000 for land; $475,000 to $525,000 for construction; $265,000 to $325,000 for equipment; $18,000 for signs; $30,000 for working capital; and $50,000 for miscellaneous expenses such as fees and permits. You'll also need to buy a liquor license, for which the price varies from state to state. You'll be responsible for obtaining the loans you'll need to finance the entire investment.

You can purchase additional restaurant franchises for $30,000 each or obtain a master franchise, but the company does not allow passive ownership of individual Ground Round restaurants. You will pay 3 percent of your gross sales to the company as a continuing royalty fee and set aside another 2 percent of gross sales for advertising. Your license agreement will grant you use of the trademarks, designs, advertising, and architectural and other unique features identified with Ground Round restaurants.

GETTING STARTED

The company will help you locate and purchase your restaurant site, which should be in an area with a relatively dense population— 50,000 has proved successful in the past—primarily in the middle-income bracket. Ground Round restaurants typically require 5,900 to 6,000 square feet and need good visibility from the street or highway. Shopping centers are profitable locations, but you could also be successful in an office building, mall, or freestanding building. An all-alcoholic-beverage license must be available, and forty-five parking spaces for each 100 patron seats are needed.

If you are converting an existing building, the company will give your architect helpful guidelines in preparing final plans and financial estimates and will consult with you, your architect, engineers, and contractor during renovation of your facility. The company will provide similar help if you choose to construct a new building. You should plan to buy 60,000 square feet of land for a new restaurant using the company's 215-seat prototype.

Ground Round believes interior decor and atmosphere can vitally affect the sales volume of your business, so company personnel will help you plan the layout and decoration for your facility. You can buy your furniture, fixtures, equipment, and expendables from local sources, but these items must meet company specifications. The company will provide you with a list of recommended local sources and link you to its distribution network for company-approved products. You can individualize your restaurant, but in all aspects of your operation you must comply with the company's guidelines and high standards for quality.

A typical Ground Round restaurant employs seventy full-time and twenty-five part-time employees. Staffing assistance is not provided as part of your franchise agreement. Before your opening you and your assistant managers will receive on-the-job, learner-controlled management training for two to three weeks at one of fifteen regional training restaurants. During the three weeks prior to your opening, a company training supervisor and a team of trainers will provide complete on-site training for your hourly personnel. You can plan to open your restaurant within four months to a year after your franchise purchase, depending on your building-construction schedule. The company will help with your grand opening.

MAKING IT WORK

As part of the advertising fee, Ground Round handles all national media coverage and maintains a library of television and radio commercials and newspaper advertisements, which you can use for complete local promotional coverage. The company will also give you mailers, seasonal displays, and promotional buttons for your waiters and waitresses to wear. And balloons, banners, flags, movies, and cartoons are supplied to brighten up the childrens' birthday celebrations. As part of an additional cooperative advertising program, you can get four-color magazine ads, billboard posters, signs, and a press package.

The company holds a national conference twice a year, regional and areawide meetings annually, and one- or two-day seminars quarterly. Four times a year, company personnel will visit your restaurant to conduct quality-assurance and internal audits and offer feedback and support. Company personnel will also be available if you should need on-site troubleshooting.

You'll receive the company's monthly newsletter, periodic product or service updates, regular reports on the company's activities, and biannual updates on trends in the restaurant industry. Your opportunity for input is guaranteed with franchisee surveys every year. The company will supply you with manuals on policy, management procedure, and customer service; forms for inventory, personnel, ordering, and accounting; and bookkeeping, inventory, and expense-analysis systems. You can buy products through the corporate food-distribution system, with its centralized purchasing and merchandising, or from outside vendors whose products meet the high quality standards specified by the Ground Round.

COMMENTS

A subsidiary of Imperial Group, Ltd., and a member of the IFA, Ground Round is seeking to increase franchise operations in most states.

GETTING MORE INFORMATION

The franchise information packet contains a brochure with high-quality photographs, a sheet on the financial aspects of franchise ownership, a letter to the potential franchisee, and samples of advertising/promotional materials. The confidential franchisee application included with the packet asks for detailed background information and extensive personal financial disclosure. For more information, write:

Lynn E. Reichel
Ground Round, Inc.
541 Main Street
South Weymouth, MA   02190–1898
(617)   331–7005

Gymboree

		AS OF		PROJECTED BY	
		1/1/85	1/1/86	1/1/87	1/1/88
NO. OF UNITS					
OWNED BY:	COMPANY	5	5	5	5
	FRANCHISEES	243	305	360	420
LOCATED:	IN U.S.	248	310	363	416
	OUTSIDE U.S.	0	0	2	9
TOTAL:		248	310	365	425
NO. OF STATES W/ UNITS		27	29	30	34

BUSINESS: parent-child developmental play program
FOUNDED: 1976
FRANCHISED: 1980
START-UP INVESTMENT: $25,385–$32,465

THE BUSINESS

When Joan Barnes first conceived her unique idea for a parent-child developmental play program in the mid-1970s, the birthrate was in a decline. Even then, Barnes found her programs in constant demand as parents passed the word about Gymboree centers. By 1979 she was operating eight centers single-handedly, so she had to franchise in order to maintain the quality of operation. Now that the baby business is booming again, so is Gymboree. The company has also benefitted from the current fitness boom toward children, many of whom are not healthy and fit, according to the President's Council on Physical Fitness. Today the corporation has over 300 centers in operation in twenty-nine states. Since 1980 its growth has exceeded 100 percent each year.

Classes at Gymboree centers cost fifty to sixty dollars for a twelve-week session in which the child and at least one parent participate in a program of self-discovery and exploration. Children are grouped by age into three classes: Babygym, for three- to twelve-month olds; Gymboree One, Two, and Three, for ten- to thirty-six-month olds; and Gymgrad, for two-and-a-half to four-year olds.

WHAT IT TAKES

Your first franchise will cost $14,000 and your second, $10,000. Since the company usually won't sell fewer than two franchises to a new buyer, your initial franchise cost will be $24,000, of which $19,385 must be paid in cash. Your total start-up investment will probably run between $25,385 and $32,465. If necessary, the company can help you meet your expenses beyond the cash amount required. You can buy a third franchise for a fee of $9,000 and a fourth for $7,000. The company does not allow passive ownership and offers master franchises only outside the United States. Your franchise agreement will apply for ten years, renewable for ten years, and will grant you a territory determined by demographic and geographic information. You'll pay a royalty fee of 6 percent and an advertising fee of 1.5 percent of your quarterly gross sales. You need no experience to own a Gymboree franchise, but a teaching background may be helpful.

GETTING STARTED

Gymboree will help you find a suitable site. Rather than building or renovating standard commercial facilities, the company has a policy of locating Gymboree centers in community buildings like churches, synagogues, or civic centers. The location you rent will need a minimum of 1,800 square feet. Gymboree will provide all the materials and supplies you'll need for recreation, teaching, and decorating and will contract the building of all wooden Gymboree equipment to local carpenters. The program format, materials, and equipment are uniform in all the franchises. You'll probably need only one full-time and one part-time employee for each gymboree center, and the company will assist you in the hiring.

The company has a rigorous franchisee selection process. Before signing the franchise agreement you will visit headquarters in Burlingame, California, for personal interviews and observation of Gymboree classes. If you qualify and remain interested, the company will send you a final contract to sign. You'll then be sent to school for nine days at headquarters, where you'll receive classroom and hands-on instruction, see videotapes, and hear presentations of case studies. You'll learn about site selection and all other aspects of business management. You can open your center within three months after signing the contract, and the company will help with your grand opening.

MAKING IT WORK

Gymboree advertises in newspapers, magazines, brochures, mailers, and television commercials. The company also markets products for home use, such as musical cassette tapes, records, and videotapes produced by nationally recognized recording companies. Children's books and the company's own line of indoor/outdoor gymnastics equipment will soon be available. R. Dakin and Company has already produced and distributed a new hand puppet and a line of stuffed toys featuring Gymboree characters. Probably the most effective marketing tool is a syndicated column called "Gymboree." Currently running in nearly 300 newspapers, the column discusses child development and offers advice to parents.

The company will send you a quarterly newsletter and a customer-oriented magazine with feature articles, columns, book reviews, and recipes. A company representative will visit your site twice during your first year to offer advice and new training. You'll also attend an annual three-day national convention and a one-day regional convention. During daily operations you can refer to your policy and procedure manuals and use the company's bookkeeping and inventory systems. Also, you can call on headquarters resource people whenever necessary. Gymboree sponsors an insurance package with general-liability and equipment coverage.

COMMENTS

A member of the IFA since 1983, Gymboree has been commended by the President's Council on Physical Fitness and recognized by the IFA for ten years in business. Gymboree was ranked 54th in *Venture* magazine's "Franchise 100" for 1986 and 187th in *Entrepreneur* magazine's "Franchise 500" for 1987. The company is seeking new franchisees in most of the United States and in Canada, Europe, and Japan.

GETTING MORE INFORMATION

The franchise information packet contains article reprints; a copy of the customer-oriented magazine; a class schedule; a gift catalog; a brochure and a list of steps to follow for potential franchisees. A franchisee profile is included for you to fill out and return with a current photograph and resume. For more information, contact:

Robert M. Jacob
Vice-President of Franchise Sales
Gymboree Corporation
872 Hinckley Road
Burlingame, CA   94010
(415)   692–8080

HairCrafters

BUSINESS: hair salon
FOUNDED: 1955
FRANCHISED: 1967
START-UP
INVESTMENT:
$71,000–$124,500

		AS OF		PROJECTED BY	
NO. OF UNITS		1/1/85	1/1/86	1/1/87	1/1/88
OWNED BY:	COMPANY	28	28	40	55
	FRANCHISEES	321	353	390	450
LOCATED:	IN U.S.	349	381	430	505
	OUTSIDE U.S.	0	0	0	0
TOTAL:		349	381	430	505
NO. OF STATES W/ UNITS		28	30	31	33

THE BUSINESS

Totaling $3.8 billion in 1976, salon-industry annual sales are projected to reach $20 billion by 1988. Yet in 1983 there were 12,000 fewer salons than in 1976. Independent, owner-operated salons are giving way to franchise salons. The franchise salon industry grew from 500 salons in 1975 to 5,000 in 1983; the projected total for 1988 is 10,000, an increase of 100 percent in five years. The dollar volume of the franchise salon industry is projected to increase 150 percent during the same five years.

HairCrafters grew from the efforts of Karl Stanley, who began his business with a single salon on Long Island nearly thirty years ago. Stanley franchised his original prototype under the name Cut & Curl, and in the mid-1970s, he created a mall-based, unisex chain called Great Expectations Precision Haircutters. The newest division, HairCrafters, responds to today's market by allowing the whole family to get fast, economical hair care at the same facility, at the same time. HairCrafters offers permanents, coloring, and haircutting services. The idea has proven to be so successful that all of the original Cut & Curl salons are being converted to HairCrafters. The average gross sales per HairCrafters salon were $195,000, with a total annual volume for all franchises at $55 million in 1985.

WHAT IT TAKES

The initial franchise fee is $18,000, and the franchise agreement, which does not offer an exclusive territory, applies for fifteen years, with a five-year renewal. The total range of your investment will be $71,000 to $124,500, with $50,000 required in cash. The company can help you finance the remaining $21,000 to $74,500. In addition to the $18,000 franchise fee you'll pay $25,000 to $50,000 for lease-hold improvements, up to $3,500 for site acquisition, up to $5,000 for lease security deposits, $5,000 to $25,000 for fixtures and equipment, $3,000 for opening inventory, and $10,000 to $20,000 for miscellaneous opening expenses.

The company encourages franchisees to think of HairCrafters not as hair salons but as investments. In fact, you do not need any hair-care experience to manage your business—or businesses. The average HairCrafters franchisee has four salons; some have as many as twenty-seven. The company encourages you to consider the benefits of committing at the outset to as many units as possible. The fee for each additional franchise is $18,000, and the ongoing royalty fee is 6 percent of gross sales.

GETTING STARTED

You will have the use of the company's system for advanced statistical analysis of demographic data to identify new salon locations with the greatest potential. You can also benefit from the company's site-selection profiles based on experience with over 500 salon locations. For an additional fee you can get detailed guidance on lease negotiations, equipment decisions, and purchase of materials and supplies. If you contract your own construction, the company can assist you for a fee; but if you prefer, HairCrafters will undertake the complete project as a turnkey operation. The typical salon is 1,200 to 1,800 square feet in a mall or shopping center. HairCrafters has specific requirements concerning equipment and signs.

You will have help selecting your staff of six full-time and three part-time people. You and your manager will receive seven to ten days of training in your salon covering employee selection and training; advertising and merchandising; marketing; bookkeeping; inventory control; and suggested accounting, data processing, and pricing practices. Your salon can be in operation three to six months after your signing of the agreement. The company will play an active part in your grand opening and will provide a tested packaged of advertising, promotional, and in-store materials to make it a success.

MAKING IT WORK

You can continue to use many of the start-up services as you add new units and new personnel. The company's research-based marketing operation uses franchisee-supplied data as well as consumer-supplied data on local competition. The research findings are used to develop a wide range of marketing materials, including brochures, newspaper ads, mailers, and point-of-purchase displays. For a fee, you can get television commercials, banners, and magazine ads.

You'll have access to the company's operations department, which develops and supplies product and training materials such as a management-training program to assist owners. Also, the company's field staff act as troubleshooters. Other resources include a toll-free hotline; policy and customer-service manuals; and standardized forms for inventory, personnel records, and accounting. A research-and-development division evaluates hair-care products for use in the salons. The company offers volume discounts through its purchasing system, giving you access to CutCo and Redkin products, although you may stock competitive brands.

HairCutters sponsors a national conference, regional conferences, and areawide franchise meetings. You will receive a quarterly newsletter and periodic product and technical updates. Your personnel will learn new styling techniques through annual on-site training sessions and a series of training videotapes. The company regularly recognizes salons with top sales and outstanding managers.

COMMENTS

Entrepreneur magazine ranked HairCrafters 83rd among its 1987 "Franchise 500," and *Venture* magazine ranked it 92nd among its 1986 "Franchise 100." A subsidiary of CutCo Industries, Inc., the company joined the IFA in 1984. HairCrafters wants to expand in a number of states and in Canada.

GETTING MORE INFORMATION

The franchise information packet includes a booklet with charts, graphs, and in-depth information on the company; a copy of the newsletter; a brochure describing the franchisee support system; an ad showing the *Entrepreneur* ranking, and a questionnaire. For more information, write or call:

Don von Liebermann
Executive Vice-President
CutCo Industries, Inc.
125 South Service Road
P.O. Box 265
Jericho, NY   11753
(516)   334–8400   (call collect)

Happy Joe's Pizza & Ice Cream Parlor

BUSINESS: pizza
restaurant
FOUNDED: 1972
FRANCHISED: 1973
START-UP
INVESTMENT:
$150,000–$400,000

NO. OF UNITS		AS OF		PROJECTED BY	
		1/1/85	1/1/86	1/1/87	1/1/88
OWNED BY: COMPANY		12	13	16	20
FRANCHISEES		72	74	78	85
LOCATED: IN U.S.		81	83	88	97
OUTSIDE U.S.		3	4	6	8
TOTAL:		84	87	94	105
NO. OF STATES W/ UNITS		9	9	9	9

THE BUSINESS

Happy Joe's Pizza and Ice Cream Parlor emphasizes community involvement and good food. Happy Joe's pizza is made of 100 percent real meats and cheeses. The menu also includes salads, pasta, soups, spaghetti, sandwiches, malts, ice cream cones, beer, and wine. In 1985, Happy Joe franchises grossed $23 million, with average gross sales per unit of $280,000 and average net income of 10 percent. The company's slogan is "old fashioned goodness made 'real' (100 %)."

WHAT IT TAKES

You will need $10,000 for the initial franchise fee. Valid for fifteen years and renewable for fifteen, the franchise agreement will establish an exclusive territory extending in a four-mile radius from your restaurant. The total investment, including the franchise fee, ranges from $150,000 to $400,000, with 30 percent of that required in cash. The company offers no direct financial assistance, but the remainder can usually be financed through conventional lending sources. Your investment will cover equipment and signs (approximately $130,000); and working capital and nonrecurring expenses such as advertising, inventory, legal expenses, deposits (about $20,000). The cost of additional franchise units varies. You may be an owner-investor, but Happy Joe's prefers that you be actively involved in the business. However, master franchises are available.

GETTING STARTED

Happy Joe's will assist with site selection, lease or purchase negotiation, facility decoration, and service and maintenance contracts. The company's construction-and-equipment department must approve all plans for remodeling or new construction and will help with facility layout for a fee. This department will provide equipment lists for competitive bidding. The typical facility is 3,000 square feet, situated in a mall, shopping center, or freestanding building. You will be required to follow all company specifications for menu, products, decor, uniforms, logos, and signs. Your restaurant will need a staff of fifteen full-time and twenty part-time employees.

The company conducts its intensive training program at various learning centers and combines in-unit training with classroom instruction on all phases of restaurant management, accounting, and food preparation. After completing the program, you will be issued an operations manual outlining each function step-by-step for easy reference. You can be open for business three to four months after buying your franchise. A Happy Joe's opening representative will be at your new restaurant prior to, during, and after your opening to assist in training your staff.

MAKING IT WORK

You will pay an advertising fee of 2 percent for local promotion and 1 percent for national coverage. Area franchise co-ops sponsor advertising for newspaper ads, black-and-white magazine ads, mailers, telephone-book ads, brochures, television and radio commercials, point-of-purchase displays, billboard posters, banners, contests, seasonal promotional materials, and incentives. Your fee will cover signs, press releases, and a public-relations/marketing manual.

Happy Joe's owners meet once a year at a national convention and three to four times a year at one-day seminars. Restaurant news is circulated via a quarterly company newsletter and monthly news-briefs on company information and market trends. Surveys are conducted periodically, and award programs honor top performance. Your administrative tasks will be simplified with regular on-site visits; on-site troubleshooting; manuals for policy and management procedure; all types of forms; and systems for bookkeeping, inventory, personnel, expense analysis, and computerized billing. An in-house department studies new products and equipment to enhance sales. Happy Joe's offers a centralized purchasing program for volume discounts, a centralized merchandising system, and company-brand products. Happy Joe's sponsors a major-medical insurance program.

COMMENTS

In *Entrepreneur* magazine's 1987 "Franchise 500," Happy Joe's was ranked 236th. The company provides an earnings claim document at a potential franchisee's personal interview. The company wants to add new franchises in nine states, as well as Egypt.

GETTING MORE INFORMATION

The franchise information packet contains brochures on the company's operations and a six-page application form. For details, contact:
Larry Whitty
Vice-President
Happy Joe's Pizza & Ice Cream Parlor, Inc.
1875 Middle Road
Bettendorf, IA   52722
(319)   359–7511

Hardee's

BUSINESS: fast-
services family
restaurants
FOUNDED: 1961
FRANCHISED: 1962
START-UP
INVESTMENT:
$632,900–$1,220,700

		AS OF		PROJECTED BY	
NO. OF UNITS		1/1/85	1/1/86	1/1/87	1/1/88
OWNED BY:	COMPANY	866	875	920	975
	FRANCHISEES	1,492	1,687	1,926	2,025
LOCATED:	IN U.S.	2,324	2,529	2,805	2,955
	OUTSIDE U.S.	34	33	41	45
TOTAL:		2,358	2,562	2,846	3,000
NO. OF STATES W/ UNITS		40	40	40	43

THE BUSINESS

The Hardee's chain, which began with a handful of North Carolina outlets in 1961 and expanded in 1982 with the acquisition of Burger Chef, has grown in less than ten years into one of the world's largest fast-food chains. The diversified Hardee's menu includes a basic hamburger line plus specialty sandwiches and a breakfast program based on a made-from-scratch biscuit, giving the company a position between a coffee shop and the traditional hamburger fast-food concept. The outlets are located principally in the southeastern, midwestern, and mid-Atlantic regions of the United States, and facilities exist in several foreign countries. The average gross sales in 1985 for individual units were $802,000, with total volume for all franchise operations of $2.2 billion.

WHAT IT TAKES

The minimum initial investment you'll need to start a Hardee's, exclusive of real estate and improvements, is $237,900, with $150,000 of this amount required in cash. This figure doesn't include expenses related to the acquisition or lease of property or to construction. The breakdown for the total initial investment is as follows:

ITEM	COST
License fee (covers Hardee's license, building plans, site-location counseling, etc.)	$15,000
Equipment and signs (50%–75% of this package usually can be financed with a lending institution)	197,400–250,700
Working capital and nonrecurring expenses (estimated costs for opening advertising, legal expenses, utility deposits, opening-change fund)	25,000– 35,000
Land for typical unit	150,000–400,000
Building costs	185,000–270,000
Land improvements	60,000–250,000
Total:	$632,900–$1,220,700

The terms of your original franchise agreement will apply for a twenty-year period, with a renewal period of ten years, and you'll be assigned an exclusive territory. You will pay an ongoing royalty fee of 3.5 percent the first five years and 4 percent the remaining fifteen years. You can purchase a single franchise, but Hardee's looks for franchisees who have the financial resources and management skills needed to develop multiple units or master franchises.

GETTING STARTED

You and a company representative will make a survey of possible locations when you are choosing a site. A typical Hardee's site has a 165-foot frontage and 210-foot depth. Once you've chosen a site and obtained Hardee's approval, the company will assist you with lease or purchase negotiations and provide plans and specifications.

The Hardee's management program will give you a complete, intensive four-week program with in-unit training and classroom instruction at an area learning center. This management internship is designed to develop the technical, supervisory, and administrative skills you will need as an entry-level manager. When you finish your training, you'll receive an operations manual, which gives a step-by-step outline of every job function in a store's operation. You can expect to hold your grand opening one year after your franchise purchase, and a Hardee's opening representative will be available to assist you in training your staff before, during, and after your opening.

MAKING IT WORK

Hardee's spends over $80 million annually on advertising campaigns and conducts sophisticated consumer research and testing for marketing purposes. The results are incorporated in both the national advertising campaigns and in many award-winning tie-in promotions with such companies as Coca-Cola and Hallmark. Hardee's also works with area ad agencies that are responsible for development of regional point-of-sale and in-store merchandising materials. Your financial participation will involve an ongoing advertising fee of 5 percent of your gross sales, which subsidizes production of materials for print-media advertising, television and radio commercials, point-of-purchase displays, contests, billboard posters, and seasonal promotionals. Although the ad fees cover the cost of producing these materials, you must pay for the actual usage of these materials. You'll be able to take advantage of co-op advertising in many cases.

The company regularly produces audiovisual materials and other job aids for your use in selecting, hiring, and training personnel; offers appraisal and performance-review systems; sponsors workshops and management seminars covering a variety of topics; and maintains two division and six area offices, fully staffed to function as resource and support systems for you. The company's sister corporation, Fast Food Merchandisers, Inc. (FFM), is responsible for the production, purchase, storage, sale, and distribution of products for eventual use at the restaurant level. You can purchase frozen foods and operating supplies from FFM at competitive prices, delivered weekly from one of nine regional distribution centers, each located in a primary market area. Goods are shipped to Hardee's units overseas from distribution centers in North Carolina and Florida.

You or your accountant will receive assistance from Hardee's in setting up your accounting system and preparing financial statements and related financial reports. You'll have immediate access to food, labor, and inventory information through your on-line data-entry cash-register terminals, which can be tied into a central station if you grow to a multilevel operation.

You'll have access to a toll-free hotline; regular on-site visits and troubleshooting from company resource persons; and a complete line of bookkeeping, management, and personnel systems. A quarterly company magazine, a bimonthly newspaper, and regional and areawide meetings will keep you apprised of developments in your field. Hardee's holds annual regional conferences and a national convention every two years.

COMMENTS

Hardee's was ranked ninth in *Venture* magazine's 1986 "Franchise 100" and fifth in *Entrepreneur* magazine's 1987 "Franchise 500." The company provides an earnings claim document prior to a potential franchisee's personal interview. Hardee's is an operating subsidiary of Imasco, USA, Inc., a division of Imasco, Ltd., of Montreal, Canada. The company has been a member of the IFA since 1976.

GETTING MORE INFORMATION

The franchise information packet contains a brochure describing the company and its operations; an annual report of the parent company, Imasco, Ltd.; single-sheet outlines describing the process of setting up a Hardee's franchise; and a franchise application requesting your personal and financial history. For details, contact:

Peter J. Charland
Director National Franchise Sales
Hardee's Food Systems, Inc.
P.O. Box 1619
Rocky Mount, NC   27081
(919)   977–2000

Health Force

BUSINESS: placement
  of temporary health-
  care workers
FOUNDED: 1975
FRANCHISED: 1983
START-UP
  INVESTMENT:
  $70,000–$100,000

NO. OF UNITS		AS OF		PROJECTED BY	
		1/1/85	1/1/86	1/1/87	1/1/88
OWNED BY:	COMPANY	5	5	6	6
	FRANCHISEES	16	31	52	75
LOCATED:	IN U.S.	21	36	58	81
	OUTSIDE U.S.	0	0	0	0
TOTAL:		21	36	58	81
NO. OF STATES W/ UNITS		11	15	20	30

THE BUSINESS

As the U.S. population continues to grow and live longer, more and more focus is being placed on health care. In 1981 health-care expenditures represented a record share of the gross national product: 9.8 percent, or $286.6 billion, which represents $1,225 per person. The temporary-health-care industry arose in response to the ever-increasing demand for both licensed and unlicensed caregivers in private homes as well as institutions. Registered nurses, licensed practical or vocational nurses, nurses' aides, homemakers, and companions in the home provide a cost-effective and humane option to institutionalized health care for the elderly, infirm, and convalescent patient. And in hospitals, nursing homes, and other health-related facilities, they can supplement permanent health-care personnel.

Health Force began in 1975 as a small segment of client services of Career Employment Services, a large, general temporary-placement organization. By 1983, Health Force had become a vigorous operation in its own right, splitting off into a separate division and offering franchise opportunities. The home-health-care industry—and Health Force in particular—has become a respected cost-saving alternative in the health-care system.

WHAT IT TAKES

Your initial franchise fee for a Health Force operation will be $39,500, and the agreement will grant you an exclusive geographic territory based on your area's population, number of hospitals, and per capita income. The term of your franchise agreement will be ten years, with a renewal period of fifteen years. If you're interested in expanding with additional franchises, your fee for each will be the same as for your initial operation. You may also invest in a Health Force franchise but hire someone else to run it for you.

The range of your total start-up investment, including the franchise fee, will be $70,000 to $100,000, with approximately $50,000 of that required in cash. However, Health Force offers in-house financing for all or part of the remaining $20,00 to $50,000.

Your royalty fee will decrease as your volume of business increases. Through Health Force's Partners in Profits system, in any calendar year that your health-care billings exceed $250,000, your share of the gross billings will increase. The more business you do, the more you earn. You'll also pay an ongoing advertising fee to participate in the company's cooperative national advertising program.

GETTING STARTED

You'll need about 800 square feet in an office building or freestanding site. Health Force will consult with you on site selection, lease negotiations, floor plans, and office layout. They'll also help you select your office furniture, equipment, and telephone system. Finally, the company will provide your initial operational forms, including applications and assignment records, time slips, letterhead stationery, envelopes, and business cards.

You'll need a staff of three full-time people, whom the company can help you hire. Then you and your assistant manager will go to the Health Force training center on Long Island for one week of intensive training. You'll begin by working with their operations manual, which covers all phases of sales, operations, recruitment, dispatching, and current management techniques. In addition, you'll get hands-on experience in a fully operational multimillion-dollar temporary service.

One week before your opening a professional trainer will come to your facility for a preopening comprehensive training program for your staff. The trainer will also help you set up your office and prepare you for your first day of business. Health Force will supply you with your preopening announcements and then help you make a list of names to send them to. You'll spend about three months getting set up and ready to open for business.

MAKING IT WORK

Many of Health Force's support services minimize the problems of placing people in temporary jobs. You will be assigned your own field-service representative, who will maintain close contact by telephone and visit you periodically to evaluate, update, and hone the skills of your staff. The field representative will review your daily operations, assist you in analyzing computerized management data, and accompany you and your sales personnel on sales visits. You will be trained in the latest sales techniques and presentations. The company also holds short seminars several times during the year and conducts franchise-owner meetings. You'll receive a newsletter, technical updates, and company updates.

One of the most helpful aspects of a Health Force franchise is assistance with cash flow. The company will finance your accounts receivable by funding your temporary payroll, freeing you from the financial burdens and uncertainties of obtaining enough dollars to fill large job orders. Bookkeeping services include preparation and mailing of the temporary-employee paychecks and client bills; preparation of all the paperwork related to worker's compensation and unemployment claims; and assistance in obtaining your required insurance and bonding, filing all government reports, and submitting all payroll taxes required by federal, state, and local laws, including W2 forms. Although you must insure your permanent staff, Health Force provides insurance coverage for all temporary employees, including liability, bonding, worker's compensation, and disability.

To assist you in sending out the most qualified temporaries in your market area, the company has put together an outstanding skills-testing package. You'll also receive management guidelines and confidential operations manual, which is updated periodically. At least monthly you will receive computerized management data in the form of sales information, client-usage information, a ranking of client activity, employee payroll reports, markup analyses, and operational reports.

You can select a variety of promotional aids from the company for use in your advertising, and Health Force offers a promotional allowance based on the sales volume of your office—the more volume you do, the more the home office contributes. Health Force constantly evaluates trends to expand the usage of temporary services and develops strategies for maximizing new markets.

COMMENTS

Health Force was ranked 424th in *Entrepreneur* magazine's 1987 "Franchise 500." A division of Career Employment Services, Inc., Health Force joined the IFA in 1982. The company donates free nursing services to needy clients. Health Force is seeking franchisees in most states.

GETTING MORE INFORMATION

The franchise information packet includes a brochure describing the benefits and services that come with a Health Force franchise, a brochure explaining the temporary-health-care industry, a color slick for a magazine ad, two publications from the IFA, and a three-page personal questionnaire.

For more information, contact:
Jerry Block
Vice-President, Marketing
Health Force
1975 Hempstead Turnpike
East Meadow, NY   11554
(516)   794–4850   (call collect)

Help-U-Sell

BUSINESS: real estate		AS OF		PROJECTED BY	
service company	NO. OF UNITS	1/1/85	1/1/86	1/1/87	1/1/88
FOUNDED: 1976	OWNED BY: COMPANY	0	0	0	0
FRANCHISED: 1976	FRANCHISEES	127	142	350	1,500
START-UP	LOCATED: IN U.S.	127	142	350	1,500
INVESTMENT:	OUTSIDE U.S.	0	0	0	0
$10,000–$50,000 plus	TOTAL:	127	142	350	1,500
franchise fee	NO. OF STATES W/ UNITS	8	10	30	50

THE BUSINESS

Described as a real estate counseling method, Help-U-Sell is a merger of traditional real estate, marketing, and counseling. The company is similar to existing firms by belonging to the Multiple Listing Service and placing some properties on it, selling other brokers' listings, advertising properties in the newspaper, obtaining financing, writing offers, and following through until closing. The company is different, however, in charging a set fee rather than a percentage commission, charging extra for showing property, not holding open houses, and counseling—pointing out bad as well as good aspects of properties. Sellers save money (with the low set fee), sell faster (using the savings to create a lower price and arrange better financing), get greater exposure through the Help-U-Sell marketing system, and gain protection through a 100 percent-satisfaction guarantee. Buyers get better prices, better financing, easier qualifications, a larger selection of properties (Help-U-Sell and multiple listings), less pressure (they can look at properties on their own), and professional counseling. The company's counseling fee is substantially less than the prevailing percentage commissions. For the broker the system creates the opportunity to operate with a lower overhead and smaller staff, and for the salespeople the method creates buyers and sellers calling in, rather than agents creating all the leads. The company spent more than $2 million developing this unique marketing system. In 1985, Help-U-Sell franchises grossed $300 million.

WHAT IT TAKES

The initial franchise fee is $275 per 1,000 population (minimum of $4,500) for an exclusive territory as selected by the franchisor and franchisee. Each franchise territory is different. The original franchise agreement is valid for five years and renewable perpetually at no additional charge. Your total investment will be the franchise fee plus $10,000 to $50,000, depending on the size territory and whether the business is new or converted from an established business. Financial assistance is available from the company. Additional franchise units will be priced the same, but you must be the operating manager. Ongoing royalty fees are 7 percent of gross income for continuing assistance and 7 percent for the mass-advertising fund. Help-U-Sell wants dedicated franchisees who have integrity and good problem-solving skills. In addition, you should have a thorough knowledge of all aspects of real estate in your area, a real estate broker's license, and enough capital to build your business. Master franchises are available.

GETTING STARTED

Help-U-Sell provides assistance with site selection; lease or purchase of equipment; and acquisition of materials and supplies. A typical facility has 1,000 to 2,000 square feet and is located in a shopping center or freestanding building. You will be required to display the company logo on your business. You'll need from three to ten full-time employees, and Help-U-Sell will assist with hiring. Five days of classroom training are held in Salt Lake City for the owner/operator and counselors, covering the Help-U-Sell marketing system and methods of managing an office, working buyers, and taking listings. It normally takes four months to open after buying your franchise.

MAKING IT WORK

The company provides samples of newspaper and black-and-white magazine ads, mailers, brochures, catalogs, television and radio commercials, point-of-purchase displays, billboard posters, signs, banners, and monthly press releases. You will be trained to create your own marketing tools. An annual convention is held for franchisees, along with regional conferences as needed and bimonthly one-day seminars. You will receive a company newsletter. Backup systems include headquarters and regional resource persons; a toll-free hotline; on-site troubleshooting; manuals on policy and management procedure; forms for inventory, personnel, and orders; and systems for bookkeeping, expense analysis, and computerized management information. Recognition programs honor outstanding service and sales.

COMMENTS

The company was ranked 163rd in *Entrepreneur* magazine's "Franchise 500" for 1987. A division of Mutual Benefit Life, Help-U-Sell is a member of the IFA. The company is seeking franchises in all states, plus Canada and Australia.

GETTING MORE INFORMATION

The franchise packet contains a fact sheet on the company's operations, a sample newsletter, a breakdown of start-up costs, various fliers on the marketing system, and an application form. For more information, write or call:

Fred Bohman
Vice-President
Help-U-Sell, Inc.
110 West 300 South, Suite 101
Salt Lake City, UT   84101
(800)   345–1990 or (801)   355–1177

Holiday Inn

		AS OF		PROJECTED BY	
BUSINESS: hotels	NO. OF UNITS	1/1/85	1/1/86	1/1/87	1/1/88
FOUNDED: 1952	OWNED BY: COMPANY	211	205	198	189
FRANCHISED: 1954	FRANCHISEES	1,490	1,480	1,446	1,425
START-UP	LOCATED: IN U.S.	1,489	1,477	1,434	1,392
INVESTMENT:	OUTSIDE U.S.	212	208	210	222
$30,000 minimum	TOTAL:	1,701	1,685	1,644	1,614
plus $49,400 to	NO. OF STATES W/ UNITS	50	50	50	50
$67,000 per room					

THE BUSINESS

Since its beginning in 1952, Holiday Inn has grown into the world's largest licensed hotel network with more than 318,000 rooms in 53 countries and territories. In 1984 the company generated revenues in excess of $5 billion, and employed more than 200,000 people around the world. Some 96 percent of all U.S. travelers have stayed at a Holiday Inn hotel, with 68 percent doing so annually. By the end of 1985, 60 percent of the system's guest rooms were no more than five years old or had undergone extensive renovation within the past five years. The international Holiday Inn hotel system, with more than 48,000 rooms, would rank as the ninth largest chain in the world. Gross sales per franchise unit in 1985 were $2 to $5 million.

WHAT IT TAKES

The initial franchise fee is $300 per room, with a $30,000 minimum. There are two types of Holiday Inns available as new constructions: the midrise prototype and the vertical prototype. The midrise prototype requires a small site of 3 to 3.5 acres and is four, five, or six stories with a moderate to high level of interior finish in the public spaces. A simple cost breakdown is as follows, based on a 184-room project:

ITEM	COST PER ROOM
Land financing cost and legal fees	$10,000
General construction	31,200
Furniture, fixtures and equipment, including special systems	8,200
Total estimated cost per room:	$49,400

The vertical prototype is more upscale, usually ten to twelve stories with the first two floors devoted to public space, lounge, restaurants, banquet facilities, and meetings rooms. Depending on the scope and concept, there will be 25,000 to 40,000 square feet of public space. The interior finish level of the public space is high. A cost breakdown is as follows:

ITEM	COST PER ROOM
Land financing cost and legal fees	$16,000
General construction	40,500
Furniture, fixtures, and equipment, including special systems	11,500
Total estimated cost per room:	$67,000

These costs will vary depending on the specific site, the general competitive state of the construction market, and other local factors. Whichever prototype hotel you choose, you'll need to have the entire amount in cash. Additional franchises are available on the same terms, and you may hold passive ownership. Your franchise term will be for twenty years, with an optional renewal period of ten years. Your ongoing royalty fee will be 4 percent of your gross room revenue. The fee for use of the Holidex reservation service is $4.20 per room per month plus a reservations-system assessment of 1 percent of gross room revenue. In order to qualify for the ownership of a Holiday Inn unit you must have experience in the field of hotel operations.

GETTING STARTED

Part of your franchise fee will cover the Holiday Inn staff's work with you in site selection, lease or purchase negotiations, staffing, and grand-opening planning. All design elements of your hotel must conform to published Holiday Inn standards. The company also offers design, supply, construction, management, and purchasing services on a competitive basis. You, your general manager, and your housekeeping manager will participate in a two-week training period at the Holiday Inn University that covers all areas of hotel operations and provides extensive preopening manuals. You'll need a staff of forty-five full-time and twelve part-time employees. It will take from eighteen to twenty-four months to open your hotel after the date of franchise purchase.

MAKING IT WORK

Your Holiday Inn franchise agreement will entitle you to use of the Holidex reservations network, advanced training for all personnel through the Holiday Inn University, sophisticated marketing-analysis and research resources, one-to-one consultations with franchise district directors, special pricing on key hotel items, a corps of service consultants to aid you in every phase of your hotel operations, and a system of telemarketing. Your advertising fee of 2 percent of your gross room revenue will cover ads for newspapers, magazines, television, and radio. You'll also have access to mailers, brochures, contests, seasonal promotional materials, a lead-referral system, a public-relations manual, and press packages.

Holiday Inn distributes a monthly magazine, a bimonthly newsletter, and periodic industry and market updates; sponsors a system-wide annual conference of owners and general managers; provides a complete and diversified set of administrative and managerial materials; and gives numerous incentive awards throughout the system.

COMMENTS

The parent company of Holiday Inn is Holiday Corporation. Holiday Inn was rated twenty-seventh in *Entrepreneur* magazine's 1987 "Franchise 500." The corporation has won numerous national and regional awards for customer service, food and beverage excellence, and competitive design. Holiday Inn is seeking franchises throughout the world.

GETTING MORE INFORMATION

The franchise information package includes a brochure with descriptions of the two prototype choices, a breakdown of costs, and background material on the corporation. For more information, contact:

Howard J. Willis
Director, Special Projects
Operations Services
System Hotels
Holiday Inn
3796 Lamar Avenue
Memphis, TN 38195
(901) 362–4663

Holiday-Payless Rent-A-Car

BUSINESS: car and
    truck rental
FOUNDED: 1971
FRANCHISED: 1982
START-UP
    INVESTMENT:
    $25,000–$100,000

		AS OF		PROJECTED BY	
		1/1/85	1/1/86	1/1/87	1/1/88
NO. OF UNITS					
OWNED BY:	COMPANY	0	0	2	5
	FRANCHISEES	160	155	175	250
LOCATED:	IN U.S.	157	150	169	245
	OUTSIDE U.S.	3	5	8	10
TOTAL:		160	155	177	255
NO. OF STATES W/ UNITS		37	36	40	45

THE BUSINESS

In the United States short-term rentals of vehicles generate over $3.5 billion in revenue each year, with business increasing in excess of 15 percent annually. The car-rental market is split roughly into two parts. The local market is made up of local firms needing extra vehicles during peak periods, individuals who do not own a car, car owners who need a larger car or station wagon for vacations or other special occasions, and insured persons who need a temporary replacement car after an accident or breakdown. The national/international travel market includes executives and salespeople who use airlines, railways, or buses to get from their home base to other cities. Also, the booming tourist trade in the United States affects the use of rental cars. Businesses and contractors often need one or more rental trucks in their everyday operations. Individual consumers, too, often need to rent trucks for household moving or general cartage.

The Payless Car Rental System, Inc., was founded in 1971, the same year that Holiday Rent-A-Car International, Inc., was established in Canada. Merged in 1982, the two companies are currently represented in major-market airports, urban areas, suburban areas, and resort markets throughout the United States, the Caribbean, Canada, and England. The company offers a wide selection of cars, wagons, and trucks to meet the total rental market. In addition, Holiday-Payless has created additional profit centers, including used-car sales, a vehicle-shipping service, tours, and leasing.

WHAT IT TAKES

You will need $5,000 to $50,000 for the initial franchise fee, which guarantees an exclusive territory established by geographical boundaries. The agreement is valid for five years and renewable in five-year increments. Your total investment, including the franchise fee, will range from $25,000 to $100,000. The company does not offer financing, and master franchises are not available. You will pay ongoing royalty fees of 5 percent and 3 percent for advertising and marketing. In most locales Holiday-Payless recommends that you fully establish your car-rental business before going into truck leasing. You may be an owner-investor without actually handling day-to-day operations. Prior car-rental experience is not necessary.

GETTING STARTED

Holiday-Payless will help with all necessary start-up details, including site selection; lease or purchase negotiations; facility layout and decoration; lease or purchase of furniture, fixtures, equipment, and vehicles; service and maintenance contracts; and acquisition of materials and merchandise. Headquarters personnel will help you pinpoint the ideal mix of vehicles for your particular market and obtain your initial supply of vehicles. The typical office is 200 to 500 square feet, located in an office building, mall, shopping center, freestanding building, commercial industrial park, or service station. Recommended suppliers handle sales of exterior signs via a number of purchase plans.

Your staff will consist of two to three full-time and one to three part-time employees. Training offered at the franchisor's office involves two to four days of classroom and on-the-job experience and covers topics such as office and counter procedures, vehicle procurement, sales calls, business development, car/truck fleet-maintenance procedures, hiring and training of personnel, and customer qualification and selection. Another three to five days of training will be held in your office for all employees. You can be renting cars within one to three months after buying the franchise. Holiday-Payless will help with your grand opening by providing a how-to kit for advertising promotion. The company's marketing personnel will accompany you on marketing calls during the first days of business.

MAKING IT WORK

Regular contacts in person and by mail with local auto-repair shops, insurance adjusters, hotels and motels, and large industries are all included in Holiday-Payless's merchandising programs. Both the U.S. and Canadian headquarters solicit business from a complete range of corporate accounts to complement the local calls made by franchisees. The company has a corporate program called the Passport Club to attract rentals by business people. A comprehensive mix of telemarketing, personal sales calls, direct mail, and advertising has made this a significant part of the company's overall business. Multinational firms that deal exclusively with Holiday-Payless and special weekend and vacation plans also boost sales.

The company's complete how-to advertising kit contains information on the best uses of all types of advertising media. You will receive promotional aids such as folders, give-aways, and display cards, all at nominal cost. The company provides national media coverage and offers radio commercials, point-of-purchase displays, signs, banners, contests, seasonal promotional materials, a lead-

referral system, contests and incentives, press releases, and a pub-
lic-relations/marketing manual. Holiday-Payless publicizes the company through advertising in in-flight, travel, and business publications, and by attendance at trade shows directed toward travel
agents.

The company sponsors a national convention every other year,
regional conferences twice a year, and areawide franchise meetings
two to three times a year. In addition, the company issues a bimonthly newsletter and offers headquarters resource persons, a toll-
free hotline, regular on-site visits and on-site troubleshooting, regularly updated manuals for setting policy and management procedure (you'll pay a deposit), inventory forms, and systems for bookkeeping and expense analysis. You'll also have access to an optional
computerized accounting system and mass-purchasing benefits for
office supplies and various operational reports. Except for rental
agreements necessary for audits, you may buy noncompany products. The company sponsors property, general-liability, and automobile insurance coverage.

COMMENTS

Holiday-Payless is affiliated with the Holiday System of Canada. In
1984, *Florida Trend* magazine ranked the company 103d in a listing
of top private companies in that state, and *Entrepreneur* magazine
ranked it 204th among the 1987 "Franchise 500." The company
wants to expand its operations in twenty-four states and in Canada.

**GETTING MORE
INFORMATION**

The franchise information packet contains copies of articles on the
company, recent Holiday-Payless ads, a brochure describing the
company's operations and support to franchises, a directory of locations, and a four-page application form.
For details, contact:
  Les Netterstrom
  President
  Holiday-Payless Rent-A-Car System
  5510 Gulfport Boulevard
  St. Petersburg, FL   33707
  (800)   541–0881 or (813)   381–2758

HouseMaster of America

BUSINESS: home-
 inspection service
FOUNDED: 1971
FRANCHISED: 1979
START-UP
 INVESTMENT:
 $27,000–$50,000

NO. OF UNITS		AS OF		PROJECTED BY	
		1/1/85	1/1/86	1/1/87	1/1/88
OWNED BY: COMPANY		0	0	0	0
FRANCHISEES		43	69	85	100
LOCATED: IN U.S.		43	69	85	100
OUTSIDE U.S.		0	0	0	0
TOTAL:		43	69	85	100
NO. OF STATES W/ UNITS		19	24	28	32

THE BUSINESS

HouseMaster of America (HMA), franchised in sixty-nine U.S. cities, assists home buyers by providing a professional property analysis before purchase. The market for professional home inspections
is growing rapidly. In 1985, HMA franchises grossed $3,617,808,
with average gross sales of $52,432 for each unit. Since 1971 the
technical staff at HMA has conducted over 25,000 inspections of
both residential and commercial properties. The inspector evaluates
the central heating and cooling systems; the plumbing; the electric-
ity; the roof; the siding; the structural soundness of walls, ceilings,
and floors; the foundation; and the built-in kitchen appliances. Some
offices also perform or arrange for termite inspections, septic-tank
and well evaluations, water-quality testing, swimming-pool inspections, and dock or bulkhead evaluations.

The HMA inspector prepares either an express report that is completed immediately or a formal narrative report that is completed in
a few days. In addition, buyers get an owners' disclosure form to
guide them in gathering further information about their potential
home. If repairs are needed, the inspector can give estimates on
repair costs. HMA also offers an optional and affordable commer-
cially insured warranty program that covers the roof, structure, and
mechanical elements of a house for a full year after the title is trans-
ferred to the buyer.

WHAT IT TAKES

The total start-up costs involve an initial franchise fee that ranges
from $17,000 to $35,000, depending on the number of owner-
occupied homes in the franchise territory, and an additional $10,000
to $15,000 to get started. The fee will buy your exclusive territory
for ten years, with subsequent ten-year renewal periods. Wherever
possible, the company will give you the right of first refusal before
selling counties adjacent to your territory to someone else. Additional franchise units can be purchased, but the company does not
offer master franchises and discourages passive ownership.

Once you're in business, the company will charge you an ongoing royalty fee of 6 percent of the monthly gross sales and an additional 4 percent advertising fee.

GETTING STARTED

An HMA franchise requires no fancy office space because customers typically order the services over the phone. Most transactions take place on a cash or credit-card basis, and bills are paid at the time of the inspection, so you'll have a minimum of hard-to-collect, costly accounts receivable.

HMA will help you with staffing and hiring. The average business needs three full-time and two part-time employees, including the owner-operator. During a week of training at Bound Brook, New Jersey, the company's inspectors will instruct you and your inspectors using an intense, technical classroom and field-training program on all aspects of house inspections. For another two days the company sales personnel will show you firsthand how the HMA marketing approach can work for you. Then you and your office manager will spend a final day learning to set up and run your office. You can expect to be in business within four to six weeks after your franchise purchase.

MAKING IT WORK

HMA supplies television and radio commercials; periodic mailers; and magazine, newspaper, and telephone-book ads; customer handouts; and a public-relations/marketing manual. In addition, you can purchase brochures, presentation books, and catalogs from the company, and you'll have access to the company's lead-referral system. The company also provides detailed illustrated technical manuals and videocassettes for your inspectors and a sales-and-promotion manual for you and your sales force. You can provide additional training for your salespeople with a series of 35-mm slide presentations.

The company's operations manual has forms and office-procedure systems. In addition, the company offers manuals on policy, management, and customer service; forms for personnel, ordering, and accounting; and a bookkeeping system. You can rely, too, on a toll-free hotline and on-site troubleshooting by company personnel when needed. HMA will send you a quarterly newsletter and updates on products and services, company information, and industry and market changes. The company constantly researches improved home-inspection methods and ways to boost local sales.

The company holds periodic one-day seminars, biannual conferences, and an annual national conference, where the company honors outstanding franchisees. HMA sponsors life and major-medical insurance for you and your employees. To protect your business from the chance inspector error, HMA offers members errors-and-omissions insurance on a pay-as-you-go basis, spreading the cost throughout the year.

COMMENTS

HMA was ranked 325th in *Entrepreneur* magazine's 1987 "Franchise 500." A member of the IFA since 1983, the company provides an earnings claim document prior to or during a potential franchisee's personnel interview. HMA wants to increase franchise operations in most of the United States as well as in Australia and Canada.

GETTING MORE INFORMATION

The franchise information packet contains two brochures that describe the home-inspection protection plan and the company itself, a sheet answering key questions about the business, a roster of HMA cities, and a one-page confidential data sheet. For details, write to:

Robert J. Hardy
President
HouseMaster of America
421 West Union Avenue
Bound Brook, NJ   08805
(800)   526–3939

H&R Block

BUSINESS: income-
tax preparation and
related services
FOUNDED: 1955
FRANCHISED: 1956
START-UP
INVESTMENT:
$1,500–$4,000

		AS OF		PROJECTED BY	
NO. OF UNITS		1/1/85	1/1/86	1/1/87	1/1/88
OWNED BY: COMPANY		4,091	4,021	4,001	3,985
FRANCHISEES		4,906	4,933	4,966	4,991
LOCATED: IN U.S.		7,672	7,560	7,549	7,548
OUTSIDE U.S.		1,325	1,394	1,418	1,428
TOTAL:		8,997	8,954	8,967	8,976
NO. OF STATES W/ UNITS		50	50	50	50

THE BUSINESS

Founded in 1955, H&R Block has grown into a network of offices forming the world's largest income-tax-preparation service. The company currently prepares approximately 10 percent of all tax returns filed in the United States and provides related services such as income-tax-preparation schools. Although major franchises are no longer available, you can participate in the company's satellite program. Each of the returns processed by a satellite office will be prepared by trained personnel, checked for accuracy, and backed by a written guarantee. Through the H&R Block satellite franchise program, you'll be able to provide convenient, dependable and accurate income-tax-preparation service to taxpayers in small communities. As a satellite owner, you'll be part of an organization that emphasizes accurate service, reasonable fees, and year-round availability, qualities that have contributed to this company's dynamic growth and have made the name H&R Block synonymous with income-tax preparation.

WHAT IT TAKES

Purchase of the initial territorial franchise requires a cash payment of $600 to $1,200 depending on the population of the franchise area. Your territory will be determined by the city, village, or town limits. The term of the original franchise agreement is five years, renewable for another five-year period. You may purchase additional franchises at a cost of $400 each. You'll pay a royalty of 60 percent of the first $5,000 in gross receipts and 40 percent thereafter. However, if you make your royalty payment within five days of the close of the reporting period, your royalty fee will be discounted by 10 percent. In addition (assuming you're current in royalty, supply, and insurance payments), your royalty rate will be reduced to 20 percent when your year-to-date gross receipts equal the average of the previous two years' gross receipts as determined on a calendar basis.

To be a successful franchisee, you must understand income taxes. The company has spent years standardizing its operations to assure clients throughout the country uniform, courteous, and accurate tax-preparation services, so H&R Block expects franchisees to maintain a businesslike atmosphere and operate with adequate office hours.

GETTING STARTED

Satellite costs include installation of signs, freight, and repair or service-maintenance contracts on copiers. The company will help you with site selection, lease negotiation, facility layout and decoration, staffing, and hiring. You'll be charged a fee for any assistance with acquisition of supplies and lease or purchase of furniture, fixtures, and equipment. Facility size, location, and number of personnel vary considerably for the franchises. You'll be able to open your business two months after the date of your franchise purchase.

MAKING IT WORK

H&R Block provides training by conducting tax courses at company-owned offices, providing training materials and tax-update bulletins, and holding seminars on both taxes and management techniques. You'll have an opportunity to attend an annual national convention, annual regional conferences, and semiannual one-day seminars; and you'll receive a yearly management analysis of your business. The company will provide you with advertising and promotional support, backing local advertising with a well-planned national campaign. In fact, H&R Block is consistently one of the nation's largest television advertisers of a single service, and the national office conducts a year-round public-relations program.

You can participate in an incentive recognition program based on performance. You'll be kept current on recent developments through a monthly company newsletter and a quarterly magazine, and you'll receive continuous training and leadership through regional and satellite directors. H&R Block furnishes all specialty supplies necessary to successfully operate your tax-preparation business except items normally found in an accounting office, and the company offers a limited deferred-payment plan for the purchase of additional supplies if needed. In addition, the company-sponsored insurance package offers property, general-liability, and errors-and-omissions coverage.

COMMENTS

H&R Block has held membership in the IFA since 1960, winning a twenty-five year recognition award from the organization. The company has franchise opportunities available in fifteen states, primarily in the South and Midwest.

GETTING MORE INFORMATION

The franchise information packet contains a six-page booklet explaining the business. For details, contact:
Christopher Meck
Director
Franchise Operations
H&R Block
4410 Main Street
Kansas City, MO 64111
(816) 753–6900

I Can't Believe It's Yogurt

BUSINESS: gourmet frozen-yogurt restaurant
FOUNDED: 1977
FRANCHISED: 1983
START-UP INVESTMENT: $104,000–$141,500

NO. OF UNITS		AS OF		PROJECTED BY	
		1/1/85	1/1/86	1/1/87	1/1/88
OWNED BY: COMPANY		9	9	9	11
FRANCHISEES		25	45	100	200
LOCATED: IN U.S.		34	54	109	209
OUTSIDE U.S.		0	0	0	2
TOTAL:		34	54	109	211
NO. OF STATES W/ UNITS		13	17	25	35

THE BUSINESS

Yogurt, or cultured milk, has been a dietary staple throughout Asia and Europe for centuries, but not until the 1970s did it begin to gain popularity in the United States in appealing, flavored versions. Today yogurt is a favorite food among Americans of all ages. I Can't Believe It's Yogurt stores serve a unique brand of soft frozen yogurt, ICBIY Softie. An all-natural, nutritious treat, it's offered in a variety of flavors served in cups, cones, sundaes, smoothies, parfaits, and other special recipes. Unlike traditional tart, custardlike yogurt, ICBIY Softie has a creamy texture and a taste just like ice cream, thanks to the company's secret recipe.

WHAT IT TAKES

You will need $20,000 for the initial franchise fee; and the franchise agreement, valid for ten years, establishes an exclusive territory extending to the city limits. Your total initial investment including the franchise fee will range from $104,000 to $141,500, with $40,000 of that required in cash. This investment covers equipment, furniture, wall menu and signs, leasehold improvements, architectural fees, inventory and supplies, deposits, an interior-design package, grand-opening expenses, and working capital. The company does not offer any financing.

The franchise fee for additional units is $15,000. The company prefers that you be a part of day-to-day operations but will permit you to be an owner-investor. There is an ongoing royalty fee of 6 percent of gross sales, plus 1 percent for advertising. No prior food-sales experience is required, but the company recommends that franchise owners have a natural ability to relate well and deal effectively with employees, customers, and the community. I Can't Believe It's Yogurt also wants franchise owners who have records of success and achievement in other fields. Master franchises are available.

GETTING STARTED

When your new franchise is granted, ICBIY will guide you every step of the way, providing a manual with detailed information concerning site selection, architectural design, construction, equipment ordering, and inventory purchasing. A location-selection package will help you in selecting your site, and ICBIY representatives will visit your proposed site to approve it. An architectural package contains a prototype floor plan, equipment list, and layout, plus complete specifications for construction and decor. An interior-decor package contains unique ICBIY wallpaper, decor art, and interior signs. The typical mall location has 400 square feet, whereas a restaurant in a shopping strip may be 1,200 square feet—these are the two prime locations for ICBIY shops. You must utilize the company's standard interior decor and employee uniforms, and have the company logo on all materials and supplies. The company will recommend sources for equipment and supplies.

You will need two full-time and eight to ten part-time employees. A six-day training school will be held in Dallas for you and a key employee of your choice. Sessions will cover store operations, human-resources management, preparation of menu items, customer service, equipment usage and maintenance, accounting procedures, budget control, inventory control and purchasing, security, and marketing. Company staff will help you plan advertising and promotions for your grand opening and attend the event, which may be held within three to six months after you purchase the franchise.

MAKING IT WORK   You will be eligible for co-op advertising funds on some marketing tools, such as newspaper ads, mailers, radio commercials, seasonal promotional materials, a lead-referral system, press releases, and a public-relations/marketing manual. ICBIY sponsors a national convention every two years, a regional conference once a year, and periodic two-day seminars. Ongoing communication comes in the form of a newsletter, periodic updates on products and company information, and surveys. You will also be assigned an advisor who will be in close contact with you, especially during the first six months of operation. Site inspections will be made once a year to keep you on track. Award programs are being designed to recognize excellent performance.

To simplify administrative tasks, ICBIY offers management-procedure manuals; inventory and order forms; and systems for bookkeeping, inventory, personnel, and expense analysis. You must use the company's brand of yogurt. ICBIY continually tests new yogurt flavors.

COMMENTS   Brice Foods, Inc., is the parent company of I Can't Believe It's Yogurt. Chairman Bill Brice and his sister Julie, president, recently placed eighteenth in a survey of the nation's top 100 young entrepreneurs conducted by the Young Entrepreneurs Organization. The awards went to owners younger than thirty whose companies had annual revenues of $100,000 or more. *Entrepreneur* magazine ranked ICBIY 364th among its 1987 "Franchise 500." A member of the IFA since 1983, ICBIY provides an earnings claim document during a potential franchisee's personal interview. The company wants to add new franchises in every state but California and in Canada.

GETTING MORE INFORMATION   The franchise information packet contains a brochure on the company and its operations, a listing of ICBIY locations, copies of recent articles on the company, and an application form. For details, contact:
Robert Schultz
Director of Franchise Development/Real Estate
I Can't Believe It's Yogurt, Inc.
P.O. Box 791908
Dallas, TX   75379–1908
(214)   392–3012

Ice Cream Churn

BUSINESS: ice cream
parlor
FOUNDED: 1973
FRANCHISED: 1979
START-UP
INVESTMENT:
$7,000

NO. OF UNITS		AS OF		PROJECTED BY	
		1/1/85	1/1/86	1/1/87	1/1/88
OWNED BY: COMPANY		2	2	2	2
	FRANCHISEES	553	784	1,000	1,250
LOCATED: IN U.S.		555	786	1,002	1,252
	OUTSIDE U.S.	0	0	0	0
TOTAL:		555	786	1,002	1,252
NO. OF STATES W/ UNITS		24	34	48	50

THE BUSINESS

Founder-owner Wendell Parker started the first Ice Cream Churn outlet at his Fina gas station in Byron, Georgia, after experimenting with a variety of unsatisfactory ice cream products. Nobody else on Interstate 75 offered hand-dipped ice cream, and Parker soon had a booming business. Outlets have spread throughout the country, not only to other gas stations who want to tap the tourist trade but also to locations such as restaurants, convenience stores, shopping malls, bowling alleys, and resorts. Ice Cream Churn sets specifications with local or regional dairies to make forty flavors of ice cream. Franchisees then carry—and advertise—the twenty-eight flavors they like best. The company figures half of sales are single dips, 40 percent are double dips, and 10 percent are triple dips. Each dip is about 2.5 ounces, or thirty dips per gallon, making each gallon worth about $20. Franchisees pay $5.25 per gallon (which includes $1-a-gallon royalty to the franchisor). In 1985, Ice Cream Churn franchises grossed $3 million, with average gross sales per unit of $45,000 and average net income of $25,000.

WHAT IT TAKES

You will need $5,000 for the franchise fee, and the agreement, valid for five years and renewable for five, will establish an exclusive territory as negotiated between you and the company. In addition to the $5,000 franchise fee you will need $1,000 for supplies and equipment and $1,000 for your initial inventory of ice cream, assuming that you already have a location. You will be responsible for any necessary remodeling. (Modular units are being designed for new sites.) You can purchase additional units for $5,000 each, and master franchises are available for Alaska, Hawaii, and foreign countries. You must be the on-site manager of the business. Your only ongoing royalty fee will be $1 per gallon of ice cream you purchase. No prior experience in selling ice cream is needed.

GETTING STARTED

Ice Cream Churn will evaluate your proposed site and help with facility layout and decoration. The company will help you get your ice cream and will provide all needed ice cream equipment, on-site signs, and roadside signs. You will need an eight-foot by fifteen-foot area for counter, cabinet, and work space, plus additional space for customers. Two refrigerated cabinets are needed for the twenty-eight three-gallon ice cream drums. The typical facility has 120 square feet for the ice cream area and is located along an interstate or major highway. New locations have recently gone into small and medium-sized towns (4,000 to 30,000 people).

One full-time employee handles ice cream and convenience-item sales at each location; two part-time workers help during busier periods (especially weekends). Your staff can be trained in four to twelve hours on site by the regional franchise agent. They will learn about set-up, dipping, profit makers, selling tips, care of ice cream, and promotions. You can dip the first ice cream cone three weeks after buying the franchise. The company will help with your grand opening.

MAKING IT WORK

There is no required advertising fee, but the company's own marketing firm develops newspaper ads, radio commercials, point-of-purchase displays, signs, banners, seasonal promotional displays, and incentives. Co-op advertising is offered for brochures. On-site training is conducted each month by the regional agent. You will also have access to headquarters resource persons and on-site trouble-shooting, if necessary. You must buy ice cream only from an approved source.

COMMENTS

Ice Cream Churn, Inc., placed fifty-first among the *Entrepreneur* magazine's 1987 "Franchise 500." The company provides an earnings claim document during a potential franchisee's personal interview. Ice Cream Churn wants to add new franchises in Alaska, Hawaii, and all foreign countries.

GETTING MORE INFORMATION

The franchise information packet contains a brochure on the company's concept and copies of articles on the business. For details, contact:

Lee Anderson
Vice-President
Ice Cream Churn, Inc.
P. O. Box 378
Byron, GA   31008
(912)   956–5880

In 'N' Out Food Stores

BUSINESS:			AS OF		PROJECTED BY	
convenience food	NO. OF UNITS		1/1/85	1/1/86	1/1/87	1/1/88
store	OWNED BY: COMPANY		0	6	12	20
FOUNDED: 1976	FRANCHISEES		22	22	28	40
FRANCHISED: 1981	LOCATED: IN U.S.		22	28	40	60
START-UP	OUTSIDE U.S.		0	0	0	0
INVESTMENT:	TOTAL:		22	28	40	60
$80,000–$160,000	NO. OF STATES W/ UNITS		2	2	3	3

THE BUSINESS

A new convenience store is a welcome sight in most neighborhoods because it offers consumers the option of quickly picking up a few necessary items without making a major trip to the local supermarket. And, as a low-risk investment, a convenience store is a rapidly growing, recession-proof option. In 'N' Out Food Stores carry thousands of food items and offer customers a clean, courteous place to shop from 7:00 A.M. until midnight or 2:00 A.M. (franchisee's choice).

WHAT IT TAKES

Your $15,000 initial franchise fee will cover a fifteen-year agreement, with a fifteen-year renewal period, and an exclusive territory within a half-mile radius of your store. The estimated costs of equipment and inventory packages shown in the following chart assume that you will lease an existing building to be remodeled. The estimated costs will differ somewhat if you buy your own building.

STORE SIZE (sq. ft.)	EQUIPMENT COST	INVENTORY COST
1,200–2,000	$50,000– 70,000	$15,000–20,000
2,200–3,800	$60,000– 90,000	$20,000–30,000
3,800–6,000	$80,000–110,000	$30,000–50,000

You must pay the first $40,000 of your total initial investment in cash, and the company will help you get financing for the remaining costs of your building, equipment, and working capital. The company will also help you get the best possible deal on buying or leasing your property. You'll pay an ongoing royalty fee of 3.75 percent of your gross sales plus another 1.75 percent of gross sales for company advertising. You need no experience to own a store, but the company looks for franchisees who have an aptitude for business and show a willingness to learn and work.

GETTING STARTED

If you don't want to start from scratch, In 'N' Out has several stores ready for operation. But if you do decide to develop your own store, the company will assist you in every way. In 'N' Out will provide you with demographic and marketing-research studies; help with the interior and exterior design of your building, construction, and installation of security systems; and help you get any licenses or permits you might need, such as building permits or liquor, beer, and wine licenses. The company has worked directly with specific manufacturers and suppliers of the equipment you'll need, and so you can save money by buying or leasing your equipment from those firms, although you can buy or lease from your own sources. The typical In 'N' Out store is 2,000 to 3,000 square feet. All stores are designed and decorated to reflect the company's image of a large, professional organization. The stores can be located in freestanding buildings as well as shopping centers and strips.

The company will help you in hiring the two full-time and two part-time people you'll probably need to operate efficiently. You and your employees will receive seven days of training—some classroom and some on-the-job—before and during your grand opening. The length of time from purchase of your franchise to your grand opening will depend on the size and location of your store.

MAKING IT WORK

You'll share the cost of advertising with all the other franchisees, so you'll get more for your advertising dollar. The cost of newspaper and magazine ads, television and radio commercials, mailers, signs, and banners are all covered by the ongoing advertising fee. The company buys merchandise in large volumes from its own list of suppliers and passes discounts on to its franchisees. If you want to buy from others, the company will approve any reputable suppliers who meet the company's minimum standards. You'll get regular follow-up training on the newest sales methods, and you'll receive periodic updates on industry trends and on developments in products and services.

In 'N' Out will supply your accountant with complete instructions for using the company's bookkeeping and accounting system. A simple but sophisticated computerized system safeguards against employee dishonesty or theft, allowing you to leave the store in charge of others without worry. You'll benefit from regular on-site visits by headquarters personnel, and you'll have access to policy manuals, management-procedure manuals, and a computerized information management system to help you run things on a daily basis.

COMMENTS

Franchises are available in areas indicated on a master franchise plan available from the home office.

GETTING MORE INFORMATION

You can request a brochure that features photographs of a store, inside and out, and gives information about the company. For more details, contact:

Eddie Zeer
Franchising Director
In 'N' Out Food Stores
19215 W. 8 Miles Road
Detroit, MI   48219
(313)   255–0100

Island Snow Hawaii

		AS OF		PROJECTED BY	
NO. OF UNITS		1/1/85	1/1/86	1/1/87	1/1/88
OWNED BY:	COMPANY	2	3	4	5
	FRANCHISEES	24	27	29	32
LOCATED:	IN U.S.	26	30	33	37
	CANADA	0	0	0	0
TOTAL:		26	30	33	37
NO. OF STATES W/ UNITS		4	4	4	6

BUSINESS: shave-ice stands and clothes and accessories
FOUNDED: 1979
FRANCHISED: 1981
START-UP INVESTMENT: $50,000–$75,000

THE BUSINESS

Capitalizing on Hawaii's image and lifestyle of exotic glamour, Island Snow Hawaii sells both shave ice cones (with or without ice cream) and accessories such as T-shirts, posters, and surfboards. Shave ice was brought to Hawaii in the 1800s by Japanese immigrant workers. Founder James Kodama envisioned the shave ice as an inexpensive lure to draw customers into his stores for T-shirts and other items, but at first Waikiki shoppers showed more interest in the thirty flavors of shave ice and tropical ice cream. Today in larger Island Snow Hawaii stores, items with the Island Snow logo account for 40 to 70 percent of total sales volume. The company reported $2.7 million in annual sales for all franchise operations in 1985, with each unit grossing an average of $100,000.

WHAT IT TAKES

You will need $10,000 for the initial franchise fee. Exclusive territories are not granted, but the franchise agreement is valid for ten years, renewable for seven. A total of $50,000 to $75,000, which includes the franchise fee, is necessary to get started, with 60 percent of that in cash. Financial assistance is not available from the company. Additional franchise units also sell for $10,000 each, and master franchises are available. You will be expected to manage the franchise yourself rather than act strictly as an investor. You'll pay 6 percent of gross sales as an ongoing royalty fee. No prior experience is needed to operate an Island Snow Hawaii franchise.

GETTING STARTED

You can expect the company to help you at no cost with site selection, lease negotiation, and general facility layout. For an additional fee the company will assist with construction; store decoration; lease or purchase of furniture and fixtures; and acquisition of materials, supplies, and merchandise. Typical facilities are 400 to 600 square feet, located in malls or resort areas. You will need one full-time and three part-time employees. Your training will consist of four days of on-site, hands-on experience, plus seven days of on-the-job training after you open. You will be taught how to make shave ice. You will also learn about time/motion studies in the store, specific products, stock levels, ordering, and sanitation. It normally takes two to three months to open for business after you buy the franchise. The company will help with your grand opening.

MAKING IT WORK

For part of your original fee you'll receive newspaper, black-and-white magazine, and telephone-book ads as well as in-house media packages with slides and videos. A cooperative advertising program provides brochures, radio commercials, national media coverage, point-of-purchase displays, billboard posters, signs, banners, contests, incentives, and seasonal promotional materials and displays. The company holds areawide franchise meetings and regional conferences once a year and on-site training twice annually to inspect and review procedures. You will receive a company newsletter and periodic updates.

You'll also have access to a resource person at headquarters, management-procedure manuals, inventory and order forms, and an inventory system. The company has divisions to produce the inventory you will carry, a central purchasing program offering volume discounts, and a centralized merchandising system.

COMMENTS

Entrepreneur magazine ranked the company 472d among its 1987 "Franchise 500." Island Snow Hawaii wants to expand in Hawaii, five southern and western states in the Continental United States and internationally.

GETTING MORE INFORMATION

The franchise information packet includes a brochure on the company and its operations, plus copies of several articles published on Island Snow Hawaii and its founder. For more information, write or call:

Lisa Sinai
Vice-President
Island Snow Hawaii
229 Paoakalani Avenue
Honolulu, HW 96815
(800) 926–1815

Jack In The Box

	AS OF		PROJECTED BY	
BUSINESS: fast-food restaurant				
NO. OF UNITS	1/1/85	1/1/86	1/1/87	1/1/88
OWNED BY: COMPANY	724	675	680	660
FRANCHISEES	67	130	175	250
LOCATED: IN U.S.	791	805	855	910
OUTSIDE U.S.	0	0	0	0
TOTAL:	791	805	855	910
NO. OF STATES W/ UNITS	7	8	10	13

BUSINESS: fast-food restaurant
FOUNDED: 1950
FRANCHISED: 1982
START-UP INVESTMENT: $500,000+

THE BUSINESS

About 20 percent of American families eat at a fast-food restaurant at least once every two weeks; most of the time they go to hamburger restaurants. But in recent years, people have wanted both more variety and more nutritional balance in their meals. A popular chain located in the western states, Jack In The Box has created its place in the fast-food market through a policy of strategic innovation. This was the first major fast-food restaurant chain to have drive-through windows on a systemwide basis, to serve breakfast sandwiches, and to expand the basic hamburger-and-fries lunch and dinner menus to include variations like tacos, pocket sandwiches, and salads.

WHAT IT TAKES

Foodmaker, Inc., which operates Jack In The Box, offers two kinds of franchise arrangements, neither of which requires previous restaurant experience for franchisees. You can either purchase an existing operation, or you can open a new facility. Either way, the franchise fee is $25,000 per location. If you choose to acquire an existing restaurant, your license will give you rights to a specific location for twenty years. Or you may want to purchase a multiple-restaurant franchise, acquiring a number of operations within a specified market area. To qualify for consideration for a single restaurant, you (and each of your partners, if any) must have a minimum net worth of $190,000. If you are looking at a multiple-restaurant deal, each investor's net worth must be $500,000. Payment must be made in cash for 40 percent of the negotiated purchase price of the restaurant(s) plus about $24,000 to $27,000 for initial inventory, working capital, and start-up expenses. After purchase, you will pay variable monthly rental on your facility, based partly on monthly gross sales. You will also pay a monthly royalty fee of 4 percent of gross sales, plus an additional 4 percent monthly marketing fee.

The arrangements for new-restaurant development are somewhat different. If applying with a partnership group, you must designate someone to personally supervise construction and operation of the restaurant(s). There are no set minimum net-worth requirements, because important factors such as market size and number of restaurants to be constructed will vary. Besides the initial franchise fee of $25,000 for the first location, you will pay a fee of $12,500 for every additional restaurant that is to be built in your development area. When each new restaurant opens, this development fee will apply toward the $25,000 franchise fee. As with franchising an existing restaurant, when you develop a new restaurant, you will be expected to pay an ongoing monthly marketing fee of 4 percent of your gross sales. Your monthly royalty fee will be only 2 percent of gross sales for the first two years after you open your new restaurant, then will go up to the standard 4 percent figure.

GETTING STARTED

If you are purchasing a new area franchise, Jack In The Box will help you gather and evaluate market data on your development area. Because all Jack In The Box restaurants must meet certain standards of design and decor, the company will work closely with you in all phases of architectural planning, construction, layout, and furnishings. Your restaurant will cover about 2,500 to 3,000 square feet.

Jack In The Box has developed a training program that emphasizes hands-on learning. You (and/or your manager) will spend eight weeks in field training at a Jack In The Box restaurant. To back up your learning experiences, you'll be given a set of operating manuals that detail all restaurant procedures. When you have successfully completed the first phase of training, you will go to San Diego for three days of classroom training covering topics like customer service, quality control, and financial management. Jack In The Box also has training programs and materials for your restaurant staff, which you can purchase for a reasonable fee.

If you are taking over an existing restaurant, it will take from three to six months after the franchise purchase for you to be in operation. If you are developing a new restaurant, you'll spend nine to twelve months preparing to open.

MAKING IT WORK

Jack In The Box will put your 4 percent advertising fee to work with newspaper and magazine advertisements, mailers, promotional displays, and television and radio commercials. The company will also participate with you and other franchisees in cooperative advertising plans, offer ongoing sales incentives, and sponsor periodic awards for superior sales and quality. You will attend city- or areawide franchise meetings every quarter and the national Jack In The Box conference once a year. You'll also receive the company newsletter on a quarterly basis. Other company communications—product or service updates, company-information updates, and franchisee questionnaires—will be sent out as needed. Your main source of information and support will be your franchise operations consultant, who will be assigned to you as soon as your franchise application is accepted. He or she will be available to help you with routine restaurant-management responsibilities as well as more serious problems.

Foodmaker will supply you with various policy, procedure, and service manuals, as well as inventory and bookkeeping systems. The company has an efficient purchasing and distribution system that will save you time, money, and effort. You can choose from over 500 products on the company's list of tested and approved products, and your order will be delivered to you from one of Foodmaker's strategically located distribution centers. Perishables can be purchased locally by the approved suppliers that you select.

Foodmaker maintains a large research-and-development department which explores everything from menu variations to restaurant decor. When a new product is developed, it is test marketed first in Jack In The Box research restaurants, then in a test city, and finally in a larger test area. To be added to the Jack In The Box menu, new items must have the potential to increase sales and be easy to prepare.

COMMENTS

Jack In The Box was ranked sixty-seventh in *Entrepreneur* magazine's 1987 "Franchise 500" and fifty-third in *Venture* magazine's 1986 "Franchise 100." A member of the IFA, the company is seeking franchisees principally in southern, southwestern, and western states, as well as outside the United States.

GETTING MORE INFORMATION

The franchise information packet consists of a pocketed folder containing six information sheets featuring photographs of Jack In The Box restaurants, personnel, and customers; an extensive application form asking for disclosure of personal, business, and financial information; a breakdown of proposed ownership interest; an authorization form allowing for release of information from your financial institutions; and authorization from your spouse for the use of all jointly held funds. For details, write to:

Sales Manager, Jack In The Box
Foodmaker, Inc.
9330 Balboa Avenue
San Diego, CA   92123
(619)   571–2200

Jani-King

BUSINESS: office-cleaning services

FOUNDED: 1969

FRANCHISED: 1984

START-UP INVESTMENT: $8,000

NO. OF UNITS			AS OF		PROJECTED BY	
			1/1/85	1/1/86	1/1/87	1/1/88
OWNED BY:	COMPANY		6	6	7	8
	FRANCHISEES		403	675	1,085	1,300
LOCATED:	IN U.S.		409	680	1,090	1,304
	OUTSIDE U.S.		0	1	2	4
TOTAL:			409	681	1,092	1,308
NO. OF STATES W/ UNITS			9	12	20	40

THE BUSINESS

According to a recent report published by the U.S. Department of Labor, the janitorial field is and will continue to be one of the fastest-growing segments of our economy for the next decade. The increasing demand in this field is due primarily to the current lack of competent personnel available for contract cleaning of business offices and facilities. In 1985, Jani-King franchises grossed $14.3 million, with average gross sales per franchise unit of $20,000.

A typical franchisee team consists of a husband and wife who work three or four hours a day, five days per week. With an assistant, they can gross about $2,500 a month. Most franchise owners schedule their cleaning crews to work between the hours of 6:00 P.M. and 11:00 P.M., Monday through Friday, and occasionally on weekends. Service contracts range from $100 per month to over $100,000 a month. Future growth will be financed by the company if necessary. Jani-King guarantees $1,000 worth of business per month for each new franchisee for the first three months of operation. The company's workers are insured and bonded.

WHAT IT TAKES

You will need $7,500 for the initial franchise fee. The agreement, which will grant you a license to operate a Jani-King business but does not guarantee an exclusive territory, will be valid for ten years, renewable for four ten-year periods. Of the total, $4,000 must be in cash, with financing for the balance available from the company. Additional units also cost $7,500 each, and master franchises sell for either $25,000 per 100,000 population (25 percent down) or $50,000 for 500,000 population (30 percent down). Master franchisees handle all billing and collections on franchisees' accounts. The company estimates that each one million in population will support approximately seventy to eighty franchises. If you buy a Jani-King franchise, you must be actively involved in the business. The company charges a 10 percent ongoing royalty fee for regular franchises and a 5 percent fee on sales made by master-franchise owners. Prior cleaning experience is not necessary.

GETTING STARTED

If you become a master-franchise owner, the company will send a representative to your city for about two weeks to help you obtain office space, equipment, furniture, and telephones; interview prospective personnel; and order initial printing and office supplies. You will also receive a starter package of office and advertising supplies to last for several months. Your training will begin with your review of training manuals covering sales, administrative, and operations functions of a regional office.

If you become a regular associate franchisee, the procedure will be similar, except that you will be trained at a regional office. Whichever franchise you select, you will attend classes for at least a week at a regional center, where you'll view videos and study contract negotiations, bookkeeping, hiring and training of personnel, the securing of new business, janitorial procedures, technical training, and public relations. You can begin to service your first customers within three months after buying the franchise.

MAKING IT WORK

For part of your franchise fee you will receive black-and-white and four-color magazine ads, telephone-book ads, national media coverage, and a public-relations/marketing manual. For a charge, you may order mailers, brochures, catalogs, presentation books, radio commercials, point-of-purchase displays, signs, and press releases. You will meet with other franchise owners at semiannual regional conferences, attend half-day seminars every three months, participate in quarterly areawide franchise meetings, and receive on-site training whenever necessary. Jani-King publishes a monthly newsletter and monthly updates on products and market information. The company sponsors award programs recognizing outstanding operations and sales.

Administrative functions are simplified with regional resource persons, a toll-free hotline, manuals on policy and customer service, accounting forms, and a bookkeeping system. Since bookkeeping is a weakness for many new business people, the company takes care of this for franchisees, billing and collecting all accounts. The company provides guidance on the few pieces of paperwork that they don't do. Regional centers cooperate with suppliers to test and approve products and programs available to franchisees. Jani-King Leasing can supply equipment that you may need, and the company also has a central purchasing program to offer volume discounts on cleaning chemicals and its own brands, but you may purchase from any source. The company sponsors property, general liability, and major-medical insurance coverage as well as fidelity bonding.

COMMENTS

Jani-King was ranked seventeenth in *Entrepreneur* magazine's 1987 "Franchise 500" and eleventh in *Venture* magazine's 1986 "Franchise 100." A member of the IFA since 1985, Jani-King wants to add new franchises across the United States and in Australia, Canada, Europe and Japan.

GETTING MORE INFORMATION

The franchise packet contains numerous articles on the company, brochures on each type of franchise, copies of recent ads, a U.S. Department of Labor report on prospects for janitorial services, and a four-page application form. For details, contact:
Kevin Spurrier
National Sales Director
Jani-King
4950 Keller Springs, Suite 190
Dallas, TX   75248
(800)   552–5264 or (214)   991–0900

Just Pants

BUSINESS: retail
  casual wear
  FOUNDED: 1969
  FRANCHISED: 1969
START-UP
  INVESTMENT:
  $118,500–$210,500

		AS OF		PROJECTED BY	
NO. OF UNITS		1/1/85	1/1/86	1/1/87	1/1/88
OWNED BY:	COMPANY	0	0	0	0
	FRANCHISEES	119	116	126	140
LOCATED:	IN U.S.	119	116	126	140
	OUTSIDE U.S.	0	0	0	0
TOTAL:		119	116	126	140
NO. OF STATES W/ UNITS		24	21	25	30

THE BUSINESS

Just Pants markets casual clothing—primarily jeans, slacks and tops—at affordable prices in sizes and styles that appeal to young people. Twenty percent of the merchandise carries the company's high-quality private label; the rest carries national and fashion labels. In 1985, Just Pants franchises sold $40,435,000 worth of merchandise with average gross sales of approximately $340,000.

WHAT IT TAKES

Just Pants charges no franchise fee. However, you'll need $10,500 to $11,500 initially to cover various deposits, some of which may be refunded later. Your total initial investment will be $118,500 to $201,500, with half of that required in cash. Besides the amount for the preliminary deposits you'll need $500 to $1,500 for a promotion fee; $7,500 to $10,000 for equipment and fixtures; $50,000 to $95,000 for construction, decorating, and leasehold improvements; $40,000 to $70,000 for inventory; and $10,000 to $15,000 for working capital and miscellaneous expenses. After you're in business, you'll be responsible for paying 5 percent of monthly gross sales as an ongoing royalty fee, and an additional 3 percent for advertising.

Your original franchise agreement will last as long as your store lease and can be renewed again for the length of the new lease agreement. Your territory will be defined by the radius clause in your lease. The company would prefer that you not simply maintain passive ownership. Master franchises are available.

GETTING STARTED

The company's real estate personnel carefully study the demographics of each potential store site, generally in an enclosed mall. The company will lease the store location in its name and sublease to you on identical terms. After getting the construction waivers, Just Pants will refund to you, or disburse on your behalf, the difference between your initial $10,000 deposit and the amount of the first month's rent. The company will design your 1,750-square-foot store according to their standardized format and will assist with the construction, decoration, and acquisition of fixtures and furniture. You can expect to open your store just three to four months after signing your franchise agreement.

With company help, you will hire two full-time and eight part-time employees. Just Pants will train you in basic business systems at the Chicago office for two days. Then you'll spend a week at an existing Just Pants store learning directly about store operations. For the first week you're open, company personnel will be by your side guiding and teaching you and your staff. The simple store layout facilitates training, and you and your employees can quickly become familiar with the unique floor-to-ceiling pants wall capable of displaying and stocking thousands of pairs of jeans and other casual pants.

MAKING IT WORK

You'll regularly receive bulletins with information about the head office, new products, market changes, and unique services. Your corporate field supervisor will visit you at least every other month for on-site training and discussion of your store's merchandise mix, inventory levels, promotional signs, and advertising. He or she will also be available to help you with problems, and you'll have the company's manuals on policy, management, and customer service. You can attend the company's semiannual national conferences, and you can rely on the company-supplied bookkeeping and inventory systems and various accounting, inventory, ordering, and personnel forms. Your 3 percent advertising fee will pay for major sales-promotion campaigns on both national and local levels. You can expect the marketing strategies to include rock concerts, athletic-team tie-ins, radio-station remote broadcasts, newspaper and telephone-book ads, and special promotional materials such as catalogs, seasonal signs, and contests. You'll also have press packages for local use.

You'll probably buy your clothing from Just Pants because the group purchasing system will allow you to sell your merchandise at lower prices than your competition. But those purchases will also be a form of advertising, as Just Pants combines funds with various manufacturers to develop big-budget co-op advertising. In addition, you may be on the licensee steering committee, which meets periodically to choose style, cut, make, and color for the company's private-label program of men's and ladies' jeans, tops, and outerwear. You'll also be free to buy from other sources if you find appropriate quality at a reasonable price.

COMMENTS

Just Pants was ranked 216th in *Entrepreneur* magazine's 1987 "Franchise 500." The company is seeking to increase operations in most states.

GETTING MORE INFORMATION

The franchise information packet includes a two-page company letter, a breakdown of financial costs, a photograph of a typical Just Pants store, a list of locations of current stores, and a two-page personal application form requiring detailed financial disclosure. For details, contact:
Harvey Olsher
Director of Franchise Development
Just Pants
201 North Wells Street, Suite 1530
Chicago, IL   60606
(312) 346–5020

K-Bob's

BUSINESS: full-service restaurant
FOUNDED: 1966
FRANCHISED: 1967
START-UP INVESTMENT: $275,000–$1,000,000

NO. OF UNITS			AS OF		PROJECTED BY	
			1/1/85	1/1/86	1/1/87	1/1/88
OWNED BY:	COMPANY		3	3	5	8
	FRANCHISEES		80	98	110	125
LOCATED:	IN U.S.		83	101	115	133
	OUTSIDE U.S.		0	0	0	0
TOTAL:			83	101	115	133
NO. OF STATES W/ UNITS			6	6	9	12

THE BUSINESS

K-Bob's started in 1966 in the heart of America's cattle country with a simple concept: serve great-tasting domestic beef accompanied by an outstanding salad wagon with full sit-down dining service in a pleasant, friendly atmosphere. The success of the original K-Bob's in Clovis, New Mexico, was followed by that of additional units; today K-Bob's, Inc., is a major regional, company-owned and franchised restaurant system with total annual dollar volume of business for all franchise operations in 1985 of $80 million, an average gross sales per unit of $800,000, and average net sales of approximately $80,000. Although grain-fed-beef steaks are featured on the menu, chicken, a salad bar, vegetable side orders, and desserts provide a generous product mix with moderate food cost. Franchisees are free to offer any menu item approved by K-Bob's, so you can respond to specific regional food favorites that would appeal to your customers.

WHAT IT TAKES

You will need $25,000 for purchase of the initial franchise. Your original franchise agreement will apply for a term of twenty years and will give you exclusive rights to a specific territory. Additional franchises cost $25,000 each. You need not manage your operation yourself. Master franchises are available. Your total development cost will vary widely depending upon the land, building, financing, and equipment costs and whether your location is a conversion or new construction. The company doesn't provide financial assistance. You'll pay an ongoing royalty fee of 3 percent of gross sales, and 1 percent of your gross sales will fund advertising. No previous food-industry experience is necessary for you or your restaurant manager, because the company has a comprehensive training program.

GETTING STARTED

K-Bob's will assist you in site selection; negotiations for lease or purchase of your location; arrangements for preliminary restaurant drawings and scale architectural blueprints; consultation with your architect or contractor; selection and ordering of food-service equipment, furniture, and signage; selection of sound systems, menu boards, and cash- and inventory-control devices; negotiation of service and maintenance contracts; purchase of materials, supplies, and merchandise; and hiring of personnel. The company will also assist in the details for your grand opening by providing advertising and promotional materials. For a fee the company will also provide assistance with lease or purchase of equipment or vehicles, or with construction.

You'll need an area of approximately 5,500 square feet located in a mall, shopping center or strip, commercial center, industrial park, or in a freestanding building. You'll need five full-time and forty part-time employees. You (and your manager, if you have one) will spend a minimum of six weeks in classroom training in Dallas, Texas, and on the job to learn about K-Bob's concept and philosophy. Through hands-on experience you'll learn about methods of food preparation, crew training, proper use of equipment, cleanliness and sanitation, merchandising, inventory control, customer service, managerial and interpersonal skills, basic accounting, cash control, profit-and-loss analysis, and record keeping. You'll be responsible for travel, meals, and lodging for yourself or your manager and one other employee, if you chose to include another person in the training program. All training materials and instruction, operation, and procedures manuals are paid for by K-Bob's, Inc. You can plan on a period of four months between your franchise purchase and your grand opening.

MAKING IT WORK

The K-Bob's advertising and marketing department will provide you with full access to the most current market research, media, promotional ideas, and radio- and television-production techniques. Marketing and advertising materials such as television commercials and black-and-white and four-color magazine ads will be available as part of your initial purchase fee. You can also use co-op funds for merchandising support such as newspaper and telephone-book ads, brochures, radio commercials, in-house media packages, and such point-of-purchase items as displays, banners, flags, balloons, and signs.

You can attend the annual national convention as well as quarterly regional conferences and semiannual one-day seminars, and you can participate in an incentive-recognition program. The company will send you a monthly newsletter, quarterly company updates, and annual updates on industry and market information. You'll receive administrative and managerial support from resource persons at both the regional and headquarters levels; a variety of policy and procedure manuals; and inventory, bookkeeping, personnel, and order forms. A research-and-development division, maintained as a part of the headquarters buying offices, offers you volume discount savings on supplies through a central purchasing system. In addition, the company-sponsored insurance package offers property, general-liability, life, major-medical, and disability coverage.

COMMENTS

K-Bob's, an operating division of the Enrec Corporation, was ranked 180th in *Entrepreneur* magazine's 1987 "Franchise 500." The company is seeking franchisees in states.

GETTING MORE INFORMATION

The franchise information packet has details on the company's marketing theme and philosophy, products, costs, training program, advertising and marketing support, and company services. For details, write or call:

Andrew C. Gunkler
Vice-President, Development
K-Bob's, Inc.
5307 Mockingbird Lane, Suite 300
Dallas, TX 75206
(214) 828–0184

Kits Cameras

BUSINESS: camera,
  video, and photo-
  finishing store
FOUNDED: 1975
FRANCHISED: 1978
START-UP
  INVESTMENT:
  $95,000–$105,000

		AS OF		PROJECTED BY	
NO. OF UNITS		1/1/85	1/1/86	1/1/87	1/1/88
OWNED BY:	COMPANY	21	26	27	30
	FRANCHISEES	30	36	38	43
LOCATED:	IN U.S.	51	62	65	73
	OUTSIDE U.S.	0	0	0	0
TOTAL:		51	62	65	73
NO. OF STATES W/ UNITS		6	6	6	6

THE BUSINESS

From its humble beginning in 1961 as a photo counter in a drugstore, Kits Cameras has evolved into the largest chain of specialty camera stores in North America. Both company growth and photo-industry growth in general are expected to continue the record climb that began in the 1970s and surpass the $12 billion sales mark achieved industrywide in 1980. Aware of the record growth trend, Kits Cameras successfully introduced—under its KitStar trade name—cameras, binoculars, and photo accessories, as well as quality picture frames. Total dollar volume of franchise operations in 1985 amounted to nearly $14 million, and Kits Cameras franchisees had an average net income per unit of $50,000.

WHAT IT TAKES

Your $15,000 franchise fee will be part of the total start-up investment costs ranging from $95,000 to $105,000, $50,000 of which must be in cash. Kits Cameras can assist you in arranging financing for the rest. Your initial franchise agreement, which will stand for ten years, with a ten-year renewal period, will entitle you to a territory within a minimum three-mile radius. Owning more than one Kits Cameras store is feasible, but the company encourages the franchisee to run his or her own shop. An additional franchise will cost you another $15,000 fee. Regardless of the number of franchises owned, you will be responsible for an ongoing royalty fee of 6 percent of gross sales. The company does not require that you have previous experience in photography sales.

GETTING STARTED

Kits Cameras will evaluate alternative sites and then ask you to choose your location. The company can negotiate leases at competitive rates in areas where you may not have been able to get in on your own. In fact, the company takes on the lease in its own name and assumes the risks that can accompany a ten- to fifteen-year lease. Kits Cameras will offer you a turnkey operation, meaning that your store will be prepared for you by retail specialists. They will order the equipment and fixtures needed to set up your shop, prepare your opening inventory, merchandise your store, and even plan your grand opening. Most Kits Cameras stores are located in either malls or strip shopping centers and are 700-square-foot facilities. You'll need two full-time and two part-time employees. Just two months after your franchise purchase you can open your shop.

Your training will involve six weeks of instruction—three weeks of classroom education at the Kent, Washington, home office and another three weeks of on-the-job training at your store location. Week one of the training covers company philosophy, management principles, photography, and product knowledge. Week two includes photofinishing training and professional sales techniques. You will learn about merchandising, store layout, and training of your sales staff in week three. Back at your store in week four, you will be shown photographic shooting sessions and other practical in-store experiences. In week five you will be instructed on executive management, including financial controls, accounting services, advertising, and marketing. The final week of training will give you additional practical experiences in store management. Successful completion of the training program is a prerequisite for a potential franchisee's final acceptance by the company as an applicant.

MAKING IT WORK

Your Kits Cameras area representative will regularly visit your store to keep you informed of new profit-making ideas. The company offers one-day seminars about six times a year and sponsors an annual national conference, quarterly regional conferences, quarterly on-site training, and periodic regional training sessions. Also, the company provides franchisees with kits containing an annual business plan with sales and profit objectives and expense budgets. Company financial advisors offer ongoing advice, and the company will maintain all bookkeeping records for you and provide monthly financial statements. Kits Cameras also sponsors various franchise achievement awards.

The company participates in a co-operative advertising program. For your ongoing advertising fee you will be shown how to promote your store locally by adapting the company's advertising programs to your own market. Advertising packets include not only formats for newspaper, radio, and television ads but also displays, price cards, window banners, and other in-store promotional materials.

You'll benefit from the company's centralized distribution system, through which you can buy directly from the company warehouse photography-related products that have been tested for profitability and customer acceptance. The computerized system at the warehouse allows easy ordering and weekly shipments. A company representative will help you maintain the most profitable blend of company merchandise. Kits Cameras also offers a limited exchange program in which you can swap out regular slow-selling merchandise in saleable shape for faster-moving, profit-generating stock. You'll get extra income, too, by taking in repairs and sending them to the company's regional service department.

COMMENTS

A subsidiary of Tri-Nek Corporation, Kits Cameras was ranked 384th among *Entrepreneur* magazine's 1987 "Franchise 500." The company provides an earnings claim document prior to a potential franchisee's personal interview. It is seeking franchisees in six western states.

GETTING MORE INFORMATION

The franchise information packet contains a brochure with color photographs of a typical franchise in all phases of operations, a pamphlet on the Kits photofinishing process, the franchisee training schedule, and a three-page application. For further information, contact:

Mike Greenen
Regional Manager
Kits Cameras
6051 South 194th Street
Kent, WA   98032
(206)   872–3688 (call collect)

KOA Kampgrounds of America

BUSINESS: campsite rental
FOUNDED: 1961
FRANCHISED: 1962
START-UP INVESTMENT: $85,000+

		AS OF		PROJECTED BY	
NO. OF UNITS		1/1/85	1/1/86	1/1/87	1/1/88
OWNED BY:	COMPANY	16	16	16	16
	FRANCHISEES	656	688	695	695
LOCATED:	IN U.S.	618	672	680	680
	OUTSIDE U.S.	54	32	31	31
TOTAL:		672	704	711	711
NO. OF STATES W/ UNITS		47	47	47	47

THE BUSINESS

Campers are a varied group, ranging from the motorcycle rider who sleeps on a bedroll to the family of six who sleeps in a tent and rents a cabin for grandmother and the television. Some campers want solitude; others want to make new friends. KOA Kampgrounds can accommodate all types of campers. Following high standards for facilities and service, each KOA campground is tailored to the needs of its campers, shaped by the geographic characteristics of its location, and stamped with the personality of its independent owner. While the early KOAs were built next to interstate highways, newer campgrounds are located off the beaten path.

KOA Kampgrounds offer—for a fee—campsites, utility hookups, and shower facilities. Some KOAs have general stores and snack bars. Many KOAs offer camping cabins with screened windows and bunk beds. Because KOAs are franchised, there are special attractions such as gift certificates, a card for 10 percent discounts, and an advance-reservation network among campgrounds.

Owning a campground can be a refreshing change. You can work outdoors, set your own hours, work with your family, and meet interesting people. Because KOA is not adding many new sites, you should expect to purchase an existing franchise.

WHAT IT TAKES

Your KOA franchise fee will be $20,000. You'll get an exclusive territory based on the area's potential market, and the term of your agreement will be five years, with a five-year renewal option. Your fee for each additional franchise will be $3,500, and the company will allow you to hire someone else as manager.

Depending on the location of your campground, your total start-up investment, including the franchise fee, will begin at $85,000, all in cash. The company suggests that the equity in your home is good collateral for financing, and many of the KOA owners selling their existing franchises will finance the sale, some offering interest rates as low as 10 percent. You'll pay a royalty of 8 percent of the weekly camper registrations and a 2 percent advertising fee. KOA doesn't require any experience in the campground industry.

GETTING STARTED

KOA will put you in touch with campgrounds that are for sale and give you an opportunity to visit them and review their operating history before deciding which to purchase. KOAs are located all across America and Canada. The facility sizes and sites vary, so the number of staff members you'll need will vary. You'll get help with any layout, decoration, and construction that might be needed. KOA has special requirements about the use of logos and the inclusion of stores and playgrounds. You will attend a three-day orientation seminar at the KOA headquarters in Billings, Montana, where you'll learn about campground management and operation—everything from registration procedures to marketing programs. If you buy an existing campground, you can open within two months after you sign the agreement. If you construct a new site, you'll need two years. KOA will help with your opening.

MAKING IT WORK

KOA offers the industry's only nationwide advertising program. From billboards to industry magazines, KOA's name is always in front of the camper. KOA discount cards, camping cabins, and reservation system all draw campers into the KOA system. Every camper who stays at a KOA gets a free 130-page directory that describes each KOA campground, its facilities, rates, seasonal opening and closing dates, phone number, owner's name, and a map with local landmarks. The magazine also contains a state-by-state atlas and general information about KOA and camping.

Each year KOA holds both a three-day national convention and district conferences for franchisees. KOA staff will visit your campground at least once a year to help you with any problems, but between visits, you can call for advice on the toll-free hotline. You'll get both the company newsletter every three weeks and periodic updates on KOA and the camping industry.

COMMENTS

A member of the IFA, KOA was ranked sixty-fifth in *Entrepreneur* magazine's 1987 "Franchise 500." The KOA Kampground Owners Association helps support eight camps for children with cancer.

GETTING MORE INFORMATION

The franchise information packet includes a campers' directory and a circular describing KOA's offerings. For more information, call or write:
Dave Johnson
Sales Manager
Kampgrounds of America, Inc.
P.O. Box 30558
Billings, MT 59114
(800) 548–7239

Kwik-Kopy Printing

BUSINESS: offset
printing and copying
service
FOUNDED: 1967
FRANCHISED: 1967
START-UP
INVESTMENT:
$89,700–$96,000

		AS OF		PROJECTED BY	
NO. OF UNITS		1/1/85	1/1/86	1/1/87	1/1/88
OWNED BY: COMPANY		0	0	0	0
FRANCHISEES		903	1,020	1,132	1,260
LOCATED: IN U.S.		714	767	867	950
OUTSIDE U.S.		189	253	265	310
TOTAL:		903	1,020	1,132	1,260
NO. OF STATES W/ UNITS		41	42	46	48

THE BUSINESS

In 1966, Bud Hadfield began to use the newly developed direct-image camera and small offset printing press in his small Houston print shop. One day an extremely satisfied customer casually remarked, "Whatever this is, you ought to franchise it." By 1970, Hadfield had sold twenty-seven franchises and become chairman of the board of Kwik-Kopy Corporation; the fellow who had made the casual remark became president.

In 1985, when the printing industry's gross sales were $3.75 billion, Kwik-Kopy's 1,000 franchises grossed $169,880,000 in sales. The phenomenal success of Kwik-Kopy is a result not only of good timing and hard work but of dependable service and high quality.

WHAT IT TAKES

Your initial franchise fee will be $41,500, but if you can pay the fee in cash, Kwik-Kopy will discount it to $35,200. If not, the company will offer financing with $10,000 down at 11 percent for ten years—$433.93 per month. If you choose to have your fee financed, Kwik-Kopy will require you to deposit $20,000 into their management fund. You will, however, get this back over a twenty-four month period, plus 11 percent interest, in payments of $932.16 per month.

Kwik-Kopy will finance the purchase of all of your equipment, which will run about $38,000 if bought from the company at cost. You'll need approximately $8,500 in cash to cover your first month's rent and deposit plus prepaid freight charges for delivery of your equipment package. You'll need another $8,000, unencumbered, for working capital. You can buy additional franchises for a reduced fee of only $7,500 each.

You'll pay a monthly royalty fee based on the amount of gross sales, as indicated by the following figures.

FEE	GROSS SALES
4%	up to $ 5,000
6%	up to $10,000
8%	over $10,000
Rebate under certain conditions	over $25,000

You will also pay an ongoing advertising fee of 2 percent of gross sales. Your franchise agreement will apply for twenty-five years, with a twenty-five year renewal period, and will guarantee for one year an exclusive territory determined by your trade area. The company does not allow passive ownership.

GETTING STARTED

Kwik-Kopy will provide detailed market- and site-analysis aids to help you assess potential locations. A corporate representative will visit your chosen site, talk with you at length, and then decide whether the site is acceptable.

Kwik-Kopy centers can be located in office buildings, commercial centers, industrial parks, shopping centers, or freestanding buildings. They're usually sized from 1,000 to 1,200 square feet. The company will help you with design and layout; selection of furniture, fixtures, and wall graphics; acquisition of equipment, supplies, and merchandise; and selection of the two full-time (and, possibly one part-time) employees you'll need.

As soon as you sign your franchise agreement, you'll receive pre-study manuals and videotapes to help you get ready for the three-week training for yourself and one other employee at the headquarters in Cypress, Texas. The company will pay all transportation and lodging expenses for you to attend classes in advertising, public relations, sales, production, work flow, pricing, record keeping, cash flow (including credit and collections), and management and marketing techniques. You'll also be given an IBM PC microcomputer, which you'll learn to use in class.

You should be able to open your store within about three months after purchase. During your grand opening the company will coordinate efforts to promote your services, including stories to the local newspaper(s) and direct mailings to local businesses. Kwik-Kopy will also give you window banners, point-of-purchase materials, and imprinted giveaway items to distribute to your customers.

MAKING IT WORK   Kwik Kopy will handle a quarterly direct-mail advertising program to reach 500 of your customers and run newspaper, magazine, and telephone-book ads, and television and radio commercials. The company will also provide brochures, presentation books, videotapes, displays, incentives, press packages, and a public-relations/marketing manual. Through a cooperative advertising program, you can get banners, flags, and, seasonal promotional materials. You can also use Kwik-Kopy's unique public-relations program called PRIDE, in which you'll use retired persons part-time to call on both your regular and prospective customers.

Kwik-Kopy sponsors an annual national convention, several regional conferences each year, as well as monthly two-day seminars, workshops, and weekend retreats. Three times each year a company representative will visit your store and provide technical and public-relations training to you and your employees. Books, audio cassettes, and videotapes are available from the company library, and you'll receive a monthly magazine, a biweekly newsletter, periodic franchisee questionnaires and surveys, periodic technical updates, and quarterly audio cassettes full of company news. The company sponsors various awards for outstanding franchisees.

A central purchasing program will enable you to benefit from volume discounts for supplies. You and your employees will be covered by group life, auto, major-medical, and disability insurance. (Disability coverage is free the first year.) You can also get property and general-liability coverage at group rates for your store.

Kwik-Kopy has eight toll-free telephone lines, and you'll get regular on-site visits and troubleshooting visits as needed. Also, if you have ongoing problems, you can request an evaluation, and the company will provide you with detailed written recommendations for remedial action. You'll get policy and procedure manuals, customer-service manuals, a complete computerized management-information and accounting system, forms to use with the computer systems, and software updates for your IBM PC.

COMMENTS

A member of the IFA, Kwik-Kopy was ranked forty-fourth in *Venture* magazine's 1986 "Franchise 100" and thirty-second in *Entrepreneur* magazine's 1987 "Franchise 500." The company is looking for franchisees throughout the world. American Wholesale Thermographers (AWT), a subsidiary of Kwik-Kopy, also has limited franchises available.

GETTING MORE INFORMATION

The franchise information packet contains a full-color brochure, a reprinted magazine article about Bud Hadfield and Kwik-Kopy, and an application for preliminary qualification. (If you're approved on the basis of the application, you may be invited to tour headquarters with company-paid overnight accommodations for two.) For more information, contact:

Gerald Hargis
National Sales Manager
Kwik-Kopy Corporation
One Kwik-Kopy Lane
P.O. Box 777
Cypress, TX   77429
(800)   231–4542 (any U.S. area outside Texas)
(800)   392–6488 (Texas, except Houston)
(713)   373–3535 (Houston)

Langenwalter Dye Concept

BUSINESS: complete carpet-maintenance service			AS OF		PROJECTED BY	
	NO. OF UNITS		1/1/85	1/1/86	1/1/87	1/1/88
	OWNED BY: COMPANY		0	0	0	0
FOUNDED: 1972		FRANCHISEES	90	101	140	200
FRANCHISED: 1980	LOCATED:	IN U.S.	88	99	138	198
START-UP		OUTSIDE U.S.	2	2	2	2
INVESTMENT:	TOTAL:		90	101	140	200
$13,500–$15,000	NO. OF STATES W/ UNITS		27	29	37	50

THE BUSINESS

Until recently homeowners with worn-looking carpeting had only two options—clean or replace their carpets. Now carpeting can be cleaned and dyed on location in a process developed by a former aerospace chemist. The Langenwalter Dye Concept has revolutionized the carpet-dyeing industry—which formerly could offer no assurance for a quality dyed carpet. Langenwalter's liquid dyes produce a solid, consistent, lasting color that dries in just a few hours. Another advantage is that the carpet can be cleaned over and over again since the dye is permanent. Although the dyeing process is about four times as expensive as the cleaning process, it's still one-fourth less the cost of replacing the same carpeting. For natural-fiber and nylon carpeting, a number of color options are available. These carpets can either be dyed back to their original color, or a color switch can be made. The only exceptions to this money-saving option are acrylic and polyester carpets, which cannot be successfully dyed. As a Langenwalter franchisee, you would also clean carpet and upholstery and perform miscellaneous carpet repairs, including working on carpets damaged by floods.

The perfect customer for Langenwalter Dye Concept is an apartment owner, who commonly replaces over 50 percent of his or her carpets because they look unsightly, despite being in good condition. The homeowner has use for these services, too, because he or she may need to dye over stains left from pets, children, food, and liquor. Once the process is complete, the nap of the carpeting is enriched, transforming old, spotted, and color-faded carpeting so that it almost looks new.

WHAT IT TAKES

Your Langenwalter carpet-service business will require a total initial investment of $13,500 to $15,000, which includes the franchise fee of $12,500 required in cash. Your territory rights will be determined by area population, and your franchise contract will last for three years, with a three-year renewal option. For another $12,500 you may open an additional territory, but you will be expected to participate actively in the operation of all of your franchises. The only royalty you'll pay will be an advertising fee of $100 a month. Langenwalter claims that all you must have to manage your franchise successfully is business sense.

GETTING STARTED

Because each Langenwalter franchise is a service business, your operating costs can be held to a minimum. In fact, many owners operate out of their homes. The company will provide you assistance with equipment leasing or purchasing and materials acquisition. The basic equipment you'll need will be a rotary single-disc carpet-cleaning machine with a solution tank. One to two full-time employees can handle your workload, or you could conceivably manage the business and do the service calls yourself.

Company training consists of classroom and hands-on training at corporate headquarters in California for one week. You will complete an intensive carpet-maintenance curriculum instructed by five

Langenwalter specialists. Coursework covers carpet and upholstery dyeing, carpet repair, flood damage, color theory, and marketing plans. Within just two to three weeks after training you will be ready for your first customer.

MAKING IT WORK

You can reach headquarters resource personnel through a toll-free telephone number if you need technical consultation. Langenwalter continually conducts research, and you will receive product and service bulletins along with a monthly company newsletter. In operating your Langenwalter franchise, you must use only company-developed carpet dyes to ensure quality service. For a small fee you can get ready-to-print telephone-book ads and a colorful flyer.

COMMENTS

A subsidiary of Langenwalter-Harris Chemical Company, the company was ranked 433d in *Entrepreneur* magazine's 1987 "Franchise 500." The company is seeking franchisees in most states and in Canada.

GETTING MORE INFORMATION

The franchise information packet includes two advertising flyers; reprints from the *Los Angeles Times, Apartment News,* and others; and literature on the Langenwalter dye process, general carpet dyeing, and the advantages of carpet restoration over replacement. For more information, contact:
John or Roy Langenwalter
Langenwalter Dye Concept
4410 East La Palma
Anaheim, CA   92807
(800)   422–4370   or   (714)   528–7610

Lincoln Log Homes

BUSINESS: log-home kits
FOUNDED: 1978
FRANCHISED: 1978
START-UP INVESTMENT: $10,000–$75,000

NO. OF UNITS		AS OF		PROJECTED BY	
		1/1/85	1/1/86	1/1/87	1/1/88
OWNED BY: COMPANY		0	0	0	0
	FRANCHISEES	417	476	540	600
LOCATED: IN U.S.		417	476	540	600
	OUTSIDE U.S.	0	0	0	0
TOTAL:		417	476	540	600
NO. OF STATES W/ UNITS		50	50	50	50

THE BUSINESS

Lincoln Log Homes has experienced a 450 percent growth in the past eight years because log homes offer an attractive alternative lifestyle for a cost up to one-third lower than that for conventional housing. Logs provide natural, quality insulation at up to six times the insulating capacity of a brick of equal thickness—and they never need painting or wallboard. The company's logs bear an uncanny resemblance to their toy namesake—Lincoln Logs. All the logs are precut to a uniform size and designed to stack easily. The stacking surfaces are flat with a lengthwise grove filled with a one-inch poly-ethylene backer rod that creates a seal. The corners join snugly together with the patent-pending Weather-Lok cut.

As a Lincoln Log Homes franchisee, you would sell and construct log homes or hire a local contractor to handle the construction. A choice of sixty log-home designs can be sent to your site in preassembled wall units or kits. All logs are numbered and correspond to blueprints supplied with each home.

WHAT IT TAKES

Lincoln Log Homes requires no franchise fee. Typically, however, franchisees are expected to buy a Lincoln Log home to use as a model. The range of investment for your model will be $10,000 to $25,000. Your total investment could range up to $75,000 if you buy a master franchise or maintain an inventory of home kits. For your initial investment you will get a territory of about 100,000 population. As a dealer, you can expect to make approximately $4,000 gross profit on each home you sell in kit form and even more from services and materials furnished in your local area. The company assesses no ongoing royalty fee.

GETTING STARTED

You will probably want to start your Lincoln Logs business by building a 2,000-square-foot log home for yourself, contracting locally for any needed services and for all building supplies except the logs. However, for a fee the company will provide your building supplies and construct your home for you. Once your home—or commercial building, if you prefer—is finished, it can serve as a model for your business. You'll receive two days of training at the home office in North Carolina to learn how to advertise, market, sell, and construct log homes. You'll get factory-construction and assembly information as well as technical and architectural drawings. In about three months you'll be ready for your grand opening. For a fee the company will send someone to help you with the opening—or you can do it on your own.

MAKING IT WORK

The company will supply you with all advertising materials, including newspaper and magazine slicks, mailers, and brochures you can use to promote the log homes. Attractive sales displays are available to put in your model home or office. The company will help you locate potential customers using their lead-referral system. National media coverage is handled by the home office, with articles in publications like *Mechanix Illustrated* and *Business Review*. You'll get a monthly newsletter and a variety of regular technical and industry updates. Personnel from the main office or from several regional offices will make routine visits and troubleshooting visits as needed. For quick information you can call the company's toll-free hotline or check the company's operations manual.

You can expect to get thirty-day delivery of logs from Lincoln Logs, and the company will advise you on buying many of your finish items locally, saving you shipping costs and giving you great flexibility when dealing with your customers. As part of a cooperative agreement between United States Solar Industries, Inc., and Lincoln Log Homes, you can install affordable solar heating and cooling in the log homes you sell.

COMMENTS

A subsidiary of Log Systems, Inc., the company ranked first in sales for the industry in 1986. Lincoln Log Homes sponsors a college scholarship fund. The company wants to expand throughout the world.

GETTING MORE INFORMATION

The franchise information packet includes fact sheets on dealer information, log homes, construction, and solar options; a price sheet; a magazine-article reprint; twenty-five sample drawings and floor plans; and a brochure answering questions about the company. A two-page personal questionnaire must be filled out before you can be given consideration as a potential dealer. For details, write to:

J. Michael Wilson
President
Lincoln Log Homes
6000 Lumber Lane
Kannapolis, N.C.   28081
(704)   932–6151 (call collect)

Lindal Cedar Homes

BUSINESS: cedar- and			AS OF		PROJECTED BY	
log-home	NO. OF UNITS		1/1/85	1/1/86	1/1/87	1/1/88
manufacturer	OWNED BY: COMPANY		6	7	9	12
FOUNDED: 1945		FRANCHISEES	115	206	300	400
FRANCHISED: 1962	LOCATED: IN U.S.		111	192	284	380
START-UP		OUTSIDE U.S.	10	21	25	32
INVESTMENT:	TOTAL:		121	213	309	412
$5,000–$200,000	NO. OF STATES W/ UNITS		50	50	50	50

THE BUSINESS

The Lindal cedar home is a contemporary post-and-beam cedar home suitable for upscale, affluent communities across the United States and Canada. The company claims that its chief competition comes from local custom builders, but Lindal offers the home buyer the same, if not more, design latitude than custom builders. Also, few builders have access to the select-grade custom cedar that Lindal's sawmill produces. The largest manufacturer of cedar homes, Lindal is a publicly held company, registered on the NASDAQ Stock Exchange.

In 1983, Lindal bought key assets of the Justus company and now offers solid-cedar log homes under the Justus name. A compact Lindal home can be shipped easily and economically from the factory to any location. Packaging where the trees grow is one of Lindal's selling points, as is the fact that the company uses Western red cedar. In 1985 the company's franchises grossed $16 million, with average sales per unit of $81,000 and an average net income of $20,000. Lindal offers not only a comprehensive warranty to customers for ordering, completion, and quality of the work but also a ten-year warranty plan covering structural integrity of the homes.

WHAT IT TAKES

When you join the Lindal team, your franchise agreement will be valid for one year, renewable yearly. Since 1983, Lindal has not charged a franchise fee, but your total investment will range from $5,000 to $200,000, depending on how many model homes you install on your site. You must have at least $5,000 in cash and arrange any financing you may need for the remaining amount. The minimum investment is for a dealer who sets up a model home as an office and also lives in it or who sets up a storefront office rather than a model home. You may be an owner-investor of a Lindal distributorship, but the company prefers that you be actively involved. No prior home-selling experience is required.

GETTING STARTED

The company will assist you with site selection, lease or purchase negotiations, construction, facility layout and decoration, lease or purchase of furniture and fixtures, and acquisition of supplies and merchandise. The typical distributorship is a 1,700-square-foot model home located near a freeway or shopping center. You will be required to use the company logo.

Your staff will consist of two full-time and two part-time employees, and the company will make suggestions on hiring. Your training will be conducted in Seattle with four days of classroom instruction covering pricing, engineering, selling, home financing, design, and advertising. In addition, you will tour the factory to see the manufacturing process. You can be selling houses six months after you buy the franchise, and the company will help with your grand opening.

MAKING IT WORK Sales literature is an important facet of Lindal's program. All new distributors receive a distributor kit tailored to fit either a Lindal or Justus business opportunity. The kit contains a starting inventory of essential four-color sales literature: planbooks, sun-room brochures, price lists, specification sheets, giveaways for home shows, magazine reprints, and so forth. A marketing manual contains reference materials on national advertising, local advertising, promotions, radio and television advertising, audiovisual aids, sales training, financial presentations, logos and art, merchandising aids, and letterhead. The kits also includes a point-of-sale display unit, which is a mock-up of the components of the building system—displaying floor, wall, and roof sections—for either Lindal or Justus.

Co-op advertising funds are offered for telephone-book ads, newspaper ads, black-and-white and four-color magazine ads, and television and radio commercials. The company conducts extensive national advertising and offers telemarketing services to follow up on new prospects. You will have a chance to meet other Lindal and Justus distributors at an annual national convention, regional conferences twice a year, and one-day seminars once a year. On-site training is conducted bimonthly. Lindal publishes a weekly company magazine, periodic newsletters, and biweekly product updates. The company distributes franchisee surveys semiannually and recognizes outstanding franchisees.

Lindal offers headquarters and regional resource persons, a toll-free hotline, regular on-site visits, on-site troubleshooting, policy and customer-service manuals, and order and accounting forms. Lindal's chairman, an inventor with thirteen U.S. patents, supervises research and development efforts for products and sales promotion. Utilizing a centralized merchandising system, Lindal divisions produce and distribute the products you will need; you must sell only company products.

COMMENTS Lindal Cedar Homes, Inc. has received a $26,000 HUD award for innovations in housing and many advertising awards, including thirteen for their planbooks and publications. Individual franchises have

high resale value. The company wants to add distributors throughout the world, except in Iron Curtain countries.

GETTING MORE INFORMATION

The franchise information packet contains extensive company literature, including a booklet on the company's homes, another booklet on franchise operations, a copy of the latest annual report, and
sales brochures. For details, contact:

Sir Walter Lindal
Chairman
Lindal Cedar Homes, Inc.
P.O. Box 24426
Seattle, WA   98124
(206)   725–0900 (call collect)

Little Professor Book Centers

BUSINESS: full-
service community
bookstore
FOUNDED: 1969
FRANCHISED: 1969
START-UP
INVESTMENT:
$76,000

NO. OF UNITS		AS OF		PROJECTED BY	
		1/1/85	1/1/86	1/1/87	1/1/88
OWNED BY: COMPANY		1	1	1	1
FRANCHISEES		75	93	115	145
LOCATED: IN U.S.		76	94	116	146
OUTSIDE U.S.		0	0	0	0
TOTAL:		76	94	116	146
NO. OF STATES W/ UNITS		· 32	32	33	36

THE BUSINESS

Recent surveys indicate that half of the adult U.S. population averaged two bookstore visits per month during the past six months,
and during the past year, one-third of all adults purchased books as
gifts. "Heavy" book readers fall between the ages of twenty-one and
forty-nine and are primarily white females. Book buyers as a whole
tend to be well educated, busy, and willing to spend discretionary
income on reading materials. Other purchases do not limit their
book buying.

Little Professor Book Centers reported a total annual dollar volume for all franchise operations of $27 million in 1985, and individ-
ual units had an average gross income of $340,000 and average net
income of $36,000. The company is the largest franchise bookstore
chain in the country.

WHAT IT TAKES

You will need $15,000 for the initial franchise fee to buy an exclusive
territory, determined by general market requirements. Your agreement will be valid for fifteen years and renewable for two ten-year
options. Your total investment will be about $76,000, with $35,000
of that required in cash. The amount beyond your franchise fee will
go for your initial inventory ($30,600); equipment and furnishings

($21,000); and leasehold improvements and other opening expenses, including cash register, freight, outdoor signs, and carpeting ($9,400). The company offers advice in applying for financial assistance.

Additional franchise units may be purchased for $3,000 each; master franchises are not available. The company permits individuals to be owner-investors but discourages the practice. You will pay an ongoing royalty fee of 2.75 percent of sales, minus sales tax, and the company will require you to spend a minimum of 2 percent of your annual gross sales for advertising and sales promotion each year. The company plans to begin collecting 1 percent of franchisees' annual gross sales for use in regional and national advertising programs. Currently, franchisees pay a fifteen-dollar monthly fee to the home office for advertising and promotional sales materials that the company supplies. Prior experience in bookselling is not necessary.

GETTING STARTED

Little Professor Book Centers will guide you with site selection, lease or purchase negotiation, facility layout and decoration, acquisition of all merchandise and fixtures, and staff hiring. In addition to yourself, you will need one or two part-time employees. A typical Little Professor store requires 1,600 square feet and is located in a mall, shopping center, or central business district. You will be expected to meet broadly defined standards for layout, fixtures, and merchandise mix.

The company store in Ann Arbor, Michigan, will be the location for your five days of initial training in daily operations, financial management, marketing, merchandising, personnel management, and salesmanship. When you open, company training will continue for four days in your store. You can be open within two months after purchasing the franchise, and you'll receive company assistance at your grand opening.

MAKING IT WORK

In return for your initial advertising fee you'll receive newspaper and black-and-white magazine ads, telephone-book ads, brochures, mailers, catalogs, television and radio commercials, point-of-purchase displays, signs, banners, seasonal promotional materials, and press releases. The confidential operating manual contains tips on public relations.

Annual national conventions are supplemented by two-day seminars twice a year; annual on-site training; monthly operational consultation; and monthly, bimonthly, and weekly publications. Recognition programs honor stores with the largest sales increases. Administrative aids include headquarters resource persons; a toll-free hotline; on-site troubleshooting; manuals on management procedure, policy, and customer service; forms for inventory, personnel, orders, and accounting; and systems for bookkeeping, inventory, and expense analysis.

Divisions of Little Professor produce or distribute equipment and supplies, and central purchasing offers volume discounts. Franchisees are not required to sell company products only, but Little Professor reserves the right to approve all products sold. The company has a primary-supplier relationship (not fiduciary) with the Ingram Book Company. Little Professor Book Centers encourages franchisees to investigate their local markets before introducing other products such as greeting cards, audio cassettes, and maps.

COMMENTS

Entrepreneur magazine ranked Little Professor Book Centers 202nd in its 1987 "Franchise 500." A division of Retail Techniques, Inc., and a member of the IFA, the company provides an earnings claim document upon request as well as a complete list of existing franchises. The company sponsors a national scholarship award program for high school seniors. Little Professor Book Centers is looking for franchisees in most states.

GETTING MORE INFORMATION

The franchise information packet contains a comprehensive brochure on bookselling and Little Professor's operations, plus a single-page application form. For more information, write or call:
Carla Garbin
Senior Vice-President
Little Professor Book Centers, Inc.
110 North Fourth Avenue
Ann Arbor, MI   48104
(800)   521–6232 or (313)   994–1212 (call collect)

Long John Silver's Seafood Shoppes

		AS OF		PROJECTED BY	
BUSINESS: fast-food	NO. OF UNITS	1/1/85	1/1/86	1/1/87	1/1/88
seafood restaurant					
FOUNDED: 1969	OWNED BY: COMPANY	818	831	860	900
FRANCHISED: 1970	FRANCHISEES	541	538	553	575
START-UP	LOCATED: IN U.S.	1,352	1,361	1,405	1,467
INVESTMENT:	OUTSIDE U.S.	7	8	8	8
$455,000–$705,000	TOTAL:	1,359	1,369	1,413	1,475
	NO. OF STATES W/ UNITS	37	37	37	37

THE BUSINESS

Nutritionists are finding new evidence to support their claim that fish is part of a healthy diet. At the forefront of fast-food preparation of seafood, Long John Silver's is currently updating and improving its image to maintain its position. The restaurants, decorated in informal, nautical style, offer a range of tempura-battered fish plus such entrees as chicken nuggets, seafood salads, and broiled fish.

Both eat-in and take-out options are offered. Franchisees currently operate about 40 percent of the Long John Silver's Seafood Shoppes. Total revenues for all franchise operations in 1985 were $246.7 million.

WHAT IT TAKES

The franchise fee is $15,000 and you must have a $300,000 minimum net worth to qualify. Start-up costs, including the franchise fee, will be about $75,000, plus the cost of real estate and equipment ($380,000 to $630,000). Single-unit franchises are available, but the company prefers for franchisees to establish multiple units. Additional units also cost $15,000 each; master franchises are not available. You may be an owner-investor if you have food-service experience. Long John Silver's requires that you have adequate capital and supporting financial statements for rapid, well-planned market development; a knowledge of retailing, preferably in food service; excellent personal and business references; and enthusiasm for the company's franchising philosophy. You'll receive an exclusive territory valid for twenty-five years for locations you own, or concurrent with the lease for a maximum of twenty-five years for leased locations. The company charges an ongoing royalty fee of 4 percent per month of gross sales.

GETTING STARTED

In return for your franchise fee, Long John Silver's will provide assistance with site selection, construction, and facility layout. The company charges, however, for assistance with facility decoration; lease or purchase of furniture and fixtures; and acquisition of equipment, materials, supplies, and merchandise. A typical Long John Silver's restaurant has 2,650 square feet and sits on 25,000 to 30,000 square feet of property located in either an office building, a mall, a shopping center, or a freestanding building.

You will need fifteen full-time and five part-time employees. In the rigorous training program you will spend several weeks working in a Long John Silver's Shoppe, then go to Lexington, Kentucky, for additional training. The length of study time varies according to position; managerial, hourly, and supervisory employees all receive training covering guest awareness, product preparation, food and plate preparation, administration, opening and closing procedures, and food ordering. With this intensive training plus construction time, you should plan on six to twelve months between purchase of your franchise and your opening. The company will help with your grand opening for a fee.

MAKING IT WORK

The company provides newspaper ads, mailers, brochures, television and radio commercials, national media coverage, point-of-purchase displays, billboard posters, signs, banners for chainwide promotions, seasonal promotional materials, and manuals on public relations and marketing. You will pay 5 percent per month of gross sales for advertising, and the company offers coop advertising. National conventions are held every other year, regional managers' meetings annually, and special one- to two-day seminars as needed. Franchise owners also meet once a year to make recommendations to the company. Quarterly magazines, quality-assurance bulletins, quarterly TV market meetings, and in-shop customer comment cards provide additional input.

A "Train the Trainer" program helps supervisors be more effective leaders and communicators, and a supervisor's seminar trains multiunit managers. Long John Silver's is the first food-service company to receive accreditation from the American Council on Education for its management-training programs, enabling graduates to receive college credit. Each year the company gives various achievement awards to franchisees. Administrative aids include headquarters and regional resource persons, regular on-site visits; on-site troubleshooting; manuals on management procedure, policy, and customer service; forms for inventory, personnel, orders, and accounting; systems for bookkeeping, inventory, personnel, expense analysis and computerized management information.

Long John Silver's maintains departments for in-depth market and product-development research. Franchisees are not obligated to purchase or lease any product from the company except for the secret-formula batter mix that coats the fish and certain other menu items. The company does have an equipment subsidiary and a central purchasing system offering food, beverages, cleaning supplies, and paper goods.

COMMENTS

Entrepreneur magazine ranked Long John Silver's 47th among its "Franchise 500" for 1987. A charter member of the IFA, the company provides earnings claim documents to potential franchisees during personal interviews. Long John Silver's and its parent company, Jerrico, Inc., have singly and jointly supported various outstanding projects—endowing a chair in management information systems at the University of Kentucky College of Business, establishing the College of Hotel and Restaurant at Transylvania University, funding an educational foundation at the National Institute for the Foodservice Industry, and actively supporting the Junior Achievement of the Bluegrass program. The company is seeking additional franchises in twenty-six states and Canada.

GETTING MORE INFORMATION

The franchise information packet contains descriptions of all phases of the Long John Silver's operation, a copy of a recent article on the company's modernization program, a history of the parent company, Jerrico, Inc., and an eight-page financial application. For more information, write or call:

Eugene O. Getchell
Vice-President, Franchising
Long John Silver's Seafood Shoppes, Inc.
101 Jerrico Drive
P.O. Box 11988
Lexington, KY   40579
(606) 268–5371

MAACO Auto Painting & Bodyworks

BUSINESS: auto			AS OF		PROJECTED BY	
painting and body	NO. OF UNITS		1/1/85	1/1/86	1/1/87	1/1/88
repairs	OWNED BY: COMPANY		1	1	0	0
FOUNDED: 1972		FRANCHISEES	372	410	450	500
FRANCHISED: 1972	LOCATED: IN U.S.		358	385	420	465
START-UP		OUTSIDE U.S.	15	26	30	35
INVESTMENT:	TOTAL:		373	411	450	500
$134,920	NO. OF STATES W/ UNITS		39	39	41	41

THE BUSINESS

Anthony A. Martino, founder of MAACO, estimates that up to 80 percent of consumers are looking for high-quality, medium-priced car-painting services. MAACO shops cater to a broad middle market, though some franchisees offer custom painting as well. In 1985, the total dollar volume for all MAACO franchises was $200,000,000, and the average gross sales for each shop were $537,000. Almost 30 percent of that business was generated by used-car fleets. A new specialty market has been created by the car manufacturers' introduction of the popular new unibodies—vehicles designed for economy and fuel efficiency. Eighty-five percent of all cars manufactured in 1985 incorporated the unibody design, spinning off a $20 billion repair market. Most MAACO shops have been equipped and trained to service unibody collision damage.

MAACO is Martino's second franchise business. The first was the highly successful AAMCO (the acronyms AAMCO and MAACO came from his initials). AAMCO, created twenty years ago, is the most successful transmission-repair chain ever founded. Martino predicts that, as unibody-repair experts, the MAACO chain of the future may become bigger than AAMCO and MAACO combined today.

WHAT IT TAKES

Your initial franchise fee will be $15,000. You must be actively involved in running your first shop. Your fee will buy the business, but not a territory, for a fifteen-year term, renewable for five-year periods. Your total initial investment, including the franchise fee, will be $134,920; and if you can pay $45,000 in cash, MAACO will help you secure financing for the remainder. You can buy additional franchises for $13,000 each. MAACO charges a royalty fee of 9 percent of gross receipts. Most MAACO owners—four out of five—have no previous experience in the car-painting business.

GETTING STARTED

You can open your MAACO shop within eight to twelve months after purchasing your franchise. Personnel from headquarters in King of Prussia, Pennsylvania, will guide your choice of a location for your 7,000 to 10,000-square-foot shop, probably in a freestanding building in the commercial area of town or in an auto mall that clusters together various independent automobile-service businesses. MAACO will also advise you on lease or purchase of your building; construction and layout; and purchase of furniture, fixtures, and the necessary specialized painting equipment, which MAACO staff will help install if you buy it from the company. In addition, MAACO will help you select and purchase your initial paint inventory and other supplies, arrange service and maintenance contracts with outside companies, and hire your eight-member staff.

You and your staff will be trained by MAACO. As owner, you'll spend an entire month at corporate headquarters, where training will be both in the classroom and in the shop prototype. You'll get a technical overview of body works, a review of shop procedures, and guidance in setting management and sales objectives. Then you or your manager will spend another week in the corporation's management-training system. Company representatives will train your crew at your shop during your first two weeks and support you with any operational assistance you may need to get started.

MAKING IT WORK

For your ongoing advertising fee of $500 a week, you'll get national exposure in television and radio commercials; newspaper, billboard, and telephone-book ads; press packages to distribute to the local media; and a manual on advertising, selling, and marketing techniques and customer relations. A headquarters or regional support team will make regular onsite visits plus troubleshooting visits as needed. You'll have access, too, to a toll-free hotline; a systems-and-procedures manual covering all aspects of a MAACO operation; inventory, personnel, and ordering forms; and an accounting system.

If you find your staff needs specialized information, company personnel will conduct training at your shop, and MAACO will send you a newsletter and a monthly magazine. The company sponsors annual regional and national conferences and gives awards for outstanding performance in public and community relations as well as sales and quality control. MAACO continually tests and develops new paints, equipment, and methods of production. You'll benefit from the company's bulk purchases of paint and supplies, although you can purchase from any outside source that meets industry standards.

COMMENTS

A subsidiary of MAACO Enterprises, Inc., and a member of the IFA since 1981, MAACO was ranked ninetieth in *Entrepreneur* magazine's 1987 "Franchise 500" and has won awards from the auto-painting industry and the Better Business Bureau. The company is seeking franchises in several southern and western states.

GETTING MORE INFORMATION

The franchise information packet consists of two photocopied sheets of information and a franchise-magazine reprint. For more information, contact:
Barbara Starr
Franchise Sales Coordinator
MAACO Auto Painting & Bodyworks
381 Brooks Road
King of Prussia, PA   19406
(800)   523–1180 or (215)   265–6606   (call collect)

The Maids International

		AS OF		PROJECTED BY	
BUSINESS: residential cleaning services	NO. OF UNITS	1/1/85	1/1/86	1/1/87	1/1/88
FOUNDED: 1979	OWNED BY: COMPANY	20	11	10	10
FRANCHISED: 1981	FRANCHISEES	123	154	190	290
START-UP	LOCATED: IN U.S.	140	160	190	280
INVESTMENT:	OUTSIDE U.S.	3	5	10	20
$30,000–$35,000	TOTAL:	143	165	200	300
	NO. OF STATES W/ UNITS	29	31	35	40

THE BUSINESS

In 1982, annual sales of home cleaning services reached $7.6 billion—up $1.2 billion in only six years—and those figures have continued to climb. With more wives working outside the home and more families headed by single parents, maid service is turning from a luxury into a necessity. A recent study made by the Washington-based Naisbitt Group predicts that between 1985 and 1990 the home-services industry will have a 20 percent annual growth rate—surpassed only by the recreational and entertainment industry. Recognizing that trend, a group of six businessmen with many years of experience in building maintenance and cleaning products put together in 1979 The Maids International, a cleaning service organized solely around the requirements for residential cleaning. By 1985 the company was producing over $800,000 in gross franchise revenues.

WHAT IT TAKES

You'll need $11,500 to buy your franchise; another $3,500 for the company's equipment package—enough uniforms, vacuum cleaners, shampooers, dusters, and cleaning chemicals to outfit two full cleaning teams; and an additional $15,000 to $20,000 to cover such start-up expenses as advertising, car leases, insurance and bonding, office supplies, telephone, legal and accounting services, and training expenses. You can purchase additional franchises for a fee of $7,500 each. The Maids also has an area-development option, which allows you to buy the rights to a larger market territory and set up multiple operations at a reduced fee per operation. Whether you choose one operation or many, you'll buy a carefully selected, exclusive territory custom tailored to match a demographic study of the kinds of households and levels of income in your business area.

You'll pay an ongoing royalty fee based upon your weekly gross earnings. The fee operates on a sliding scale—7 percent for gross sales up to about $3,800, then 6 percent from $3,800 to $7,700 gross sales, and 5 percent for weekly gross sales above $7,700. You'll also pay a regular advertising fee of 2 percent of your weekly gross sales.

GETTING STARTED

Since you'll be taking services to your customers, you'll need only 400 to 700 square feet of office and storage space, typically in an industrial or commercial park but also possibly in a shopping strip. The company will help you find the best location and will provide all of the initial equipment and supplies you'll need. The Maids has arranged a fleet-leasing program with Ford Motor Company to supply you with the yellow and green station wagons your cleaning crews will use. The arrangements with the manufacturer are direct, but you'll be serviced by a local dealer. The company has also arranged business-computer leasing with a number of different manufacturers.

Besides knowing how to clean everything from bathrooms to balustrades quickly, thoroughly, and safely, you'll have to be able to run a complex business operation. You'll train from eight to eleven weeks on both the technical and administrative sides of your operation. Six weeks of counseling will prepare you, your managers, and your technical supervisors for an intensive six-day course covering accounting, pricing, scheduling, advertising, and hiring—plus efficient cleaning in all sorts of situations. When you get home, the company will follow up with another one to three weeks of consultation.

The Maids will provide materials you can use to train your employees. With videotapes and technical manuals you'll be able to show your cleaning teams not only how to make bathrooms and kitchens sparkle but also how to handle such special projects as cleaning up after parties. Other audiovisual training aids will help you promote sales by improving your telephone sales techniques and teaching you how to market to apartment complexes and home builders.

MAKING IT WORK

The Maids will keep you well supplied with advertising and promotional materials—from special start-up and seasonal promotionals to ongoing advertising campaigns. You'll get direct-mail brochures; ad slicks for newspapers, magazines, and telephone books; billboard posters and signs; and radio and TV commercials. Through a cooperative advertising program the company pays production costs on approved outdoor advertising, and The Maids has lighted portable displays you can use at local home shows and exhibits. You'll receive a monthly newsletter plus regular technical bulletins and updates. The company hosts an annual convention and semiannual regional conferences, with both technical seminars and informal idea sharing.

The company's computerized management information system will help you keep track of such aspects of your business as the percentage of your money that goes into labor, supplies, or auto expenses. You'll be able to develop job estimates and work schedules, calculate employee hours and payroll, and prepare income and tax reports. In addition, The Maids sponsors a complete business insurance package, including property, general-liability, automobile, worker's compensation, life, major-medical, and dental insurance coverage. You can also arrange for third-party bonding of your employees through this package.

The Maids has a toll-free hotline; and if you have an emergency, a trained manager or technical supervisor will come to your site within seventy-two hours. Also, field representatives will visit your location on a regular basis to see how things are going. When you need to order cleaning supplies and add to your equipment inventory, you'll save money and guarantee high quality by ordering through The Maids distribution system, with seven regionally located warehouses.

COMMENTS

The Maids was ranked 81st in *Venture* magazine's 1986 "Franchise 100" and 193rd in *Entrepreneur* magazine's 1987 "Franchise 500." A member of the IFA since 1985, the company is seeking franchisees throughout the United States and in Australia and Canada.

GETTING MORE INFORMATION

The franchise information packet contains a brochure with extensive information about corporate personnel and services, a sample copy of the company newsletter, reprints of articles, and a franchise application form asking for your personal, business, and financial history. For more information, contact:

Rebecca Bishop
Director of Marketing
The Maids International, Inc.
5015 Underwood Avenue
Omaha, NE   68132
(800)   THE–MAID or (402)   558–8797

Mail Boxes Etc. USA

BUSINESS: mailbox			AS OF		PROJECTED BY	
rental/postal services	NO. OF UNITS		1/1/85	1/1/86	1/1/87	1/1/88
FOUNDED: 1980	OWNED BY: COMPANY		0	0	1	4
FRANCHISED: 1981		FRANCHISEES	145	241	416	661
START-UP	LOCATED: IN U.S.		145	241	417	665
INVESTMENT:		OUTSIDE U.S.	0	0	0	0
$46,000–$73,000	TOTAL:		145	241	417	665
	NO. OF STATES W/ UNITS		21	32	43	50

THE BUSINESS

Mail Boxes Etc. (MBE) began as a mailbox-rental operation offering customers the prestige of a street address and suite number. The company has evolved into a service-center operation offering a broad range of postal, business, and communications services. MBE centers are full-service postal operations with twenty-four-hour access; call-in mail-status service; mail receiving, forwarding, and posting services; packaging services; and receiving and distributing services for express-delivery companies like United Parcel Service and Federal Express. MBE centers also offer a wide range of business and communications services—from word processing and photocopying to telephone answering. The centers also offer telegram, telex, and facsimile transmission; sell stamps, envelopes, packing materials, and other postal and business supplies and perform various convenience services, like making passport photos, processing film, making keys, and wiring flowers. The average annual gross sales per franchise unit total about $110,000. Of all the MBE franchises that have opened since 1981, 98 percent remain in operation today.

WHAT IT TAKES

Your franchise fee for an individual operation will be $15,000, and the agreement will give you an exclusive territory for ten years, renewable for another ten years. Additional units cost from $10,000 to $12,500, and MBE offers master franchises. With a master franchise you could subfranchise MBE centers in your region and collect your cut of the individual franchise fees and the ongoing franchise royalties (7 percent of gross revenue). The cost of your area franchise will depend on the size of your territory.

Beyond the franchise fee, your approximate start-up costs for opening an individual center will include the following: $21,000 for leasehold improvements, including an optional 10 percent construction-management fee paid to MBE or an area franchisee; $6,000 for equipment and supplies; $3,000 for deposits; $3,000 for prepaid business expenses like insurance, equipment rental, and fees; $4,000 for grand-opening promotions; and $8,000 for a cash reserve. These figures represent averages, so your total initial investment, including your franchise fee, could range from about $46,000 to about $73,000. The company offers financing for from $30,000 to $50,000 of these start-up costs.

GETTING STARTED

The basic Mail Boxes Etc. center has 800 to 1,200 square feet—enough room for 250 mailboxes plus the office-supply, secretarial, communications, and photocopy operations. MBE offers not only facility-selection and construction assistance but also a standard prefabricated construction design and graphics package. You'll also have the option of getting all your equipment and start-up supplies from the company, and MBE will help you establish your accounts with service companies like Western Union and Purolator Courier.

While your center is under construction, you (and/or your manager, if you're not going to run the operation yourself) will attend the company's intensive two-week training program, which covers every aspect of MBE-center operation. You'll also get a comprehensive step-by-step operations manual, which the company will update regularly. When you are ready to open, the company will give you a grand-opening promotional package, including advertising and marketing materials.

MAKING IT WORK

Two percent of your ongoing royalty fee will be earmarked for advertising support. MBE has an in-house advertising/public-relations agency that will supply you with everything from flyers and brochures to commercials and print ads. If there are other MBE centers in your city, you can form advertising coalitions to get the most value from these materials. The company sponsors an annual national conference, quarterly regional conferences, and monthly areawide franchise meetings. You'll receive quarterly newsletters, weekly updates on new MBE concepts, and regular product and service updates.

In addition to the headquarters resource persons, you'll be able to call on regional personnel, who will make both regular on-site visits and troubleshooting visits as needed. If any problem comes up, you'll be able to reach the company on their twenty-four-hour business hotline. Because the company purchases equipment and supplies in volume, it can pass along these savings to you. You may offer other products that meet the company's quality standards. You'll also receive practical financial-data forms and convenient order forms.

COMMENTS

MBE was ranked forty-sixth in *Venture* magazine's 1986 "Franchise 100" and ninety-ninth in *Entrepreneur* magazine's 1987 "Franchise 500." A member of the IFA, the company is seeking franchisees in almost all parts of the United States but not in other countries.

GETTING MORE INFORMATION

The franchise information packet has a brochure with color photographs showing various parts of an MBE center in operation; information about the advantages of an MBE franchise; clips from several articles about franchising and MBE franchisees; a detailed, itemized breakdown of estimated start-up costs; a general application form asking for information about your personal, business, and financial background; and a separate detailed personal financial statement. For details, write to:

Tony DeSio
President and Chief Executive Officer
Mail Boxes Etc. USA
7690 El Camino Real, Suite 206
Carlsbad, CA   92008
(619) 452–1553

Management Recruiters International

		AS OF		PROJECTED BY	
BUSINESS: executive search and placement firm	**NO. OF UNITS**	1/1/85	1/1/86	1/1/87	1/1/88
	OWNED BY: COMPANY	40	40	42	44
FOUNDED: 1957	FRANCHISEES	356	380	393	406
FRANCHISED: 1965	LOCATED: IN U.S.	395	419	434	449
START-UP	OUTSIDE U.S.	1	1	1	1
INVESTMENT:	TOTAL:	396	420	435	450
$30,000–$50,000	NO. OF STATES W/ UNITS	48	48	48	48

THE BUSINESS

The personnel-placement business has changed dramatically since it began shortly after World War II. Rather than dealing primarily with people who are out of work, Management Recruiters International (MRI) specializes in locating and recruiting those who already have jobs and have proven their abilities. Candidates do not pay a fee; all fees are assumed by the employer clients. MRI is the world's largest search firm, with gross billings exceeding $150 million per annum (ten years ago revenues were $35 million). The company has over 400 offices in the United States, employing more than 2,500 account executives. Approximately 10 percent of the offices are company owned, and the balance are franchised. MRI has two major operating divisions: Management Recruiters (approximately 300 offices), and Sales Consultants (about 100 offices) which is the only national network of its size specializing in the sales field. There are separate divisions for clerical (Office Mates 5) and data-processing (CompuSearch) personnel. In 1985, MRI franchises grossed $120 million, with average gross sales per unit of $300,000 and average net income of $100,000.

WHAT IT TAKES

Your franchise fee of $16,000 to $25,000 will cover an exclusive territory determined using the latest issue of Sales and Marketing Management Survey of Buying Power. The agreement holds for at least five years, and renewal is not necessary. Your total initial investment will be from $30,000 to $50,000, with the franchise fee required in cash. MRI offers no financial assistance. The fee for additional units is negotiable, but master franchises are not available. You must operate the business if you buy an MRI franchise. The company charges an ongoing royalty fee of 5 percent of gross revenues plus 0.5 percent for advertising. No experience in the field is necessary.

GETTING STARTED

MRI will assist you in obtaining necessary state and local licenses, securing office space and negotiating the lease, planning the layout and design of your office, selecting and purchasing office furniture and equipment, selecting your telephone system, and contracting for newspaper advertising rates and terms. The typical MRI office has 800 square feet and is located in an office building, a freestanding building, or a commercial industrial park.

You will need one part-time and three full-time employees, whom MRI will help recruit, hire, and train. You will attend three weeks of training at the corporate offices for hands-on and video sessions, followed by five weeks with your employees in your office. You will study all facets of candidate recruitment, office management, and formulation of an advertising program. You can expect to be open for business within six weeks after purchasing your franchise. MRI will help you seek employer clients when you are ready to open.

MAKING IT WORK

MRI provides a complete file of advertising layouts, mailing pieces, and promotional materials. The company also offers co-op advertising funds. You'll receive a personalized public-relations program that includes contact lists of reporters and editors in your local media market, brochures, presentation books, mailers, catalogs, in-house media packages (slides, videotapes), national media coverage, a lead-referral system, and incentives.

MRI sponsors biannual national conventions and regional conferences, as well as regular areawide franchise meetings. The company will offer frequent seminars and intensive on-site training during your first year of operation, and you will receive a VHS videocassette recorder, a television, and twenty-two videocassettes on various facets of the business to review in your office. MRI distributes a monthly magazine; a weekly newsletter; updates on services, company information, and the market; and a customer-oriented magazine. Each year the company offers awards in numerous categories to franchisees and their employees.

Administrative backup includes headquarters and regional resource persons; a toll-free hotline; regular onsite visits and onsite troubleshooting; manuals on policy, management procedure, and customer service; forms for inventory, personnel, and accounting; and systems for bookkeeping, personnel, expense analysis, computerized management information, and computerized billing. You can get a volume discount for printing and operating forms by ordering through the MRI printers, although you can use noncompany suppliers. Company-sponsored insurance programs offer life, major-medical, and disability coverage.

COMMENTS

A division of CDI Corporation and a member of the IFA, MRI was ranked 118th in *Entrepreneur* magazine's 1987 "Franchise 500." MRI provides an earnings claim document during a potential franchisee's personal interview. The company has won numerous business awards. MRI wants to develop new franchises throughout the United States.

GETTING MORE INFORMATION

The franchise information packet contains brochures on the company's operations, principal officers, and award winners; an IFA brochure titled "Investigate before Investing"; samples of dozens of MRI ads run in publications such as the *Wall Street Journal;* brochures from each division; and a directory of MRI offices. For details, contact:

Douglas Bugie
Director, Franchise Advertising
Management Recruiters International
1127 Euclid Avenue, Suite 1400
Cleveland, OH   44115
(800)   321–2309

Mazzio's Pizza

		AS OF		PROJECTED BY	
BUSINESS: pizza restaurant	NO. OF UNITS	1/1/85	1/1/86	1/1/87	1/1/88
FOUNDED: 1963	OWNED BY: COMPANY	40	48	53	58
FRANCHISED: 1979	FRANCHISEES	66	90	99	109
START-UP	LOCATED: IN U.S.	106	138	152	167
INVESTMENT:	OUTSIDE U.S.	0	0	0	0
$243,000–$1,062,000	TOTAL:	106	138	152	167
	NO. OF STATES W/ UNITS	13	13	18	22

THE BUSINESS

Mazzio's pizzas have been called untraditional because they contain higher-quality ingredients and more meat and cheese than many other pizzas, and the company emphasizes the nutritional value of its pizzas. Mazzio's Pizza has set trends by introducing new pizzas like taco and barbecue. Within the rapidly growing fast-food industry, pizza leads all types of food in sales, unit growth, and share gains of food dollars spent outside the home. In 1985 the total volume of franchise business for Mazzio's Pizza reached $25 million.

WHAT IT TAKES

The initial franchise fee is $20,000. The same amount applies for additional franchise units, and many franchisees who started with one unit are now multiple-unit owners. Approved owner-investors may take advantage of a multiple-unit exclusive license agreement. However, Mazzio's Pizza has the discretionary right to grant additional franchises, and one condition for your opening more franchises would be satisfactory operation of your existing units. Each case is decided individually.

The initial fee will allow you to be a Mazzio's Pizza franchise owner for twenty years. If at some point you want to sell your franchise, the company retains the first right of refusal and the right to review and approve the purchaser. You may be a passive owner, but Mazzio's Pizza encourages you to be active in the operation and administration of your restaurant. Although helpful, prior restaurant training and experience are not necessary.

If you construct your restaurant, your total initial investment will be approximately $468,000 to $1,062,000. In addition to the $20,000 franchise fee you'll pay approximately $125,000 to $250,000 for equipment and signs, $300,000 to $750,000 for real estate and leasehold improvements, $8,000 to $17,000 for inventory, and $15,000 to $25,000 for working capital. If you lease an existing building rather than constructing a new one, your investment will decrease by $225,000 to $500,000. You'll also pay an ongoing royalty fee of 3 percent of sales, and 1 percent of that will go to an advertising cooperative.

GETTING STARTED

You will need approximately 3,000 square feet, either a freestanding building or a company in a shopping center. The company will help you find a suitable site and will guide you in planning for costs and building procedures. Your restaurant will have a distinctive logo and neon signs, an appealing interior, electronic games, and a twenty-four-item salad bar. Many restaurants also offer a drive-through service.

As soon as you've signed the agreement, service representatives will begin working with you on pricing structure, evaluation of competition, and marketing. You'll be sent to the company-owned restaurant in Tulsa, Oklahoma for a hands-on training program that lasts from one to three months and covers all aspects of basic restaurant management. You will also receive a complete instruction guide covering construction through opening and a detailed operations manual. Before you open, company representatives will look over your restaurant at least twice.

Depending on the size of your facility, you will need at least six full-time and as many as fifty part-time employees. Company representatives will conduct a five-day onsite training session for your employees and usually will stay at your restaurant through the third week of business to assure a smooth beginning.

MAKING IT WORK

Mazzio's Pizza sponsors annual national franchise meetings and seminars plus additional regional training seminars. It has a franchise service department and a quarterly magazine to tell you of company and industry news and trends. The company develops and tests many new menu items, and two independent research firms carry out special research projects.

You'll receive an operations manual covering product preparation, customer service, security procedures, administration, profitability, and personnel management. Your franchise package also includes bookkeeping, inventory, and personnel systems—with all the necessary forms—and a computerized management information system. A company-sponsored insurance package offers most forms of coverage.

Most franchisees take advantage of the in-house computer and the services of locally based independent suppliers who provide weekly distribution of food products, paper products, and operating supplies. You may use other product sources that the company has approved. Trained marketing and advertising personnel will assist you with marketing and advertising plans. Throughout the year you may purchase pre-packaged advertising campaigns that utilize television, radio, four-color-print, and newspaper ads. Encouraging experimentation and change in marketing approaches, Mazzio's Pizza has offered such promotions as a "Weekdays Are Free Days for Moms" deal. Another marketing incentive stimulates enthusiasm and participation by awarding a grand prize of a trip for two to the supervisor/manager who wins the most points. One Mazzio's Pizza restaurant worked a cooperative promotion with a local radio station to give away concert tickets.

COMMENTS

A member of the IFA since 1977, Mazzio's Pizza was ranked 198th in *Entrepreneur* magazine's 1987 "Franchise 500." The company which is a subsidiary of Ken's Restaurant Systems, Inc., makes available an earnings claim document prior to or during a potential franchisee's personal interview. Mazzio's Pizza wants to expand in the Southwest and Southeast.

GETTING MORE INFORMATION

The franchise information packet includes a KRS information booklet, a company magazine, a four-page brochure, a summary of a franchisee's estimated initial investment, and a guideline for franchisee application. For more information, contact:
Brad Williams
Senior Vice-President, Franchising
Mazzio's Pizza (KRS, Inc.)
4441 South 72 East Avenue
Tulsa, OK 74145
(918) 663–8880

McDonald's

		AS OF		PROJECTED BY	
NO. OF UNITS		1/1/85	1/1/86	1/1/87	1/1/88
OWNED BY: COMPANY		2,053	2,165	N/A	N/A
FRANCHISEES		6,251	6,736	N/A	N/A
LOCATED: IN U.S.		6,595	6,972	N/A	N/A
OUTSIDE U.S.		1,709	1,929	N/A	N/A
TOTAL:		8,304	8,901	N/A	N/A
NO. OF STATES W/ UNITS		50	50	N/A	N/A

BUSINESS: fast-food restaurant
FOUNDED: 1955
FRANCHISED: 1955
START-UP INVESTMENT: $62,680–$384,500

THE BUSINESS

Founded in 1955, McDonald's has become the largest food-service organization in the world.

WHAT IT TAKES

There are three ways you can acquire a McDonald's franchise: purchase a new restaurant business, purchase an existing business from the company, or purchase an existing business from the present franchisee. Your franchise agreement, which applies for twenty years, will allow you to operate a McDonald's facility and to use the company's trademarks and service marks; designs for restaurant decor; signs and equipment layout; formulas and specifications for menu items; and methods of operation, inventory control, bookkeeping, accounting, and marketing. In return, you must agree to operate your business in accordance with the standards set by the company. You'll pay an ongoing monthly fee based on your restaurant's sales performance (currently 3 percent of the monthly sales) plus a minimum monthly fee, or 8.5 percent of monthly sales, whichever is greater. McDonald's grants franchises only to individuals, not to corporations or partnerships. For your investment you will need to combine personal funds and loans from traditional sources, because McDonald's doesn't provide financing or loan guarantees, nor will it allow you to be an absentee investor.

There are two kinds of franchise agreements available. The costs and fees for the conventional franchise agreement would total $325,000 to $384,500. The breakdown of expenditures would be as follows:

ITEM	INITIAL COSTS
Initial fee earned by McDonald's at the time the restaurant is ready for occupancy. Paid to McDonald's.	$12,500
Interest-fee security deposit for acceptable operation of the franchise, refundable at the expiration of the franchise. Paid to McDonald's and subject to refund.	$15,000
Approximate cost of kitchen equipment, not including taxes, delivery, and installation. Paid to supplier.	$139,500–$145,000
Approximate cost of signs, not including taxes, delivery and installation. Paid to supplier.	$30,000
Approximate cost of seating and decor, not including taxes, delivery, and installation. Paid to supplier.	$35,000– $40,000
Approximate cost for taxes, delivery, and installation of the signs, equipment, seating, and decor. Amount varies depending on state and local taxes, distance, etc. Paid to supplier.	$23,000– $27,000
Approximate cost of cash-register system. Paid to supplier.	$20,000– $40,000

ITEM	INITIAL COSTS
Approximate cash requirements for miscellaneous equipment, franchisee's construction options, landscaping, operating cash, safe, first month's rent, training, preopening expenses, etc. Paid to supplier.	$50,000– $75,000
Total:	$325,000–$384,500

If you don't want to buy a conventional franchise, you might qualify for the business facilities lease program available to a limited number of potential franchisees who excel in their qualifications but are unable to meet the financial requirements. The costs of developing and equipping the restaurant are the same as for a conventional franchise. However, McDonald's will purchase the signs, equipment, and decor and lease them to you. The total investment of approximately $62,680 must be funded from nonborrowed personal resources.

Your costs to participate in the business facilities lease program would be as follows:

Initial Costs: The following costs will vary depending on individual circumstances.

$15,000—security deposit
 12,000—inventory
  3,380—first month's rent
  5,000—moving expense
  6,000—management training
  7,000—crew training
  4,500—uniforms
  3,600—preopening advertising
  5,000—landscaping
  1,200—operating supplies/miscellaneous equipment

Total: $62,680

Term: 3 years

Ongoing Fees: A monthly fee based upon the restaurants's sales performance (currently 3% of monthly sales) plus a minimum monthly fee, or 13% of monthly sales, whichever is greater.

Purchase Option: Available in the second and third years of the term (assuming full compliance with franchise).

Option Price: The higher of the following:
(a) $350,000
(b) a percentage of annual sales calculated as follows:

SALES VOLUME	PERCENT OF SALES
$999,999 or less	41
$1,000,000–$1,099,999	42
$1,100,000–$1,299,999	44
$1,300,000 and higher	46

plus

(c) the cost of any additional equipment or leasehold improvements purchased by McDonald's, leased to you, and installed after your restaurant has opened for business.

If you exercise your option, the franchise agreement for the business facilities lease applies for twenty years and your ongoing fees will be those in effect for a conventional franchise.

If after initial interviews with company representatives you are still interested in obtaining a franchise, you'll work in a McDonald's facility for fifty hours to give the company an opportunity to further evaluate you in the restaurant environment and to give you a closer look at McDonald's. As a McDonald's franchisee, you must be prepared to relocate. The company will try to honor your geographical preferences but cannot accept your request for a specific location or city. Site selection is based on an extensive evaluation by company real estate personnel.

GETTING STARTED   Once you and McDonald's agree to proceed, you'll enter a formal training program. Covering eighteen to twenty-four months, the training occurs on a part-time basis and involves several phases, most of which take place in a McDonald's restaurant convenient to your home. In addition, you'll take part in four formal classroom sessions of one to two weeks in duration; one of these takes place at the McDonald's Hamburger University. McDonald's will also provide you with seminars, conferences, one-on-one sessions with corporate personnel, and sophisticated audiovisual training.

After you successfully complete your first phase of training, which normally lasts about eight months, the company will register you and collect a $4,000 registration fee, which will be applied to your franchise fee. If for any reason you withdraw from the program or the company removes you, this fee will be refunded. McDonald's will formally offer the franchise to you only when you've completed the training. You'll pay the cost of your time and expenses during the training period, but the company will pay the cost of the training materials. All of your employees will also receive extensive training from the company through classroom courses, videotapes, and filmed and programmed training materials.

MAKING IT WORK

For ongoing support each region is staffed with field-service specialists. These resource persons will work directly with you not only with the opening of the restaurant but also on an ongoing basis, and they will visit your operation regularly. McDonald's will not sell food, paper products, equipment or other supplies to you, but it will help you get them elsewhere with discounts through high-volume purchasing. The corporation continually creates and tests new products for the restaurants.

Your advertising dollars will be pooled with those of other franchisees to promote the McDonald's system and image regionally and nationally. You'll be expected to become involved in your community's civic and charitable activities as part of the McDonald's philosophy that the company and its franchisees should contribute to the communities in which they do business.

COMMENTS

A member of the IFA, McDonald's was ranked second in *Venture* magazine's 1986 "Franchise 100" and fifth in *Entrepreneur* magazine's 1987 "Franchise 500." McDonald's provides an earnings claim document prior to a potential franchisee's personal interview. The company is seeking franchises in all states and most foreign countries, except Africa.

GETTING MORE INFORMATION

The franchise information packet includes a brochure outlining the general requirements for a prospective franchisee, a detailed breakdown of costs for both types of franchises, a list of regional licensing offices (you'll send your franchise application to the licensing office responsible for the region in which you live), and an application form requesting personal and detailed financial information and a history of your business experience.

For more information, contact:
Franchise Licensing
McDonald's
McDonald's Plaza
Oak Brook, IL   60521
(312)   575–6196

The Medicine Shoppe

		AS OF		PROJECTED BY	
BUSINESS: retail	NO. OF UNITS	1/1/85	1/1/86	1/1/87	1/1/88
pharmacy	OWNED BY: COMPANY	0	0	0	N/A
FOUNDED: 1970	FRANCHISEES	499	583	660	N/A
FRANCHISED: 1971	LOCATED: IN U.S.	499	583	660	N/A
START-UP	OUTSIDE U.S.	0	0	0	N/A
INVESTMENT:	TOTAL:	499	583	660	N/A
$65,000–$75,000	NO. OF STATES W/ UNITS	46	47	48	N/A

THE BUSINESS

As the nation's largest independent chain of prescription centers, The Medicine Shoppe has a goal of opening 1,000 new franchises before 1990. The company's approach is to put knowledgeable pharmacists into their own businesses. Medicine Shoppe stores are exceptionally compact prescription centers, but the number of prescriptions filled daily in the average Medicine Shoppe exceeds the national average for chains and independents. Ninety percent of Medicine Shoppe's business is prescriptions (not comic books, motor oil, or flashcubes). The rest includes over-the-counter drugs, vitamins, and health-related supplies. In 1985 the company's franchises grossed $230 million, with average gross sales per unit of $500,000. The company tries to combine the best aspects of both the old-fashioned pharmacist and today's sophisticated management techniques and systems.

WHAT IT TAKES

You will need $18,000 in cash for the initial franchise fee, with the agreement establishing an exclusive territory for twenty years, renewable for ten. Your total investment, including the franchise fee, will be $65,000 to $75,000. Shop conversions will require a smaller investment. The company provides direct financial assistance (and went public in 1983 to secure funds to do so). Additional units may be purchased, and you may be an owner-investor. Master franchises are not available. The Medicine Shoppe charges an ongoing royalty fee of 5 percent of sales and is considering adding an advertising royalty. Medicine Shoppe owners are generally pharmacists.

GETTING STARTED

You can expect assistance with site selection; lease or purchase negotiation; construction; facility layout and decoration; lease or purchase of furniture, fixtures, and equipment; and acquisition of supplies and merchandise. The company will help thoroughly evaluate the area in which you wish to locate. Opening inventory, fixtures, and equipment will be provided as part of your franchise fee. The typical Medicine Shoppe is 1,000 square feet, located in a shopping strip or freestanding building. You will be expected to make consistent use of trademarks, signs, and copyrights. The interior decor and layouts are directed and approved by the franchisor. Fixtures and furniture are available from the company, as are more than 200 private-label items.

Your staff will consist of one to two part-time employees in addition to the full-time owner/manager. You will receive one week of training in accounting, marketing, advertising, purchasing, customer relations, public relations, and daily operations at corporate headquarters in St. Louis. You will also learn to conduct a variety of health-care screening tests; achieve high inventory turnover; control overhead, salaries, and hours; and maximize profits and product margins.

It generally takes nine months to open a new Medicine Shoppe location. The company has developed a six-week grand-opening program to generate exposure for your new business. During this period, Medicine Shoppe's store-opening coordinator and district manager will help you detail doctor's offices and contact local companies and businesses.

MAKING IT WORK
The company's public-relations department will provide press releases, news articles, promotional programs, publicity in trade journals, and a public-relations/marketing manual. The company also creates newspaper ads, mailers, telephone-book ads, brochures, television and radio commercials, national media coverage, point-of-purchase displays, signs, banners, seasonal promotional materials, incentives, posters, shelf talkers, bag stuffers, and advertising manuals. Cooperative advertising funds are available.

The company holds national conventions plus yearly regional and district conferences, and semiannual areawide franchise meetings. The Medicine Shoppe publishes a newsletter every other month, as well as updates on products, service, company, and market information as needed. Two franchise owners from each region serve on an owner's advisory council. The sponsor of various award programs in sales, community relations, and public relations, the company has itself won awards for both advertising and public-relations health-awareness programs.

The company pays all developmental and production costs for the materials needed in screenings for colon-rectal cancer, diabetes, glaucoma, skin cancer, and hearing problems. Administrative backup services include headquarters resource persons; a toll-free hotline; regular onsite visits and troubleshooting; manuals on policy, management procedure, and customer service; forms for inventory, personnel, and accounting; and systems to handle bookkeeping, inventory, expense analysis, and computerized billing and management information. Medicine Shoppe has a research and development department, a division to distribute merchandise, and a central purchasing program offering volume discounts. You may sell both Medicine Shoppe's private-label brands and national ones.

COMMENTS

The Medicine Shoppe was ranked fifty-ninth in *Entrepreneur* magazine's 1987 "Franchise 500" and forty-third in *Venture* magazine's 1986 "Franchisor 100." A member of the IFA since 1975, the company provides an earnings claim document upon request. The Medicine Shoppe plans to expand throughout the United States.

GETTING MORE INFORMATION

The franchise information packet contains brochures describing the company's operations plus an article on current concepts in retail pharmacy management. For details, contact:

J. F. Atkinson
Vice-President, Marketing
The Medicine Shoppe
Medicine Shoppe International, Inc.
10121 Paget Drive
St. Louis, MO   63132
(800)   325–1397 or (314)   993–6000

Meineke Discount Mufflers

BUSINESS: repair and replacement of car exhaust systems, brakes, and shock absorbers
FOUNDED: 1972
FRANCHISED: 1972
START-UP INVESTMENT: $45,000

		AS OF		PROJECTED BY	
NO. OF UNITS		1/1/85	1/1/86	1/1/87	1/1/88
OWNED BY:	COMPANY	1	1	1	1
	FRANCHISEES	516	714	814	912
LOCATED:	IN U.S.	516	713	813	911
	OUTSIDE U.S.	1	2	2	2
TOTAL:		517	715	815	913
NO. OF STATES W/ UNITS		38	40	44	46

THE BUSINESS

With new-car sales dropping and people keeping their cars longer, the automotive aftermarket is more in demand. Specializing in mufflers has made it possible for Meineke to offer fast, low-cost, quality service to customers in this market. The company also offers services for and replacement of dual-exhaust systems, custom bending, shock absorbers, and brakes. The average Meineke shop open for over two years grosses $280,620 per year, and the total dollar volume for all shops in 1985 was $118 million in gross sales.

WHAT IT TAKES

To buy your first Meineke shop you'll need $22,500 for the initial franchise fee. A second shop is the same price, but after that the price is discounted 25 percent. Your franchise agreement will last for fifteen years, with a fifteen-year renewal period, and will guarantee a territory of 50,000 current motor-vehicle registrations. Total start-up expenses, including the franchise fee, will come to about

$45,000. The company wants cash for the full amount; however, Meineke will assist you in arranging financing with Allied Lending Corporation. Meineke requires that you manage the shop yourself, and no previous industry experience or knowledge is needed. You'll pay a royalty fee of 7 percent of gross sales plus an advertising fee of 12 percent.

GETTING STARTED

A Meineke shop usually requires about 2,500 square feet and can be located in a commercial center, shopping center, freestanding building, or even an old gas station that has been converted. The company will help you select the best site, offer advice on lease or purchase agreements, provide you with all the necessary supplies, arrange for you to get initial inventory, and help you with the shop's layout. If your shop needs construction, or if you need to lease or purchase a company vehicle, Meineke will make recommendations. You'll need three or four full-time employees, whom Meineke will help you select.

The in-depth training you'll receive covers marketing, management, operations, and technical procedures for installing exhaust systems and shock absorbers and for doing brake jobs. You'll spend one week in classroom training and two and a half weeks in hands-on training at the company's corporate training center. Then, after you've opened your shop you'll get one more week of on-the-job training.

Within approximately four to seven months after purchasing your franchise you'll be ready to begin business. Company representatives will be available to assist with your grand opening.

MAKING IT WORK

Your advertising fee will pay for a comprehensive advertising package. Meineke advertises in newspapers, magazines, telephone books, and mailers, as well as on radio and television. The company will provide you with free catalogs, point-of-purchase displays, and signs.

Meineke staff members will provide you and your employees with continuous onsite training whenever needed. You'll be constantly updated on improved marketing, operational, and technical operations by representatives as well as through meetings and seminars. The company holds an annual national conference, regional conventions three times a year, quarterly seminars, and periodic citywide meetings. The company newsletter will also keep you informed of company news and industry trends.

You won't be limited to selling Meineke products as long as the other products are approved by the company and meet their specifications. When you order merchandise, you can use the central merchandising system and get volume discounts through the central purchasing program. The company's unique inventory system will allow you to fill 98 percent of your orders from stock, and it allows you to adjust your stock each year to weed out obsolete parts.

Meineke's management personnel are available at all times for assistance and troubleshooting. You can consult your policy, procedure, and customer-service manuals or call the company's toll-free hotline whenever you have questions. You'll get a bookkeeping system, a computerized management information system, and forms for personnel and inventory. Meineke can arrange an insurance package for you and your employees with property, general-liabilty, major-medical, disability, and worker's compensation coverage available. The company continually explores ways to diversify Meineke's operations.

COMMENTS

A division of Parts Industries Corporation and a member of the IFA, Meineke was ranked twenty-sixth in *Entrepreneur* magazine's "Franchise 500" for 1987 and twenty-fourth in *Venture* magazine's 1986 "Franchise 100." The company is seeking new franchisees in most states and in Canada.

GETTING MORE INFORMATION

The franchisee information packet contains a brochure with photographs of Meineke shops, a list of dealers with their locations and phone numbers, a current data sheet listing average gross sales, and a qualification sheet. For more information, contact:

Ron Smythe
President
Meineke Discount Mufflers
128 South Tryon Street, Suite 900
Charlotte, NC   28202
(800)   231–9877 or (704)   377–8855

Merry Maids

BUSINESS: residential		AS OF		PROJECTED BY	
		1/1/85	1/1/86	1/1/87	1/1/88
cleaning service NO. OF UNITS					
FOUNDED: 1980 OWNED BY: COMPANY		1	1	1	1
FRANCHISED: 1980 FRANCHISEES		194	289	424	549
START-UP LOCATED: IN U.S.		195	290	425	550
INVESTMENT: OUTSIDE U.S.		0	0	0	0
$25,000–$30,000 TOTAL:		195	290	425	550
NO. OF STATES W/ UNITS		35	40	42	45

THE BUSINESS

In 1983, service franchises, such as housecleaning, grew twice as fast as traditional franchises and are predicted to continue their explosive growth. Merry Maids, one of the top six service franchises, is the largest company in the franchise residential-cleaning-service industry. In 1985 each Merry Maids franchise unit grossed an average of $200,000. Seventy-five percent of the new Merry Maids franchise owners have been referred to the company by a present owner.

WHAT IT TAKES

For a $25,000 to $30,000 cash investment, including your $15,500 franchise fee, you will obtain an exclusive territory encompassing the geographic boundaries of 30,000 to 40,000 households, applicable for five years and renewable in five-year periods thereafter. Additional territories can be purchased for $15,500 each, but the company prefers that you not be a passive owner. Seven percent of your gross sales must be returned to the company as a royalty fee. Merry Maids does not require its franchisees to have any prior experience in the housecleaning business.

GETTING STARTED

The company's research consultants will help you select a site and target a market, and other company personnel will help you negotiate the best lease agreement. Your facility could be located in a shopping center, an office building, a freestanding building, or a commercial or industrial center. You will want your Merry Maids office to have about 800 square feet with washer and dryer hookups.

Company staff will also help you set up and stock the office. You'll need an IBM computer to run the management software system and a television with a videocassette recorder to show the employees video training program. With the help of the company resource center, you'll stock the 250 cleaning-related products available to franchise owners. For your cleaning staff you'll get two sets of team equipment and the distinctive company uniforms. You will probably need two full-time and twenty part-time employees, whom you will hire with company assistance.

As a new Merry Maids franchise owner, you and/or your managers will get five days of training at corporate headquarters in Omaha, Nebraska. You'll learn about hiring, training, marketing, selling, and scheduling. Corporate personnel will also help you establish an individualized business plan, operating guidelines, and systems to increase profits. Your personnel should be cleaning homes within thirty days after you sign your franchise agreement. Company representatives will participate in your opening-day activities.

MAKING IT WORK

Merry Maids promotes its franchises through corporate advertising in national newspapers and magazines and develops materials you can use locally, either on your own or cooperatively. Merry Maids sponsors an annual national conference in Omaha, Nebraska, and makes awards for top sales. Four times a year Merry Maids holds meetings in each of its fourteen regions. The company's Buddy Program will match you, a new owner, with a nearby established franchise owner who can help during your crucial beginning months. Your regional coordinator—who is also a franchise owner—will visit regularly, and headquarters personnel will call you at least once a week.

Every month you'll get the company's newsletter, and your employees will receive a quarterly tabloid. You'll also have the company's policy, management-procedure, and customer-service manuals, which are updated yearly. The company-tested bookkeeping, inventory, personnel, and computerized billing systems—and the accompanying forms—all supplement the computerized management information system. You can save money by purchasing the company's chemicals and cleaning supplies, although you are free to buy equivalent items locally. The Merry Maids insurance package includes property, general-liability, automobile, life, major-medical, worker's compensation, and third-party-bonding coverage.

Expect innovative programs from the Merry Maids headquarters. The latest is a joint national marketing program with U-Haul International. Merry Maids cleans U-Haul's rental vans, and all U-Haul centers refer business to Merry Maids. Resort referral cards, free from the company, have been designed to thank resort customers and refer them to Merry Maids service when they get home. Other programs have been negotiated with Daybridge Learning Centers and Cardinal Industry's Condominium Hotels.

COMMENTS

Merry Maids was ranked ninety-fifth in *Entrepreneur* magazine's 1987 "Franchise 500." A member of the IFA since 1985, the company wants to increase franchise operations throughout the United States and in Canada and Japan.

GETTING MORE INFORMATION

The franchise information packet includes a brochure, a press release, article reprints, and sample newsletters. For details, write to:
Dale Peterson
Executive Vice-President
Merry Maids, Inc.
11117 Mill Valley Road
Omaha, NE 68154
(800) 345–5535 or (402) 498—0331

M.G.M. Liquor Warehouse

BUSINESS: retail
  liquor stores
FOUNDED: 1971
FRANCHISED: 1979
START-UP
  INVESTMENT:
  $210,000–$350,000

		AS OF		PROJECTED BY	
NO. OF UNITS		1/1/85	1/1/86	1/1/87	1/1/88
OWNED BY: COMPANY		3	3	4	5
FRANCHISEES		20	27	35	45
LOCATED: IN U.S.		23	30	39	50
OUTSIDE U.S.		0	0	0	0
TOTAL:		23	30	39	50
NO. OF STATES W/ UNITS		5	5	5	5

THE BUSINESS

M.G.M. Liquor Warehouse is one of the largest liquor retailers in the country and the leader in franchising package stores.

WHAT IT TAKES

You have several options in purchasing an M.G.M. Liquor Warehouse franchise. For $25,000 you can buy an existing franchise. A new franchise for a single store costs $25,000 to $50,000, depending on the state. Your franchise agreement will give you an exclusive territory based on square-mile radius and population, and applies for fifteen years, renewable for subsequent ten-year periods. Another option is to buy a franchise for a particular territory, which would allow you to develop more than one store. In that case, your initial fee will be $25,000 for the first two businesses and $20,000 for each subsequent business. But you must plan to run each one actively because the company does not allow passive ownership. You need no prior experience in the retail liquor business to be a successful M.G.M. manager.

Depending on the size of your store, you'll need $55,000 to $160,000 to improve and equip an existing building. That price includes the cost of outdoor signs, equipment, leasehold improvements, and cash registers. Another $155,000 to $210,000 will be necessary for initial working capital to cover the purchase of your initial inventory, licenses, starting salaries, and insurance. You'll need $50,000 of your initial investment cash. You must find your own financing. You will pay the company a flat royalty fee and/or a percentage of the monthly gross sales, depending on the state you locate in.

GETTING STARTED

M.G.M. Liquor Warehouse requires a marketing survey prior to approval of any new store site. The company will evaluate the population trends in your area, the per capita spending, and the market potential of the primary and secondary trade areas around the proposed site. Typically, you'll want a site that offers 5,000 to 8,000 square feet in a shopping center or freestanding building.

All aspects of the development of the building's exterior and interior are determined by company standards. On the outside, Liquor Warehouse stores are more attractive than the typical liquor store; on the inside, they are more efficient, with floor space planned to minimize operating costs and maximize profit. You will use the company logo, uniforms, and cash-register displays, all purchased through a centralized buying system.

Besides yourself, you'll need one full-time and five-part time employees. You and/or your manager will be trained for two weeks at the corporate office in St. Paul, Minnesota. Afterwards, you'll have your own set of confidential operations manuals outlining administrative policies and business procedures. You'll also study cash management, the variety of liquor products, employee motivation, and store operations. You'll need about six months from the time of the purchase of your franchise until your opening. Company officials will visit your store and work with you during your grand opening.

MAKING IT WORK

You'll pay M.G.M. Liquor Warehouse 1 percent of your monthly gross sales for advertising. Most of that money will support the company-sponsored Wine Club, which your customers can join to participate in tastings, receive regular newsletters about wines, and qualify for discounts on wine purchases. The company will handle all administrative details—producing the newsletter, designing the wine tastings, and so on. You'll also pay additional charges for cooperative major-media campaigns sponsored by the franchisees as a group.

You'll meet with company personnel and other owners in your area at monthly regional franchise advisory councils to discuss buying, merchandising, advertising, promotion, and new products. Approximately fifteen two-hour seminars are offered every year on business and product updates. All franchisees gather annually at the national council meeting. Twice a year the company will send you a newsletter to supplement its monthly company updates and weekly information about the industry as a whole. In addition to making regular visits, corporate experts will come to your store as needed to offer operational advice, and you can regularly refer to the company operations manuals. The company will provide not only your business systems for expense analysis, inventory, and bookkeeping but also forms for inventory, personnel, ordering, and accounting.

Perhaps the foundation of each franchise is the company's volume purchases of liquor. The company requires that M.G.M. stores display and sell only a limited selection of private and exclusive labels. Even though you can save money by buying from the company's wholesale house, you can also buy from other sources.

COMMENTS

The company wants to increase franchise operations in a small selection of western, midwestern, and southern states.

GETTING MORE INFORMATION

The franchise information packet consists of ten photocopied pages of information. For details, write to:
Ms. Carolyn M.E. Gill
National Franchise Coordinator
M.G.M. Liquor Warehouse
1124 Carpenteur Avenue West
St. Paul, MN   55113
(612)   487–1006

MicroAge Computer Stores

BUSINESS: sales and support of multiuser computer and office-automation systems
FOUNDED: 1976
FRANCHISED: 1980
START-UP INVESTMENT: up to $300,000

		AS OF		PROJECTED BY	
NO. OF UNITS		1/1/85	1/1/86	1/1/87	1/1/88
OWNED BY:	COMPANY	2	2	5	10
	FRANCHISEES	133	141	155	175
LOCATED:	IN U.S.	125	133	146	150
	OUTSIDE U.S.	10	10	14	35
TOTAL:		135	143	160	185
NO. OF STATES W/ UNITS		32	37	40	45

THE BUSINESS

The market potential for personal and business computer systems is still largely untapped. Federal government statistics identify approximately 50 million white-collar professionals, less than 10 percent of whom have personal computers at their work sites. The microcomputer, or personal computer (PC), has the capability of becoming as important to these individuals as the calculator. In 1984, the United States shipped over 7.5 million PCs, and by 1989 approximately 18.7 million will be shipped, an increase of 249 percent in five years.

Sales to computer stores are likely to remain a critical first step in distribution. In 1983 computer stores commanded 29.5 percent of micro-unit shipments and 48.1 percent of the dollar value of shipments. In the future, sales of computers through computer stores will increase significantly. By 1989 service-oriented computer stores will dominate mass merchandisers, wholesalers, and direct sales in number of personal systems sold by commanding 38.1 percent of total sales. The PC store is giving way to the systems store, an operation capable of solving data- and voice-management problems in small to large corporations by integrating data processing and communications technologies.

There are three levels of MicroAge Systems Stores. A level-one systems store services the data-management needs of individuals and businesses through personal computers, multiuser systems, networks, and micro-to-mainframe communications. The level-two store incorporates data and voice management with business phone systems. The level-three systems store ties together both computer and communications using wide area networks, voice/data computers, and advanced multiuser technology. The total dollar volume for all franchise outlets in 1985 was $232,162,000.

WHAT IT TAKES

The initial franchise fee is $30,000, and the franchise agreement runs for a term of ten years. You'll receive an exclusive territory of a fifteen-square-mile area with the store at the center. The total investment required of you can be up to $300,000, with $125,000 to $150,000 needed in cash. The company provides no financial assistance, so you'll have to make your own arrangements with financial institutions.

A conversion store franchise requires a considerably lower initial investment than for a new store. Actual costs depend on your geographic location, desired size of store, condition of the present facility, current inventory levels, and inventory lines to be added. MicroAge management prefers to review each situation on an individual basis before estimating the costs of transition from your present operation to a MicroAge facility.

You'll be paying an ongoing percentage of the gross income of your store, plus an ongoing advertising fee of 1 percent of your gross sales.

GETTING STARTED

A typical MicroAge store requires 3,500 square feet and is located in an office building, shopping center, or commercial and industrial park. You'll need from six to twenty full-time employees. MicroAge will help you with site selection, lease or purchase negotiation, facility layout and decoration, staffing and hiring, acquisition of supplies and materials necessary for your operation, and the grand opening. MicroAge expects franchisees to meet specific requirements to insure consistent quality of image, products, and services.

You'll receive training at the company headquarters in Arizona: a three-day business planning session for you as owner and for your manager, and a two-week session of classroom work and hands-on experience covering financial management, sales, management, technical information, store operations, service-center management, vertical markets sales and management, and product selection and management. It will take approximately five months from the signing of your agreement until the day you open for business.

MAKING IT WORK

Your training will continue with quarterly regional conferences and an annual national conference. Field seminars are held monthly via satellite, and you'll receive onsite sales training twice a year. MicroAge, as part of its standard support to you, will provide a full range of advertising packages, including newspaper and magazine ads, mailers and brochures, telephone-book ads, catalogs, TV and radio commercials, point-of-purchase displays, a lead-referral system, and incentive packages.

You'll be able to take advantage of customer accounts-receivable financing and central purchasing and merchandising systems. The company operates a major distribution business to support your product needs. You'll receive the quarterly company newsletter and monthly product updates and have access to toll-free hotlines and headquarters resource people. MicroAge will also give you policy, procedure, and customer-service manuals; inventory, personnel, accounting, and order forms; a bookkeeping system; and computerized billing and management information systems.

COMMENTS

A member of the IFA, MicroAge was rated 60th in *Venture* magazine's 1986 "Franchise 100." The company is seeking franchisees throughout the United States and in Canada and Europe.

GETTING MORE INFORMATION

The franchise package includes a brochure describing the company's services and a preliminary qualification review form requesting personal and financial information. For more information, contact:

Tom Krawczyk
  or
Peter Haltgren
Franchise Development
MicroAge Computer Stores, Inc.
2308 South 55th Street
Tempe, AZ   85282
(602)   968–3168, extension 323

Mifax

BUSINESS: office
   systems and billing
   and collection
   services for the
   healthcare industry
FOUNDED: 1969
FRANCHISED: 1979
START-UP
   INVESTMENT:
   $16,340 (plus a
   $10,000-20,000 line of
   credit)

		AS OF		PROJECTED BY	
NO. OF UNITS		1/1/85	1/1/86	1/1/87	1/1/88
OWNED BY:	COMPANY	0	0	0	0
	FRANCHISEES	62	71	92	114
LOCATED:	IN U.S.	62	71	92	114
	OUTSIDE U.S.	0	0	0	0
TOTAL:		62	71	92	114
NO. OF STATES W/ UNITS		25	29	33	47

THE BUSINESS

Most patients may think of their doctor or dentist as a health-care professional whose greatest concern is taking care of people, but this is only part of the picture. As business executives, they must also oversee the management of their office and practice. Mifax Service and Systems, Inc., serves these professionals by keeping track of daily business activities, completing insurance forms, recording charges and payments, sending monthly statements, and following up on unpaid balances. The Mifax automated Accounts Receivable Management System (ARMS) helps reduce late payments, thus increasing receivables.

The number of physicians in this country continues to grow steadily each year, making a ready market for Mifax services. The company's data service is tailored to the individual's needs, providing comprehensive computerized management reports each month. In addition, Mifax pays the physician after statements are prepared, thus eliminating the wait for patients to pay. For the twelve months ending 31 March 1986, Mifax reported that franchisees' earnings ranged from $41,000 to $125,000, with a third averaging $67,000. Mifax dealerships sell Control-o-fax office systems, billing and collection services, and computer services.

WHAT IT TAKES

You will need $8,500 for the initial franchise fee. This does not ensure a nonexclusive territory, but the company has never put two dealers in one territory. The franchise is considered to be continuous with no renewal necessary. You should expect to spend a total of $16,340, with a backup line of credit for $10,000 to $20,000 to cover expenses during the first six months. The franchise fee must be in cash, and the company will provide direct financial assistance for the remainder. There are no ongoing royalty fees. Neither master franchises nor additional franchises are available.

You will be expected to manage the business yourself. Mifax recommends that you have the following: four or more years of successful sales experience, with a minimum of two of those years involving sales to the health-care industry (calling on doctors' offices); a working knowledge of the business side of a doctor's practice; a demonstrated desire to own your own business; and evidence of your ability to save money.

GETTING STARTED

The company will help you with acquiring necessary materials, supplies, and merchandise. Besides yourself, you will need two full-time and two part-time employees, whom the company will help you hire. The following training is given at company headquarters: at least a two-day workshop on policy and procedure orientation; at least five days of classroom training on basic sales, including product knowledge, selling, and market awareness; at least five days of classroom training and practical application of sales techniques; a telemarketing seminar; at least five days of classroom instruction on selection and training of salespeople; and at least five days of classroom training and motivation of salespeople. Also, your sales personnel will receive five days of classroom training covering principles and techniques of telephone sales and customer service. You can open about a month after buying your franchise.

MAKING IT WORK

Although there is no advertising fee, the company provides newspaper ads, black-and-white and four-color magazine ads, brochures, presentation books, catalogs, in-house media packages (slides and videotapes), contests, seasonal promotional materials, a lead-referral system, incentives, and press releases. Regional conferences are held quarterly. You will receive a company newsletter every three months, updates on products and services periodically, company-information updates every week, and industry and market information monthly. The company sponsors various awards each year.

Backup systems include headquarters and regional resource persons; a toll-free hotline; regular onsite visits; onsite troubleshooting; manuals for policy, management procedure, and customer service; forms for inventory, personnel, and orders; and a bookkeeping and computerized billing system. The company maintains a research-and-development department. Mifax does all the receivables on behalf of franchisees and is totally responsible for collecting them.

COMMENTS

Mifax was ranked 266th in *Entrepreneur* magazine's 1987 "Franchise 500." A member of the IFA since 1985, the company provides an earnings claim document. The company participates in both United Way and Big Brothers/Big Sisters. Mifax is planning to expand in several states across the country.

GETTING MORE INFORMATION

The franchise information packet contains a brochure on the health-care industry's need for business systems and Mifax's services, copies of recent business articles on the company, and a four-page application form. For more information, write or call:

Deanne DeLange
Franchise Coordinator
Mifax Service and Systems, Inc.
3022 Airport Boulevard, Box 5800
Waterloo, IA   50704
(319)   234–4896

Miracle Auto Painting & Body Repair

BUSINESS:			AS OF		PROJECTED BY	
automobile painting	NO. OF UNITS		1/1/85	1/1/86	1/1/87	1/1/88
and body repair	OWNED BY: COMPANY		3	5	3	1
FOUNDED: 1953	FRANCHISEES		45	44	50	55
FRANCHISED: 1964	LOCATED: IN U.S.		48	49	53	56
START-UP	OUTSIDE U.S.		0	0	0	0
INVESTMENT:	TOTAL:		48	49	53	56
$150,000–$200,000	NO. OF STATES W/ UNITS		6	6	8	15

THE BUSINESS

Many cars on the road are five to eight years old, and the number is increasing. Part of the automotive aftermarket, Miracle Auto Painting provides top-quality automobile painting and body repair. Miracle sees their result as "better quality and more reasonably priced than any of the other 'competitive' production paint shops." The company has been under the same leadership since its founding in 1953. In 1985 the company's franchise operations grossed $40 million, with individual units grossing an average of $815,000 and netting an average of $97,000.

WHAT IT TAKES

Your initial franchise fee of $35,000 will buy an exclusive territory determined by population, number of registered vehicles, and vehicles per person. The original franchise agreement is valid for ten years and renewable for five-year periods. Your total initial investment will range from $150,000 to $200,000, and $75,000 of that must be in cash. Miracle will help arrange financing from a variety of sources. The cost of additional franchises is negotiable, and master franchises are available. Passive ownership is permitted but discouraged. You will pay an ongoing royalty fee of 5 percent of annual gross sales, exclusive of sales tax.

GETTING STARTED

Miracle will provide guidance in locating the best high-traffic site and assistance in evaluating a potential site before you enter into a formal lease agreement. Prototype design plans will be provided for your architects, contractors, and equipment installers to see that the building or remodeling and installation details are completed. The company will offer discounts on your initial orders of equipment, paint, and materials; your total initial inventory will cost $5,000 to $7,500. A typical facility is 10,000 square feet, located in a freestanding building or commercial industrial park or center.

You'll need to hire eleven full-time and three part-time employees. Franchisees do not need any previous experience in the industry. Complete two-week training programs, tailored to the individual, are provided in the flagship store in San Mateo, California, or at a location closer to your home. Training covers shop building, shop set-up, personnel, estimating, accounting, advertising, and public relations. The time between your purchase of the franchise until your opening will be about three months. Miracle will assist with your grand opening.

MAKING IT WORK

The franchise fee covers a variety of marketing aids, ranging from newspaper, magazine, and telephone-book ads to mailers and radio and television commercials. The company also has billboard designs, signs, banners, and in-house media packages. The company sponsors annual regional advertising campaigns to boost sales. Co-op programs include seasonal promotional materials, brochures, catalogs, and presentation books. Annual national and regional conventions are supplemented by seminars held three times a year. Miracle also publishes newsletters quarterly, issues product and service updates regularly, and recognizes franchisees' accomplishments.

You'll receive ongoing support from company representatives who make regular onsite visits and from headquarters resource people by telephone. The company provides policy and customer-service manuals, bookkeeping and inventory systems, and preprinted forms. A company subsidiary makes volume purchases of equipment and supplies, which Miracle will offer to you at low prices. To insure that high-quality materials are used, the company will give you an authorized product list. The company offers an insurance program with property, general-liability, automobile, life, major-medical, dental, disability, worker's compensation, and third-party-bonding coverage.

COMMENTS

Miracle was ranked 249th in *Entrepreneur* magazine's 1987 "Franchise 500." Multiple Allied Services, Inc., is the parent company. The company wants to expand in several western and southern states.

The franchise packet contains a brochure describing franchise operations and support, a three-page release with questions frequently asked about Miracle, and a four-page application form. For more information, call or write:
> Jim Jordan
> Marketing Director
> Miracle Auto Painting and Body Repair
> 1065 East Hillsdale Boulevard #110
> Foster City, CA   94404
> (800)   331–0404, or in California (800)   233–8090

Miracle-Ear

BUSINESS: hearing-
aid manufacturing
and marketing
FOUNDED: 1948
FRANCHISED: 1984
START-UP
INVESTMENT:
$25,000

		AS OF		PROJECTED BY	
NO. OF UNITS		1/1/85	1/1/86	1/1/87	1/1/88
OWNED BY:	COMPANY	11	14	20	25
	FRANCHISEES	139	214	280	325
LOCATED:	IN U.S.	150	228	300	350
	OUTSIDE U.S.	0	0	0	0
TOTAL:		150	228	300	350
NO. OF STATES W/ UNITS		42	44	50	50

THE BUSINESS

An innovator in the hearing-aid field, Miracle-Ear sold its products for thirty-six years through a network of independent multiline dealers before opening up franchised and company-owned retail stores. The company is the primary supplier of hearing aids to Sears, Roebuck and Company, which sells these products under the Sears name in its larger retail stores. Miracle-Ear also operates the hearing-aid departments in twenty Sears retail stores on a concession basis as part of a pilot program. Miracle-Ear's "Micro" model, introduced in 1986, is believed to be the world's smallest hearing aid. In addition, in 1986 the company introduced the world's first programmable hearing aid and unique Spectrum hearing aid, offering an advance in effective background-noise reduction.

Miracle-Ear's total dollar volume for 1985 was more than $31 million. The franchise system is unique in the hearing-aids industry. Miracle-Ear manufactures and markets high-quality hearing aids and other hearing-aid accessory products and replacement parts. In addition, the company markets audiometers and hearing-aid batteries.

WHAT IT TAKES

The initial franchise fee is $12,500, and the agreement covers an exclusive territory determined by population. Your franchise agreement will be valid for twenty years, with no provision for renewal.

The total initial investment of $25,000, which includes the franchise fee, must be in cash. The company does not offer financial assistance. The fee for additional units is the same as the first; master franchises are not available. Passive ownership is permitted but discouraged. The company charges an ongoing royalty fee of $31.50 per unit. Some experience in the field is considered helpful.

GETTING STARTED

Miracle-Ear assists in site evaluation and makes available signs, furnishings, space planning, and assistance in acquiring merchandise. The typical facility is 1,000 square feet, with locations in everything from office buildings to shopping malls. You will be required to use the company's complete identity program. The number of employees varies depending in the market size. A complete, professional training program is available to take a new franchisee from basic audiology to license exam. You can be in business within three months after purchasing your franchise. The company will help with your grand opening.

MAKING IT WORK

Miracle-Ear offers national advertising and local promotion planning. Annual national conventions, regional conferences, and on-site training every six months keep employees motivated and informed. Company-sponsored recognition programs make awards in three categories, and a company magazine and newsletter explain advances in the field. The company will provide you with seasonal promotional materials, displays, and contests. A computerized billing system, software, and computer training are provided to larger franchises. The computer systems are also used to generate leads for you. All types of forms and manuals are offered, as well as bookkeeping, inventory, and personnel systems. Committed to developing state-of-the-art products, the company maintains research and development departments. You may sell competitive brands (2 to 5 percent of total inventory) to accommodate referral business. You will be eligible for major-medical and dental insurance programs.

COMMENTS

Miracle-Ear was ranked 26th in *Venture* magazine's 1986 "Franchise 100" and 174th in *Entrepreneur* magazine's 1987 "Franchise 500." A recipient of the Sears Partners in Progress Award, the company is seeking new franchisees in all states except Hawaii, Minnesota, Nebraska, and Tennessee.

GETTING MORE INFORMATION

The franchise information packet contains the company's annual report and a brochure showing interior display systems available to franchisees. For more information, write or call:

Norman L. Blemaster
Executive Vice-President of Franchising
Miracle-Ear
7731 Country Club Drive
Golden Valley, MN 55427
(800) 328–0626

Miracle Method

BUSINESS: bathtub			AS OF		PROJECTED BY	
and tile refinishing	NO. OF UNITS		1/1/85	1/1/86	1/1/87	1/1/88
and chip repair	OWNED BY: COMPANY		0	0	0	0
FOUNDED: 1977		FRANCHISEES	35	44	68	120
FRANCHISED: 1980	LOCATED: IN U.S.		26	28	38	60
START-UP		OUTSIDE U.S.	9	16	30	60
INVESTMENT:	TOTAL:		35	44	68	120
$20,000–$25,000	NO. OF STATES W/ UNITS		7	8	14	20

THE BUSINESS

Miracle Method's unique process using molecular bonding and infrared light can repair chipped porcelain bathroom fixtures or refinish or change the color of tile. A heavy, durable, glossy layer of material either in the old color or a new one is bonded to the old surface. Since all porcelain twenty years or older could benefit from refinishing, a major portion of the market consists of an estimated 35 million bathtubs throughout the country in private homes, hotels, motels, apartment complexes, refurbishing contractors' businesses, and government housing projects. The average refinishing job runs between $225 and $425 per tub. Custom coloring, stripping a competitor's failed job, or removing and reinstalling shower doors are extra. Tile refinishing usually costs from $3 to $6 per square foot, and chip or crack repair is $50 to $150. You can also offer customers repair and restoration of fiberglass or plastic shower stalls, tubs, hot tubs, and spas. The prices you can charge will vary depending on the local economy. You can expect to average a gross income of about $66,800 and net about $24,000 annually for each franchise you own. The total dollar volume for all Miracle Method franchises in 1985 was $2,808,000.

WHAT IT TAKES

The franchise fee for your first Miracle Method operation will be $15,750, which will cover your equipment. Ensuring an exclusive territory, the agreement applies for five years, with a five-year renewal period. Your total initial investment may be between $20,000 and $25,000, which must be paid in cash. If you want to buy more franchises, the fee will be discounted to $12,650, and you can get master franchises. You don't need any experience or skills in ceramics, plumbing, or business to operate a Miracle Method successfully. You'll pay an ongoing royalty fee of 7.5 percent of your gross income. The company prefers but does not require that you be actively involved in running your franchise.

GETTING STARTED

A Miracle Method franchise is a very low overhead operation; you can use a room in your home as an office. But if you need to find an office outside your home, the company will help you locate one. You'll need about 500 square feet to run your business, and since you can buy most of your supplies at local stores, you won't need to keep a large inventory. It's a good idea to get a small pickup truck to carry your equipment and chemicals to the job site. Miracle Method will provide you with company-logo signs for your vehicles, plus uniforms, invoices, and letterhead with the logo. You can pay helpers by the job, so it isn't necessary to hire regular employees. You may choose to start out as a one-person operation and expand later, hiring a secretary, bookkeeper, and team of workers.

The company will send a representative to your site to help you set up your business and offer you two to three weeks of intensive on-the-job training, in which you'll learn the basic techniques of restoration and ways to refine and perfect your work. The representative will not only show you how to find potential customers and direct effective advertising to your market but also will accompany you on sales calls at homes, hotels, and construction sites. You'll get everything you need to restore the first twenty tubs. You should be able to start up within two months after your purchase.

MAKING IT WORK

Miracle Method will provide you with a lead-referral system, press packages, and a marketing manual to help you build your business. If you want advertising materials like mailers and newspaper ads directed specifically to your area, you can pay a fee of 3 percent of your gross sales. You'll receive frequent marketing bulletins with specific how-to tips, a quarterly company newsletter, and weekly technical updates. The company holds an annual national convention.

Company representatives will visit your site regularly, and regional and headquarters personnel can answer your questions by phone. You'll also receive policy and procedure manuals, forms for bookkeeping, and systems for expense analysis and computerized information management.

If you want to branch out, the company will allow you to sell any home-restoration services or products. You can buy your porcelain restoration supplies from local stores (except the Miracle Method bonding agent), or you can buy everything through a central company purchasing program to share in volume discounts. The Miracle Method product and your workmanship will be backed by a five-year nationally certified limited warranty, which will assure your customers that they are doing business with a large professional organization—licensed, bonded, and fully insured. The company continually conducts research on materials and delivery systems.

COMMENTS

Entrepreneur magazine ranked Miracle Method 378th among its "Franchise 500" for 1987. The company is seeking new franchisees in most parts of the United States and in other countries.

GETTING MORE INFORMATION

The franchise information packet includes a brochure with a photo insert showing tubs, sinks, and tile before and after restoration; a sample invoice/receipt, and a sample certified warranty. For more information, contact:

Robert D. Gray
President
Miracle Method, Inc.
1280 Monument Boulevard
Concord, CA   94520
(415)   680–8850 (call collect)

Molly Maid

BUSINESS: residential maid service
FOUNDED: 1980 (Canada), 1984 (U.S.)
FRANCHISED: 1980
START-UP INVESTMENT: $16,900

		AS OF		PROJECTED BY	
NO. OF UNITS		1/1/85	1/1/86	1/1/87	1/1/88
OWNED BY:	COMPANY	0	0	0	0
	FRANCHISEES	110	161	233	333
LOCATED:	IN U.S.	1	28	78	138
	OUTSIDE U.S.	109	133	155	195
TOTAL:		110	161	233	333
NO. OF STATES W/ UNITS		1	11	25	35

THE BUSINESS

Molly Maid, Inc., an exclusive residential maid service, uses two-person teams of uniformed, bonded, and insured maids. According to the company, Molly Maid offers a high rate of return on the initial investment with minimal risk. In 1985, Molly Maid's annual dollar volume for all franchise operations was $10 million, with average gross sales per unit of $150,000 and average net income per unit of $35,000.

WHAT IT TAKES

You will need an initial franchise fee of $12,900 plus $2,400 for a starter kit of supplies. The franchise agreement will give you an exclusive territory, determined by geographic area and census tracts, for ten years, renewable for five-year periods. Of the total $16,900 initial investment, $11,400 must be in cash; the company can provide financial assistance for the remainder. Additional units can be purchased for $10,000 each, but master franchises are not available. If you decide to hire a manager, the company must approve the person you select. Ongoing royalty fees are graduated—8 percent for sales up to $500,000; 6 percent for sales between $500,000 and $700,000; and 4 percent for sales over $750,000. You need no prior experience in maid service.

GETTING STARTED

Molly Maid will help you purchase or lease the vehicles needed for the cleaning teams, give instruction on staffing and hiring, and help you procure equipment and supplies. Your office will be in your home to reduce overhead. Molly Maid will require you to use the company logo and designated uniforms.

The number of cleaning teams necessary varies from franchise to franchise, but you will handle all the bookkeeping, scheduling and sales. You will attend school at corporate headquarters in Ann Arbor, Michigan, for five days of training covering marketing, production, accounting, and employee hiring and training. After purchasing your franchise, you can expect to be in business within a month. Molly Maid will help with your grand opening.

MAKING IT WORK

Your ongoing advertising fee of 2 percent of sales provides a variety of resources: newspaper ads, black-and-white and four-color magazine ads, mailers, telephone-book ads, brochures, catalogs, presentation books, press releases, in-house media packages (slides and videotapes), and billboard posters. You may also participate in co-op advertising programs for television and radio commercials, seasonal promotional materials, and contests. Molly Maid holds a national convention once a year, spring and fall regional conferences, and periodic one-day seminars. The company also provides a minimum of three days of onsite training each year for every franchise.

Molly Maid offers a variety of special awards each year. The company provides full backup service via newsletters; magazines; a toll-free hotline; onsite troubleshooting; manuals on policy, management, and customer service; forms for personnel, orders, and accounting; and systems for bookkeeping, personnel, expense analysis, and computerized billing. You will not be required to use specific cleaning products, although Molly Maid will suggest the best types. Molly Maid sponsors insurance packages with property, general-liability, automobile, life, major-medical, worker's compensation, and third-party-bonding coverage.

COMMENTS

Ranked 201st in *Entrepreneur* magazine's 1987 "Franchise 500," Molly Maid has been a member of the IFA since 1984. The company participates in the Santa's Helper and Toys for Tots program and serves as the official maid service for Ronald McDonald House. Molly Maid wants to add franchises throughout the United States and in Africa, Asia, Australia, Canada, Europe, Japan, Mexico, and South America.

GETTING MORE INFORMATION

The franchise information packet contains a copy of the franchise agreement and details about the initial package furnished to franchisees. For details, write or call:

Cathy Meeker
Director of Franchise Sales
Molly Maid, Inc.
707 Wolverine Tower
3001 South State Street
Ann Arbor, MI   48104
(800)   331–4600

Money Mailer

BUSINESS: direct-mail
  marketing
  FOUNDED: 1979
  FRANCHISED: 1979
START-UP
  INVESTMENT:
  $17,000–$200,000

		AS OF		PROJECTED BY	
NO. OF UNITS		1/1/85	1/1/86	1/1/87	1/1/88
OWNED BY: COMPANY		0	0	0	0
	FRANCHISEES	70	102	180	250
LOCATED: IN U.S.		70	102	180	250
	OUTSIDE U.S.	0	0	0	0
TOTAL:		70	102	180	250
NO. OF STATES W/ UNITS		12	22	43	50

THE BUSINESS

According to A. C. Nielsen, 72 percent of consumers surveyed nationwide report using the direct-mail coupons they receive. Money Mailer was founded in 1979 to tap into this market and now mails over 200 million coupons and advertisements to U.S. homes annually. The high-quality precut coupons, delivered in distinctive envelopes, lead to the highest redemption rates in the industry. In 1985 the total dollar volume for the company's franchise operations was $4,496,537, with individual units averaging a gross income of $150,000 and a net income of $100,000 to $110,000.

The Money Mailer system is made up of regions, which are divided into local franchises. Each regional master franchisee purchases the right to operate in a given territory having at least 180,000 mailable addresses. The regional office, in turn, sells local franchisees the right to mail in areas of 30,000 to 40,000 domiciles.

WHAT IT TAKES

In addition to needing previous experience in marketing, sales, and advertising, you will need from $17,000 to $200,000 for the initial franchise fee, based on the number of residences that receive mail and the type of franchise you want. For the $17,000 franchise fee the entire amount must be in cash, and for amounts above $50,000, 30 percent must be cash. The company can provide financial assistance. The fee for additional franchise units is based on the number of addresses receiving mail. The original franchise agreement extends for fifteen years and is renewable every five years. Passive ownership of your first franchise is allowed but discouraged. The company charges no ongoing royalty fees.

GETTING STARTED

Money Mailer provides assistance with site selection; purchase negotiation; facility layout; decoration; lease or purchase of furniture, fixtures, and equipment; acquisition of materials and supplies; and staffing and hiring. You can borrow, lease, or purchase a MacIntosh Plus computer and MacIntosh LaserWriter from the franchisor. You will need 500 to 700 square feet for your office. Typical locations include office buildings or freestanding buildings. Money Mailer provides all standards and logos, a uniform office layout, and logos to put on clothing.

Besides yourself, you will need four full-time and three part-time employees, whom the company will help you hire. You'll receive two weeks of training in your office, with instruction both in the classroom and from manuals. You will cover product knowledge, sales, use of computers, art sales methods, procedures, and hiring and training of employees. You'll spend another week in the field calling on potential clients. As a local franchisee, you can plan to open about three weeks after purchasing your franchise; regional franchisees can plan on a two-month period. Money Mailer will assist with your grand opening.

MAKING IT WORK

Money Mailer charges no ongoing advertising fee but offers advertising, marketing, and promotional materials for a price. The company not only sponsors annual national conventions and biannual regional conferences and seminars but also sends franchisees a quarterly magazine, customer-oriented publications, and regular updates on service and sales ideas. Videotapes are also available for your ongoing education. Money Mailer sponsors various recognition programs and provides a toll-free hotline; regular onsite visits; onsite troubleshooting; policy, management-procedure, and customer-service manuals; inventory, personnel, order, and accounting forms; and systems for expense analysis, computerized management information, and computerized billing. Money Mailer has a research-and-development department as well as divisions that prepare, print, and mail coupons; a central purchasing system offering volume discounts; and a centralized merchandising system. The company sponsors insurance for property, general-liability, automobile, major-medical, dental, and worker's compensation needs.

COMMENTS

Money Mailer has been a member of the IFA since 1979. The company wants to expand operations in twenty-three states and in Canada, Australia, and Japan.

GETTING MORE INFORMATION

The franchise information packet contains a sample mailing package, a brochure and fliers on the company's training and operations, listings of major clients, and four-page application with authorization for a credit check. For more information, write or call:
Stan Levy
Vice-President
Money Mailer, Inc.
15472 Chemical Lane
Huntington Beach, CA   92649
(800)   MAILER + 1

Mr. Build

BUSINESS: trade and service contractors in residential and commercial properties
FOUNDED: 1981
FRANCHISED: 1981
START-UP INVESTMENT: $7,000–$20,000

		AS OF		PROJECTED BY	
NO. OF UNITS		1/1/85	1/1/86	1/1/87	1/1/88
OWNED BY:	COMPANY	0	0	0	0
	FRANCHISEES	480	485	630	950
LOCATED:	IN U.S.	450	450	570	850
	OUTSIDE U.S.	30	35	60	100
TOTAL:		480	485	630	950
NO. OF STATES W/ UNITS		20	25	35	50

THE BUSINESS

Sales for construction and home services franchises is projected to grow at an annual rate of 20 percent for the next several years. The Mr. Build franchise system includes fifty home-service trades, ranging from roofing and other construction professions to maintenance and related services for residential and commercial properties.

WHAT IT TAKES

In order to be considered for a Mr. Build franchise, you must be fully qualified in the contracting trade or service for which you are planning a franchise—plumbing, roofing, electric contracting, or masonry, for example. Your initial fee for a Mr. Build franchise will be from $6,000 to $10,000, depending on the type of service you want to offer and your local conditions. Your additional investment will run from $1,000 to $10,000 to convert trucks, signs, and other items to Mr. Build formats. The percentage of this amount that you'll need in cash will also vary, depending on local factors. Financial assistance is available to you through the Mr. Build regional offices. You may purchase additional franchises and either act as manager or hire someone to fill that position. You may also acquire a master franchise. Your original franchise agreement will apply for five years but will not grant an exclusive territory. The ongoing royalty fee is determined according to the conditions and situation of each individual franchisee.

GETTING STARTED

Mr. Build International will help you with the negotiations for vehicle lease or purchase; acquisition of materials and supplies; hiring of additional staff; and formulation of service and maintenance contracts for your equipment. The Mr. Build International headquarters staff also will provide information and guidance for you in the decoration of your office facility. As a Mr. Build International franchise operator, you'll use the standard company logo on business signs, cards, stationery, vehicles, and uniforms. Mr. Build International has arranged low-cost, quick service for you from a variety of suppliers.

MAKING IT WORK

Mr. Build International holds one-day training sessions at the annual national convention for you as franchise owner and for your manager. In addition, you and your employees will have access to regular seminars and workshops at the regional level. The sessions include training in the areas of sales presentations, generation of leads, business management, advertising and image development, hiring and training personnel, and time management, plus others.

The ongoing monthly advertising fee of $300 is applied to a national advertising program. From this pool of advertising dollars Mr. Build International will provide you with newspaper and black-and-white magazine ads, mailers, brochures, telephone-book ads, presentation books, TV and radio commercials, national media coverage, in-house media packages, point-of-sale displays, billboard posters, a public-relations and marketing manual, and a series of press releases for use in your local media. Also, you can purchase four-color magazine ads and catalogs.

You'll receive a company magazine and newsletter, product and service updates; industry and market information; a customer-oriented newsletter; policy and procedure manuals; inventory, order, and accounting forms; and expense-analysis, computerized-billing, and management information systems. In addition to these operational tools, Mr. Build International has a company insurance program that offers property, general-liability, life, major-medical, disability, third-party-bonding, and theft coverage.

COMMENTS

Mr. Build International was rated 156th in *Entrepreneur* magazine's "Franchise 500" for 1987. The company is seeking franchisees in most of the United States and in Japan.

GETTING MORE INFORMATION

The franchise information packet contains a copy of the company magazine and copies of the company newsletter and convention issue news. For more information, contact:

Sherman Tarr
Director of Public Relations
Mr. Build
One Univac Lane
Windsor, CT 06095
(203) 285-0766

National Video

BUSINESS: home video rentals and sales

FOUNDED: 1977

FRANCHISED: 1981

START-UP INVESTMENT: $39,500–$250,000

NO. OF UNITS		AS OF		PROJECTED BY	
		1/1/85	1/1/86	1/1/87	1/1/88
OWNED BY: COMPANY		2	3	5	15
FRANCHISEES		400	624	1,100	1,400
LOCATED: IN U.S.		295	480	900	1,200
OUTSIDE U.S.		107	147	205	215
TOTAL:		402	627	1,105	1,415
NO. OF STATES W/ UNITS		50	50	50	50

THE BUSINESS

Recently the home video entertainment market has grown dramatically. National Video's family-oriented stores tap into this market by offering a large selection of competitively priced rental movies, plus sales and rentals of related products. The company's annual dollar volume for all franchises was $92 million in 1985, with average gross sales per unit of $180,000. Over 25 million videocassette recorders have been sold in the United States—one VCR in every 3.5 households with a TV. By 1988, 65 percent of all homes are expected to own at least one VCR. The retail market for the sale and rental of prerecorded videocassettes has been exploding, with sales of over $3 billion in 1985. Experts predict that sales will top $5 billion.

WHAT IT TAKES

Depending on the population of the area to be served, National Video offers three options in franchising: a Class I store for markets with over 10,000 population (with a franchise fee of $19,900; a "super store" version is also available for large market areas); Class II, a scaled-down version for areas under 10,000 population (with a franchise fee of $14,900), or the Movie Express Kiosk, a National Video store within a grocery store or convenience store (total price of $39,500, which includes the $12,000 franchise fee). Master franchises are available in each category.

Your start-up costs for Class I and Class II stores would be:

	STORE TYPE	
ITEM	CLASS I	CLASS II
Initial franchise fees	$19,900	$14,900
Real property	$750–5,000/mo.	$750–4,000/mo.
Equipment, fixtures, signs, fixed assets, leasehold improvements, computer systems, decorating costs	$8,900–75,000	$8,900–49,000
Inventory, supplies	$56,000–90,000	$25,000–31,000
Security deposits, prepaid expenses, working capital	$3,750–25,000	$3,750–6,000
Insurance	$300–500	$500–1,500
License costs, attorney fees, accounting fees, sales tax bonds, and recruiting expenses	$1,500–7,000	$1,500–5,000
Advertising and public relations	$400–13,100	$400–2,600
NVI annual convention deposit, employee wages, utility costs, miscellaneous costs	$2,000–12,000	$2,000–6,000
Total:	$93,700–$250,000	$57,700–$120,000

For each of the three options, the total initial investment must be paid in cash; the company offers no assistance with financing. You may buy additional franchises for 50 percent or less of the original fees, depending on the number purchased. More than half of National Video franchise owners have opened additional stores; 20 percent now own five or more stores. Passive ownership is allowed. Your monthly royalty fee (4.9 percent of gross sales of nonhardware items) can be eliminated for part of your sales through a quarterly discount based on volume. Royalties are not paid on sales of videocassette recorders, televisions, and certain other equipment. You'll also pay an advertising fee of 3 percent of gross sales. Previous video sales experience is not required.

GETTING STARTED   National Video's regional operations managers offer assistance with site selection, lease negotiation, construction, setup, and staffing. The stores typically require 1,800 square feet in a freestanding building or shopping center. There are strict requirements for store decor. You will need three full-time and five part-time employees. You or your store managers will attend a week-long training class at the corporate training school in Portland, Oregon. A support team will assist you with everything from initial store inventory to grand opening displays and personnel training. You can plan to open within three to four months after purchasing the franchise. The company will provide preopening and grand-opening advertising packages to simplify the process.

MAKING IT WORK   The company's ongoing national advertising and public-relations campaigns, such as national contests and sweepstakes, put National Video franchises in the limelight. In addition to advertising, merchandising, and purchasing assistance you'll receive an in-house news magazine twice a month. National Video sponsors regular seminars, conferences, and numerous recognition programs. Regional operations managers will contact you regularly to answer questions and offer assistance. The company provides a multivolume operations manual; inventory, bookkeeping, and personnel systems; and a variety of forms. Volume purchasing will permit you to buy products at reduced prices, and a custom-designed computer system will provide daily management reports on sales and key operating information. You will not be required to use or sell company products only. A variety of insurance packages offer everything from property to major-medical and disability coverage.

COMMENTS   In *Entrepreneur* magazine's "Franchise 500" National Video was ranked fortieth, number one in the videocassette rental stores classification; and in *Venture* magazine's 1986 "Franchise 100" it was ranked twelfth. The company received a special citation from President Reagan for its Operation Safe Child, a video identification program, and National Video is a national Easter Seals sponsor. The company wants to open new franchises throughout the United States and in Canada.

GETTING MORE INFORMATION   The franchise packet includes several copies of features from national magazines on the company, a brochure describing its operations, two brochures explaining specific programs and comparing its franchise fees with others', and a three-page business application. For more information, write or call:

Sue Laws
Director, Sales Administration
National Video, Inc.
P. O. Box 18220
Portland, OR   97218
(800)   547–1310 or (503)   284–2965 (call collect)

Nation-wide General Rental Centers

		AS OF		PROJECTED BY	
	NO. OF UNITS	1/1/85	1/1/86	1/1/87	1/1/88
	OWNED BY: COMPANY	1	1	2	2
	FRANCHISEES	126	153	188	210
	LOCATED: IN U.S.	127	154	190	212
	OUTSIDE U.S.	0	0	0	0
	TOTAL:	127	154	190	212
	NO. OF STATES W/ UNITS	34	35	36	37

BUSINESS: rental center
FOUNDED: 1977
FRANCHISED: 1977
START-UP INVESTMENT: $98,500

THE BUSINESS

In America today more people are renting rather than owning many items. Do-it-yourselfers can save money by renting important labor-saving tools, recreation gear, and other equipment. Contractors, too, are turning to renting. Like homeowners, professionals know that they can rent occasionally needed items economically, without tying up needed capital. This frees them from the worries of maintenance, and they get quality equipment in top condition, earning tax benefits at the same time. Nation-wide General Rental Centers offer not only a full line of items for the contractor and do-it-yourself home owner but also home health supplies, lawn and yard tools, painters' equipment, party and banquet supplies, plumbers' tools, sanding machines, and household equipment. In 1985 the company's franchises grossed approximately $17,351,300, with average gross sales per unit of $137,706 and net income per store of 10 to 22 percent.

WHAT IT TAKES

The company does not charge a franchise fee, but you will have an exclusive territory for a three-mile radius from your location. Your agreement will be valid for three years and renewable year by year. Your total investment will be $98,500, with $25,000 of that required in cash. This total covers $88,000 for inventory plus funds for the training program; business-preparation package; shelf, pegboard, and fixtures allowance; and grand-opening advertising allowance. The company does not offer financing but will provide guidance on the subject. The balance of your investment can be financed with a five-year loan. After you open your rental center, you will be able to obtain additional growth inventory through the company's leasing program, with 100 percent financing. Master franchises are available. You may be an owner-investor of your store. General Rental Centers does not charge any ongoing royalty fees. No prior rental or retail experience is necessary to be successful.

GETTING STARTED

The company will help you with site selection, lease and purchase negotiations, and facility layout. You will pay for equipment lease or purchase and acquisition of supplies and merchandise. A business-preparation package contains everything you'll need to open for business, including a "Grand Opening" pennant, decals for equipment, 10,000 advertising handouts, 10,000 rental contracts, rate guide books, "Rent Me" signs, forms, personalized statements, stationery, matches, and more. Your building must be 2,000 to 4,000 square feet, with 2,000 to 15,000 square feet outside that can be fenced for additional storage, allows for good traffic flow, and can handle parking for six to ten cars.

During the first year you can run the business with one full-time and one part-time employee, and the company will assist with hiring. You or your manager will attend five days of on-the-job training at a rental center in either Columbia, South Carolina, or Reno, Nevada, where you'll learn about proven methods of handling customers (over the counter and on the telephone), maintenance, record keeping, insurance, and many other aspects of management. You can be open within forty-five days after buying your franchise. The company will help with your grand opening.

MAKING IT WORK

You will receive newspaper ads, mailers, telephone-book ads, radio commercials, signs, banners, press releases, and a public-relations/marketing manual. There are no national conventions, but you will receive onsite training as needed. The company publishes product and service updates and market-information updates periodically. The company sponsors award programs for top sales and excellence in service. Administrative services include headquarters resource persons, a toll-free hotline, regular onsite visits, onsite troubleshooting, policy manuals, inventory and accounting forms, and a bookkeeping system. The company offers a central purchasing program for volume discounts but does not require franchisees to sell company products exclusively. Insurance programs offer property, general-liability, life, major-medical, and dental coverage.

COMMENTS

Nation-wide General Rental Centers will provide an earnings claim document during a potential franchisee's personal interview. The company wants to add new franchises across the United States.

GETTING MORE
INFORMATION

The franchise information packet contains projections of a franchisee's expenses and income for the first three years, details of the company's operations, and a three-page application form. For more information, contact:

I. N. Goodvin
President
Nation-wide General Rental Centers, Inc.
1684 Highway 92 West, Suite A
Woodstock, GA   30188
(800)   227–1643 or (404)   924–0057

Nitro-Green Professional Lawn and Tree Care

BUSINESS: tree- and lawn-care services		AS OF		PROJECTED BY	
	NO. OF UNITS	1/1/85	1/1/86	1/1/87	1/1/88
FOUNDED: 1977	OWNED BY: COMPANY	0	0	0	0
FRANCHISED: 1979	FRANCHISEES	30	35	43	50
START-UP	LOCATED: IN U.S.	30	35	43	50
INVESTMENT:	OUTSIDE U.S.	0	0	0	0
$26,000–$30,000	TOTAL:	30	35	43	50
	NO. OF STATES W/ UNITS	11	11	13	16

THE BUSINESS

Americans who are proud of their homes want to have attractive yards, but they may not have enough time to devote to the task. That time crunch, coupled with the discretionary income to pay to have the job done right, is fueling the growth of lawn-care services. Nitro-Green specializes in liquid-spray fertilization and control of damaging insects and unsightly weeds. The program consists of four applications per year at a cost competitive with do-it-yourself methods. Customers thus avoid having to select, haul, store, and apply the materials themselves. Nitro-Green claims a 75 percent renewal rate among clients. Nitro-Green reports average gross sales per franchise unit of $100,000 to $150,000. The company estimates that only a quarter of the potential market is currently receiving professional lawn and tree care.

WHAT IT TAKES

You will pay a $14,000 franchise fee plus another $4,000 for pre-opening costs and working capital. After buying or leasing a one-ton truck, you will need to buy a spray rig for approximately $5,000. The total initial cost will be about $26,000 to $30,000. Franchisees have an exclusive area, effective for twenty years and then renewable for another ten. Of the initial investment, $23,000 must be in cash; indirect financial assistance is available. Fees to buy additional franchise units are negotiable, and you do not have to be the operator of the business. Nitro-Green charges an ongoing royalty fee of 7 percent of gross sales. No prior experience in the field is necessary.

GETTING STARTED

Since this is a service business, you will not need an office. Nitro-Green suggests one full-time employee and one part-time. You'll receive standard uniforms for all employees, and your trucks must be equipped according to company standards and appearance. Training begins in the home office with one week of classroom and on-the-job experience for the owner, followed by one week of training for the owner and employees in their franchise area. Videotapes provide additional education for all employees as needed. The initial training covers bookkeeping, products, advertising, spraying instruction, equipment, and technical information. Nitro-Green estimates that it should take one to two months to open your business after you've purchased a franchise.

MAKING IT WORK

For part of the original fee, Nitro-Green provides newspaper ads, black-and-white and four-color magazine ads, mailers, telephone-book ads, brochures, and presentation books. In addition, television and radio commercials, billboard posters, signs, contests, seasonal promotional materials, a lead-referral system, incentives, a public-relations/marketing manual, and press releases will also be available to you at no additional charge. The company conducts an annual four-day convention, one- or two-day seminars once a year, and on-site training two or three times a year. A monthly newsletter, quarterly questionnaires and surveys, and an annual customer-oriented newsletter provide information throughout the year. Nitro-Green also sponsors various recognition programs.

Backup programs include headquarters and regional resource people; a toll-free hotline; regular onsite visits; onsite troubleshooting; manuals on policy, customer service, and management procedure; forms for inventory, personnel, orders, and accounting; and systems for bookkeeping, inventory, personnel, and computerized management information, a computerized billing, and expense analysis. A research-and-development department strives to update products and knowledge. Franchisees must use company products, which are provided through Nitro-Green's centralized purchasing program offering volume discounts. Company-sponsored insurance offers property, general-liability, automobile, life, and major-medical coverage.

COMMENTS

Nitro-Green will provide an earnings claim document upon request. *Lawn Care Industry* has listed Nitro-Green for several years as one of the "Million Dollar Lawn Care Companies." The company wants new franchisees in western and central states.

GETTING MORE
INFORMATION

The franchise information packet contains a brochure explaining the Nitro-Green system, a letter to potential franchisees with additional details, an inventory checkoff list, and a four-page financial application form. For more information, call or write:

Roger Albrecht
President
375 East Horsetooth Road
Shores Four #102
Fort Collins, CO   80525
(800)   621–8387 (outside Colorado) or (303)   223–8873

Norrell

BUSINESS:			AS OF		PROJECTED BY	
temporary-help	NO. OF UNITS	1/1/85	1/1/86	1/1/87	1/1/88
services	OWNED BY: COMPANY	150	156	171	189
FOUNDED: 1961	FRANCHISEES	81	90	120	150
FRANCHISED: 1966	LOCATED: IN U.S.	224	239	279	319
START-UP	OUTSIDE U.S.	7	7	12	20
INVESTMENT:	TOTAL:	231	246	291	339
$30,000–$55,000	NO. OF STATES W/ UNITS	34	34	40	42

THE BUSINESS

Today, temporary services is one of the nation's fastest growing industries. The total sales volume has topped $6 billion, nearly doubling in four years. Businesses have continued to demand a wider variety of skills in their supplemental work force. Temporary-help services are today providing engineers, nurses, word processors, accountants, marketing assistants, and many other kinds of highly trained and skilled professionals. In fact, in 1985 typists and file clerks accounted for only about one-half of the total sales of temporary-help firms. Norrell Services franchises grossed $53 million in 1985. The company emphasizes consultation with companies to help them adjust to changes in their work-force and employee needs. Also, Norrell offers a forty-five-minute response to emergency requests for temporary workers and an unconditional guarantee of satisfaction. Norrell addresses all categories of temporary help but caters to the secretarial and office-automation functions.

WHAT IT TAKES

Norrell charges no franchise fee, but the original franchise agreement, valid for fifteen years, does assure an exclusive territory determined by county or population. Your total initial investment will be $30,000 to $55,0000, with $20,000 of that required in cash. Your investment will cover leasing of office space, decorating, purchase of furniture and equipment, salaries, rent, utilities, insurance, advertising, promotion, and legal and accounting services. You'll pay an ongoing royalty fee based on a percentage of your monthly gross margin. Master franchises are not available. You must be the operating manager of the business. Prior knowledge of the industry is not necessary.

GETTING STARTED

Norrell will assist you with site selection, facility layout and decoration, and lease or purchase of furniture and fixtures; and the company will furnish your initial printed supplies. The typical Norrell office is 1,000 square feet, located in an office building or freestanding building. Your office must meet Norrell's standards as a professional business, and the site is subject to Norrell's approval. You will need two to three full-time employees, including yourself, and Norrell will assist with hiring. Training for all employees begins in Atlanta with one week of classroom instruction on operations, sales, and management in the temporary-help industry followed by 100 days of field training. Consultation will continue after you open, and you will return to the training/learning center for eighty-four hours of additional training annually. You can be in business two months after signing your franchise agreement. Norrell will assist with your grand opening for a fee.

MAKING IT WORK

The company offers co-op advertising for black-and-white and four-color magazine ads, television and radio commercials, and billboard posters. You'll receive at no charge mailers, presentation books, catalogs, national media coverage, in-house media packages, contests, seasonal promotional materials, a lead-referral system, incentives, press releases, and a public-relations/marketing manual. You may purchase newspaper ads, telephone-book ads, brochures, point-of-purchase displays, signs, and banners. There is no ongoing advertising fee. After your initial training you will also receive a self-study course augmented by national conventions held each year, annual regional conferences, quarterly two-day seminars, regular onsite training, and areawide franchise meetings held every three months. Company publications include a magazine issued twice a year; monthly and quarterly newsletters; periodic updates on service, company, and market information; and a quarterly customer-oriented magazine. Surveys are made annually, and award programs honor excellence in office performance.

Backup services include headquarters and regional resource persons; a toll-free hotline; regular onsite visits; onsite troubleshooting; manuals for policy, management procedure, and customer service; all types of forms; and systems for bookkeeping, inventory, expense analysis, computerized management information, and computerized billing. A marketing department develops new and better ways of servicing client firms as well as temporary employees. Franchisees are required to promote only Norrell Temporary Services but are not required to purchase supplies from Norrell. The company offers accounts-receivable financing and sponsors life, major-medical, and dental insurance coverage.

COMMENTS

Entrepreneur magazine ranked Norrell 137th in its 1987 "Franchise 500." Norrell is a member of the IFA and the Georgia Alliance for the Arts and donates 1 percent of its revenues to charities. The company seeks to expand franchise operations in all 50 states and Canada.

GETTING MORE INFORMATION

The franchise packet contains a copy of Norrell's annual report, samples of four-color ads placed in magazines such as *Time* and *Business Week,* fliers explaining the company's operations, copies of articles on the temporary-help field, and a two-page biographical sketch form for you to fill out. For more details, contact:
Dennis Fuller
Director, Franchise Development
Norrell Services
3092 Piedmont Road
Atlanta, GA   30305
(800)   334–9694 or (404)   262–2100

One Hour Moto-Photo

		AS OF		PROJECTED BY	
BUSINESS: one-hour photo-processing centers	NO. OF UNITS	1/1/85	1/1/86	1/1/87	1/1/88
	OWNED BY: COMPANY	2	3	18	35
FOUNDED: 1981	FRANCHISEES	149	181	215	245
FRANCHISED: 1982	LOCATED: IN U.S.	151	184	231	275
START-UP	OUTSIDE U.S.	0	0	2	5
INVESTMENT:	TOTAL:	151	184	233	280
$179,000–$279,000	NO. OF STATES W/ UNITS	18	22	27	30

THE BUSINESS

Today one-hour photo-processing establishments make up 20 percent of the $3.5 billion photo-finishing market. Industry experts predict that the photo-finishing market will double in size over the next seven years, with one-hour processing growing to 50 percent of this market by the end of the 1980s. Moto-Photo, America's largest franchisor of one-hour stores, offers its customers quick, on-site photo finishing, as well as other photo-related services such as enlargements, albums, frames, reprints, video transfer, and portraits. Total sales for One Hour Moto-Photo franchises in 1985 were $40 million, with an average gross income of $240,000 per unit and average net income of $72,000.

WHAT IT TAKES

You don't need a technical or photo-finishing background, but you must have a good credit rating and work experience. Your total initial investment will include $35,000 for the franchise fee, up to $500 for professional fees, up to $12,000 for lease deposits, $20,000 to $60,000 for leasehold improvements, $86,000 to $104,000 for equipment, $6,000 to $7,000 for opening advertising, $500 to $3,500 for initial training, $25,000 to $50,000 for working capital, and $6,500 to $7,500 for opening inventory. You'll need 25 percent of the total investment in cash. Financial assistance is available through Bank One of Ohio. Your exclusive territory will be determined by the market area for your store. You'll pay an ongoing royalty fee of 6 percent of gross sales. You'll be able to purchase additional units for $20,000 each. Master franchises are available.

GETTING STARTED

Moto-Photo will directly assist you with site selection, store design, training, technical needs, and installation of equipment. Also, a company representative will work with you during your first week of operation. You will need a location that provides approximately 1,200 square feet in a mall, shopping center or strip, or a freestanding building. You'll set up your facility according to a uniform Moto-Photo layout using approved materials and supplies. Some of the items necessary for your business are private-label items. The company negotiates discount prices with most vendors for start-up and ongoing supplies.

You'll need three full-time and four part-time employees. Moto-Photo's initial two-week training period takes place in Dayton, Ohio, and combines classroom and hands-on learning. You'll learn about accounting, sales training, marketing, merchandising, personnel management, and technical aspects of your equipment. This is followed by a week of on-the-job training for you and your staff at your facility. Plan on three to six months from signing the franchise agreement to opening your store.

MAKING IT WORK

Your franchise fee will cover a $650 rebate for your travel expenses during the training period, as well as substantial discounts on expenses for equipment, supplies, chemicals, leasehold improvements, architectural plans, and demographic studies. You can realize a direct cost savings of 5 to 10 percent of gross sales on purchases of everyday operating supplies. You'll also receive purchasing assistance based on consumer-demand research. You'll receive a monthly visit from a company representative who will provide technical assistance and ongoing training, and the company will not only develop a marketing and advertising plan tailored for your store and market area but also help you plan your market activities.

Your advertising fees will total 6 percent of your gross sales, with 5.5 percent for local co-op advertising and .5 percent to Moto Photo for development of advertising materials for your use. These include TV and radio commercials, newspaper ads, flyers, and direct-mail pieces. You'll have an opportunity to attend an annual national convention as well as annual regional conferences, and you can participate in a company awards program. You'll receive an informative newsletter six times a year, and product and technical updates periodically. Moto-Photo has a company-sponsored insurance program that includes property, general-liability, life, and major-medical coverage.

COMMENTS

Moto-Photo was ranked 87th in *Venture* magazine's 1986 "Franchise 100" and 265th in *Entrepreneur* magazine's 1987 "Franchise 500." A member of the IFA since 1985, the company provides an earnings claim document prior to a potential franchisee's interview. Moto-Photo wants to add franchises in most states and Europe.

GETTING MORE INFORMATION

The franchise folder includes a concise question-and-answer sheet with information on all phases of a franchise, a questionnaire requesting personal and financial information, and a number of articles about the company and its founder reprinted from business and financial publications. For more information, contact:

Paul Pieschel
Vice-President, Franchise Sales
One Hour Moto-Photo
4444 Lake Center Drive
Dayton, OH   45426
(800) 346-6686 or (513)   854–6686

Packy The Shipper

BUSINESS: packaging
and shipping service
FOUNDED: 1976
FRANCHISED: 1981
START-UP
INVESTMENT:
$995–$1,295

		AS OF		PROJECTED BY	
NO. OF UNITS		1/1/85	1/1/86	1/1/87	1/1/88
OWNED BY: COMPANY		0	0	0	0
	FRANCHISEES	800	1,200	1,800	2,500
LOCATED: IN U.S.		800	1,200	1,800	2,500
	OUTSIDE U.S.	0	0	0	0
TOTAL:		800	1,200	1,800	2,500
NO. OF STATES W/ UNITS		45	48	48	48

THE BUSINESS

Packy the Shipper franchises offer simplified packaging and shipping for both individuals and businesses—and increased sales for the existing businesses in which they are located. The franchise sites serve as drop-off points for packages to be shipped by United Parcel Service or Emery Air Freight. Profit margins can be as high as 90 percent or more, and nearly 44 percent of Packy the Shipper customers make another purchase while in the store. In 1985, Packy the Shipper franchises grossed $4 million.

WHAT IT TAKES

You will need $995 to $1,295 to buy a Packy the Shipper franchise, and the agreement will assure you of an exclusive territory with a perpetual franchise (no renewal necessary). The higher initial fee covers more supplies, such as fliers and sales contracts. The fee must be paid in cash; no financial assistance is available from the company. Additional franchises cost the same amount. Master franchises are not offered. You may acquire a franchise without being the manager of the unit. An ongoing royalty fee is based on the number of packages shipped. Individual units set their own handling charge (ranging from $1.25 to $2 per package) and add that to the shipping charge. No previous knowledge or experience is required.

GETTING STARTED

Since Packy the Shipper units are designed to go into existing businesses, the company will not get directly involved with your facility in any way. Locations range from office buildings to malls. In addition to yourself, only one part-time employee is necessary. A two- to three-hour training program is provided at your location, explaining the total operation, packaging, and how to fill out sales contracts. It will take only two to four weeks to open after you purchase the franchise.

MAKING IT WORK

As part of a cooperative advertising program you will have access to newspaper ads, mailers, telephone-book ads, brochures, television and radio commercials, signs, and press releases. The company conducts onsite training every ninety days for the sales group and sends franchisees a newsletter every six months plus company and market updates every ninety days. Backup services include headquarters and regional resource persons, a toll-free hotline, onsite troubleshooting, order and accounting forms, and systems for bookkeeping and computerized billing. The company will insure shipments for you, offer claim payment and services, audit and pay shippers' bills, provide a tracer service, give an insurance rebate on unspent funds (a secondary profit center), file necessary reports with the Interstate Commerce Commission, maintain your account history and records for one year, and eliminate the UPS charge for weekly pickup (currently $3.25 to $4.25 per week). The company-sponsored insurance offers general-liability coverage. The company offers a profit-sharing plan for franchisees.

COMMENTS

PNS, Inc., is the parent company of Packy the Shipper, which was ranked thirteenth in *Venture* magazine's 1986 "Franchise 100" and thirtieth in *Entrepreneur* magazine's 1987 "Franchise 500." The company wants to add new franchisees in the forty-eight contiguous states. It provides an earnings claim document prior to or during a potential franchisee's personal interview.

GETTING MORE INFORMATION

The franchise packet contains two brochures on the company's operations and profit-sharing plan plus a franchise agreement. For more information, write or call:

R. W. Harrison
President
PNS, Inc.
409 Main Street
Racine, WI   53403
(800)   54 + PACKY

Papa Aldo's Take & Bake Pizza Shops

		AS OF		PROJECTED BY	
BUSINESS: take-and-bake pizza	NO. OF UNITS	1/1/85	1/1/86	1/1/87	1/1/88
FOUNDED: 1981	OWNED BY: COMPANY	2	3	5	8
FRANCHISED: 1982	FRANCHISEES	22	35	60	82
START-UP	LOCATED: IN U.S.	24	38	65	90
INVESTMENT:	OUTSIDE U.S.	0	0	0	0
$70,000–$100,000	TOTAL:	24	38	65	90
	NO. OF STATES W/ UNITS	2	2	4	5

THE BUSINESS

Papa Aldo's Take & Bake Pizza Shop has introduced a new slant on the pizza market by providing freshly made, uncooked pizza to take home and eat hot from the oven. Papa Aldo's pizza needs only twelve to fifteen minutes home baking time, because the crusts have been partially baked in a central bakery before being shipped to the franchise shop. Customers have a choice of thin and crispy or thick and chewy crusts. And all Papa Aldo's pizzas are generously topped with only fresh ingredients. Customers can watch as a carry-out, unbaked meal is prepared in an assembly-line process that produces a pizza every thirty seconds. Since labor costs and overhead are lower for Papa Aldo's shops, the company's products are priced 30 to 35 percent lower than those of other pizzarias.

Papa Aldo's franchise operations did $5.5 million worth of business in 1985. Annual gross sales for individual shops ranged from $101,000 to $295,000, with an average of $185,000 (break even is about $110,000). The average net income per franchise was $27,750.

WHAT IT TAKES

Your initial franchise fee of $15,000 must be in cash. Constructing, decorating, and equipping your shop will cost you an additional $55,000 to $85,000. Your franchise agreement will last for ten years, with five-year renewal periods, and will give you exclusive control of a territory determined by population. If you decide to expand, additional franchises will only cost $12,500 each. If you prefer to invest as a passive owner, you may arrange for someone else to run your operation. You'll pay both an ongoing royalty fee of 5 percent of gross sales, minus coupon discounts, and another 5 percent to the cooperative advertising and promotions fund.

GETTING STARTED

You will receive assistance from Papa Aldo's with virtually everything from site selection to the grand opening, which usually takes place about four months after the franchise purchase. Papa Aldo's experts will help you locate the best shop site—typically in a shopping center—and assist with lease or purchase negotiations and construction. The interior of your shop will be 800 to 1,000 square feet.

Architectural consultants will show you how to custom-tailor your site, emphasizing an old-world charm with Italian accents. You won't need huge ovens or extensive seating, but you will need slicers, scales, and preparation equipment. The staff of Papa Aldo's will help you find sources for the equipment, supplies, and services you'll need.

Your full week of training at the headquarters in Portland, Oregon, will cover quality control, personnel management, marketing, financing, insurance, permits, and other legal requirements of your new business. You will probably need four part-time employees, whom Papa Aldo's staff will help you hire and train. The company will provide expert advertising and promotion for your grand opening.

MAKING IT WORK

A detailed operations manual includes forms, maintenance procedures, guides for record keeping, and more. You'll get a regular newsletter and manual supplements, as well as advertising and business aids to keep you up-to-date. An area representative will visit your shop regularly. Annual national conferences and periodic seminars will provide you with continuing educational support. Your ongoing advertising fee will provide for newspaper and magazine ads, television commercials, brochures, catalogs, signs, contests, and other advertising and promotional aids.

You also will benefit from a central purchasing program that offers volume discounts for the prebaked pizza crusts. Sauces for the pizzas are blended from spice packages supplied by Papa Aldo's, so a uniform quality is guaranteed. Frequent announced and unannounced visits from corporate personnel enforce strict standards in proportions of topping ingredients. The company sponsors a variety of franchisee recognition programs.

COMMENTS

A member of the IFA, Papa Aldo's received one of *Restaurant Hospitality* magazine's national design awards in May 1986. The company is seeking franchisees in the northwestern and southwestern United States and in Canada.

GETTING MORE INFORMATION

The franchise information packet includes a brochure, information sheets, and reprints of several restaurant-magazine articles. For more information, write or call:

John A. Gundle
Chief Executive Officer
Papa Aldo's Take & Bake Pizza Shops
1519 SW Sunset Boulevard
Portland, OR   97201
(503)   246–7272

Paul Davis Systems

		AS OF		PROJECTED BY	
BUSINESS: insurance		1/1/85	1/1/86	1/1/87	1/1/88
restoration-	NO. OF UNITS				
management services	OWNED BY: COMPANY	0	0	0	0
FOUNDED: 1966	FRANCHISEES	65	70	171	311
FRANCHISED: 1970	LOCATED: IN U.S.	65	70	160	300
START-UP	OUTSIDE U.S.	0	0	11	11
INVESTMENT:	TOTAL:	65	70	171	311
$40,000	NO. OF STATES W/ UNITS	23	24	40	50

THE BUSINESS

Insurance restoration contracting is a field situated between the insurance industry and the construction business. Paul W. Davis Systems, Inc. (PDS), provides this unique service to insurance adjustors. When a property owner reports a loss due to fire or other calamity, a PDS representative surveys the scene and assesses the damage according to a detailed checklist and evaluation sheet. Using specialty computer software, the PDS staff member quickly generates a detailed estimate of repair and restoration costs and works to arrive at the lowest equitable price on which adjustor and home owner can agree. When the adjustor approves the amount, the PDS representative generates a computer printout of all work orders for the independent contractors.

PDS is a conservative company with well-established roots in a permanent industry. In 1985 the sixty-five PDS franchises grossed a total of $18 million, with an average gross per unit of $691,000 and average net income of over 20 percent. In 1980 total reported fire losses were $5.5 billion, or $23.77 for every individual in the United States. Multiply $23.77 by the population of your area, and you'll have a reasonable annual market projection of fire losses in that area. This figure doesn't include damages caused by wind storms, vehicles, water, or small unreported fires, which all require service. Given such occurrences, the insurance restoration business is resistant to recession.

WHAT IT TAKES

Operation of a PDS franchise requires two people. There are many husband-and-wife teams throughout the company. No previous experience is necessary. The cash investment required to start a PDS franchise is $40,000, which includes the franchise fee of $35,000. The agreement will give you an exclusive territory that can include a population up to 300,000, and this will apply for an initial period of five years, with an option for a one-year renewal. You can invest in additional units at the same price.

Of the total franchise fee, $15,000 must be paid to the company as down payment. PDS will finance the remainder in monthly installments of 2.5 percent of business collections or a minimum of $400 per month, whichever is greater, after the start of operations. The note you will sign is a corporate note, so you will have no personal liability. A franchise territory with a population of less than 12,000 sells for $20,000. In this case, you would pay $10,000 down and have a note for $10,000 with the same terms as those just described. You'll pay a monthly royalty fee of 2.5 percent of your gross sales.

GETTING STARTED

Your business will function on a fixed sales price tied to a fixed cost, resulting in an operation with low overhead. No commercial office space is necessary; only a simple two-section office is required. Your home or garage apartment would be adequate. Your office furnishings will consist of two desks, two file cabinets, a telephone, and your computer system. You will have no inventories or perishables and no support cost for national advertising.

You'll attend three weeks of classes at the PDS training school in Jacksonville, Florida, where you'll learn about the computer system, accounting, onsite damage estimating, and business psychology. After your training is completed, you'll return to your home office for a further week of training in setting up operations. You can be open for business one month after signing the franchise agreement.

MAKING IT WORK

PDS has more than 150 computer software programs designed to assist every phase of your business operations. In addition, as a new owner, you'll be supplied with a series of contracts that are derived from twenty years of business experience. You'll also receive a public-relations and marketing manual, brochures and presentation materials, and a quarterly newsletter. The company holds periodic areawide franchise meetings and sponsors an insurance package that offers property, life, and major-medical coverage.

COMMENTS

Paul W. Davis Systems, Inc., was rated 194th in *Entrepreneur* magazine's 1987 "Franchise 500." A break-even analysis and earnings claim document are available to potential franchises. The company is seeking franchises in almost all states.

GETTING MORE INFORMATION

The franchise information packet includes a franchise disclosure document, franchise disclosure document exhibits, a copy of the standard franchise purchase agreement, an initial application form, a complete description of operations and requirements, and a reprint of a magazine article about the company. For more information, contact:

Patrick Kienel
Franchise Sales Director
Paul Davis Systems, Inc.
1900 The Exchange #655
Atlanta, GA   30339–2028
(800)   722–3939 or (404)   951–0056

P&D/Premier Auto Parts

BUSINESS:			AS OF		PROJECTED BY	
			1/1/85	1/1/86	1/1/87	1/1/88
automotive-parts	NO. OF UNITS					
delivery and service	OWNED BY: COMPANY		0	0	0	0
FOUNDED: 1919		FRANCHISEES	22	24	28	33
FRANCHISED: 1980	LOCATED: IN U.S.		22	24	28	33
START-UP		OUTSIDE U.S.	0	0	0	0
INVESTMENT:	TOTAL:		22	24	28	33
$35,000–$50,000	NO. OF STATES W/ UNITS		17	17	21	25

THE BUSINESS

P&D began designing and manufacturing ignition parts in 1919 with ignition points for the Maxwell automobile. Evolving with the auto industry, P&D is now the oldest independent ignition company. A delivery and service system, P&D provides quality merchandise at factory direct prices to independent garages, service stations, fleet shops, and car dealers. A wide array of products is available to service domestic cars, foreign cars, and light- and heavy-duty trucks. A franchisee buys approved automotive parts directly from the manufacturer through P&D and stocks and delivers these parts to customers in the franchise territory. The franchisee normally stocks his or her automotive parts at home in a garage or basement and delivers them in a fourteen- to sixteen-foot step van. Competition in the aftermarket is strong, P&D reports, particularly from the local jobber/parts stores. Franchisees counter this with prices that are 25 to 30 percent lower than the local jobber can offer. Gross profits for franchisees traditionally range between 35 and 42 percent of annual gross sales.

WHAT IT TAKES

You will need $8,900 for the initial franchise fee. The agreement provides you with an exclusive territory that will include at least 500 prospective customers (independent garages, fleet shops, etc.). Your total investment, including the franchise fee, will be $35,000 to $50,000 to cover the following: $2,000 for the down payment on your truck (unless you can find a used vehicle); $12,000 to $14,000 for the initial parts inventory; and the remainder for operating capital. For a bigger return later, the company recommends reinvesting most of your income into your business during the first three to six months of operation. You must arrange any financing that you may need. Additional franchise units are also $8,900. Master franchises are not available. You may buy a franchise without actually running the business, but P&D does not encourage the practice. You will pay an ongoing royalty fee based on a percentage of purchases. Prior knowledge of the industry is not necessary.

GETTING STARTED

P&D offers assistance with vehicle lease or purchase; truck layout; and acquisition of supplies, materials, and merchandise. Since you will be operating from your home, you will not have any need for an additional office. You will be expected to display the company's standard graphics with logo on all company vehicles. The business will be a one-person operation, at least at the beginning. The company will train you for one week at the Carmel, Indiana, corporate offices in a classroom setting. Topics covered will include establishing a route, truck layout, history of the automotive parts aftermarket, competition and interchanges, salesmanship, bookkeeping, product knowledge, and inventory control. After this first week of training you can expect to receive all of your inventory within about a month. Before the inventory arrives you can begin making contacts in your territory. When you are ready to go into the territory to sell, a sales and marketing person from P&D will work with you for the first week.

MAKING IT WORK

P&D offers mailers, brochures, presentation books, catalogs, point-of-purchase displays, contests, seasonal promotional materials, a lead-referral system, and press releases at no charge. Also, there is no advertising fee. Incentive programs, signs, and special motivational cassette tapes are also available. The company sponsors annual national conventions, and you will receive onsite training every three months as needed. P&D issues a quarterly company newsletter; regular updates on products, company information, and market information; and franchisee surveys as required. Recognition programs honor top-selling franchises. Backup systems include headquarters resource persons, regular onsite visits, manuals for policy and management procedures, all types of forms, and systems for bookkeeping and inventory. You will benefit from a central purchasing program with volume discounts, a centralized merchandising system, and company brands. Company-sponsored insurance programs offer property, general-liabilty, automobile, life, and major-medical coverage.

COMMENTS

P&D was ranked 485th in *Entrepreneur* magazine's "Franchise 500" for 1987. The company is seeking franchises in forty-seven states.

GETTING MORE INFORMATION

The franchise information packet contains a history of P&D, a product-line sheet, samples of the newsletter and a franchisee news bulletin, information on vehicle requirements, a franchise questionnaire, and a brief data report. For more information, write or call:

Don E. Boyle
President
P&D/Premier Auto Parts, Inc.
470 Gradle Drive
Carmel, IN   46069
(317)   848–1016

Pearle Vision Centers

BUSINESS: retail
optical company
FOUNDED: 1962
FRANCHISED: 1980
START-UP
INVESTMENT:
$50,000–$300,000

NO. OF UNITS		AS OF		PROJECTED BY	
		1/1/85	1/1/86	1/1/87	1/1/88
OWNED BY: COMPANY		405	400	410	420
FRANCHISEES		470	530	575	620
LOCATED: IN U.S.		875	930	985	1,040
OUTSIDE U.S.		0	0	0	0
TOTAL:		875	930	985	1,040
NO. OF STATES W/ UNITS		42	44	46	47

THE BUSINESS

The largest retail eye-care company in the world, Pearle Vision has its own regional laboratories to supply retail outlets with surface grinding and special-order items. To emphasize its commitment to quality and customer satisfaction Pearle offers a guarantee: for one year from purchase a Pearle Vision Center will repair or replace broken eyeglass frames and lenses at no charge. Each customer receives the guarantee automatically with every pair of prescription glasses. Contact lenses are also a major part of Pearle's inventory. In 1985, Pearle's franchise operations grossed a total of $175 million, with average sales per unit of $330,000 and net income of $60,000.

WHAT IT TAKES

You will need $15,000 for the initial franchise fee. The original franchise agreement extends for ten years, renewable for another ten, but does not offer an exclusive territory. You will need a total of $50,000 to $300,000, depending on whether you convert a business you already own, purchase another to convert, or build a new facility. Ten percent of your total investment must be in cash, and Pearle offers direct financial assistance for the balance. Additional units cost $15,000 each. Master franchises are not available. You must take an active part in managing the business. An ongoing royalty fee is based on 8.5 percent of gross sales, and you'll also pay an 8 percent of gross sales advertising fee to support the company's extensive national advertising. You must be a licensed optometrist or optician to be considered for a franchise.

GETTING STARTED   Pearle provides assistance with establishing service and maintenance contracts and acquiring materials and supplies. For a fee Pearle will help with site selection, lease negotiation, construction, facility layout and decoration, and lease or purchase of furniture and fixtures. A typical Pearle Vision Center is 1,500 square feet, located in a mall, shopping center, or freestanding building. Except for converted locations, all Pearle offices have a uniform layout. Including yourself, your staff will consist of one part-time and two full-time employees. You will go to Dallas for three days of training, in which you'll learn about material cost controls, the labs and distribution system, personnel, business management, financial reporting, and accounting systems. You can open your franchise in as little as one month if you're converting a store or four months if you're opening a new facility. Pearle will provide a grand-opening advertising campaign to help you get under way.

MAKING IT WORK   Your advertising fee will be split 6 percent for national and 2 percent for local efforts. To support your local advertising and marketing program, you'll receive newspaper and telephone book ads, mailers and brochures, television and radio commercials, in-house media packages (slides, videotapes), point-of-purchase displays, billboard posters, signs, banners, contests and incentives, press releases, and a public-relations and marketing manual. Pearle holds a national convention once a year, regional conferences every three months, and seminars three times a year. The company sends quarterly newsletters and monthly product updates. Various award programs recognize franchise success.

Backup systems include headquarters and regional resource persons; regular onsite visits and onsite troubleshooting; manuals for policy, management procedures, and customer service; all types of forms; and systems for bookkeeping, inventory, personnel, expense analysis, computerized management information, and computerized billing. Research and development departments focus on marketing and merchandising. Pearle has not only centralized labs and distribution facilities offering volume discounts but also real estate and construction subsidiaries. You may buy from other suppliers as long as the labs are approved by Pearle and the frames are in Pearle's frame line. Pearle sponsors insurance packages for property, general-liability, life, major-medical, dental, and disability coverage.

COMMENTS   Pearle was ranked thirty-ninth in *Venture* magazine's "Franchise 100" for 1986. Pearle is a member of the IFA. The company is seeking to expand franchise operations in forty-three states, Canada, Europe, and Japan.

GETTING MORE INFORMATION

The franchise information packet contains a brochure on Pearle's operations and a franchise inquiry questionnaire. For more information, write or call:

Steve Berkman
Director of Franchise Sales
Pearle Vision Centers, Inc.
2534 Royal Lane
Dallas, TX   75229
(800)   Pearle–1 or (214)   241–3381

PIP Postal Instant Press

BUSINESS: offset printing, copying, and related printing services
FOUNDED: 1965
FRANCHISED: 1968
START-UP INVESTMENT: $82,000

		AS OF		PROJECTED BY	
		1/1/85	1/1/86	1/1/87	1/1/88
NO. OF UNITS					
OWNED BY:	COMPANY	6	4	2	1
	FRANCHISEES	953	1,041	1,107	1,215
LOCATED:	IN U.S.	916	989	1,048	1,145
	CANADA	43	56	61	71
TOTAL:		959	1,045	1,109	1,216
NO. OF STATES W/ UNITS		45	45	45	45

THE BUSINESS

Businesses increasingly recognize that their literature reflects directly on the quality of their company, so a growing number want excellent printing services for their materials. The quick-print industry is one of the fastest growing in the country and Postal Instant Press (PIP) is the world's largest printing chain, with over 1,000 locations. The company reports that 98 percent of all PIP franchises opened in the past twenty years are still operating. In 1985 the company's franchise operations grossed a total of $195 million, with average gross sales per unit of approximately $200,000 a year.

WHAT IT TAKES

You will pay a $40,000 franchise fee. The agreement, valid for twenty years and renewable for the same period, guarantees an exclusive territory covering approximately 1,500 business licenses, depending on the geography and types of businesses in the area. Your total initial investment will be about $82,000, including $42,000 for equipment and working capital. You should expect to have $15,000 of the total in cash, and the company can provide financial assistance through PIP Capital, Inc., a wholly owned subsidiary, for the remainder. A second franchise in the same territory may be bought for $2,500, or $7,500 for limited circumstances out of the territory. International master franchises are also available. You must manage the day-to-day operations of your franchise. Ongoing royalty fees will be 6 percent on the first $4,000 of gross sales and 8 percent on gross sales in excess of $4,000 a month. More than 98 percent of the company's franchise owners have not been involved in printing before buying a PIP franchise.

GETTING STARTED

The company will assist with site selection; lease negotiation; facility layout; decoration; furniture and fixture lease or purchase; equipment lease or purchase; service and maintenance contracts; and acquisition of materials, supplies, and merchandise. The typical facility is 1,200 square feet, and is located in an office building, shopping center, freestanding building, and commercial industrial park. You will be expected to use the company's standard facility unit and service marks, and your equipment must conform to certain standards.

A PIP franchise needs two full-time employees, including the owner/manager. Training will begin with two weeks for the owner/manager at the PIP training center in Los Angeles. Classroom and hands-on lessons will cover press and camera work, store operations, printing knowledge, company orientation, and financial and marketing operations. You can plan to open about three months after buying a franchise. The company will assist with your grand opening.

MAKING IT WORK

Your ongoing advertising fee of $500 a month, plus 1 percent of gross sales (which the company will match), will cover newspaper and black-and-white magazine ads, brochures, mailers, television and radio commercials, national media coverage, and billboard posters. In addition, the company provides telephone-book ads, point-of-purchase displays, presentation books, catalogs, in-house media packages of slides or videotapes, signs, banners, contests, seasonal promotional materials, a lead-referral system, press releases, and public-relations/marketing manuals. You will be kept up-to-date with biannual conventions, annual regional conferences, periodic one-day seminars, and quarterly onsite training. The company distributes a bimonthly company newsletter and regular updates pertinent to the business.

PIP sponsors various recognition programs and provides such backup services as headquarters and regional resource persons; a toll-free hotline; regular onsite visits and troubleshooting; manuals for policy, management procedure, and customer service; forms for inventory, personnel, ordering, and accounting; systems for bookkeeping, inventory, expense analysis, computerized billing, and computerized management information; and electronic publishing. PIP franchises have the benefit of national equipment and supplies contracts with PIP divisions that produce or distribute merchandise, and a central purchasing system offers volume discounts. Franchisees are not required to use or sell only company products; however, materials must be approved by the company. PIP offers insurance programs for property, general-liability, automobile, major-medical, dental, and worker's compensation coverage.

COMMENTS

PIP was ranked thirty-fourth in *Entrepreneur* magazine's 1987 "Franchise 500" and forty-eighth in *Venture* magazine's 1986 "Franchise 100." A member of the IFA since 1971 and recipient of the first Annual IFA Franchise Relations Award, PIP participates in March of Dimes campaigns and encourages extensive PIP owner involvement in community affairs. The company seeks to increase franchise operations in forty-nine states, Australia, Canada, Europe, Japan, and Mexico.

GETTING MORE INFORMATION

The franchise information packet contains materials on marketing, investing, advertising, the printing industry, and the people of PIP; a four-page financial application; and a listing of all PIP franchises. For more information, write or call:

L. Anthony Rubin
Vice-President/General Counsel
Postal Instant Press
8201 Beverly Boulevard
Los Angeles, CA   90043
(800)   421–4634 (in California);
(800)   638–8441 or (213)   653–8750 (outside California)

The Pit Pros

BUSINESS:
automobile-
maintenance service
FOUNDED: 1981
FRANCHISED: 1981
**START-UP
INVESTMENT:**
$54,350–$80,650

		AS OF		PROJECTED BY	
NO. OF UNITS		1/1/85	1/1/86	1/1/87	1/1/88
OWNED BY: COMPANY		0	0	0	0
FRANCHISEES		96	128	275	450
LOCATED: IN U.S.		96	128	275	450
CANADA		0	0	0	0
TOTAL:		96	128	275	450
NO. OF STATES W/ UNITS		7	8	11	15

THE BUSINESS

The automotive-service industry in the United States makes almost $95 billion in sales annually—over $13 billion in services alone—and is growing at an annual rate of more than 9 percent. Because of economic conditions, the nature of the automotive-service industry has been changing. Over 95,000 service stations have closed since

1972. By the end of the 1980s more than 65 percent of the remaining stations will be self-service only, without maintenance or repair services. At the same time, people are keeping their cars longer and maintaining them better. Many of them have purchased cars with small or diesel engines—cars that need frequent oil changes to stay in good running condition.

This market data inspired the founding of the Pit Pros (under its original name Lube N GO) by a group of businessmen who wanted to capitalize on a potentially profitable yet undeveloped franchise market. Their franchise concept is based on the criteria of low start-up cost, low overhead, low capital investment, low inventory needs, low risk, and no previous experience—but with simple and fast training, high profit margins, and a cash or credit-card payment system. Their service strategy is to provide oil and filter change, lubrication, fluids replenishment, tire-pressure check, and windshield cleaning in less than ten minutes using a two-person crew. By servicing without a long wait and for a fixed fee all kinds of automobiles—foreign or domestic, standard or diesel, family cars or recreational vans—in clean facilities located in suburban neighborhoods, The Pit Pros has established itself as one of the founding companies in the oil- and lube-service franchise market. In 1985 annual gross sales per franchise unit averaged $275,000 with average net income at about $55,000.

WHAT IT TAKES

The Pit Pros franchise fee is $15,000, which will buy you a protected location within a two-mile radius of your shop for the twenty-five-year term of your agreement. In addition to the franchise fee you can expect to pay $17,900 to $32,900 for equipment, tools, fixtures, and signs; $5,700 to $13,000 for building renovation; $3,200 for the opening inventory; $1,750 for grand-opening expenses; and $10,800 to $14,800 for working capital and deposits.

Although you must pay your franchise fee in cash, The Pit Pros can help you locate financing for the remainder, either through the Small Business Association or a local bank. Although master franchises are not available, you can purchase additional single-unit franchises at a 10 percent reduction in the fee. For each franchise you'll pay an ongoing royalty fee amounting to 5 percent of your gross sales. Passive ownership of an initial franchise is allowed but discouraged, because part of The Pit Pros operational design is to increase profits by making it easy for owners to run the business themselves, without the expense of trained mechanics.

GETTING STARTED

Company experts will assist you with selection of the most advantageous site, lease or purchase negotiations, and (at cost to you, if you want this service) supervision of the remodeling and/or construction of your facility. Your facility will be a freestanding building covering about 1,500 square feet and located in a shopping center or strip. The company has standard blueprints for your use, as well as standard interior and exterior decor and graphics. The company will help you with the lease or purchase of all the furniture, fixtures, equipment, supplies, and merchandise you'll need to get started. Also, the company will advise you on hiring the two full-time and four part-time employees you'll need and will provide you with the standard The Pit Pros uniforms.

You and your manager, if you have one, will attend a two-week training program at The Pit Pros' Chicago offices, where you'll have both classroom sessions and hands-on learning experiences covering technical and management information. You'll also receive policy, management-procedure and public-relations/marketing manuals, bookkeeping, inventory, expense-analysis, and personnel systems; and all the necessary forms. Within four to nine months after signing the franchise agreement, you'll be ready for your grand opening. The Pit Pros will supply you with grand-opening advertising materials—banners and flags, newspaper ads, radio and/or TV commercials, a press package, etc.—and send a company resource person to help out. All the planning and preparation should begin to pay off for you in about six months—that's how quickly many The Pit Pros franchisees begin to show a profit.

MAKING IT WORK

Your ongoing royalty fee will help pay for the development and production of a variety of advertising and marketing materials. You'll receive ad slicks for telephone-book and newspaper advertisements, billboard posters, and radio and television commercials. The company sponsors employee contests regularly and offers a lead-referral system. The Pit Pros sponsors yearly regional conferences, regular citywide or areawide franchisee meetings, monthly half-day seminars, and special onsite training as requested. The company also sends franchisees a newsletter and periodic technical updates on products and services. The Pit Pros has negotiated national purchasing contracts that will give you volume discounts on materials and supplies. Headquarters-based resource people will visit your facility regularly, and they will offer onsite troubleshooting, financial counseling, and continuous assistance on management, marketing, and technical matters.

COMMENTS

The Pit Pros was ranked 493rd in *Entrepreneur* magazine's 1987 "Franchise 500." The company makes an earnings claim document available prior to or during a potential franchisee's personal interview. The Pit Pros is seeking franchises in a dozen midwestern and southern states.

GETTING MORE INFORMATION

The franchise information packet consists of a brochure covering basic industry and business information, including a page of professional references and brief resumes of the corporate officers; photocopies of various articles on the oil- and lube-service industry and franchising in general; and an application form requesting your basic personal and financial data. For details, write to:

Timothy Whyte
President
The Pit Pros
9657 Distribution Avenue
San Diego, CA   92121
(619)   566–2690

Pizza Inn

BUSINESS: pizza
  restaurant
  FOUNDED: 1961
  FRANCHISED: 1963
START-UP
  INVESTMENT:
  $150,000–$225,000

		AS OF		PROJECTED BY	
NO. OF UNITS		1/1/85	1/1/86	1/1/87	1/1/88
OWNED BY:	COMPANY	287	255	265	275
	FRANCHISEES	419	472	525	575
LOCATED:	IN U.S.	691	707	760	800
	OUTSIDE U.S.	15	20	30	50
TOTAL:		706	727	790	850
NO. OF STATES W/ UNITS		30	29	32	35

THE BUSINESS

Pizza is one of the fastest growing segments in the growing $100 billion restaurant business. Pizza Inn offers a pizza-plus restaurant serving spaghetti, lasagna, hot and cold sandwiches, and salad in addition to their Italian pies. Besides seated dining, Pizza Inn offers take-out and delivery services. Since opening for business in 1961, the company has expanded not only in the United States but also in the Far East, the Middle East, and Africa. In 1984, Pizza Inn restaurant operations generated sales of more than $250 million. The average sales per store were more than $350,000.

WHAT IT TAKES

The company requires all franchisees to have a net worth of at least $150,000. If you qualify, you'll need $17,500 to pay your Pizza Inn franchise fee. This will buy you one restaurant with a one-mile protected territory. Your total investment will vary depending upon whether you want a delivery-only operation ($150,000) or a full-service restaurant ($225,000)—but for either you must have a minimum of $75,000 available in cash. Pizza Inn will help you arrange financing of the balance with Westinghouse Credit Corporation or some other investment lending organization.

If you want to buy more than one operation, the franchise fee for each of two to five additional units will run only $12,500; for units six through ten only $7,500 each; for units eleven through fifteen only $5,000 each; and only $2,500 each for all additional units. Fees for franchises outside the United States are higher and vary depending upon the country.

In addition to your initial fee, you'll pay a 4 percent royalty on gross sales (reduced to 3.5 percent for sixteen or more units and 3 percent for twenty-one or more units) plus an additional 1.5 percent royalty for national advertising support. You're also required to set aside 1.5 percent for local advertising. Your agreement will expire in twenty years, but you can renew it then for no additional fee. You don't need to know anything about restaurants—or even cooking—to qualify for a Pizza Inn franchise.

GETTING STARTED

You'll need to hire five full-time and fifteen part-time employees. During a five-week training program, staff at the company training center in Dallas will teach you and your key personnel about every aspect of franchise operation—from dough making to inventory and food cost controls. You'll attend classroom sessions, view videotapes, and get plenty of hands-on experience. When you get back home, you'll be able to use the H.O.T. (Hourly Operations Training) Program—videotapes, an instructional text, and written tests—to prepare your employees.

The company's development team will assist you throughout every phase of getting into business, from site selection and negotiation to building construction and equipment acquisition. Typically, your restaurant will cover 2,990 square feet—only 800 to 1,200 square feet if it's a delivery-only operation—located in a shopping center, mall, or office building. It will be constructed according to one of several prototype designs and decorated with one of four decor packages. Pizza Inn has a construction subsidiary that you can use to build your facility, or you can work with a local contractor. When your restaurant is ready for business—usually within four to six months—a company opening team will help you with all the details of your grand opening.

MAKING IT WORK

As a Pizza Inn franchisee, you'll become a member of the Pizza Inn advertising plan, which provides national media support for the chain. You'll get professionally prepared television commercials, newspaper ads, and flyers to use locally. You'll also receive a public-relations guide, point-of-purchase and seasonal displays, balloons, flags, banners, and signs. Ongoing company market research will keep you up-to-date on all the latest food-service-industry trends. If you have any special marketing questions or problems, you'll be able to turn to your Pizza Inn representative, who will visit your restaurant regularly.

Your representative will also help you set up your operating and accounting procedures; and the company will provide the systems and forms you'll need to generate daily cash reports, weekly and monthly inventories, food and labor analyses, consumption-rate statistics, operational controls, and employee performance reports. You'll also have complete policy, management-procedure, and customer-service manuals to refer to for day-to-day operations, but for unanswered questions you can contact headquarters personnel on the toll-free hotline.

Your store will be equipped with a videotape player so that you or your store manager can schedule ongoing H.O.T. Program training sessions as needed to fit your particular operation. The company sponsors one- to two-day seminars on a weekly basis and onsite training by a field consultant four times a year. You'll also have the opportunity to attend two regional conferences and two national conferences (one company sponsored, the other franchisee sponsored) each year. Between issues of the bimonthly company magazine, you'll receive regular updates on company and industry news as well as product or service developments.

Pizza Inn's research-and-development laboratory not only tests and evaluates new recipes and products to offer customers but also better ways to prepare and serve foods. Quality Sausage Company, Branch Cheese Company, and Norco Manufacturing and Distributing Company—the company's food and distribution subsidiaries—will give you the convenience of one-stop shopping for your supplies as well as the cost savings of volume purchasing. Finally, Pizza Inn sponsors a comprehensive insurance package that includes general-liability, property, and automobile coverage for your business, and life, major-medical, dental, disability, and worker's compensation coverage for your employees. Third-party bonding is also included.

COMMENTS

Pizza Inn was ranked seventy-sixth in *Entrepreneur* magazine's 1987 "Franchise 500." A member of the IFA since 1985, the company wants to expand throughout the United States as well as in Canada and Mexico and overseas.

GETTING MORE INFORMATION

The franchise information packet contains data sheets giving the specifics of Pizza Inn's franchise operation and showing color photographs of foods, restaurants, personnel, and various operations;

an annual report; and a four-page application form that asks for extensive business and financial information. For more information, contact:

Paul R. Brown
Vice-President
Pizza Inn, Inc.
2930 Stemmons Freeway
P. O. Box 660193
Dallas, TX   75266–0193
(800)   527–1483 or (214)   638–7250

P.k.g.'s

BUSINESS: packaging
and shipping service
FOUNDED: 1983
FRANCHISED: 1983
START-UP
INVESTMENT:
$30,000–$40,000

		AS OF		PROJECTED BY	
		1/1/85	1/1/86	1/1/87	1/1/88
NO. OF UNITS					
OWNED BY:	COMPANY	1	3	4	6
	FRANCHISEES	24	30	42	66
LOCATED:	IN U.S.	25	33	46	72
	OUTSIDE U.S.	0	0	0	0
TOTAL:		25	33	46	72
NO. OF STATES W/ UNITS		6	8	12	16

THE BUSINESS

A unique packaging, shipping, and gift-wrapping service, P.k.g.'s serves individuals, hotels, motels, antique dealers, computer service centers, retail shops, and manufacturers who want to ship everything from golf clubs to stereos. The company has no exclusive agreements with any shipper, so it can select the most economical shipping method for customers. P.k.g.'s provides custom cartons and crates, packs fragile items with a foam-in-place system, sends gifts, packages perishable items, sells cartons and packing materials, and makes daily shipments via United Parcel Service, motor and air freight, and the U.S. Postal Service. The company reported $2.3 million in annual sales for franchise operations in 1985, with average gross sales per unit of $70,000.

WHAT IT TAKES

You will need $10,000 for the franchise fee. The original agreement, which extends for ten years and is renewable for ten, will guarantee an exclusive territory within a two-mile radius of your store location. Your total investment, including the franchise fee, will be $30,000 to $40,000, and $30,000 of that must be in cash. Two thousand of the total amount will be for preopening advertising. Additional units also sell for $10,000, and master franchises are available. You will pay an ongoing royalty fee of 4 percent of gross sales, payable monthly. The company prefers that you be the on-premises manager. Previous experience is not necessary.

GETTING STARTED

P.k.g.'s will help with site selection. A typical facility has 1,000 square feet and is located in a shopping center. You will be expected to follow the uniform store design, using specified equipment, fixtures, and inventory. The company will furnish you with a store interior layout adapted from their standard design. Upon your approval, they will then provide you with leasehold improvement materials (wall and floor coverings and lighting fixtures) and detailed instructions for installation. Upon completion, P.k.g.'s store-installation manager will deliver and install all of the store cabinetry, equipment, displays, supplies, and inventory. The onsite, turnkey installation normally takes four days.

If you can act as the full-time manager, you'll need only one part-time employee. Training lasts for one week in a company-owned store and covers operations, sales, marketing, policies and procedures, and your preopening schedule. In addition, you and your employees will receive at least three days of training in your store. You can expect to open two months after buying your franchise. The company will help with your grand opening.

MAKING IT WORK

Your advertising fee will entitle you to newspaper and black-and-white magazine ads, mailers, telephone-book ads, brochures, presentation books, catalogs, television and radio commercials, billboard posters, signs, banners, contests, seasonal promotional materials, a lead-referral system, incentives, press releases, and a public-relations/marketing manual. An annual convention is held for franchisees. The company publishes a biweekly newsletter and updates on products, service, company information, and industry information.

Administrative support includes headquarters resource persons; a toll-free hotline; regular on site visits; on site troubleshooting; manuals on policy, management procedure, and customer service; all types of forms; and an expense-analysis system. The company-owned locations constantly try new products, services, and marketing techniques to pass along to franchisees. A central purchasing program offers volume discounts, and company brands are available. You may use other types of products as long as they meet franchise specifications. Company-sponsored insurance offers property and general-liability coverage.

COMMENTS P.k.g.'s was ranked 453rd in *Entrepreneur* magazine's 1987 "Franchise 500." The company is seeking franchisees in thirty-one states.

GETTING MORE INFORMATION The franchise information packet contains a brochure on company operations, question-and-answer sheets, and a preliminary franchise application. For more information, write or call:

Thomas R. Sizer
President
P.k.g.'s
7681 Montgomery Road
Cincinnati, OH 45236
(800) 543–7547 or (513) 793–4460 (call collect)

Precision Tune

BUSINESS:			AS OF		PROJECTED BY	
specialized car tune-	NO. OF UNITS		1/1/85	1/1/86	1/1/87	1/1/88
up service	OWNED BY: COMPANY		5	2	0	0
FOUNDED: 1975		FRANCHISEES	235	283	335	435
FRANCHISED: 1977	LOCATED: IN U.S.		240	285	335	435
START-UP		OUTSIDE U.S.	0	0	0	0
INVESTMENT:	TOTAL:		240	285	335	435
$97,000–$113,300	NO. OF STATES W/ UNITS		30	30	34	38

THE BUSINESS The high price of new automobiles has motivated many motorists to keep their cars longer and spend more dollars maintaining them. People with new cars find the increasingly complex electronic systems far too complicated for the do-it-yourselfer to maintain. There has been a dramatic drop in the number of facilities that offer automotive service and repair. More and more service stations have become self-service gas stations, and the number of automotive dealerships has decreased significantly because of falling sales of new cars. A pioneer in its field, Precision Tune has emerged as the nation's largest franchisor of specialty automotive tune-up centers. In 1985 total dollar volume for franchise operations was $72 million, with individual units grossing approximately $300,000.

Precision Tune centers use state-of-the-art electronic diagnostic and testing equipment. Each one backs up its work with a warranty good in Precision Tune centers coast to coast that guarantees both parts and labor for six months or 6,000 miles. Over 70 percent of all Precision Tune franchisees are multiple center owners.

WHAT IT TAKES

You will need $15,000 for the initial franchise fee. Your agreement will be valid for ten years and renewable for five, but will not guarantee an exclusive territory. Your total investment, including the franchise fee, will range from $97,000 to $113,300 for equipment, leasehold improvements, insurance, signs, installation of equipment, travel expenses for employees to attend training school, initial advertising, and working capital. This does not include the cost of freight or of land and construction if a new facility is built. Of the total investment $30,000 must be in cash; financing for the remainder is available through Allied Lending. Subsequent units are $15,000 each, and master franchises are available. You may buy a franchise without actually being involved in day-to-day operations, but Precision Tune discourages the practice. Your ongoing royalty fee will be 7.5 percent of gross sales. Prior knowledge of the field is not required.

GETTING STARTED

The company provides assistance with site selection and lease negotiation. A typical facility is 2,500 square feet in a shopping center or a freestanding building. You may convert an existing service station. Approvals are required on sites, facilities, services, signs, advertising, marketing materials, uniforms, and equipment. Including you, the center will need one part-time and four full-time employees. Two weeks of training will be arranged for you and your employees at corporate headquarters in Beaumont, Texas, where you'll learn about center operations, marketing, and technical and policy procedures in both classroom and hands-on training. You can open about six months after purchasing a Precision Tune franchise. You will receive assistance with your grand opening.

MAKING IT WORK

For part of your 9 percent advertising fee you'll receive newspaper ads, mailers, telephone-book ads, brochures, television and radio commercials, in-house media packages, and a lead-referral system. An annual convention and a local representative available in most markets will keep you in touch with company happenings, and area-wide franchise meetings are held as needed. In addition, you'll receive a bimonthly newsletter; a film library on management, operations, and technical topics; and weekly technical bulletins. Awards are given for technical training.

Backup systems include headquarters and regional resource persons; regular onsite visits; onsite troubleshooting; manuals for policy and management procedures; forms for inventory, ordering, and accounting; and an inventory system. Precision Tune offers a complete parts distribution service and warehouse; a central purchasing system for volume discounts; and company brands of spark plugs, filters, and promotional items. You will not be required to sell only company products, but you must select products that meet Precision Tune's specifications.

COMMENTS

Precision Tune was ranked 106th in *Entrepreneur* magazine's 1987 "Franchise 500" and 85th in *Venture* magazine's 1986 "Franchise 100." A member of the IFA since 1979, the company is seeking to expand operations in forty-nine states, Canada, Europe, and Japan.

GETTING MORE INFORMATION

The franchise information packet contains fliers on all aspects of the company's operations and the automotive aftermarket, interviews with individual franchisees, a map of locations, and a qualification form. For more information, write or call:

Steve Goff
Director of New Center Development
Precision Tune, Inc.
P. O. Box 6065
755 South 11th Street
Beaumont, TX   77705
(800)   231–0588 or (409)   838–3781 (call collect)

PrintMasters

BUSINESS: instant printing center
FOUNDED: 1976
FRANCHISED: 1976
START-UP INVESTMENT: $99,500

NO. OF UNITS	AS OF		PROJECTED BY	
	1/1/85	1/1/86	1/1/87	1/1/88
OWNED BY: COMPANY	0	0	1	1
FRANCHISEES	30	40	55	100
LOCATED: IN U.S.	30	40	56	101
OUTSIDE U.S.	0	0	0	0
TOTAL:	30	40	56	101
NO. OF STATES W/ UNITS	2	2	2	3

THE BUSINESS

Primarily concentrated in southern California, PrintMasters is an instant printing center that services small businesses, law firms, medical and professional offices, and manufacturers. Emphasizing a marketing approach to expand business, PrintMasters sees every business as a potential user of printing. The centers prepare mostly medium-volume runs of simple copy and related services such as collating, binding, stapling, and folding. Through arrangements with other companies, franchisees can offer many printing services that they do not specialize in. In 1985, PrintMasters franchises grossed $8.5 million, with average sales per unit of $216,000.

WHAT IT TAKES

Your initial franchise fee will be $24,500. Guaranteeing an exclusive territory determined by zip code (at least 1,000 business licenses), the franchise agreement is valid for twenty years and renewable for twenty. Your total investment will be about $99,500 to cover the fee, equipment ($45,000), and working capital ($30,000). Your working capital must be in cash, but the remainder may be financed. Additional units cost half as much as the first; master franchises are not available. You may be a nonoperating manager, but PrintMasters does not encourage the practice. Ongoing annual royalty fees are a fixed amount: $250 the first year, increasing up to $550 in years four through twenty. No prior experience is necessary.

GETTING STARTED

PrintMasters offers a turnkey operation and assists with site selection, lease and purchase negotiation, construction, facility layout and design, and acquisition of all equipment and supplies. The company will also do an in-depth marketing study for you and obtain all licenses and permits necessary to open. The typical facility is 1,000 square feet, located in an office building, shopping center, freestanding building, or commercial or industrial park. PrintMasters will hire the three full-time employees you'll need. You and your employees will learn all aspects of printing and managing a business in four weeks of training held in both the PrintMasters corporate offices and your PrintMasters shop. After you buy a franchise, you may be in full operation within three to four months. The company will help with your grand opening by providing an ad campaign for direct mail, personal solicitation, and print media.

MAKING IT WORK

PrintMasters plans to implement an ongoing advertising fee of 2 percent of gross sales to cover mailers, brochures, presentation books, catalogs, in-house media packages, point-of-purchase displays, banners, seasonal promotional materials, a lead-referral system, incentives, press releases, and a public-relations/marketing manual. Co-op advertising money is offered for telephone-book ads. The company holds regional conventions once a year, one-day profit-management seminars every six weeks, financial and accounting counseling sessions, and onsite training as needed.

Additional information comes from a company newsletter plus periodic updates on products, service, company news, and industry activities. City and areawide franchise meetings are held and franchisee surveys conducted as needed. Backup services include headquarters resource persons, a toll-free hotline, onsite troubleshooting, manuals on policy and management procedures, forms for inventory and ordering, and a bookkeeping system. PrintMasters has a central purchasing system to offer volume discounts, and you may sell noncompany products as long as they meet quality standards set by PrintMasters. Company-sponsored insurance offers property, general-liability, and medical coverage.

COMMENTS   PrintMasters was ranked 324th in *Entrepreneur* magazine's 1987 "Franchise 500." The company wants to add franchises in Arizona, California, and Texas.

GETTING MORE INFORMATION   The franchise information packet contains question-and-answer sheets on company operations, a detailed list of required equipment, an application questionnaire, and a six-page application form. For more details, contact;
Thomas P. Vitacco
President
PrintMasters, Inc.
350 South Crenshaw Boulevard, Suite A–106
Torrance, CA   90503
(800)   221–8945 or (213)   328–0303

Putt-Putt Golf Courses

BUSINESS: miniature golf courses
FOUNDED: 1954
FRANCHISED: 1955
START-UP INVESTMENT: $70,000–$900,000

		AS OF		PROJECTED BY	
NO. OF UNITS		1/1/85	1/1/86	1/1/87	1/1/88
OWNED BY: COMPANY		8	8	9	10
FRANCHISEES		399	407	417	429
LOCATED: IN U.S.		356	359	368	379
OUTSIDE U.S.		51	56	58	60
TOTAL:		407	415	426	439
NO. OF STATES W/ UNITS		39	39	40	40

THE BUSINESS   Putt-Putt golf courses have been providing fun for sports enthusiasts, young and old, for more than thirty-two years. The idea for the company was born when businessman Don Clayton, under doctor's orders to rest and relax, found an outlet in miniature golf. The largest franchisor of miniature golf courses, Putt-Putt offers golf only or golf and advanced electronic gamerooms and Scoop-Scoop Ice Cream Shoppes. The company recommends the fifty-four- or seventy-two-hole Putt-Putt golf courses for large metropolitan areas and thirty-six-hole courses for smaller cities. Because of low profit returns on eighteen-hole locations, Putt-Putt no longer recommends construction of these small courses. For courses with hired management, Putt-Putt reports an average net income of 21 percent of total revenues and 32 percent net operating income for owner-operated courses. In 1985, Putt-Putt franchises grossed $25 million, with average gross sales per unit of $62,500.

WHAT IT TAKES　　　You will need $10,000 for the initial Putt-Putt Golf Course franchise fee, $5,000 for a Putt-Putt Golf and Gameroom franchise, or $15,000 for both. Guaranteeing you an exclusive territory extending in a four-mile radius from your golf course, the original agreement will be valid for forty years and renewable year to year after that. Options for the golf course may be taken for sixty days at $2,000, the gameroom only for sixty days at $2,000, and both for ninety days at $3,000. Your total investment will range from $70,000 to $900,000 with the cost to open a thirty-six-hole course estimated to average $130,000 and that for a fifty-four-hole course to average $195,000. Fifteen to 20 percent of the total must be in cash, with no financial assistance available from the company. Additional units will cost the same amount; master franchises are not available. You may be an owner-investor, but the company recommends that you run the business. You will pay 5 percent of gross ticket sales for an ongoing royalty fee, with 3 percent of that considered a service fee and 2 percent for national advertising. No prior experience is needed to operate a Putt-Putt franchise.

GETTING STARTED　　　The typical Putt-Putt location is 60,000 square feet, located near a mall or shopping center. Your location must be zoned for miniature golf and not situated immediately adjacent to a residence. After approving a local site for your course, the Putt-Putt home office will design a custom golf-course layout. For the company staff to design your course properly, you must furnish topographical maps of the land and obtain information on local regulations regarding, for example, curb breaks and setback lines. When the course is designed, Southern Golf Distributors, Inc., will provide a list of materials and supplies necessary for the construction to meet full Putt-Putt requirements. You can expect to receive these materials within three weeks. Putt-Putt will also help you stock the course with necessary supplies and merchandise. You will be required to conform to all copyright design and trademark standards.

　　　The course will be staffed by two full-time and five part-time employees, and Putt-Putt will assist with hiring. When you are ready to open, the home office will furnish you a manager's manual to assist you in the proper training of your personnel. The company schedules regional training schools on a regular basis. If a regional school scheduled prior to your course opening, the company will require your personnel to attend. If a school is not scheduled prior to your opening, the company will encourage your personnel to participate in five days of intensive training at an approved home-office course location. Your contract will require you, as the owner, or your principal manager to attend the first annual national convention and/or the first training school held following your opening. You can expect to be open within three months after purchasing a Putt-Putt franchise. The company will help you with your grand opening.

MAKING IT WORK

Your advertising fee will cover a myriad of marketing tools: newspaper, telephone-book, and black-and-white and four-color magazine ads; mailers; brochures; presentation books; television and radio commercials; in-house media packages (slides, videotapes); point-of-purchase displays; billboard posters; signs; contests; seasonal promotional materials; incentives; press releases; and a public-relations/marketing manual. Co-op funding is offered for banners, flags, and balloons. The company sponsors an annual national convention, an annual regional owners' meeting, two-day seminars every two months, regular areawide franchise meetings, and onsite training as needed. Communication will continue with a quarterly company magazine; a weekly newsletter; updates on service, company and market information as needed; a customer-oriented magazine four to five times a year; franchisee surveys three times a year; and an annual catalog.

Putt-Putt sponsors various award programs and offers backup administrative services including headquarters and regional resource persons; regular onsite visits; onsite troubleshooting; manuals for policy and management procedure; all types of forms; and systems for bookkeeping, inventory, personnel, expense analysis, computerized management information, and computerized billing. Putt-Putt maintains divisions to produce and distribute merchandise, equipment, and supplies; and it has a central purchasing program offering volume discounts, a centralized merchandising system, company brands, and exclusive purchase protection of trade-name materials. You must use products approved by Putt-Putt. The company offers customer accounts-receivable financing, and sponsors insurance programs for property, general-liability, automobile, life, major-medical, dental, disability, worker's compensation, third-party bonding, and product-liability coverage.

COMMENTS

Putt-Putt was ranked 112th in *Entrepreneur* magazine's 1987 "Franchise 500." The company provides an earnings claim document upon request. The winner of numerous beautification and charity awards, Putt-Putt sponsors national, state, and local tournament programs offering over $400,000 in prize money through the Professional Putters Association. The company wants to expand its franchise operations throughout the United States.

GETTING MORE INFORMATION

The franchise information packet contains a copy of the company magazine, a letter describing the company's operations, a breakdown of construction costs and operating expenses, and an eight-page application form. For more details, contact:

Bob Owens
National Franchise Director
Putt-Putt Golf Courses of America, Inc.
3007 Fort Bragg Road
Fayetteville, NC   28303
(919)   485–7131

Rainbow International Carpet Dyeing & Cleaning Company

BUSINESS: carpet-
dyeing and -cleaning
services
FOUNDED: 1980
FRANCHISED: 1981
START-UP
INVESTMENT:
$11,505

NO. OF UNITS		AS OF		PROJECTED BY	
		1/1/85	1/1/86	1/1/87	1/1/88
OWNED BY: COMPANY		1	3	4	5
FRANCHISEES		700	847	1,000	1,500
LOCATED: IN U.S.		691	825	974	1,405
OUTSIDE U.S.		10	25	30	100
TOTAL:		701	850	1,004	1,505
NO. OF STATES W/ UNITS		50	50	50	50

THE BUSINESS

Rainbow franchises provide the services consumers need to refurbish possessions that require a high capital investment. Rainbow has perfected their own formulas for the chemicals and techniques to dye, tint, and colorize carpets on location. The company performs the following services: dyeing, tinting, chemical shampooing, steam cleaning, fiber protection, carpet repair, flood and water restoration, odor control, furniture cleaning and dyeing, and drapery cleaning. Rainbow's system uses chemical and mechanical actions. Every carpet cleaned is colorized. The combination of optical brighteners and color enhances the appearance of every carpet treated.

WHAT IT TAKES

The minimum franchise fee is $15,000 based on $300 for every 1,000 population. Establishing an exclusive territory by population and serviceable mileage involved, the agreement is valid for ten years and renewable for ten. The company will finance 76 percent of the franchise fee (at 12 percent interest), and you may also finance your van. Your typical start-up expenses totaling $11,505 would include $3,800 for the franchise fee down payment; $5,405 for supplies and equipment; $1,000 for the van down payment; $350 for truck signs; $450 for training, travel, and expenses; and $500 for miscellaneous expenses. Additional units cost the same; master franchises are not available. You may be an owner-investor, but Rainbow prefers that you be actively involved in the business. Ongoing royalty fees will be figured at 7 percent of gross receipts (total receipts less sales taxes). No prior carpet-cleaning experience is necessary.

GETTING STARTED   Rainbow will help you lease or purchase vehicles and equipment and acquire your supplies. Most franchise owners work out of their homes, although some opt for setting up a small office. You must use standard uniforms for all employees and place the company logo on all vans. You will need to hire one full-time employee. You and your employee will go to the Waco, Texas, headquarters for a week of training covering equipment use; application of tinting solutions and dyes; techniques of shampooing, tinting, and dyeing various carpet fabrics; upholstery and drapery cleaning; and carpet repair. You will also receive a training program for use in weekly training sessions. You can be ready for business a month after buying your franchise, and Rainbow will offer help with your grand opening.

MAKING IT WORK   Rainbow charges no advertising fee, but you can participate in a lead-referral system and receive newspaper ads, brochures, presentation books, contest materials, and seasonal promotions. The company sponsors an annual national convention, regional conferences twice monthly, and one-day seminars twenty times a year. Rainbow publishes a bimonthly magazine and a monthly newsletter, and it sponsors various franchisee award programs. You will have access to headquarters resource persons and a toll-free hotline. Home-office executives make it a point to congratulate top franchisees by phone or to call routemen who may need special encouragement or motivation. Rainbow continually field-tests new techniques, products, and marketing ideas. The company has divisions that produce or distribute equipment and supplies, but you may sell noncompany products as long as Rainbow International approves their use.

COMMENTS   Rainbow was ranked thirty-third in *Entrepreneur* magazine's 1987 "Franchise 500" and eighth in *Venture* magazine's 1986 "Franchise 100." (*Entrepreneur* recently ranked Rainbow first among maintenance-products and service companies.) A member of the IFA, Rainbow provides an earnings claim document upon request. The company has received many civic honors. Rainbow wants to add new franchises throughout the United States, except in Texas, and in foreign countries.

GETTING MORE
INFORMATION   The franchise information packet contains a brochure on the company's operations, a breakdown of expenses, copies of recent articles on Rainbow, criteria for sales contests, customer brochures, and the company's code of values. For details, contact:
   Donald J. Dwyer
   President
   Rainbow International Carpet Dyeing & Cleaning Company
   1010 University Parks Drive
   Waco, TX   76707
   (800)   433–3322 or (817)   756–2122

RainSoft Water Conditioning Company

BUSINESS: water-		AS OF		PROJECTED BY	
conditioning and	NO. OF UNITS	1/1/85	1/1/86	1/1/87	1/1/88
drinking-water-	OWNED BY: COMPANY	0	0	0	0
systems sales	FRANCHISEES	205	260	315	370
FOUNDED: 1953	LOCATED: IN U.S.	200	250	300	350
FRANCHISED: 1958	OUTSIDE U.S.	5	10	15	20
START-UP	TOTAL:	205	260	315	370
INVESTMENT:	NO. OF STATES W/ UNITS	40	44	46	46
$20,000–$50,000					

THE BUSINESS

In recent years Americans have shown a growing awareness of and concern about the purity of their water supplies. According to a study conducted by the federal Environmental Protection Agency of more than 3,000 adults in metropolitan and rural areas, 84 percent felt that water pollution is a major national problem. In a Harris poll two-thirds of the respondents felt that water pollution is a very serious problem. A Gallup poll found that in hard-water areas 70 percent of the residents do not have water-treatment equipment—and 32 percent expressed interest in getting treatment equipment.

The RainSoft Water Conditioning Company manufactures products to soften, filter, decontaminate, and purify water, making cooking and drinking water tastier and healthier. The company claims that homes using their water purification system save money in every room of the house by using less soap, replacing valves and fixtures less often, needing fewer appliance repairs, and using less energy to heat water. Promoting the slogan to its franchisees of "Yes, a glass of water can make you rich!", the company grossed $60 million in franchise operations during 1985. In that year average gross sales per unit were $300,000 to $400,000, with average net income per unit of $75,000 to $125,000.

WHAT IT TAKES

You will need $2,000, $4,000 or $7,000 for your franchise fee, depending on the population of your market. The agreement guarantees an exclusive territory, and the company does not set a limit on duration of the franchise. Your total investment, including the franchise fee, will range from $20,000 to $50,000, with approximately half of that required in cash. Master franchises are not available. You may be an owner-investor, but RainSoft prefers that you be the operating manager. You will pay no ongoing royalty fees. The company recommends that you have a background in direct selling.

GETTING STARTED

RainSoft will help you lay out your facility and acquire merchandise. The typical RainSoft location is 1,200 square feet, situated in a shopping center, freestanding building, or commercial industrial park.

You will need ten full-time and four part-time employees, whom the company will help you hire. As owner-manager, you will attend a week of classroom training at RainSoft headquarters to learn about site layout, hiring, training, sales, accounting, and water-treatment technology. You and your employees will spend two weeks in the field for hands-on experience. Your new business could be open a month and a half after you buy the franchise, and RainSoft will help with your grand opening.

MAKING IT WORK

You will pay no advertising fee, but included in your franchise package is a supply of newspaper, black-and-white and four-color magazine ads, mailers, telephone-book ads, brochures, presentation books, catalogs, television and radio commercials, in-house media packages (slides, videotapes), point-of-purchase displays, billboard posters, signs, banners, seasonal promotional materials, and a public-relations/marketing manual. There is no charge for the company's lead-referral system or press releases. The company holds a national convention every eighteen months, an annual regional conference, monthly one-day seminars, and monthly one- to two-day onsite training sessions.

The company will send you a monthly newsletter plus regular updates on products, service, company information, and market information. Award programs recognize top salespeople and top dealerships. Administrative backup systems include headquarters and regional resource persons; onsite troubleshooting; manuals for policy, management procedures, and customer service; all types of forms; and systems for bookkeeping, inventory, personnel, and expense analysis. RainSoft emphasizes research and development, and it requires franchisees to sell RainSoft products only.

COMMENTS

RainSoft was ranked 129th in *Entrepreneur* magazine's 1987 "Franchise 500." A member of the IFA, RainSoft wants to add new franchises throughout the world.

GETTING MORE INFORMATION

The franchise information packet contains numerous articles on water pollution, brochures on the company's products and operations, testimonials from franchise owners, a copy of the company's Dun & Bradstreet rating, copies of articles on the company, and a one-page application form. For details, contact:

Dave Cole
Dealer Development Coordinator
RainSoft Water Conditioning Company
2080 Lunt Avenue
Elk Grove Village, IL   60007
(312)   437–9400

Rax Restaurants

BUSINESS: quick-
service restaurants
FOUNDED: 1978
FRANCHISED: 1978
START-UP
INVESTMENT:
$625,000–$725,000

	AS OF		PROJECTED BY	
NO. OF UNITS	1/1/85	1/1/86	1/1/87	1/1/88
OWNED BY: COMPANY	141	162	174	186
FRANCHISEES	253	315	403	528
LOCATED: IN U.S.	394	477	577	714
OUTSIDE U.S.	0	0	0	0
TOTAL:	394	477	577	714
NO. OF STATES W/ UNITS	35	35	35	35

THE BUSINESS

Rax Restaurants feature a limited menu in an upscale atmosphere—a quick-service dining experience offered in a dining room with pickup and drive-through conveniences. The company caters to customers aged twenty-five years and older who have average to above-average incomes. Originally a roast-beef restaurant, Rax has added a selection of lighter, contemporary food products. Emphasizing the nutritional value of its selections, Rax provides a four-color take-home brochure showing the menu items available with check marks by those selections prepared according to dietary guidelines of the American Heart Association. In 1985 the total annual dollar volume of all franchises was $175,071,500, with average gross sales per unit of $627,000 and average net income per unit of $29,000.

WHAT IT TAKES

Your initial franchise fee will be $25,000 per unit, due when construction begins. Your exclusive territory determined by county will be granted for a period of twenty years. The company estimates that land costs will average $175,000 to $300,000. Rax will provide working drawings and specifications for their standard building, which you must have altered to fit your local needs. The average building cost is $211,500 to $230,000, and site preparation will average $80,000. Rax must approve the site you select, but the actual purchase or leasing of the site will be your responsibility. Your total investment will run between $625,000 and $725,000, with $100,000 of the amount due in cash. The company offers no financial assistance. Additional units are available for $25,000 each, or you can expand your investment with a master franchise. The company does not allow passive ownership of franchises. Equipment costs for your facility will vary depending on the options you select and local codes, but a typical breakdown is as follows:

EQUIPMENT	COST
Hood systems	$11,200
Kitchen equipment	95,000
Smallwares package	8,900

EQUIPMENT		COST
Electronic cash registers		13,300
Dining room furniture		22,400
Uniforms		1,600
Drive-through window system (intercom)		2,500
Sign package		10,700
Greenhouse shades		3,400
Music system		1,500
Subtotal:		170,500
Optional breakfast package	$2,700	
Optional breakfast buffet package	2,900	
		5,600
Total:		$176,000*

*Price does not include sales tax, freight, or installation.

Other costs associated with preopening training for hourly employees, inventory, deposits, and working capital total approximately $50,000. Your monthly royalty fee will be 4 percent of your gross sales with an additional 4 percent of the gross required for advertising and promotion. You'll need from three to five years of previous restaurant-business experience to qualify for a Rax franchise, although the company has accepted applications from those without restaurant experience who have a demonstrably strong business background.

GETTING STARTED

You'll need a 3,500-square-foot freestanding building plus a 36,500-square foot parking lot. Rax will assist you with purchase negotiation, facility decoration, service contracts, and equipment lease or purchase. The company will require you to use corporate-approved uniforms, supplies, and equipment. The corporation negotiates purchase agreements for most items, and you will have the option to utilize these contracts. You'll have your choice of three locations for your five-week training period: Columbus, Ohio; Orlando, Florida; or St. Louis, Missouri. You'll have three weeks of in-restaurant training, beginning with production and service training and basic management functions, followed by two weeks of classroom sessions focusing on supervisory skills and administration. A company supervisor will visit you on a quarterly basis to give additional on-site training. Plan on a staff of fifteen full-time employees and twenty-five to thirty part-time ones. Company representatives will help you staff your facility and make arrangements for your grand opening.

MAKING IT WORK

For your 4 percent monthly advertising fee the company will provide you with newspaper ads, mailers, television and radio commercials, point-of-purchase displays, billboard posters, banners, press releases, and a public-relations/marketing manual. Rax will require you to use and sell only company products, but the company's central purchasing and merchandising program will enable you to take advantage of volume discounts. In addition, you'll be able to utilize such administrative resources as the regional and headquarters personnel, management-procedure and customer-service manuals, and computerized inventory and billing systems. The company holds an annual national convention and semiannual regional conferences.

COMMENTS

Rax Restaurants were rated seventy-fifth in *Entrepreneur* magazine's 1987 "Franchise 500." The chain was recently ranked #1 in *Restaurants and Institutions Tastes of America* among fast-food chains with varied menus. The company provides an earnings claim document. Rax is seeking franchises in thirty-five states.

GETTING MORE INFORMATION

The franchise information packet includes a copy of a brochure listing the Rax menu items, a directory of existing facilities, an outline of the franchise program, and a preliminary profile application that requests personal and financial information. For more information, contact:

William J. Dolan
Vice-President, Franchising
Rax Restaurants, Inc.
1266 Dublin Road
Columbus, OH   43215
(614)   486–3669

Realty World

BUSINESS: real estate
  sales
  FOUNDED: 1974
  FRANCHISED: 1975
START-UP
  INVESTMENT:
  $5,000–$15,000

	AS OF		PROJECTED BY	
NO. OF UNITS	1/1/85	1/1/86	1/1/87	1/1/88
OWNED BY: COMPANY	0	0	0	0
FRANCHISEES	1,250	1,500	1,800	2,500
LOCATED: IN U.S.	1,160	1,400	1,675	2,350
OUTSIDE U.S.	90	100	125	150
TOTAL:	1,250	1,500	1,800	2,500
NO. OF STATES W/ UNITS	50	50	50	50

THE BUSINESS

Today more than 15,000 professional real estate brokers and sales associates in the United States and Canada regularly use the Realty World system. Over 1 million properties with a value in excess of $57 billion have been sold by the company. Developed in the mid-1970s Realty World's system was created as an alternative to an antiquated real estate system that was constantly limited by an inability to expand significantly beyond its own natural geographical location. Financial institutions are part of Realty World's three-tiered system, along with independent real estate brokers. One element of the Realty World system is RealScope, a program showing the potential seller's home in great detail with at least eight color photographs. Another is the RealSafe guarantee, a limited home-warranty program covering major repair bills on all major appliances and mechanical elements and systems during the first year after purchase. A program called the ReaLine International Referral System allows sellers to list in their own community and begin to search for a location in a new town simultaneously. In 1985, Realty World franchises grossed $4.4 billion.

WHAT IT TAKES

Your initial franchise fee will be approximately $10,000 for a nonexclusive territory valid for five years and renewable for five. Your total investment will be $5,000 to $15,000, with 50 percent of that required in cash. The remainder may be financed through various financial institutions. The cost for additional units is about $5,000. Master franchises, called territorial licenses, are available. You must act as manager of the business. Your ongoing royalty fee will range between 3 to 6 percent of gross commissions. You must have a state license as a real estate broker and be in good standing.

GETTING STARTED

Normally converting existing businesses to its program, Realty World will offer assistance with layout and decoration of your offices and with acquisition of materials and supplies through approved suppliers. The typical Realty World office is 1,500 to 2,000 square feet, located in a mall, shopping center, or freestanding building. You will be required to use consistent logos, trademarks, and registrations. Clothing using company logos is available and its use is highly encouraged. You will need ten to fifteen full-time employees, and Realty World will assist with hiring. Training begins at the international headquarters near Washington, D.C., and continues in local academies for brokers, managers, sales associates, referral coordinators, and administrative personnel. Realty World will help with your grand opening.

MAKING IT WORK

For your advertising fee of 2 percent of gross commissions (maximum $321 a month), you will receive newspaper ads, black-and-white and four-color magazine ads, telephone-book ads, brochures, television and radio commercials, national media coverage, billboard posters, a lead-referral system, press releases, and a public-relations/marketing manual. An annual convention brings brokers together, as do quarterly regional conferences, monthly areawide franchise meetings, and seminars that may be as short as four hours or as long as thirty. Onsite business consulting is held monthly. Realty World conducts surveys and publishes a customer-oriented quarterly magazine, a monthly newsletter, and updates on service and market news as needed.

Numerous awards honor top performance. Backup systems include headquarters resource persons; a toll-free hotline; onsite troubleshooting; manuals on policy, management procedure, and customer service; personnel and accounting forms; and systems for bookkeeping, expense analysis, and computerized management information. The company emphasizes research and development of new programs and services. Company-sponsored insurance programs offer life, major-medical, and third-party-bonding coverage.

COMMENTS

Realty World was ranked twenty-fourth in *Entrepreneur* magazine's 1987 "Franchise 500" (first among realty companies) and twenty-third in *Venture* magazine's 1986 "Franchise 100." A division of Thomson McKinnon, Inc., the company is a major sponsor of United Cerebral Palsy and encourages franchisees to participate in community affairs. Realty World wants to expand franchise operations throughout the world.

GETTING MORE INFORMATION

The franchise information packet contains numerous brochures on the company's operations, a copy of the *Entrepreneur* "Franchise 500," and a sample of the Realty World newsletter. For more details, contact:

Gae S. Johnson
Director of Public Relations
Realty World
7700 Little River Turnpike
Annandale, VA   22003
(703) 631-9300

RE/MAX

BUSINESS: real estate
  sales
  FOUNDED: 1973
  FRANCHISED: 1976
START-UP
  INVESTMENT:
  $7,500–$30,000

		AS OF		PROJECTED BY	
NO. OF UNITS		1/1/85	1/1/86	1/1/87	1/1/88
OWNED BY: COMPANY		0	0	0	0
FRANCHISEES		540	772	1,042	1,440
LOCATED: IN U.S.		358	474	640	850
OUTSIDE U.S.		182	298	402	590
TOTAL:		540	772	1,042	1,440
NO. OF STATES W/ UNITS		38	42	48	50

THE BUSINESS

RE/MAX International, Inc., is the second largest real estate organization in both the United States and Canada in terms of gross volume. RE/MAX sales associates are the highest producers in the industry, outproducing agents of other major real estate companies three to one. This international real estate network has independent member offices located throughout the United States and Canada. RE/MAX offers a full-service relocation company, an asset-management company, and an insuring outlet in addition to the real estate organization. The company emphasizes that its success is based upon its innovative management concept and quality of sales agents attracted to the system. Agents are given 100 percent commissions and may set smaller commissions to secure listings; agents also set their own advertising schedule, thus permitting sellers greater exposure than competing firms offer. Following the belief that only a few agents in most real estate offices make the majority of sales, RE/MAX accepts only top-selling agents to create a sales momentum to be shared by the entire office, not decreased by inactive agents. The company estimates that its franchise operations earned a total of $504 million in 1985.

WHAT IT TAKES

RE/MAX franchise fees vary, but you will have an exclusive territory determined by demographics. The length of the agreement is variable, as is the renewal period. Your total investment will be $7,500 to $30,000 with 25 to 33 percent of that required in cash. RE/MAX can provide financial assistance for the remainder. The fee for additional units also varies. Master franchises are available. RE/

MAX franchisees must be actively involved in the business. Ongoing royalty fees will be a fixed dollar amount for each sales associate working under the RE/MAX service mark. You must have a real estate broker's license to purchase a RE/MAX franchise.

GETTING STARTED

RE/MAX will help you with site selection; lease negotiation; facility layout and decoration; lease or purchase of furniture, fixtures, and equipment; service and maintenance contracts; and acquisition of materials and supplies. The typical office is 2,500 to 3,000 square feet, located in an office building, shopping center, freestanding building, or professional park. You will be required to follow mandatory protection guidelines for trademarks and to use them properly.

Your staff will consist of one part-time and two full-time employees. You will attend one week of training in Denver, where you will study business establishment, identity and exposure, growth, retention, office environment, methodology, quality control, accounting and bookkeeping, and general management techniques. After buying a RE/MAX franchise, you can be open for business in three to four months. The company will help with your grand opening.

MAKING IT WORK

Your signs and banners will be provided as part of your franchise fee. Cooperative advertising funds are available for marketing tools such as newspaper and magazine ads, mailers, telephone-book ads, brochures, presentation books, catalogs, radio and television commercials, national media coverage, and billboard posters. A lead-referral system and public-relations/marketing manual are also provided at no charge. Your ongoing advertising charge will be $50 per month, per sales associate. RE/MAX sponsors national conventions twice a year, regional conferences every three months, monthly areawide franchise meetings, and one-day seminars as necessary, and it assists with onsite training when needed. The company also publishes a quarterly magazine, a monthly newsletter, a customer-oriented magazine every three months, and company information updates as necessary. RE/MAX conducts franchisee surveys quarterly and sponsors numerous award programs.

Backup managerial systems include headquarters and regional resource persons; a toll-free hotline; regular onsite visits; onsite troubleshooting; manuals for policy and management procedure; forms for inventory, personnel, and accounting; and systems for bookkeeping, expense analysis, computerized management information, and computerized billing. As a franchisee, you will cooperate with other real estate brokers in selling their inventory as well. The company sponsors insurance programs for property, general-liability, automobile, life, major-medical, dental, disability, and errors-and-omissions coverage.

COMMENTS

RE/MAX was ranked twentieth in *Entrepreneur* magazine's 1987 "Franchise 500" and fifty-ninth in *Venture* magazine's 1986 "Franchise 100." RE/MAX owns the world's largest hot-air balloon fleet (thirty), which it uses to publicize the company during participation in community events. A member of the IFA since 1983, RE/MAX wants to develop franchises throughout the United States and Canada.

GETTING MORE INFORMATION

The franchise information packet contains reprints of recent articles on the company, a copy of the latest annual report, and sample magazines published by RE/MAX. For details, contact:
Daryl Jesperson
Vice-President
RE/MAX
P.O. Box 3907
Englewood, CO   80155
(800)   525–7452 or (303)   770–5531

Rent-A-Dent

BUSINESS: used-car rental
FOUNDED: 1977
FRANCHISED: 1979
START-UP INVESTMENT: $150,000–$200,000

		AS OF		PROJECTED BY	
NO. OF UNITS		1/1/85	1/1/86	1/1/87	1/1/88
OWNED BY: COMPANY		2	3	5	7
FRANCHISEES		49	55	75	100
LOCATED: IN U.S.		51	58	80	107
OUTSIDE U.S.		0	0	0	0
TOTAL:		51	58	80	107
NO. OF STATES W/ UNITS		13	16	25	39

THE BUSINESS

Constantly increasing new-car prices have forced major new-car rental companies to escalate their rental rates to keep pace with rising vehicle prices. These increased rental rates have, in turn, spawned a whole new industry—the rental of used cars at affordable rates. Customers range from tourists and business travelers to insurance clients, residents needing a second or replacement vehicle, body repair shops, garages, service stations, motels, hotels and travel agencies. The industry currently grosses more than $4 billion annually. Car rental experts are projecting that total industry income will double by 1990, with an ever-increasing share going to aggressive operators with quality used cars.

Using all top-quality, late-model used cars (no dents) Rent-A-Dent reports a franchise retention rate of 97 percent. Seventy percent of each unit's business comes from repeat business. Rent-A-Dent cars have power steering and brakes, air conditioning, rear-window defoggers, and often AM/FM stereo radios with tape decks.

WHAT IT TAKES

Your initial franchise fee may be as low as $7,500 or as high as $30,000, depending on location. The ongoing franchise agreement ensures an exclusive territory, and no renewal is necessary. Your total investment will range from $150,000 to $200,000, with half of that required in cash. The company offers indirect assistance with financing through a lease company. Additional franchises may be purchased at half the cost of your original unit, and master franchises are available. It is possible to own the franchise without being the day-to-day manager. The ongoing royalty fee will be 7 percent of rental time and mileage charges plus an ongoing national advertising fee of 2 percent. You need not be familiar with the rental-car industry to buy a Rent-A-Dent franchise.

GETTING STARTED

The company provides assistance with site selection, vehicle lease or purchase, acquisition of materials and supplies, staffing, and facility layout. The typical facility contains 1,000 square feet and is located in a freestanding building. Rent-A-Dent will require you to use their signs, uniform printing, company logo, and standard uniforms for employees. The number of employees varies depending on the size of the operation. Training includes five days in the Seattle headquarters for all employees in a classroom setting, followed by five to seven days on location in your new business. All aspects of car rental and day-to-day operations will be covered. Rent-A-Dent representatives will assist with planning and staffing your grand opening.

MAKING IT WORK

For your advertising fee you'll receive black-and-white and four-color magazine ads, mailers, brochures, and radio and television commercials. Co-op funding covers telephone-book ads. Ongoing training includes an annual national convention and onsite training. A company newsletter comes out six times a year. You will also receive periodic questionnaires and updates on products, services, company information, and industry and market information. Various recognition programs honor outstanding franchisees.

Backup services include headquarters resource persons; a toll-free hotline; regular onsite visits; onsite troubleshooting; customer-service manuals; systems for bookkeeping, inventory, expense analysis, and computerized billing; and all types of forms. Before you open, the company will send out a marketing team to introduce your business to local prospects, including travel agencies. The company maintains a research-and-development department. When your credit is approved, you'll have access to a variety of fleet-acquisition programs for either new or used vehicles. A twenty-four-hour reservation service, group buying power, and special MasterCard and Visa service with a discount rate under two percent are other benefits. Rent-A-Dent sponsors insurance for automobile, major-medical, dental, and general-liability coverage.

COMMENTS

Rent-A-Dent was ranked 366th in *Entrepreneur* magazine's 1987 "Franchise 500." The company is seeking to expand in all fifty states.

GETTING MORE INFORMATION

The franchise information packet contains a full list of franchises, information about all aspects of operation, copies of recent newspaper features on the company, and fliers on promotional clothing and other supplies available. For more information, write or call:

Charles A. Scherbaum
President
Rent-A-Dent Car Rental Systems, Inc.
19415 Pacific Highway South, Suite 413
Seattle, WA   98188
(800)   426–5243 or (206)   226–0268

ROMAC

BUSINESS:
accounting, finance, banking, and data-processing personnel recruitment and placement
FOUNDED: 1966
FRANCHISED: 1976
START-UP
INVESTMENT:
$75,000–$100,000

NO. OF UNITS		AS OF		PROJECTED BY	
		1/1/85	1/1/86	1/1/87	1/1/88
OWNED BY: COMPANY		0	0	2	4
FRANCHISEES		32	36	44	52
LOCATED: IN U.S.		32	36	46	56
OUTSIDE U.S.		0	0	0	0
TOTAL:		32	36	46	56
NO. OF STATES W/ UNITS		17	21	22	25

THE BUSINESS

Personnel recruitment is one of the fastest-growing industries in the United States. Today both companies and job seekers have recognized the time and cost-effectiveness of using personnel consulting firms. ROMAC was founded in 1966 in Newton, Massachusetts, by two former IBM executives. The firm specializes in the placement of qualified professionals in accounting, finance, data processing, and banking and uses an extensive screening process and ROM-NET, a highly refined computerized multiple-listing system, to match applicants and clients expertly. Total dollar volume of RO-MAC franchises in 1985 was $12.5 million, with an average gross sales per unit of $379,000.

WHAT IT TAKES

In order to qualify for a franchise, you should have a background in either accounting, finance, banking, or data processing. The capital you'll need to set up a ROMAC franchise will depend on your ability to negotiate setup costs such as deposits, leases, furniture, and supplies and to control operating expenses. Of the total investment, $50,000 to $75,000 must be in cash. The company can provide direct financial assistance if necessary. Your original franchise term will be for ten years, with renewal periods of ten years available. During this time you'll have exclusive rights to a geographically determined territory, and you can open additional franchise units in your territory for no additional fee. You'll pay an 8 percent annual royalty fee, assessed against the gross revenue of your franchise.

If during the setup time you, as owner, and an administrative manager are working full-time, your cash start-up investment can be estimated as follows:

ITEM	MINIMUM ESTIMATED CASH REQUIRED	MAXIMUM ESTIMATED CASH REQUIRED
START-UP NEEDS:		
Franchise fee (minimum when 50% is financed, maximum when paid in full)	$20,000	$40,000
Rent deposit (750–900 sq. ft. @ $11–$22 psf)	825	1,500
License, bond, and legal fees to incorporate	500	1,500
Telephone installation and deposit (3 lines)	500	1,500
Computer terminal (minimum—lease deposit; maximum—purchase)	130	1,500
Business insurance (minimum is for insurance required pursuant to franchise agreement)	800	1,500

ITEM	MINIMUM ESTIMATED CASH REQUIRED	MAXIMUM ESTIMATED CASH REQUIRED
Office and printed supplies	1,000	2,000
Travel/lodging for training	500	1,500
Miscellaneous	1,000	2,000
Furniture (minimum assumes lease; maximum assumes purchase)	500	6,000
Office equipment (minimum assumes lease; maximum assumes purchase)	200	4,000
Total:	$25,955	$63,150

ESTIMATED MONTHLY OPERATING EXPENSES

FIXED EXPENSES:

Rent	825	1,650
Telephone ($300–$500 per consultant)	300	100
Postage	75	100
Office supplies	75	100
ROMNET license plus computer usage	80	140
Accounting/legal	100	200
Advertising	750	1,500
Administrative manager	900	1,300
Payroll tax (8% of gross)	72	104
Leased furniture	150	Purchased
Leased computer equipment	35	300
Leased office equipment (copier, typewriter)	250	Purchased
Franchise fee payments if 50% of franchise fee is financed at 12%	941	Purchased

ITEM	MINIMUM ESTIMATED CASH REQUIRED	MAXIMUM ESTIMATED CASH REQUIRED
Miscellaneous	100	300
Total:	$4,653	$6,194

ESTIMATED VARIABLE EXPENSES
(as a percentage of gross receipts)

	MINIMUM	MAXIMUM
Consultant commissions—year one*	30.0%	40.0%
Payroll tax (8% of commission)	2.4%	3.2%
Royalty	8.0%	8.0%
Advertising royalty (minimum $100 per month)	1.0%	1.0%
Total:	41.4%	52.2%

SUMMARY OF CAPITAL REQUIREMENTS

	MINIMUM	MAXIMUM
Start-up costs	$25,955	$63,150
Monthly fixed expenses	18,612	24,776
Additional capital**	10,000	14,000

*Commission paid on all placements made at collection.
**Additional capital to cover living expenses for the first four months of operation, and relocation expenses if applicable.

GETTING STARTED

ROMAC and Associates, Inc., will assist you in locating and securing the best site for your franchise. Typical sites occupy 1,000 to 2,000 square feet of space in an office building. Once you and RO-MAC are satisfied with the proposed location and costs, the franchise staff will help in the lease negotiations and final styling of the facility, based on a standard ROMAC plan.

ROMAC will provide you with a two-week training session covering interviewing techniques, hiring and training your staff, developing controls and business plans, contracts, professional sales techniques, accounting, personnel management, and the interoffice system. Five days of this training will take place in classrooms at corporate headquarters, and ten days will be on-the-job training at your location with a company consultant. You'll need to hire five to seven full-time employees. The length of time from signing the franchise agreement to the opening of your office will be from two to three months.

MAKING IT WORK

The ROMAC advertising consultants have designed numerous ads, and the company will provide you with a comprehensive advertising program. Field representatives will advise you on many phases of your franchise operations, from daily operations to motivating personnel, and you can utilize a toll-free hotline for immediate assistance. The company sponsors an annual national conference, regional conferences and seminars, and continuing onsite training. You will receive a quarterly company newsletter, as well as a company magazine, technical updates, and industry and market information. The company sponsors various recognition programs. As a ROMAC franchisee, you'll be eligible for the company-sponsored insurance program offering life, major-medical, dental, and disability coverage.

COMMENTS

ROMAC was ranked 388th in *Entrepreneur* magazine's 1987 "Franchise 500" and has been a member of the IFA since 1981. The company is seeking franchises in 27 states, mostly in the Midwest and West.

GETTING MORE INFORMATION

The information packet includes a description of the company, copies of the eight-page company newsletter, a franchise evaluation form that requests personal and financial information, and information on the advantages of franchising. For more information, contact:

Gerard P. Giguere, Jr.
Vice-President
ROMAC and Associates, Inc.
Box 7469 DTS
183 Middle Street, Third Floor
Portland, ME   04112
(800)   341–0263 or (207)   773–6387

Round Table Pizza

BUSINESS: pizza		AS OF		PROJECTED BY	
restaurant	NO. OF UNITS	1/1/85	1/1/86	1/1/87	1/1/88
FOUNDED: 1959	OWNED BY: COMPANY	2	10	6	11
FRANCHISED: 1962	FRANCHISEES	412	445	564	619
START-UP	LOCATED: IN U.S.	414	455	570	630
INVESTMENT:	OUTSIDE U.S.	0	0	0	0
$250,000–$300,000	TOTAL:	414	455	570	630
	NO. OF STATES W/ UNITS	10	11	11	11

THE BUSINESS

Pizza chains are growing faster than hamburger or chicken franchise restaurants. Round Table Pizza is the biggest pizza chain in the West and the fifth largest in the nation. Emphasizing an intimate, relaxed atmosphere, Round Table Pizza restaurants serve sandwiches, hamburgers, and salads in addition to pizza. In 1985 the company reported total sales for its franchises of $196,500,000, with average gross sales per unit $456,000.

WHAT IT TAKES

You will need $20,000 for the initial franchise fee. The original franchise agreement, valid for fifteen years and renewable for another fifteen, establishes an exclusive territory in some cases, with a minimum one- to two-mile limit between restaurants, depending on population density. Your total investment, including the franchise fee will be $250,000 to $300,000, depending on variations in renovation and construction costs. Of the total, you must have $80,000 to $100,000 in cash. The company does not offer financial assistance. Additional units are sold for $10,000 each; master franchises are not available. You must be the operating manager of your franchise. Ongoing royalty fees will be 4 percent of monthly net sales, plus 3 percent for advertising. Prior restaurant experience is preferred but not required.

GETTING STARTED

Round Table Pizza will help you select a site; negotiate for lease and purchase; handle construction; lay out and design the facility; arrange for lease or purchase of furniture, fixtures, and equipment; and acquire supplies and merchandise. The typical Round Table Pizza restaurant has 2,400 to 3,500 square feet and is located in a mall, shopping center, or freestanding building. You will need four full-time and fourteen part-time employees. To be trained as a manager, you will go to Culver City, California, for two weeks of lessons on operations and product preparation, one week on accounting, and one week on management development. A portion of your training will be conducted in a Round Table Pizza restaurant to make sure that you are thoroughly familiar with day-to-day operations. You can open a year to a year and a half after buying your franchise.

MAKING IT WORK

Round Table Pizza provides the following resources in return for your advertising fee: newspaper ads, mailers, telephone-book ads, brochures, television and radio commercials, in-house media packages (slides, videotapes), point-of-purchase displays, signs, banners, seasonal promotional materials, press releases, and a public-relations/marketing manual. You will meet with other franchise owners at an annual convention and attend semiannual one-day seminars. You may also request training films, manuals, and support information to use in training employees and reviewing procedures.

Round Table publishes a monthly magazine and offers headquarters and regional resource persons; regular onsite visits; onsite troubleshooting; manuals on policy and management procedure; all types of forms; systems for inventory, personnel, expense analysis; and makeup charts. The Round Table Supply Company sells equipment, furniture, fixtures, and small wares. A central purchasing program offers volume discounts. You may buy from noncompany suppliers as long as their products are of comparable quality, but the pizza spice blend and dough must come from a designated supplier. Round Table sponsors insurance for life, dental, and major-medical coverage.

COMMENTS

Round Table was ranked sixty-sixth in *Entrepreneur* magazine's 1987 "Franchise 500" and eighty-ninth in *Venture* magazine's 1986 "Franchise 100." The company wants to expand its operations in Arizona and California.

GETTING MORE INFORMATION

The franchise information packet contains full-color brochures explaining the company's operations, breakdowns of capital needed, copies of recent articles on the company, and an application form. For details, contact:
  Kimberley Bachelder
  Coordinator, Franchise Sales
  Round Table Franchise Corporation
  601 Montgomery Street, Suite 500
  San Francisco, CA   94111
  (415)   392–7500

Roy Rogers

BUSINESS: fast-food restaurant
FOUNDED: 1929
FRANCHISED: 1968
START-UP INVESTMENT: $750,000–$1,000,000

NO. OF UNITS		AS OF		PROJECTED BY	
		1/1/85	1/1/86	1/1/87	1/1/88
OWNED BY: COMPANY		345	360	382	412
FRANCHISEES		147	187	206	250
LOCATED: IN U.S.		492	547	588	662
OUTSIDE U.S.		0	0	0	0
TOTAL:		492	547	588	662
NO. OF STATES W/ UNITS		16	16	16	16

THE BUSINESS

A division of the Marriott Corporation, Roy Rogers restaurants are described as fast-food restaurants. Using standard menus and operating systems, they feature roast beef, hamburgers, fried chicken, and salad and sandwich-fixings bars. In 1985 these franchises grossed $136,943,000, and average sales for a single unit were $910,355.

WHAT IT TAKES

The initial franchise fee of $25,000 purchases a nonexclusive territory valid for twenty years and renewable for twenty. Your total investment will be between $750,000 and $1 million, depending on land and construction costs; $150,000 of the total must be in cash. Financial assistance is not available. Additional units may be bought for the same amount, and master franchises are available. You must actively manage the business. You will pay an ongoing royalty fee of 4 percent of gross sales. The company recommends prior experience in the food-service field and requires a combined net worth of not less than $500,000, exclusive of principal residences and other personal property. If two or more persons apply jointly for a franchise, one must be principally responsible and hold a minimum 50 percent equity position in the operating assets.

GETTING STARTED

You will receive guidance on facility layout at no charge, but you must pay for assistance with purchase negotiation, construction, facility decoration, lease or purchase of furniture fixtures and equipment, and acquisition of materials and supplies. The typical restaurant is 3,000 square feet, often located near a college campus or an airport. You will be required to have a specially designed building; to obtain standard fixtures, equipment, containers and other items used in serving and dispensing food products; to use the company's signs, emblems, trade names, trademarks, and service marks; and to use particular food products which meet quality standards. Marriott subsidiaries sell equipment and supplies.

You can expect to hire twenty full-time and thirty part-time employees. The training program is extensive, entailing 500 hours for the franchise in the Washington, D.C., headquarters on skills and management. Two employees will each receive 400 hours of similar training in the regional office. Training will cover day-to-day operations of a Roy Rogers restaurant, including technical operation of equipment, management of employees, accounting procedures, and the preparation of records and reports relating to the operation. It normally takes twelve to sixteen months to open after purchasing your franchise. The company will assist with the grand opening.

MAKING IT WORK

For your ongoing advertising fee—4 percent regional, 1 percent local for the Baltimore, Washington, Philadelphia, and New York areas— you'll receive newspaper ads, mailers, brochures, presentation books, television and radio commercials, in-house media packages such as slides and videotapes, point-of-purchase displays, seasonal promotional materials, press releases, and public-relations manuals. The company sponsors an annual national convention, regional conferences every three months, and quarterly city- and areawide franchise meetings. A franchise consultant will be assigned to assist you with additional training or problem-solving after you open.

The company sponsors recognition programs and provides monthly newsletters and periodic product, service, and company-information updates. Backup services include regional and headquarters resource persons plus manuals on policy, management procedure, and customer service. The company continually researches new products. The parent company, Marriott, has not only divisions that distribute merchandise, equipment, and supplies but also a centralized merchandising system and company brands. You will not be required to sell only company products.

COMMENTS

Roy Rogers was ranked 100th in *Entrepreneur* magazine's 1987 "Franchise 500." A member of the IFA since 1972, the corporation and local stores make a commitment to community service. Roy Rogers is seeking new franchisees in eleven states in the northeast and mid-Atlantic regions.

GETTING MORE INFORMATION

The franchise information packet contains descriptions of the company's operations, site criteria, a four-page application form, and the IFA code of ethics. For more information, write or call:
Richard Parker
Director of Franchise Development
Roy Rogers
1803 Research Boulevard, Suite 101
Rockville, MD   20850
(800)   423–2409, extension 6129 or (301)   251–6129

Sara Care

		AS OF		PROJECTED BY	
BUSINESS: home care	NO. OF UNITS	1/1/85	1/1/86	1/1/87	1/1/88
personnel services					
FOUNDED: 1978	OWNED BY: COMPANY	0	0	0	2
FRANCHISED: 1982	FRANCHISEES	24	31	44	70
START-UP	LOCATED: IN U.S.	24	31	44	72
INVESTMENT:	OUTSIDE U.S.	0	0	0	0
$35,975–$48,475	TOTAL:	24	31	44	72
	NO. OF STATES W/ UNITS	11	12	22	25

THE BUSINESS

Sara Care was founded in El Paso, Texas, when two needs were combined: working women who needed help and retirees not wanting to retire completely. Founder Sara Addis developed the idea of sending retirees to handle a variety of services such as waiting for the television repairman, baby sitting, tutoring, pet sitting, driving children to and from school, shopping for daily needs, and running errands. In addition, Sara Care employees regularly visit elderly and shut-in persons who live alone, watch homes when people are on vacation, maintain yards, and visit people in the hospital. The largest franchisor of non-nursing-home service personnel, Sara Care was organized as a temporary personnel service, one of the fastest-growing fields in the country. Assignments can be on an hourly, daily, weekly, or live-in basis. Bonded and insured through the franchisee, sitters must be certified in CPR and first-aid techniques.

In 1985, Sara Care franchises grossed $3,707,629, with average gross sales per unit of $123,587. The charge for most services retirees do is $5 an hour, except for professional care of the sick. Most clients are working couples who prefer to hire others to do their work around the house so that they are free to pursue their careers. The registered retirees are chosen from among those with backgrounds full of rich life experiences and honesty. According to Addis, "They wish to work in order to share their usefulness, not only for the money." Sara Care claims to move the art of companion and sitting service from the commonplace to a new level of professionalism.

WHAT IT TAKES

You will need $12,500 to $25,000 for the initial franchise fee, depending on the population of the community in which you locate. You will be granted an exclusive territory with perpetual term. Your additional setup costs for rent, licenses, permits, deposits, furniture, fixtures, a typewriter, a copier, Chamber of Commerce dues, telephone deposit and installation, small equipment, miscellaneous office supplies, insurance and bonding, legal and accounting services, and expenses to attend training will be about $13,800. You will also need about $9,675 for operating costs during the first three months. The franchise fee must be in cash, but the company offers financing for the remainder. Additional units are priced the same; master franchises are available. You may be an owner-investor of the business. Sara Care charges an ongoing royalty of 5 percent of gross sales, calculated monthly. No prior experience in the industry is necessary.

GETTING STARTED

Sara Care will assist you with site selection; lease negotiation; facility layout and decoration; lease or purchase of furniture, fixtures, and equipment; service and maintenance contracts; and acquisition of supplies. The typical office is 450 to 500 square feet, located in an office building, shopping center, or home (although the company encourages the use of an office). All forms and materials must contain the company logo and meet the franchisor's specifications. In addition to you, your staff will consist of one full-time and one part-time employee, and Sara Care will give you tips on hiring. You will spend eight business days in El Paso, Texas, to learn the history of Sara Care, office procedures, preopening procedures, recruitment of field employees and orientation, trademark usage, advertising and promotion, forms, bookkeeping, and payroll. You can be open for business two months after buying the franchise. The company will help with your grand opening.

MAKING IT WORK

You must spend 3 percent of your gross sales on local advertising. When Sara Care initiates its national advertising campaign, you will pay 1 percent of gross sales to that fund and reduce local advertising to 2 percent. Covered by your franchise fee is a supply of newspaper ads, black-and-white magazine ads, mailers, telephone-book ads, brochures, radio commercials, billboard posters, seasonal promotional displays, press releases, and a public-relations/marketing manual. Sara Care sponsors an annual national convention and onsite training as needed. The company publishes a newsletter and regular updates on company information and market trends, and it conducts surveys and sponsors award programs.

Franchisee packets are distributed monthly to share ideas in marketing and to note accomplishments of Sara Care franchisees. Backup services include headquarters resource persons; a toll-free hotline; onsite troubleshooting; policy and management manuals; forms for personnel, orders, and accounting; field-employee manuals; and systems for bookkeeping and personnel. The marketing department concentrates on ideas to increase sales. The company's central purchasing program offers volume discounts on supplies you will use frequently, and you may sell only services approved by Sara

Care. Company-sponsored insurance offers property, general-liability, automobile, third-party-bonding, and professional-liability
coverage.

COMMENTS

Sara Care was ranked 429th in *Entrepreneur* magazine's 1987 "Fran-
chise 500," first among the sitting/home-care services. President
Sara Addis has received various national and international honors.
A member of the IFA since 1983, Sara Care wants to develop new
franchises in all but nine states, and in Australia, Canada, and
Japan.

**GETTING MORE
INFORMATION**

The franchise information packet contains a company history, details of the company's concept and operations, numerous copies of
articles on the business from major magazines and newspapers, and
an application form. For details, contact:
    Sandra Palmer
    Director of Sales
    Sara Care Franchise Corporation
    1200 Goden Key Circle, Suite 368
    El Paso, TX   79925
    (800)   351–CARE or (915)   593–5071 (call collect in Texas)

Scandia Down Shops

		AS OF		PROJECTED BY	
BUSINESS: retail	NO. OF UNITS	1/1/85	1/1/86	1/1/87	1/1/88
bedding outlets					
FOUNDED: 1980	OWNED BY: COMPANY	0	0	0	0
FRANCHISED: 1980	FRANCHISEES	67	77	97	127
START-UP	LOCATED: IN U.S.	67	77	97	127
INVESTMENT:	OUTSIDE U.S.	0	0	0	0
$75,000–$150,000	TOTAL:	67	77	97	127
	NO. OF STATES W/ UNITS	32	35	38	45

THE BUSINESS

A Scandia Down Shop is a complete bedroom shop featuring down
and feather comforters and pillows, European and domestic linens,
wool pads, custom-sewn accessories, European classic brass beds,
and contemporary designer beds. The company has shown continual sales growth from $2.0 million in 1980 to $15.8 million in 1985.
The average gross sales per franchise unit in 1985 were $249,000.

WHAT IT TAKES

To open a Scandia Down Shop you'll pay a franchise fee of $25,000.
Your other initial expenses will include $20,000 to $30,000 for opening inventory, $23,000 to $67,000 for start-up costs, $2,000 to $8,000
for grand-opening expenses, and $5,000 to $20,000 for working/op-

erating capital. Start-up costs include rent and security deposits, utilities, insurance, business permits, locally purchased furniture, decor and supplies, travel and lodging for training, and the largest variable, construction costs. Of your total initial investment of $75,000 to $150,000 you'll need to pay $50,000 to $75,000 in cash. For the balance the company will provide a loan-application guide, and if you qualify, will assist you in obtaining financing through commercial institutions.

Your initial franchise agreement will cover a term of ten years, with a renewal period of ten years available. You may hold passive ownership of your first franchise and purchase additional locations at $25,000 each, or you may purchase a master franchise. There are no exclusive territories granted by the company. Your royalty fee will be 5 percent of your gross sales. Scandia Down Corporation has tested and selected an inventory package, and the amount of inventory varies with shop square footage. You need not have any previous industry knowledge or experience to become a Scandia Down franchisee.

GETTING STARTED

Your store will require 1,000 square feet, preferably in a mall, shopping center, or downtown storefront; and you will need a staff of one full-time and three part-time employees. Your original franchise fee will entitle you to the use of the Scandia Down Shop name, logo, trademarks, and copyrighted material; assistance in site selection and lease negotiation; training; operations manuals; shop setup; advertising materials; and grand-opening assistance. The company can also help you with construction, acquisition of supplies and merchandise through a central purchasing program, and facility layout and decoration following a standard floor plan. Scandia Down will also provide assistance for your grand opening, which you can expect to hold three months after signing your franchise agreement. Your two-week classroom session held at corporate headquarters in Seattle will give you training in product knowledge, sales, advertising, marketing, accounting, inventory control, purchasing, store decor, and staff selection and training. You'll follow up this initial period with two days of staff sales training in a shop.

MAKING IT WORK

You'll pay a 3 percent ongoing advertising fee, for which you'll receive national media coverage, in-house media packages, newspaper and telephone-book ads, and black-and-white and four-color magazine ads. Through a co-op ad program you can get brochures, catalogs, billboard space, signs, and seasonal promotional materials. The company maintains a product research and marketing division. You will learn about new products and developments through a quarterly company newsletter, industry and market information provided monthly, and weekly service and company updates. Managerial and administrative resources provided by the company include regular onsite support visits by headquarters personnel; policy and procedure manuals; forms for accounting; personnel, orders, and inventory systems; and a bookkeeping system. Scandia Down Corporation holds an annual conference and sponsors special regional and sales-recognition awards.

COMMENTS

Scandia Down Shops was ranked 312th in *Entrepreneur* magazine's 1987 "Franchise 500." A member of the IFA, the company provides an earnings claim document prior to a potential franchisee's personal interview. Scandia Down shops wants to expand franchise operations in most states.

GETTING MORE INFORMATION

The franchise information packet includes a brochure, color catalog of products, a national directory of existing franchises, two press releases, material from the IFA, a listing of start-up costs, and an application form requesting personal and financial background information. A stamped, addressed reply envelope is included for the application. For more information, contact:

Tom Hansen
Director, Franchise Development
Scandia Down Shops
P.O. Box 88819
Seattle, WA   98188
(800)   237–5337 or (206)   251–5050

Schlotzsky's

		AS OF		PROJECTED BY	
BUSINESS: sandwich shop	NO. OF UNITS	1/1/85	1/1/86	1/1/87	1/1/88
FOUNDED: 1971	OWNED BY: COMPANY	8	8	10	20
FRANCHISED: 1976	FRANCHISEES	160	180	205	250
START-UP	LOCATED: IN U.S.	168	188	215	270
INVESTMENT:	OUTSIDE U.S.	0	0	0	0
$110,000–$115,000	TOTAL:	168	188	215	270
	NO. OF STATES W/ UNITS	17	20	24	26

THE BUSINESS

Since the first store opened in Austin, Texas, in 1971, Schlotzsky's has retained the original recipe for its famous Schlotzsky sandwich. Considered by the owners to be their key to success, the one-of-a-kind sandwich comes with freshly baked sourdough buns, three spicy meats, three melted cheeses, marinated olives, lettuce, tomatoes, and secret ingredients. By 1977 the business had grown to twenty shops with total annual sales of $2.4 million. Now Schlotzsky's has almost 200 shops in seventeen states and annual sales of nearly $43 million. President of the company, John Wooley, plans to double these figures by mid-1989. Annual sales average over $240,000 per shop.

WHAT IT TAKES

Schlotzsky's charges an initial franchise fee of $15,000. The franchise agreement, applicable for twenty years with a ten-year renewal option, will grant you an exclusive territory based on your financial ability to develop a targeted geographic area. Total start-up investment, including the franchise fee, ranges from $110,000 to $115,000. The company will require you to pay 30 to 40 percent of the total in cash but will help you obtain financing for the remainder. You can buy additional franchises for only $7,500 each. You may either run the shop yourself or hire a manager. You'll pay a royalty fee of 4 percent of gross sales, an additional 1 percent for the company's national advertising and marketing fund, and an additional 3 percent for local advertising. Master franchises are available.

GETTING STARTED

A Schlotzsky's sandwich shop is simple to open and operate. Since there's no frying, there's no expensive equipment or complicated machinery involved. Shops are usually 1,000 to 2,000 square feet and are located in malls, shopping centers, or freestanding buildings. The company will help you select a site and negotiate a lease or purchase agreement. You'll also receive help with construction, shop layout, decorating, and lease or purchase of furniture, fixtures, and equipment. The cost of most of these items will be covered by your initial investment. You'll also have the option of adding a soup and salad bar to your shop, plus four new sandwiches to the menu.

You'll need two full-time and eight part-time employees, whom the Schlotzsky's staff will help you hire. The company provides all new franchisees with a three-week training program. You and your manager, if you hire one, can go to the San Antonio Training Center for three weeks of classroom and hands-on instruction. You'll study crew training, purchasing, hiring, accounting, advertising, marketing, and equipment maintenance. Within two to three months you'll be ready for business. Just before your grand opening the company will send a three-member crew to assist you during your first week of business.

MAKING IT WORK

The company's national advertising and marketing fund provides a yearly advertising and marketing plan plus advertising in newspapers, magazines, telephone books, mailers, and on radio and television. You can also get videotapes, point-of-purchase displays, seasonal promotionals, billboard posters, signs, banners, press packages, and manuals with tips and techniques for advertising. The company has an Elected Franchisee Council (EFC), a board of five representatives that maintains an open dialogue between company and franchisees, builds a consensus with franchisees, and contributes to all decision making from menu changes to advertising campaigns. Every sixty days members of the council are brought to company headquarters in Austin, at the company's expense, to meet with the corporate team and discuss current issues.

The company sponsors an annual national convention and annual one-day seminars and produces a monthly newsletter that has been cited as one of the most informative and comprehensive in the franchise trade. You'll also receive monthly industry and market-information updates, and you can get a complete videotaped training program for your employees.

Schlotzsky's franchise service representatives will visit your site regularly to insure that quality-control and systemwide standards are met, offer merchandising and sales analyses, coordinate annual diagnostic business reviews, supervise special marketing programs, and troubleshoot any difficult problems you may face. You'll receive the company's manuals on operations, training, policy, and management procedure; systems for personnel, inventory, bookkeeping, and expense analysis; a state-of-the-art computer system; and forms for accounting, personnel, inventory, and ordering. You can buy all nonrequired food items from your own sources as long as they meet company specifications. When you buy required food items, you can save money through the company's central purchasing program, which will pass volume discounts on to you. Schlotzsky's sponsors a recognition program for outstanding franchisees and conducts ongoing research on and development of new products.

COMMENTS

Schlotzsky's has won national design awards. It participates in numerous local fund-raising activities and contributes to several charities. Schlotzsky's was ranked 171st in *Entrepreneur* magazine's 1987 "Franchise 500." The company is seeking new franchisees primarily in the midwest and southwest.

GETTING MORE INFORMATION

The franchise information packet includes an eight-page brochure with photographs and an article excerpted from *Restaurant News*. For more information, contact:

Karl D. Martinez
Senior Vice-President of Marketing and Franchise
Schlotzsky's, Inc.
200 West 4th Street
Austin, TX   78701
(512)   480–9871

Scottish Inns, Red Carpet Inn, Master Hosts Inns

BUSINESS: motels			AS OF		PROJECTED BY	
FOUNDED: 1982	NO. OF UNITS		1/1/85	1/1/86	1/1/87	1/1/88
FRANCHISED: 1982	OWNED BY: COMPANY		0	0	0	0
START-UP		FRANCHISEES	190	213	250	300
INVESTMENT:	LOCATED: IN U.S.		188	211	248	290
$600,000 up		OUTSIDE U.S.	2	2	2	10
	TOTAL:		190	213	250	300
	NO. OF STATES W/ UNITS		20	22	27	30

THE BUSINESS

Hospitality International is the umbrella company that operates, directs, and controls the Red Carpet Inn, Master Hosts Inns, and Scottish Inns motel systems. All three chains have existed for more than fifteen years and have a strong base of loyal, repeat customers. Hospitality has combined its coverage of the motel market with budget (Scottish Inns), full-service (Red Carpet Inns) and resort facilities (Master Hosts Inns) to achieve the greatest efficiency. The momentum and customer base of all three systems are intended to benefit everyone. With three options available, you can select the identity that's right for your property and your market. Hospitality International reported $201.7 million of business for all its franchise operations in 1985.

WHAT IT TAKES

You will pay $5,000 for a Scottish Inns franchise, $8,000 for Red Carpet, and $10,000 for Master Hosts. Your original franchise agreement will be valid for five years with a five-year renewable period, but no exclusive territories are granted. Your total investment will be $600,000 and up, depending on the size and complexity of the project, and all of this must be in cash. Additional units carry the same price tag. You may invest in one of these franchises without being the on-premises manager. Your ongoing royalty fee based on monthly gross receipts will be 2 to 3 percent. The monthly reservation-system fee is two dollars per guest room. Prior hotel experience is not required.

GETTING STARTED

Hospitality International will assist you in all phases with planning, feasibility studies, design, furnishing, construction, supplies, and equipment. The typical facility has 35,000 square feet and is located near a commercial or industrial center. You must follow the company's minimum specifications regarding room size, decor, and other details. You will need thirteen full-time and four part-time employees. Training for owner-managers is held for three days in Atlanta, Georgia, and covers housekeeping, security and safety, front-office operations, inventories, standards of operation, advertising, sales, and management of a successful restaurant. It normally takes three months to open after you've purchased a franchise. The company will help with your grand opening.

MAKING IT WORK

For your advertising fee you will receive newspaper ads, black-and-white and four-color magazine ads, mailers, telephone-book ads, brochures, presentation books, catalogs, television and radio commercials, national media coverage, in-house media packages, an exterior sign program, group and tour sales, in-room promotional pieces, participation in special business-builder programs, and assistance in developing a comprehensive marketing plan. The ongoing advertising fee is based on gross receipts. A national convention is held each year, supplemented by three-day seminars every two months, and onsite training twice a year covering housekeeping and front-desk operations. The company issues a quarterly newsletter, conducts customer surveys regularly, and sponsors various award programs. Backup resources include a toll-free hotline, policy and management-procedure manuals, and a computerized management information system.

COMMENTS

Hospitality International was ranked 123d in *Entrepreneur* magazine's 1987 "Franchise 500." The company regularly sponsors activities in the Midtown Atlanta Senior Citizens Center and has been adopted as their "grandchild" along with the Atlanta Braves and Atlanta Ballet. New franchises are being sought in all states except those on the west coast and in the northwest.

GETTING MORE INFORMATION

The franchise information packet contains a directory of Hospitality International motels, reprints of recent articles on the firm, question-and-answer sheets on various aspects of the motels' operation, and sample newsletters. For more information, contact:

Richard H. Rogers
President
Hospitality International
1152 Spring Street, Suite A
Atlanta, GA   30309
(800)   251–1962

Second Sole

BUSINESS: sales of
athletic shoes and
clothing; resoling and
repair of athletic
shoes
FOUNDED: 1976
FRANCHISED: 1978
START-UP
INVESTMENT:
$75,000–$150,000

NO. OF UNITS		AS OF		PROJECTED BY	
		1/1/85	1/1/86	1/1/87	1/1/88
OWNED BY:	COMPANY	37	24	3	3
	FRANCHISEES	21	36	69	81
LOCATED:	IN U.S.	58	60	72	84
	OUTSIDE U.S.	0	0	0	0
TOTAL:		58	60	72	84
NO. OF STATES W/ UNITS		8	9	12	12

THE BUSINESS

Since 1976 the athletic-shoe industry has been growing at a phenomenal rate into what is now a multibillion-dollar industry. Second Sole
was the first company in the United States to sell, resole, and repair
athletic shoes. It originally began as a small athletic-shoe resoling
outlet in Claremont, California. The company ventured into retail
sales just as the industry exploded. Sales for the little Claremont
store that first year were a remarkable $351,290 gross. When the
company later purchased Action Footwear, a group of Athlete's
Foot stores in Los Angeles, it expanded into shopping malls. Although this expansion reached a much greater market, the company's goals were and still are to be the best, not the largest. Second
Sole customers who shop at mall locations are a mix of about 50
percent athletes and 50 percent nonathletes. Strip centers attract
about 70 percent athletes. Generally, customers tend to be between
eighteen and forty-four years old, and about 70 percent are males.

As owner of a Second Sole store, you can offer your customers
the finest-quality name-brand shoes, as well as sports clothing.
While many other athletic-shoe stores overspecialize in one sport
shoe, such as running shoes, Second Sole offers customers footwear
for almost any sport. In 1985 sales for all franchises combined totaled $20,000,000, with the average gross sales per franchise of
$350,000 and average net of about 10 percent.

WHAT IT TAKES

The fee for your initial Second Sole store will be $10,000, but the
amount is discounted to $5,000 for additional stores. Including the
franchise fee and other start-up costs (building costs, inventory, and
fixtures), your total investment will be between $75,000 and
$150,000. You'll need at least 25 percent of the total in cash (from
$18,750 to $37,500), but Small Business Association loans and financing packages may be available for costs over the cash amount.
Your franchise agreement will apply for ten years, with a ten-year
renewal. You'll have an exclusive territory within a five-mile radius

of your store. Master franchises are available, and passive owner-ship is acceptable. Although most owners make their living working in their stores, others choose to hire managers or let family members run the store. Previous experience is not required, but it is helpful. The company charges a 3 to 5 percent ongoing royalty fee based on monthly net sales, plus another .5 percent for national advertising.

GETTING STARTED

Second Sole staff will help you choose a site and negotiate a lease or purchase. For your store's design you can get blueprints that have been used and proven successful by other Second Sole stores. Most stores are between 1,200 and 2,000 square feet in malls and shopping centers or strips. You'll need to hire from two to four full-time and four to eight part-time employees, and Second Sole personnel will help you choose the best applicants. The company will also help you buy your inventory, lay out merchandise, and decorate your store. Second Sole suggests that you set aside a portion of your initial investment for pre-grand-opening advertising, and Second Sole will help you produce an effective ad campaign.

You'll be trained for one week at the corporate office in San Diego, then a Second Sole executive will work with you in your store for two-day follow-up session. You'll learn about all aspects of running a retail business, including store design, management, sales techniques, bookkeeping, accounting, and advertising. You'll also learn all about the products you'll sell and about resoling. By the end of training you'll be fully qualified to operate your own store. You can have the grand opening within two to three months after you purchase the franchise.

MAKING IT WORK

The company has a staff of marketing and advertising executives to help you plan your advertising, whether you need a single ad or an entire campaign. Your .5 percent fee will go toward placing black-and-white and four-color ads in national magazines such as *Runner* and *Runner's World*. You'll get promotional posters and advertising slicks, radio and television commercials, banners and seasonal promotional materials—all covered by your advertising fee.

The company will send you a bimonthly newsletter, and an ongoing sales training program will provide you and your staff with a technical understanding of the latest developments in athletic shoes. You'll attend areawide franchise meetings and an annual national convention. You'll also get manuals covering management procedures, policies, and customer service, plus forms for inventory, ordering, accounting, and personnel.

Although you may buy company brands at volume discounts through a central purchasing program, you won't be limited to selling only Second Sole products. You may buy merchandise from any company-approved supplier. Second Sole staff will help with merchandising, advise you on product mix, and assist you with purchasing decisions. Second Sole can use its strong position in the industry to get priority shipments of products that are so popular they might otherwise be difficult to get. If a customer has a problem with a pair of shoes purchased at your store, you'll be able to fix it, usually free of charge, or replace it, no questions asked.

COMMENTS

Second Sole was ranked 319th in *Entrepreneur* magazine's 1987 "Franchise 500." The company is seeking new franchises in all states.

GETTING MORE INFORMATION

The franchise information packet contains fourteen pages of information on buying a Second Sole franchise, several full-page advertisements, and a four-page application. For more information, contact:

Mr. Dana P. Smith
Vice-President
Second Sole, Inc.
9605 Scranton Road, Suite 840
San Diego, CA   92121
(619)   458–0761 (call collect)

Security Alliance

BUSINESS: alarm-
system installation
FOUNDED: 1976
FRANCHISED: 1983
START-UP
INVESTMENT:
$57,000–$67,000

NO. OF UNITS		AS OF		PROJECTED BY	
		1/1/85	1/1/86	1/1/87	1/1/88
OWNED BY: COMPANY		0	0	0	0
FRANCHISEES		74	96	150	250
LOCATED: IN U.S.		74	96	150	250
OUTSIDE U.S.		0	0	0	0
TOTAL:		74	96	150	250
NO. OF STATES W/ UNITS		31	34	50	50

THE BUSINESS

According to the 1980 census, there are more than 86 million housing units—homes, apartments, and mobile homes—across the country. Yet it is estimated that only 8 to 9 percent of those homes have security devices of any kind, leaving nearly 80 million homes unprotected. In 1980 one in every four households was burglarized, and fires caused more than 4,000 deaths and over $3 billion in residential property losses.

Security Alliance is a national network of alarm-installing companies specializing in residential and small-business security. New franchises may be either newly created companies or companies that have been in business for years but are not growing rapidly enough. Security Alliance works with manufacturers of security systems to design products that are both effective and affordable. The total dollar volume in 1985 for all Security Alliance franchise operations was $30 million, and the average gross sales per franchise were $100,000, with a net income of $30,000.

WHAT IT TAKES

Your initial Security Alliance franchise fee will be $17,500, which must be in cash. In addition to the fee, you will need a minimum of $40,000 in working capital to start up your business. (This does not apply to existing alarm-installation companies who are switching their businesses over to Security Alliance—their start-up costs and procedures will be different.) The company will work with you in putting together a business plan to present to various lending institutions or the Small Business Association for financing. The term of your agreement will be five years, with a fifteen-year renewal, giving you an exclusive territory with a minimum of 250,000 people and 80,000 dwellings. You will pay 6 percent of revenues monthly as a royalty. The fee for additional franchises is negotiable, but the company discourages absentee ownership in most cases. Master franchises are available. Experience in the security business is not required, but the company prefers that you be an aggressive "doer" with a proven record of business success.

GETTING STARTED

You will need about 1,000 square feet of store space in a mall, office building, shopping center, or industrial park. You'll have company assistance with site selection, layout and design of your store, lease or purchase negotiation, decorating, and furnishing. The company has requirements about standardized uniforms and vehicles.

You'll spend two weeks at the Chicago headquarters for the Security Alliance management seminar, in which you'll learn about recruitment and compensation of personnel, fundamental techniques of sales and general management, time management, budgeting guidelines, business organization, inventory guidelines, and employee evaluation. Your sales managers and sales staff will get a week of instruction to learn how to develop prospects, make a sales presentation, conduct a security survey, and to close a sale. Your technical and service employees will have an additional week of training. You can open your Security Alliance dealership three months after signing the agreement.

MAKING IT WORK

You'll receive a series of detailed, comprehensive manuals to help you operate your Security Alliance dealership. The operations manual covers topics such as managing your business, financial management, bank financing, credit and collection, insurance requirements, inventory control, marketing techniques, advertising procedures, and time management. After your sales personnel have completed the sales seminar, you will be able to reinforce their training with the sales manual and an ongoing onsite sales training program, with assistance from the company's field-support personnel. You'll also get personnel manuals with comprehensive information on recruiting procedures, evaluation techniques, the selection process, and ongoing training programs. Incentive, motivation, and compensation packages are described in detail. Your manuals also contain a comprehensive set of master forms for every phase of your operation. You'll have a general-liability insurance package through the company.

You'll get special pricing on professionally developed promotional materials, ranging from sophisticated brochures to direct-mail advertising and telemarketing programs. Security Alliance has an effective lead-generation program, and it provides an assortment of business builders—national ad reprints, color brochures with tips on crime prevention and fire safety, a checklist for personal inventory, and so on. Consumer leads generated by the extensive national advertising campaign are passed directly to franchisees.

Emphasizing a strong headquarters-franchisee relationship, Security Alliance will send you a confidential franchisee newsletter, another newsletter for up-to-date technical installation information and ideas, and an ongoing series of bulletins and idea stimulators. Company executives will help you and your staff make sales calls and manage business operations, and you can call for assistance on the toll-free hotline. The company holds an annual national convention and regional meetings and sponsors various recognition awards.

You'll benefit from Security Alliance's centralized merchandising system and volume discounts. Many of the products are designed especially and exclusively for Security Alliance by ADEMCO, a multi-million-dollar manufacturer with worldwide distribution centers. A new product line is manufactured by Mitsubishi.

COMMENTS

Security Alliance was ranked 387th in *Entrepreneur* magazine's 1987 "Franchise 500" and 82d in *Venture* magazine's 1986 "Franchise 100." A member of the IFA since 1984, the company also belongs to the National Burglar and Fire Alarm Association. New franchisees are sought throughout the world.

GETTING MORE INFORMATION

The franchise information packet includes brochures with information about the company, an application, a list of franchisee benefits, and article and ad reprints. For more information, call or write:

Ron Davis
President
Security Alliance Corp.
1865 Miner Street
Des Plaines, IL   60016
(800)   323–7601 or (312)   298–7300

ServiceMaster

			AS OF		PROJECTED BY	
BUSINESS: cleaning and lawn-care services	NO. OF UNITS		1/1/85	1/1/86	1/1/87	1/1/88
	OWNED BY: COMPANY		0	0	0	0
FOUNDED: 1948		FRANCHISEES	2,987	3,287	3,637	3,917
FRANCHISED: 1948	LOCATED:	IN U.S.	2,401	2,599	2,829	3,014
START-UP		OUTSIDE U.S.	586	688	808	903
INVESTMENT:	TOTAL:		2,987	3,287	3,637	3,917
$10,700–$19,800	NO. OF STATES W/ UNITS		50	50	50	50

THE BUSINESS

The demand for qualified cleaning professionals continues to grow, and ServiceMaster offers four different franchises to meet the need. The carpet and upholstery franchise uses modern, work-saving ServiceMaster products and equipment in customers' homes, apartments, condominiums, offices, banks, hotels, motels, retail stores, nursing homes, funeral homes, schools, and airports. Some licensees sell their services and products through local retail stores. Much of the work is on a project basis, although there is a growing trend toward having ServiceMaster cleaning services done on a regularly scheduled basis. The second franchise, called the on-location type, specializes in cleaning and maintaining floors, walls, carpeting, and upholstery. This franchise also serves insurance adjusters, home and condominium owners, and apartment and building managers by restoring property damaged by fire, smoke, or water. Contract services, the third franchise type, provides housekeeping for offices, schools, institutions, and similar buildings on a contract basis. This franchise handles the cleaning and maintenance of floors, walls, furniture, windows, and restrooms, along with other light cleaning functions. In this franchise you will be a professional dealing with building managers to provide continuing services on a contract basis. You will be a manager, hiring and managing your own part-time and full-time employees. (With the first two franchises you add employees as the business grows.) And fourth, ServiceMaster takes care of the outside of properties with a lawn-care franchise. In 1985, ServiceMaster franchises grossed $229 million, with average gross sales per unit of $77,000.

WHAT IT TAKES

For franchise fees you will need $5,450 for the carpet and upholstery franchise, $11,500 for the contract services type, or $11,500 for the on-location type. The agreement, valid for five years and renewable for five, does not grant an exclusive territory. Your total investment will range from $10,700 (carpet and upholstery) to $19,800 (contract services or on-location), with half of that required in cash. Direct financial assistance is available from the company. Your investment will cover training material and aids, promotional materials (including a blazer with ServiceMaster logo), professional equipment, supplies and tools, professional chemicals, and the franchise fee. Master franchises are available. You must be the manager of your franchise. Ongoing royalty fees will be 4 to 10 percent of sales monthly. No prior cleaning-business experience is necessary.

GETTING STARTED

You will run the business from your home or small office. Depending on the franchise, you may have about seven full-time and two part-time employees. Your first two weeks of training will begin in your home office using the company manual and visuals, to be followed by two and a half weeks of technical and sales education after you have opened for business. You will also attend the Academy of Service for a week of classroom and hands-on training. Through these various courses you will learn all aspects of operating a small business. You can open within six weeks after buying your ServiceMaster franchise.

MAKING IT WORK

Your franchise fee will cover newspaper ads, mailers, brochures, radio commercials, national media coverage, in-house media packages (slides, videotapes), and a lead-referral system. Co-op advertising is available for telephone-book ads. ServiceMaster holds an annual national convention, annual regional conferences, eight area-wide franchise meetings each year, and various one-day seminars. ServiceMaster also offers onsite training as needed, distributes a monthly newsletter and periodic product/service technical and market updates, conducts surveys twice a year, and sponsors various award programs.

As backup resources ServiceMaster offers headquarters and regional resource persons; a toll-free hotline; regular onsite visits and onsite troubleshooting; manuals on policy, management procedure, and customer service; and systems for bookkeeping, computerized management information, and computerized billing. A research-and-development department studies new products, equipment, and systems. The company has divisions to produce and distribute merchandise, equipment, and supplies; a central purchasing program offering volume discounts; a centralized merchandising system; and company brands. You may use noncompany products. Service-Master offers customer accounts-receivable financing and sponsors insurance for property, general-liability, automobile, life, major-medical, dental, disability, worker's compensation, and third-party-bonding coverage.

COMMENTS

ServiceMaster was ranked ninth in *Entrepreneur* magazine's 1987 "Franchise 500" and sixteenth in *Venture* magazine's 1986 "Franchise 100." A division of ServiceMaster Industries Inc., ServiceMaster has been a member of the IFA since 1959. The company wants to add franchises throughout the United States and in Australia, Canada, Europe, and Japan.

GETTING MORE INFORMATION

The franchise information packet contains sample brochures, break-downs of cost for each franchise (except lawn care), an overview brochure explaining the company's operations, a contract services training manual, the offering in the form required by the FTC, two evaluation tests for you to complete, and a one-page application form. For more details, contact:
Denis V. Horsfall
Vice-President, Sales
ServiceMaster Residential and Commercial Corporation
2300 Warrenville Road
Downers Grove, IL   60515
(312)   964–1300

Service Personnel

		AS OF		PROJECTED BY	
	NO. OF UNITS	1/1/85	1/1/86	1/1/87	1/1/88
	OWNED BY: COMPANY	0	0	0	0
	FRANCHISEES	20	30	40	50
	LOCATED: IN U.S.	20	30	40	50
	OUTSIDE U.S.	0	0	0	0
	TOTAL:	20	30	40	50
	NO. OF STATES W/ UNITS	10	10	10	10

BUSINESS: permanent and temporary employment agency
FOUNDED: 1980
FRANCHISED: 1983
START-UP INVESTMENT: $6,000–$7,000

THE BUSINESS

The personnel-placement industry is now rated the third fastest growing service industry in the United States. Temporary placement alone has grown from a $481 million industry in 1971 to a $4 billion one today. Service Personnel has combined temporary and permanent placement services in one company to produce an even more profitable and dynamic business. The company has such a low start-up cost and quick return on investment that it is well suited to small towns and suburban areas as well as cities. In 1985 total sales came to $1,000,000 for all Service Personnel franchises combined, and the average per franchise was $80,000 gross and $25,000 net.

WHAT IT TAKES

You'll pay a fee of $3,500 for your first franchise. Other expenses can run between $2,500 and $3,500, and include one month's rent of office space, telephone installation, supplies, license and bonding, insurance, furniture and decor, travel for training, and other miscellaneous items. The estimate doesn't include prepaid items, security deposits, and working capital. Although the company can assist you with financing these costs, they recommend you start out with at least $5,000 or $6,000 cash for operating funds. Your operating costs, including salaries, will run approximately $1,920 to $3,730 monthly, plus you'll pay a royalty fee of 10 percent of gross sales.

Your franchise agreement will apply for ten years, with five-year renewal periods. Passive ownership is permitted, but the company strongly suggests you know how to manage the office so you can step in and take over if necessary. You can buy a territory bounded by streets, city limits, or even county lines. If you buy a large territory you can get additional franchises for no fee and sell them in your area.

GETTING STARTED

Service Personnel offices are always located in office buildings and require from 200 to 300 square feet of space. The company will help you with site selection, lease negotiation, layout, decoration, acquisition of materials and supplies, and acquisition of a state license. If you choose to manage the office, you'll need, at most, two full-time employees, whom the company will help you hire. A manager and a communicator usually run the office as a team. A third person can make outside calls, help develop new business, and work in public relations, as well as fill in for the manager when necessary.

You'll spend a week in classroom training at the Murfreesboro, Tennessee, facilities learning about advertising, recruiting, management, bookkeeping, interviewing, and operations. You'll get another week of on-the-job training at an office already in operation and a third week at your own office after start-up. Before your grand opening, Service Personnel staff will train you in public relations and promotions. You can probably open your office about a month after purchasing the franchise.

MAKING IT WORK

Part of your 10 percent royalty fee will go toward ongoing training, consulting, and guidance. You'll pay no advertising fee for the newspaper and magazine ads, brochures, mailers, and presentation books you'll get. You can also get media packages such as slides and videotapes, displays, and press packages, and you can participate in contests. Company staff will make regular visits to your office, and regional company personnel will be available for consultations with you at your office. You'll receive a weekly newsletter and quarterly surveys, and your customers will get a monthly newsletter.

The company sponsors yearly national meetings, quarterly regional conventions, and areawide franchise meetings. You'll also have policy manuals and bookkeeping and expense-analysis systems for daily use. You and your employees will get an insurance package with life, major-medical, dental, and disability coverage, and your business will have general-liability coverage. If you refer a franchise applicant to the company, you'll get a referral fee if the applicant buys a franchise or territory. The company also has recognition programs for top employees and offices.

COMMENTS

Service Personnel makes an earnings claim document available to potential franchisees. The company is seeking franchisees in twelve states.

GETTING MORE INFORMATION

The franchise information packet includes eight pages of franchise information and a cover letter from the president of the company. To get more information, contact:

Richard Hughes
President
Service Personnel, Inc.
826 Memorial Boulevard, Suite 209
Murfreesboro, TN   37130
(615)   896–1501 (call collect)

Servpro

BUSINESS: cleaning and restoration service
FOUNDED: 1967
FRANCHISED: 1968
START-UP INVESTMENT: $29,000–$42,151

		AS OF		PROJECTED BY	
NO. OF UNITS		1/1/85	1/1/86	1/1/87	1/1/88
OWNED BY:	COMPANY	0	0	0	0
	FRANCHISEES	550	590	640	700
LOCATED:	IN U.S.	550	590	640	700
	OUTSIDE U.S.	0	0	0	0
TOTAL:		550	590	640	700
NO. OF STATES W/ UNITS		48	48	49	50

THE BUSINESS

Servpro is a cleaning business specializing in fire, flood, and vandalism restoration as well as carpet, furniture, and drapery cleaning. Servpro also markets janitorial service, maid service, carpet dyeing, ceiling cleaning, and deodorization service. The company provides services to home owners, insurance companies, retail stores, real estate and property-management firms, and commercial and institutional buildings. In 1985, Servpro franchises grossed $52 million, with average sales per unit of $95,000. The company also markets some products for home use.

WHAT IT TAKES

Your initial franchise fee will be either $26,500 or $31,500, depending on which services you plan to offer (the complete package includes carpet dyeing and ceiling cleaning). Covering a nonexclusive territory based on demographics, the franchise agreement is valid for five years and automatically renewable for five-year terms. Your total initial investment will range from $29,000 to $42,151, with up to 50 percent financing available from Servpro Industries upon approval of your credit background. Additional units carry the same initial franchise fee. You may be an investor-owner, but the company discourages the practice. Master franchises are available. Your ongoing royalty fee will be 5 to 10 percent, based on gross volume, and type of work. Prior experience is not necessary.

GETTING STARTED

Servpro will assist with site selection; facility layout and decoration; lease or purchase of furniture, equipment, and vehicles; service maintenance contracts; and acquisition of supplies and merchandise. You may operate from your home or a warehouse. You will need three to five full-time employees, including yourself. Your training will involve your study of the company manuals for two weeks; two weeks of on-the-job training (with compensation); seven days of management, sales, and financial training in the national classroom with an expense allowance for transportation, meals, and lodging; and, finally, two days of setup training when you open. You can be open within a month and a half after purchasing a Servpro franchise. The company will help with your grand opening.

MAKING IT WORK

Servpro offers catalogs, television and radio commercials, billboard posters, and incentives to enhance your business as well as a co-op advertising program. The company issues both a monthly newsletter with management tips and periodic updates on service, products, and market information. The company holds monthly areawide franchise meetings, conducts surveys as needed, and sponsors various award programs.

   Backup services include headquarters and regional resource persons; a toll-free hotline; regular onsite visits; onsite troubleshooting; manuals for policy, management procedure, and customer service; all types of forms; and systems for bookkeeping, expense analysis, inventory, personnel, and computerized billing. Servpro has two chemists working full-time on research and development of new products, and the company prefers that franchisees use company products, but approval for other products and equipment may be granted. The company produces and distributes merchandise, equipment, and supplies and utilizes a central purchasing and merchandising system for volume discounts.

COMMENTS

Servpro was ranked sixty-ninth in *Entrepreneur* magazine's 1987 "Franchise 500." A member of the IFA, the company wants to increase franchise operations across the United States and in several foreign countries.

GETTING MORE INFORMATION

The franchise information packet contains numerous brochures on the company's services, various cleaning-package options, a list of the products included in the packages, and a six-page application form. For more details, contact:
Richard Isaacson
Director of Marketing
Servpro Industries Inc.
11357 Pyrites Way
Rancho Cordova, CA   95670–0050
(800)   826–9586 or (916)   635–3111

7-Eleven

BUSINESS:			AS OF		PROJECTED BY	
convenience grocery	NO. OF UNITS		1/1/85	1/1/86	1/1/87	1/1/88
stores	OWNED BY: COMPANY		4,526	4,498	N/A	N/A
FOUNDED: 1927		FRANCHISEES	6,412	6,656	N/A	N/A
FRANCHISED: 1964	LOCATED:	IN U.S.	7,635	7,675	N/A	N/A
START-UP		OUTSIDE U.S.	3,303	3,479	N/A	N/A
INVESTMENT:	TOTAL:		10,938	11,154	N/A	N/A
$52,579	NO. OF STATES W/ UNITS		41	41	N/A	N/A

THE BUSINESS

Usually open for business twenty-four hours a day, seven days a week, 7-Eleven stores are small, compact, easily accessible convenience grocery stores. A division of Southland Corporation, a pioneer of the convenience store, 7-Eleven has stores throughout the United States. Since the dollar volume, gross sales, and net income per unit vary widely, general figures are given in the Franchise Offering Circular available from the company.

WHAT IT TAKES

Your total investment will vary, depending on the store type and location. The initial franchise fee varies for each store; however, the fee is computed for each store as follows: (1) The initial franchise fee for a store that has not been continuously operated for the preceding twelve calendar months is an amount equal to 15 percent of the previous calendar year's annualized average per-store monthly gross profit (excluding gross profit from gasoline) for all stores located within the district in which the franchised store is or is to be located. (2) If the store has been continuously operated for at least the preceding twelve calendar months, the franchise fee is an amount equal to 15 percent of that store's gross profit (excluding gross profit from gasoline) for the immediately preceding twelve calendar months. The company does not allow passive ownership, nor are master franchises available. The franchise agreement will give you a single store at a specific location, not an exclusive territory.

You'll also need a minimum additional investment of $12,500. Your minimum cash payment required will be the applicable franchise fee for the store plus the minimum investment, with the balance of your total investment paid out of your store's operation over a reasonable time period. Your investment requirements for a 7-Eleven franchise will include the cost of the inventory, the cash-register fund, and all necessary operating licenses. The exact amount will vary depending on the location of your store and the inventory requirements. As of December 1985, the average total investment in the inventory for a 7-Eleven Store was $38,806, the average cash-register fund was $773, and the approximate cost of licenses and permits was $500. The company will finance a portion of the investment if you are a qualified applicant.

You'll share a percentage of the gross profit from your store with 7-Eleven as a continuing charge for rental of the store building, equipment, utilities, advertising, and bookkeeping, as well as for merchandising and general advisory assistance. From your share of the gross profits you'll pay all other operating expenses, including items such as payroll, store supplies, telephone, laundry, bad checks, payroll taxes, cash variation, advertising, employees' group insurance, security expense, bad merchandise, inventory variation, equipment repair, general maintenance, janitorial service, interest expense, and taxes and license. The amount remaining after payment of the operating expenses will be your net income.

GETTING STARTED

The location of your store will be researched and selected by 7-Eleven real estate representatives. After the company buys or leases a site, the completed 7-Eleven store will be leased to you. A typical 7-Eleven facility occupies 2,400 square feet and is located in or near office buildings, commercial or industrial parks or centers, shopping centers, or malls. All equipment in the store, including heating and air conditioning, vaults, shelving, cash registers, and refrigerated cases, will be included in your lease, and you'll be responsible for maintaining it. You'll receive assistance from 7-Eleven in the arrangement of initial inventory for the store; afterwards you'll be responsible for all ordering and stocking of merchandise. The number of employees you'll need will vary, depending on the size, location, and type of unit you choose.

Before your final acceptance as a franchisee you'll be required to complete successfully the 7-Eleven store-operations training program, which includes two weeks of actual experience in a training store. You'll follow up this training with one week of classroom work at the regional training center, where you'll learn about a variety of essential management skills, techniques, and procedures. The cost of these sessions is included in your initial franchise fee. You can plan on opening within two to three months after purchasing your franchise.

MAKING IT WORK

The company provides television, radio, magazine, and newspaper advertising. You'll have access to the 7-Eleven network of administrative resources through a company accounts-receivable financing program, optional merchandise and supply benefits, central purchasing program, company publications and bulletins, business forms, and resource persons. The company will prepare a list for you of recommended merchandise, retail selling prices, and vendors, some of whom may be affiliated with 7-Eleven or handle merchandise produced by divisions of Southland Corporation. You'll be free to purchase merchandise from any vendor and to establish retail prices. You'll receive credit for all discounts and allowances on merchandise purchased. Bookkeeping records on your operation will be kept for you by 7-Eleven. You'll make daily cash deposits of sales receipts, and from these 7-Eleven will pay for all operating expenses and merchandise purchases you have approved in connection with the operation of the store. You, your family, and your employees will be eligible to participate in a group insurance program that provides dental, sickness, disability (only for you, as a franchisee), and life coverage. In most areas you can opt for an H.R. 10 retirement plan.

COMMENTS

7-Eleven Stores was ranked eighth in *Entrepreneur* magazine's 1987 "Franchise 500." Southland Corporation, 7-Eleven's parent company, has been a member of the IFA since 1964. A Uniform Franchise Offering Circular is available to potential franchisees upon request. The Southland Corporation supports many community service programs, such as the Muscular Dystrophy Association and the March of Dimes. The company is seeking franchisees in a number of East and West Coast states.

GETTING MORE INFORMATION

The franchise information packet includes a franchise offering circular with all disclosure information and forms necessary to complete a franchise agreement, a color folder with an outline of franchise procedures, and an insert sheet describing the operations. For more information, contact:

Wayne Beeder
Manager, Franchise Systems
Southland Corporation
2828 North Haskell Avenue
Dallas, TX   75221
(214)   828–7763

Sheraton Inns

BUSINESS: hotel
  FOUNDED: 1937
  FRANCHISED: 1962
START-UP
  INVESTMENT:
  $30,000 + $150 per
  room over 100 rooms

NO. OF UNITS		AS OF 1/1/85	AS OF 1/1/86	PROJECTED BY 1/1/87	PROJECTED BY 1/1/88
OWNED BY:	COMPANY	134	142	152	182
	FRANCHISEES	339	345	348	358
LOCATED:	IN U.S.	350	369	366	394
	OUTSIDE U.S.	123	118	134	146
TOTAL:		473	487	500	540
NO. OF STATES W/ UNITS		50	50	50	50

THE BUSINESS

The network of Sheraton hotels, inns, and resorts currently extends to 60 countries, everywhere from Argentina to Zimbabwe. The hotel chain hosts 21 million guests a year and serves more than 136 million meals annually. In 1985 the chain's room business grossed more than $812 million among its franchises, with average room sales per unit of $2,354,127 and net income per unit of $117,706. Acquired by the ITT Corporation in 1968, Sheraton is increasing its market share by the expansion and promotion of such features as its advanced reservations system, personalized food service (gourmet and specialty restaurants), luxury hotel-within-a-hotel Towers units, and a variety of fitness facilities and programs.

WHAT IT TAKES

You will need $30,000 for the franchise fee, plus $150 per room over 100 rooms. The fee for additional franchises is the same, and master franchises are available. Your exclusive territory will be valid for ten years and renewable for ten-year periods. You will need all investment capital in cash, because Sheraton offers no financing, although it will assist you in preparing loan applications. You may be an owner-investor of a Sheraton franchise. The company charges an ongoing royalty fee of 5 percent of gross room sales, plus a monthly fee for the Reservatron III reservation system of 1.6 percent of gross room sales. Prior hotel experience is not required.

GETTING STARTED

Sheraton's staff will monitor the progress of your project from its initial stages through its grand opening. As part of your application for a franchise, you will be required to obtain from an independent research firm a feasibility study projecting the number of guest rooms and type of facility best suited for the market area. Sheraton will provide guidance for facility layout and decoration. Sheraton facilities are located in all types of areas—near highways, in malls and shopping centers, or in commercial industrial parks. Staff sizes vary greatly. Sheraton will help you find a qualified general manager to direct the activities of the property. The five-day training program will instruct the general manager and the sales and room personnel in Sheraton's programs and industry practices. It normally takes two years after a franchise purchase to develop and open a new Sheraton hotel. You will receive full assistance with your grand opening.

MAKING IT WORK

Co-op advertising funds are available for newspaper ads, black-and-white and four-color magazine ads, mailers, telephone-book ads, radio commercials, national media coverage, a lead-referral system, and press releases. You will also receive a public-relations/marketing manual. The company's sales force is staffed with specialists in corporate, industrial, tour, travel, associations, incentive, union, and government sales. A group room-availability information bank speeds reservations for travel agencies and meeting planners. Sheraton holds regional conferences twice a year, five-day seminars on sales development and marketing management five times a year, onsite training sessions three times a year, and areawide franchise meetings twice a year.

Sheraton publishes a monthly magazine and newsletter; periodic updates on service, company news, and market information; and a monthly customer-oriented magazine. Award programs recognize hotels for excellence in service, sales, and tenure. Your administrative tasks will be simplified with headquarters and regional resource persons; a toll-free hotline; regular onsite visits; onsite troubleshooting; manuals for policy, management procedure, and customer service; and forms for inventory and orders. Sheraton divisions produce and distribute merchandise, equipment, and supplies and offer volume discounts through a central purchasing and merchandising system for company brands. There is no requirement to sell company products only, but you must use the Sheraton logo on products.

COMMENTS

Sheraton was ranked sixty-fourth in *Entrepreneur* magazine's 1987 "Franchise 500." A member of the IFA since 1974, the company wants to develop new hotels throughout the world.

GETTING MORE INFORMATION

The franchise information packet contains a booklet describing architectural requirements for a Sheraton hotel, brochures on the franchise program, fact sheets on the company's hotels, a directory of Sheraton properties, an FTC required offering, an IFA booklet on franchises, and information on the company's background. For more details, contact:

Michael F. Bloomer
Director of Franchising Division
The Sheraton Corporation
60 State Street
Boston, MA   02109
(617)   367–5300

Sir Speedy Printing Centers

BUSINESS: printing			AS OF		PROJECTED BY	
services	NO. OF UNITS		1/1/85	1/1/86	1/1/87	1/1/88
FOUNDED: 1968	OWNED BY: COMPANY		0	0	0	0
FRANCHISED: 1968		FRANCHISEES	500	605	750	900
START-UP	LOCATED: IN U.S.		496	595	725	825
INVESTMENT:		OUTSIDE U.S.	4	10	25	75
$116,000	TOTAL:		500	605	750	900
	NO. OF STATES W/ UNITS		34	38	42	45

THE BUSINESS

Each year more and more individuals, small businesses, and large corporations need sophisticated color printing, typeset copy, and a multitude of detailed business forms. As a result of this "paper explosion," sales from the 5,000 printing franchises in the United States exceeded $800 million. In 1985, Sir Speedy's franchises accounted for $150 million of that total, and the average per franchise was $298,200 in gross sales. Sir Speedy Printing specializes in printing promotional materials, instruction sheets, bulletins, maps, charts, graphs, menus, letterheads, and all kinds of business forms. The company's services are designed to bridge the gap between small in-house photocopiers and large-scale commercial printshops.

WHAT IT TAKES

The franchise fee for a Sir Speedy Printing Center is $17,500, $5,000 of which must be paid when you apply for a franchise. The remaining $12,500 will be due before you attend the company's training program. You'll pay another $18,500 for start-up costs to cover your training, site location and preparation, and market research. This also will be due before you attend training. Your equipment cost will be $50,000, and you can get everything you need in a package through the company, which will let you lease the equipment package at below-market leasing rates for five years. After that time you can buy the equipment for 10 percent of its original value. The company can help you get a Small Business Association loan for the remainder of your startup costs. You should have on hand a cash amount of about $30,000 to cover costs during the first few months of operation. Your franchise agreement, valid for twenty years with a ten-year renewal option, will entitle you to a territory based on market surveys of your area. You do not have to have any previous experience in printing to be a franchisee.

You can get additional centers for $5,000 each, and master franchises are available. The company will permit you to hire a manager but prefers that you run the center yourself. You'll pay a reduced royalty fee of 4 percent of gross sales your first year and 6 percent thereafter. However, the company has a royalty incentive program that will reduce the royalty if your sales volume reaches a certain level.

GETTING STARTED

You can have a Sir Speedy center in an office building, shopping center, commercial center, or freestanding building. You'll need 1,000 to 1,200 square feet, and company representatives will help you choose the best site. Sir Speedy will also help you with lease or purchase negotiations for the property and layout, decoration, and furnishing of your center. All Sir Speedy centers display the company colors and logo. The initial equipment and supply package you'll get will provide you with all the tools, equipment, and supplies needed to begin producing high-quality printing immediately. The company will also help you select the two full-time employees you'll need to hire.

You'll receive two weeks of classroom training at the Laguna Hills, California, National Training Center. Part of your fee will cover the cost of travel and accommodations for two. You'll study business operations, sales, equipment operations, accounting, marketing and advertising. For the first two weeks you're open, a Sir Speedy representative will provide further training at your center. You can also get an optional week of training at another established location. You'll get practical experience in personnel management, outside sales, counter sales, pricing, and paper recognition.

MAKING IT WORK

The advertising fee of 2 percent of your monthly gross sales will cover magazine and telephone-book ads, brochures, mailers, point-of-purchase displays, signs, banners, and press packages. The company will also produce radio and television commercials and sponsor contests, and the lead-referral system and public-relations manual will help you do more effective local marketing. You can also participate with other Sir Speedy franchisees in cooperative advertising campaigns.

The company sponsors various recognition programs and holds yearly national and regional conventions, as well as bimonthly, half-day seminars at owners' association meetings. A field representative will visit your center regularly and consult with you on problems, plus you can call a specially trained troubleshooter on the company's toll-free hotline. You'll be provided with a bookkeeping system, accounting forms, and policy and procedure manuals for daily operations. A variety of publications—such as the company newsletter, technical product updates, and surveys—will be sent to you regularly.

When you buy supplies, you can team up with other franchisees to get volume discounts through the company's central purchasing program. You can get discounts up to 40 percent below retail prices on some supplies. You and your employees will get insurance at group rates through the company's insurance package, which offers automobile, life, major-medical, dental, disability, property, and general-liability coverage.

COMMENTS

Sir Speedy Printing was ranked forty-ninth in *Entrepreneur* magazine's 1987 "Franchise 500" and thirty-second in *Venture* magazine's 1986 "Franchise 100." A member of the IFA, the company is seeking franchisees throughout in the United States, and in Asia, Australia, Canada, Japan, and Mexico.

GETTING MORE INFORMATION

The information packet comes with a brochure about Sir Speedy Printing centers, an insert about costs and financing, a list of centers throughout the country, and a qualification report for you to fill out and return. For details, contact:

Harold C. Lloyd
Vice-President of Sales
Sir Speedy, Inc.
23131 Verdugo Drive
Laguna Hills, CA   92653
(800)   854–3321

Slender Center

BUSINESS: weight-			AS OF		PROJECTED BY	
loss consultation	NO. OF UNITS		1/1/85	1/1/86	1/1/87	1/1/88
FOUNDED: 1979	OWNED BY: COMPANY		3	3	3	3
FRANCHISED: 1980		FRANCHISEES	40	40	46	56
START-UP	LOCATED: IN U.S.		43	43	49	59
INVESTMENT:		OUTSIDE U.S.	0	0	0	0
$16,500–$34,000	TOTAL:		43	43	49	59
	NO. OF STATES W/ UNITS		3	4	5	7

THE BUSINESS

Permanent weight loss is an achievement that has eluded most people who've tried such methods as fad diets and torturous exercise programs. Yet 73 percent of Slender Center's clients succeed in losing weight and keeping it off. The company's innovative program is safe for men, women, adolescents, vegetarians, and even nursing mothers. Also, physicians often refer obese patients to Slender Center, where their weight losses can be closely monitored.

The Slender Center Program has been approved by the head of nutritional sciences at the University of Wisconsin. The program uses a combination of low calorie intake (about 800 calories per day to start) using foods from the four food groups, vitamin supplements, and behavior-modification techniques such as relaxation, imagery, and affirmations. Clients are given a 246-page manual that includes a cookbook, instructions, and a recommended self-help reading list.

Once clients achieve their weight goals, they join a stabilization and maintenance program in which an ideal calorie intake is determined and their weight is monitored for another four months. For a small fee clients can then join a program in which they're given updates on new low-calorie recipes, continuing moral support, and behavior-modification consultations. As a Slender Center franchisee you can expect to net from 20 to 70 percent of your gross annual income.

WHAT IT TAKES

The fee for your Slender Center franchise will run from $12,000 to $27,000, with no fee for additional franchises. Your five-year agreement, with five-year renewals, will grant you an exclusive territory based on the population in your area. The company allows passive ownership but prefers that you manage the center yourself. Your total initial investment, including franchise fee and lease or purchase of a site, will range from $16,500 to $34,000, which you'll need to pay in cash. You'll also pay an ongoing royalty fee of 6 percent of your first $2,500 of gross monthly sales. For sales above $2,500 you'll pay only 4 percent. (There is a minimum fee of $165 per month.)

You don't need any experience to operate a Slender Center, but empathy and an energetic personality are important. (Many consultants, like their clients, have had a weight problem in the past.) It is helpful but not necessary to have experience in teaching, sales, fitness, or business.

GETTING STARTED

As soon as Slender Center has evaluated your area and made a preliminary decision to locate a center in your area, it will help you negotiate the lease or purchase of your site, which should be between 400 and 900 square feet in a freestanding building, shopping center, or office building. The company will also start to work on your grand-opening advertising campaign and help you staff your office. You'll need at least one half-time employee and, if you choose not to manage the center yourself, a full-time manager. The company's consultants will help you decorate, furnish, and lay out your center and will supply you with all the initial materials and merchandise you'll need.

You and your employees will receive five days of training at the company's school in Madison, Wisconsin. You'll learn about marketing, advertising, accounting, sales, consulting and motivation techniques, and nutritional education. There are also three company-owned centers where you'll go for on-the-job training during your five-day visit. You should be ready for your grand opening within six to eight weeks after buying your franchise.

MAKING IT WORK

Slender Center charges no ongoing fees for advertising but provides, free of charge, newspaper and magazine ads, telephone-book ads, mailers, brochures, and more. The company sends franchisees a monthly company newsletter and semiannual surveys, and customers receive a quarterly publication oriented to their special needs and interests. The company sponsors biannual regional conferences, city- or areawide franchise meetings, and periodic one-day seminars.

Headquarters personnel will visit your center on a regular basis; help with troubleshooting; show you systems for bookkeeping and expense analysis; and give you forms for inventory, ordering, and accounting. You'll also receive management procedure and policy manuals. Slender Center sponsors various performance awards and regularly tests new low-calorie recipes for your clients.

COMMENTS

Slender Center was ranked 466th in *Entrepreneur* magazine's 1987 "Franchise 500." A member of the IFA since 1985, the company is seeking franchisees in eleven states.

**GETTING MORE
INFORMATION**

The franchise information packet contains a client-oriented brochure, a report to prospective franchisees, a list of references you
can call, and an application. To get more information, contact:
Jean Geurink
President
Slender Center, Inc.
9 Odana Court
Madison, WI   53719
(608)   273–2086 (call collect)

Sounds Easy

BUSINESS: retail
  video rental
    FOUNDED: 1980
    FRANCHISED: 1981
START-UP
  INVESTMENT:
  $80,000–$150,000

NO. OF UNITS		AS OF		PROJECTED BY	
		1/1/85	1/1/86	1/1/87	1/1/88
OWNED BY: COMPANY		0	1	1	1
FRANCHISEES		66	81	100	150
LOCATED: IN U.S.		66	82	101	151
OUTSIDE U.S.		0	0	0	0
TOTAL:		66	82	101	151
NO. OF STATES W/ UNITS		19	20	21	22

THE BUSINESS

The home video rental market is one of the fastest-growing industries of the 1980s. The electronics and movie industries are concen-
trating more on the home entertainment market now than ever before. In fact, combined with the highly successful, continually
growing rental industry, home video rentals has the number one
business opportunity in America. In 1985 the total sales for Sounds
Easy franchises were $6,984,945, and the average gross sales per
franchise were estimated to be $108,536. Sounds Easy maintains a
family image in the services it offers and its movie selections. Customers can choose from thousands of VHS movie tapes.

WHAT IT TAKES

The initial franchise fee for a Sounds Easy store is $13,500. The
agreement is for ten years, with two five-year renewal periods. No
exclusive territory is guaranteed, but you may build a master franchise area as large as your state, if you qualify. Additional stores
cost $6,000 each. Total startup costs, including franchise fees, may
run from $80,000 to $150,000. The company will assist you in obtaining a conventional or Small Business Association loan, then
leave the amount of cash down payment you'll be required to pay
up to the lending institution. Sounds Easy will permit you to hire a
manager to run your store, but they prefer that you manage it yourself. You'll pay an ongoing royalty fee of 5 percent of gross sales.

GETTING STARTED

Sounds Easy stores usually have from 1,500 to 2,000 square feet and are located in malls or shopping centers. The company will work closely with you in choosing a suitable site. Once you've settled on a location for your store, Sounds Easy will help you negotiate the lease, then help you lease or purchase your equipment, furniture, and fixtures. You'll probably need one full-time and two part-time employees, whom the company will help hire.

You'll attend school at the company's new National Training Center in Orem, Utah, for five days of intensive study. Throughout the discussions, lectures, videotaped presentations, and on-the-floor experience, emphasis is placed on how to develop a successful business. Seminars cover the Sounds Easy concept, facility design and layout, personnel, customer relations, budgeting, merchandising, operations management, sales techniques, maintenance of VCR machines and tapes, and advertising. Upon successful completion of the course, you'll receive a diploma to display in your store. Within about six weeks after purchasing your franchise, you should be able to have your grand opening, which the company will help you plan.

MAKING IT WORK

All franchisees participate in a cooperative advertising program to help stimulate sales. Sounds Easy will supply newspaper ads, mailers, point-of-purchase displays, banners, seasonal promotions, and radio commercials. The company sponsors a yearly national convention and regional meetings, and it offers follow-up training programs through videotaped presentations. The company newsletter, technical and industry updates, and surveys will also keep you up to date. If you have any problems or questions, you can call the company's toll-free hotline. Company personnel will also visit your site regularly and offer support and training in new areas of development.

You'll be trained to use the company's expense-analysis system and computerized management information system, and Sounds Easy will supply you with accounting and ordering forms and policy and procedure manuals. Sounds Easy will help you choose your merchandise from over 12,000 video movies now available, and you'll get group discounts through volume purchasing with other franchisees. The company's budgeting and financial-planning programs will help you increase sales and control expenses. Sounds Easy sponsors various performance awards.

COMMENTS

Sounds Easy was ranked 347th in *Entrepreneur* magazine's 1987 "Franchise 500" and 77th in *Venture* magazine's "Franchise 100." The company is seeking new franchises in most states.

GETTING MORE INFORMATION

The franchise information packet features a discussion of reasons for and benefits of owning a Sounds Easy franchise, an overview of the training program, and an application. For more information, contact:

David A. Meine
President
Sounds Easy
2230 North University Parkway, Suite 2F
Provo, UT 84604
(800) 437–4363 or (801) 375–7527

Sport-About

BUSINESS: specialty sporting-goods store
FOUNDED: 1978
FRANCHISED: 1978
START-UP INVESTMENT: $100,000

		AS OF		PROJECTED BY	
NO. OF UNITS		1/1/85	1/1/86	1/1/87	1/1/88
OWNED BY:	COMPANY	1	1	1	1
	FRANCHISEES	10	25	70	150
LOCATED:	IN U.S.	11	26	71	151
	OUTSIDE U.S.	0	0	0	0
TOTAL:		11	26	71	151
NO. OF STATES W/ UNITS		6	18	28	35

THE BUSINESS

Today, a growing number of people are participating in athletics during all seasons—from racquetball to snow skiing. Sport-About, a retail franchise featuring a complete range of sporting-goods equipment, footwear, and activewear, is seeking to capture its share of the $25 billion consumers spend annually on sports activities. Increased awareness of the need for personal fitness is expected to fuel the trend toward mass participation in sports and the need for sports equipment and accessories.

WHAT IT TAKES

To start your Sport-About franchise, you will need $100,000 to $140,000, which includes a $20,000 franchise fee. Your other start-up costs will include the following average figures: $5,000 for a computer system; $11,500 for fixtures, equipment, and supplies; $50,000 for initial inventory; $6,000 for operating capital and preopening expenses; $5,000 for grand-opening advertising and setup; and $2,500 for leasehold improvements. Approximately 30 percent of your total investment must be in cash, but company financial experts will assist you in obtaining a loan from your local lending institution or the Small Business Administration. The franchise agreement will entitle you to exclusive territorial rights for ten years, with a renewal period of five years.

Since you do not have to manage the units that you own, you can also own a master franchise, involving your subfranchising of several locations within your territory for a portion of the ongoing royalty fee of 4 percent of gross sales. Sport-About franchises are available not only to newcomers to the sporting-goods industry but also to current operators of independent sporting-goods stores through a special conversion package.

GETTING STARTED

Sport-About's staff will conduct a comprehensive market study to evaluate the best location, assist with lease negotiations, and advise you on store layout. You and your manager will be sent to Minneapolis for a two-week training seminar consisting of both classroom and in-store instruction. The training will provide you with a thorough education in product features, ordering procedures, and accounting and financial reporting. A portion of your training time will be spent in an operating Sport-About store, where you will be shown good customer-service techniques, approaches to staffing and scheduling of personnel, local advertising promotions, and proper merchandising of your store. Then later, at your own store, your manager and your two full-time employees will review similar topics on site but will focus primarily on customer service and merchandise familiarity.

Your 1,500- to 2,000-square-foot store will either be located in a mall or a strip shopping center. You can expect to be open for business within three months after purchasing your franchise, and for a fee you can have company assistance in planning your grand opening.

MAKING IT WORK

Planned and designed advertising layouts, cooperative advertising with certain brand-name manufacturers, and seasonal promotions are just some of the benefits you'll receive from your advertising fee of 1.5 percent of gross sales. Sport-About also conducts two trade shows a year, enabling you to learn directly from suppliers about new products and improvements in merchandise programs. At quarterly budget meetings, frequently held at the franchises, home-office personnel will provide an in-depth analysis of your business plan. These sessions will be available to you during your first year of operations to help keep your business thriving. Other ongoing assistance is available through a WATS telephone line for consultation on merchandising promotions, inventory control, and other concerns. Onsite training will be provided to you every three months if needed.

Managing your inventory will be simplified by Sport-About's customized computer system and software package which will enable you to record inventory and sales transactions as they occur. With this capability you will always be aware of what's selling so you can reorder quickly from the company's central warehouse, which enables you to purchase a large selection of fast-moving products at a volume discount during any season. In addition, national and regional buying programs exist with over 100 major suppliers of sporting goods and accessories. As a Sport-About owner, you will have instant access to merchandise and an approved line of credit with such big-name manufacturers as Wilson, Nike, and Spalding. For additional revenue you can offer imprinting of sportswear, trophy and award engraving, racquet restringing, and bat regripping.

COMMENTS

Sport-About was ranked 304th in *Entrepreneur* magazine's 1987 "Franchise 500." A member of IFA since 1986, the company is seeking franchisees throughout the United States.

GETTING MORE INFORMATION

The franchise information packet has brochures and booklets on frequently asked questions about the company, franchise operations, and the sporting-goods industry; several reprints from national publications; a one-page application form; and names and addresses of recent franchise owners. For further information, write or call, toll-free or collect:

Debbie Kneeland
Administrative Assistant
Sport-About, Inc.
1557 Coon Rapids Boulevard
Minneapolis, MN   55433
(800)   328–2502 or (612)   757–8414

Sport Shack

		AS OF		PROJECTED BY	
BUSINESS: sports	NO. OF UNITS	1/1/85	1/1/86	1/1/87	1/1/88
equipment and clothing store	OWNED BY: COMPANY	0	0	1	1
FOUNDED: 1974	FRANCHISEES	70	80	87	105
FRANCHISED: 1975	LOCATED: IN U.S.	70	80	88	106
START-UP	OUTSIDE U.S.	0	0	0	0
INVESTMENT:	TOTAL:	70	80	88	106
$85,000–$105,000	NO. OF STATES W/ UNITS	35	37	38	42

THE BUSINESS

In all areas of the country men, women, and children of all athletic skill levels and all income groups buy and use sporting equipment and clothing. Sport Shack is a national franchise of multiline retail sporting-goods stores carrying brand-name athletic and physical-fitness equipment, active sportswear, and athletic footwear for sports and everyday wear. The product lines include jackets; uniforms; warm-ups; caps; swimwear; a complete range of footwear; trophies; and equipment for baseball, racquetball, golf, and other sports. The stores carry major brands such as Reebok, Converse, Speedo, Spalding, Wilson, Nike, and MacGregor. In 1985, Sport Shack had $20 million in total dollar volume, and the average gross sales per franchise were $250,000.

WHAT IT TAKES

Your initial franchise fee will be $10,000. The term of your agreement will be ten years, and you'll get an exclusive territory based on population. You will need $25,000 in cash and the ability to finance $60,000 to $80,000. The company will advise you on how, where, and under what terms to secure financing, and it will help with the preparation of the loan-application documents. You can hire someone else to manage your store, and you can add additional stores for a lower franchise fee—only $5,000 each. Ongoing fees include a royalty of 3 percent and an advertising fee of 1 percent of gross sales.

GETTING STARTED

The typical Sport Shack store is 2,000 to 3,500 square feet in a mall or shopping center. You will get consultation and assistance with finding the proper store location and negotiating a lease, and the company will give you custom plans and blueprints to help with the store layout. Sport Shack has a national account-pricing program with major store-fixture manufacturers. You can take advantage of pricing programs for custom interior and exterior signs and equipment; and you can get a discount on a computer package, including the printer, supplies, and software for inventory control and general-ledger accounting.

You will need one full-time and three part-time employees. Your store manager will spend five days at the Sport Shack headquarters in St. Paul, Minnesota. The training includes classroom instruction and store visitation and covers merchandising, selecting fixtures, store layout, advertising, employee training, sales techniques, and accounting. If you need special assistance, headquarters staff will visit your store prior to opening and provide a detailed, itemized recommended opening inventory for your store. You can open your Sport Shack store three to six months after buying your franchise, and the company will help with your grand opening.

MAKING IT WORK

You will have the guidance of the Sports Advisory Board, headed by Herb Brooks, coach of the 1980 Olympic Gold Medal–winning U.S. hockey team. The company holds regional meetings in conjunction with trade shows and publishes a monthly newsletter, merchandising bulletins, and other periodic information releases. Headquarters personnel will make onsite visits or answer your questions on the toll-free hotline.

Your 1 percent advertising fee will bring you mailers, television and radio commercials, and billboard posters. The company has a national jingle for broadcast media that features their slogan, "Sport Shack . . . where America goes into action!" Your visibility will be enhanced with imprinted shopping bags, logo shirts, caps, key tags, balloons, pens, and other handouts.

You will receive a complete manual that not only explains store policies and procedures but also covers such operating practices as display, accounting, advertising, buying, and sales techniques. You will have custom purchase-order and sales-invoice forms, envelopes, letterhead, business cards, and accounting and inventory forms. Group health insurance is available for health, property, and liability coverage. With Sport Shack you'll benefit from national buying directly from major sporting-goods suppliers who will give you volume discounts and other advantages. Sport Shack interstore inventory balancing is coordinated by headquarters. You'll be a part of the first national sporting-goods chain to adopt the Universal Sports Code method of pricing and inventory control.

COMMENTS

A member of the IFA since 1986, Sport Shack was ranked 278th in *Entrepreneur* magazine's 1987 "Franchise 500." The company is seeking franchises in most states.

GETTING MORE INFORMATION

The franchise information packet includes a letter and a brochure that describes company support and programs. For more information, write or call:

William Montgomery
Vice-President
Sport Shack, Inc.
1310 East Highway 96
St. Paul, MN   55110
(800)   328–8322, extension 130 (outside Minnesota)
(612)   426–0072 (in Minnesota)

Spring Crest Drapery Centers

BUSINESS: custom-
   drapery sales,
   installation, and
   cleaning
FOUNDED: 1955
FRANCHISED: 1968
START-UP
   INVESTMENT:
   $29,800–$78,900

		AS OF		PROJECTED BY	
NO. OF UNITS		1/1/85	1/1/86	1/1/87	1/1/88
OWNED BY:	COMPANY	0	0	0	1
	FRANCHISEES	275	285	300	315
LOCATED:	IN U.S.	185	195	205	215
	OUTSIDE U.S.	90	90	95	101
TOTAL:		275	285	300	316
NO. OF STATES W/ UNITS		37	38	38	39

THE BUSINESS

A growing number of homeowners are choosing a Spring Crest Center to help them decorate or redecorate their windows. With the number of two-income families on the rise, decorating services are becoming more popular and affordable. Spring Crest offers its customers an exclusive brand of pleated draperies plus a complete array of window treatments. Customers may choose from hundreds of fabrics and get wallpaper and accessories to match. The aesthetic appeal of the company's products plus a full ten-year limited warranty have made Spring Crest popular with both residential and commercial buyers. The company also offers drapery repair and alteration, protective treatments, and drapery and upholstery cleaning. Insurance jobs and commercial projects are also a source of business for Spring Crest.

In 1985, Spring Crest franchise sales totaled $40,000,000. The average center made $146,000 gross and $36,500 net for that same year. Company surveys show that 97 percent of Spring Crest's customers are satisfied with their draperies. Those customers generate another 60 percent of sales in referrals and repeat business.

WHAT IT TAKES

Your franchise fee for a Spring Crest center will be between $7,500 and $12,500, depending on the size of your protected territory, as determined by population. Applicable for ten years, the agreement allows passive ownership, although the company prefers that you run the store yourself.

Start-up expenses, listed as follows, can vary.

ITEM	COST
Opening advertising	$1,000–$ 3,000
Samples, sales aids, and printed material	2,000– 4,000
Leasehold improvements, displays, fixtures, outside sign	5,700– 11,000

ITEM	COST
Lease advance	1,000– 3,000
Miscellaneous (utility deposit, business license, insurance, freight, office supplies, etc.)	2,500– 3,500
Inventory	4,500– 7,700
Tools and cleaning equipment	1,600– 6,700
Computer system	0– 5,500
Vehicle	0– 14,000
Working capital	4,000– 8,000
Franchise fee	7,500– 12,500
Total: initial investment	$29,800–$78,900

Fifty to 75 percent of your total initial investment must be paid in cash. The company will help you secure a loan for the balance from a bank or other lending institution. You can buy additional stores for only $7,500 each. You'll pay an ongoing royalty fee of 3 percent of your gross sales.

GETTING STARTED

You'll need a site with about 1,200 square feet in a shopping center or freestanding building. The company will help you make the best choice and will assist you with the construction, layout, and decoration of your store. Whether you decide to lease or purchase your site, they'll help you negotiate to get the best price. Before your grand opening Spring Crest will make sure you have all the equipment, supplies, merchandise, and personnel you need. The company has a list of preferred suppliers you can buy from, if you choose.

You will probably need two full-time employees. You and your employees will spend two weeks at the home office in Brea, California, learning about the products and studying design, measurement, installation, and estimation techniques. You'll also learn about store management, selling, and advertising. Expert decorator techniques for window problems and state-of-the-art cleaning techniques for draperies and upholstery will also be covered. After your classroom training you'll get another one and a half weeks of on-the-job training from a franchise-development manager.

Spring Crest personnel will ensure that by grand opening your showroom will be filled with a vast array of attractive fabrics and full-sized displays of draperies. Also, your workroom will be completely equipped to fill orders. You should be able to have your grand opening within two months after your franchise purchase.

MAKING IT WORK

Spring Crest has its own advertising agency to develop effective programs for your area. You'll participate in the company's advertising programs for a fee of 2 percent of your gross sales. Some of the advertising materials you will get are newspaper and magazine ads, telephone-book ads, mailers, and radio and television commercials. In a cooperative advertising program you'll also have access to an audiovisual drapery fashion show, national media coverage, banners, signs, brochures, catalogs, a marketing manual, and a lead-referral system. Spring Crest publishes a monthly franchise newsletter, a bimonthly company magazine, technical product updates, and company-information updates. The company sponsors annual national and regional conventions, where workshops are a regular feature.

The combined buying power of all the Spring Crest centers will enable you to get supplies at volume discounts by ordering through the company's central purchasing program. You save even more money because the company sells its own brand-name products, produced by a division of Spring Crest. As a result, your prices may be lower than those of major department stores. However, you won't be limited to selling only Spring Crest products. In fact, most franchisees sell all types of window treatments. But only Spring Crest Windoware is backed by a ten-year written warranty honored by all Spring Crest locations.

To run your business, you'll be provided with a set of manuals covering policies, management procedures, and customer service. You can also get the forms you need for managing inventory, ordering supplies, and accounting. The company will provide you with their systems for bookkeeping, expense analysis, and inventory, as well as their computerized management information system. You can use the company's toll-free hotline to reach headquarters or regional personnel, who will also make routine and troubleshooting visits to your center. You and your employees can take advantage of the company's recognition programs and a benefits package that includes life, major-medical, dental, and disability insurance coverage.

COMMENTS

A member of the IFA since 1974, Spring Crest was ranked 120th in *Entrepreneur* magazine's 1987 "Franchise 500." The company makes available an earnings claim document. Spring Crest is seeking franchisees throughout the United States and in Africa, Australia, Canada, and Europe.

GETTING MORE INFORMATION

The franchise information packet contains a brochure with a code of ethics, a list of references, a directory of centers worldwide, and a questionnaire for confidential evaluation. Also in the packet are the company's product guide, with installation instructions and limited warranty, and a newspaper magazine insert with numerous color photographs. For more information, contact:

Jack Long
President
Spring Crest Drapery Centers
505 West Lambert Road
Brea, CA   92621
(800)   552–5523

Spring-Green Lawn Care

BUSINESS: lawn-care services		AS OF		PROJECTED BY	
	NO. OF UNITS	1/1/85	1/1/86	1/1/87	1/1/88
FOUNDED: 1977	OWNED BY: COMPANY	3	3	3	3
FRANCHISED: 1977	FRANCHISEES	73	104	139	184
START-UP	LOCATED: IN U.S.	76	107	142	187
INVESTMENT:	OUTSIDE U.S.	0	0	0	0
$17,945–$29,000	TOTAL:	76	107	142	187
	NO. OF STATES W/ UNITS	13	15	17	19

THE BUSINESS

A beautiful yard is one of the least-expensive enhancements to residential property values. Trees and shrubs can add as much as 20 percent to the appraised value of a home. Fertilizer and pesticide-treatment services have been available since the mid-1960s—usually at a high cost from landscapers. In recent years, however, two-career suburban families—pinched for leisure time—have created a sizable middle-class market for lawn-care services. By 1984 the industry's annual sales topped $2.1 billion. With a market of 20 million home-owned yards in the United States, the growth potential is staggering.

Spring-Green Lawn Care provides a full range of guaranteed lawn services for residential and commercial customers. The lawn-care program includes weed control; pest control; fertilizer application; and aeration for lawns, trees, and shrubs. In one year a typical lawn would have four to five fertilizer applications and weed- and insect-control treatments along with four treatments of tree and shrub root fertilizer and insecticides. Spring-Green Lawn Care franchises had $10 million in gross sales in 1985.

WHAT IT TAKES

Your franchise fee will be $12,900, with your total initial investment ranging from $17,945 to $29,000. You'll be able to get indirect financial assistance through the company's truck- and equipment-leasing program. Applying for ten years, with a ten-year renewal option, the agreement will grant you an exclusive territory with a minimum of 20,000 single-family households at or above a specified income level. You can purchase additional units for $11,900 each, but you must be prepared to manage all your operations actively, because the company discourages absentee ownership. You'll have an on-going royalty payment of 7 percent of gross sales and an advertising fee of 2 percent of gross sales.

GETTING STARTED

Your Spring-Green facility can be in your home, because it only requires about 600 square feet. If you choose to locate in a commercial or industrial park, the company will help you select the site and design the layout and will advise you during lease or purchase negotiations. You will also have help with leasing or purchasing equipment, trucks, materials, and merchandise. Your equipment will include a 300-gallon lawn-spraying unit, a high-pressure hose, and a fertilizer spreader. You will need two full-time and four part-time employees, whom the company will help you select.

In Spring-Green's intensive training program you'll begin pre-training with video modules that explain basic concepts. Then you'll spend five days at corporate headquarters in Plainfield, Illinois, alternating classroom sessions with practical training at Spring-Green's own local franchise. You'll train with Spring-Green application equipment; evaluate actual lawn characteristics and problems; encounter real management, marketing, and accounting situations; and become familiar with the Spring-Green sales system. Your training will continue with on-location startup assistance in your franchise territory. The company will help with your grand opening, which will be one to two months after you sign the franchise agreement.

MAKING IT WORK

Spring-Green will design a customized marketing plan for your territory and then send a direct-mail brochure to the areas in your territory with the best prospects. The replies from the brochures will go directly to your office. One marketing tool of the Spring-Green sales system is a brochure that describes Spring-Green's tree and shrub treatment and has space for the results of your free survey of the condition of the potential customer's trees and shrubs.

Your training will continue through your reviews of the audiovisual and reference materials. Spring-Green holds an annual national convention, three regional conferences, one-day seminars about five times a year, and citywide franchise meetings four times a year. Regular field-service visits by headquarters staff will provide you with hands-on guidance and counsel in operations, marketing, and management. You'll receive Spring-Green's professional newsletter, with technical portions written by company agronomists; an employee newsletter; and periodic updates on the industry, new products, and company information.

Spring-Green will provide you with a complete accounting and financial program. You'll receive weekly computer-generated reports that provide valuable operational data about your franchise. When your company reaches a size that requires computerization, you can get computer programs and systems currently being used by larger franchises. Among the supplies you can purchase from the company are personalized forms and operating manuals. Spring-Lawn has a central purchasing program that offers volume discounts and a central merchandising system. You can use Spring-Green products as well as any other equipment, supplies, and materials that meet the company's quality-control standards. Your insurance package will include property, liability, disability, auto, life, and major-medical coverage. The company awards program recognizes several operational and sales categories.

COMMENTS

A member of the IFA since 1979, Spring-Green was ranked 246th in *Entrepreneur* magazine's 1987 "Franchise 500." A founding member of the Professional Lawn Care Association of America, the company encourages franchisees to participate in local community projects and get involved in industry activities. Spring-Green is seeking franchises in central and northeastern states.

GETTING MORE INFORMATION

The franchise information packet contains a card series that describes Spring-Green and the lawn-care industry, a list of corporate references, several article reprints, a statement of the company's philosophy, samples of merchandising brochures, and a get-acquainted questionnaire. For more information, call or write:

James Gurke
Director of Franchise Marketing
Spring-Green Lawn Care
11927 Spaulding School Drive
Plainfield, IL   60544
(800)   435–4051 or (815)   436-8777

Stained Glass Overlay

BUSINESS:			AS OF		PROJECTED BY	
			1/1/85	1/1/86	1/1/87	1/1/88
decorative-glass	NO. OF UNITS					
applications	OWNED BY: COMPANY		0	0	0	0
FOUNDED: 1974	FRANCHISEES		130	255	340	500
FRANCHISED: 1981	LOCATED: IN U.S.		120	240	320	400
START-UP	OUTSIDE U.S.		10	15	20	100
INVESTMENT:	TOTAL:		130	255	340	500
$45,000–$60,000	NO. OF STATES W/ UNITS		20	40	48	50

THE BUSINESS

Stained glass is in demand among architects, builders, contractors, and interior designers. Stained Glass Overlay (SGO) has a patented process that transforms everyday glass into designer glass. With the overlay process, colored film and strips of lead are bonded to a single piece of glass, producing the same three-dimensional feel and look of stained glass without the weight and other disadvantages. The finished product is seamless, airtight, waterproof, and fade resistant and contains ultraviolet inhibitors. The overlay process can be applied to windows (without removing them), mirrors, restaurant booth dividers, van and auto windows, china cabinets, and many other surfaces.

In addition, Stained Glass Overlay offers customers unlimited design and color options. SGO also carries a line of handcrafted oak or mahogany entry doors and side panels with windows that can be decorated with the overlay process or beveled glass, which SGO franchises also carry. Recently SGO franchises began offering sandblasted glass and designer area rugs, too.

In 1981, with no advertising, the company sold 70 franchises. By 1983 revenues were up to $1 million, and three businessmen had bought SGO purposely to develop and support the franchises. By 1985 revenues were well over $3 million.

WHAT IT TAKES

The $34,000 franchise fee is part of the minimum initial investment of $45,000 required in cash. Your total investment can be up to $60,000, depending on your facility. Part of that total cost also is an average of $8,000 for the franchise package with training information, initial forms, supplies, marketing tools, and sample doors. Another $3,000 of the total covers materials, including sheets of color and lead.

Your SGO franchise agreement will guarantee an exclusive territory that has approximately 200,000 people or clear growth potential. You also can do business in an area not covered by another franchise if you get prior approval; you can also serve any customer, no matter where the project is, as long as you do not solicit, measure, or install in another franchisee's exclusive territory. The term of the franchise agreement is five years, with a five-year renewal and a $1,000 tax-deductible renewal fee. The fee for each additional franchise is $34,000, and master franchises are available. You may take a hands-on approach to running your SGO franchise, or you may use it as an investment and hire crews to do the actual application. Each month you'll pay a royalty fee of 5 percent of gross sales and an advertising fee of 2 percent of gross sales.

GETTING STARTED

Although many overlay applications can be done at the job site, you will need a small preparation area. You could work out of your home, but the company recommends that you set up a showroom. The typical SGO workshop/showroom is 1,000 square feet in a shopping center or freestanding building. Once you have found a site, SGO will help you with layout and decoration and will advise you about buying materials and supplies. The company also recommends that you have a van. With overlay windows and your business name painted on the side, a van is a continuous, low-cost, tax-deductible advertising tool.

You'll need four full-time employees. Your entire staff can go to the SGO offices in Costa Mesa, California, for five days of training. You'll learn about the overlay application techniques, the products, sales, marketing, bookkeeping, and administration. You can be open for business within one month after your franchise purchase.

MAKING IT WORK

Your advertising fee will bring you national attention with four-color ads in such general magazines as *House Beautiful* and such trade magazines as *Glass Digest,* as well as in several airline publications. Press releases are mailed to building and decorating trade magazines and to decorating editors at consumer magazines. If you want to run a local advertising campaign, the company will give you newspaper and magazine slicks and a schedule of their national ad campaign so that you can run yours simultaneously. You can also buy videotaped television commercials with space at the end for you to add your company name and address. You'll be part of a listing in Sweet's Source Catalog, used by over 60,000 builders, architects, and decorators in the U.S.—and SGO will give you a list of Sweet's Catalog users in your territory. Your franchise fee will bring you a supply of catalogs, mailing brochures, and a videotape to attract customers at home shows and fairs. You can buy more of these items from the company as needed, and you can buy presentation and photo albums.

The company sponsors yearly national and regional conferences and publishes a monthly newsletter. SGO recently formed a franchise advisory board that publishes its own newsletter. You'll get business forms, a check-writing system, a bookkeeping system, printed instructional materials, and management and customer-service manuals. The company also maintains a toll-free hotline. Stained Glass Overlay has a research-and-development department.

Your starter package of color film and lead stripping is enough for $30,000 in sales (the cost of materials is about 10 percent of the price to the customer). You'll get volume discounts when you order more materials from the company. Your franchise agreement guarantees that the price of materials will not increase more than 15 percent each year. You can also use other brands as long as you get company approval.

COMMENTS

Stained Glass Overlay was ranked 101st in *Entrepreneur* magazine's 1987 "Franchise 500" and 36th in *Venture* magazine's 1986 "Franchise 100." A member of the IFA, the company is seeking franchisees primarily in the eastern and western parts of the United States.

GETTING MORE INFORMATION

The franchise information packet includes a brochure about the company, a newsletter, sample story boards of television commercials, photos and listings of franchise equipment, photos of restoration work and equipment, and a confidential questionnaire. For more information, contact:

Jim Fitzpatrick
Marketing Director
Stained Glass Overlay, Inc.
151 Kalmus Drive, Suite J–4
Costa Mesa, CA   92626
(800)   654–7666 or (714)   957-8188

Steamatic

		AS OF		PROJECTED BY	
		1/1/85	1/1/86	1/1/87	1/1/88
NO. OF UNITS					
OWNED BY: COMPANY		11	11	11	11
FRANCHISEES		166	164	210	257
LOCATED: IN U.S.		122	116	143	172
OUTSIDE U.S.		55	59	78	96
TOTAL:		177	175	221	268
NO. OF STATES W/ UNITS		27	27	30	35

BUSINESS: restoration and cleaning service
FOUNDED: 1968
FRANCHISED: 1968
START-UP INVESTMENT: $37,000–$43,000

THE BUSINESS

Steamatic is a restoration business with the expertise and equipment to repair water and fire damage at approximately 25 percent of the cost of replacement. Large-scale commercial catastrophes are handled by a mobile staff of restoration experts who work with—and pay a fee to—the local franchisee. Steamatic is known particularly for its nonemergency home cleaning of carpets, draperies, furniture, and air ducts.

WHAT IT TAKES

Your initial franchise fee of $28,000 will cover a five-year renewable agreement with a territory determined by population. The smallest market classification will give you a business that can be run by you and your family members. With some management experience and capital, however, you can set up a larger operation. You'll need an additional $9,000 to $15,000 to start your business. (Those figures are low partly because your equipment is leased rather than purchased.) Though the first $15,000 must be in cash, personnel at headquarters can assist you in financing the remainder through a local bank. The franchise fee for each additional territory is $28,000. Company officials prefer that you actively run your Steamatic franchises. After the first five years the royalty fee you'll pay to the company will decrease from 10 to 5 percent of gross revenues. You'll pay no ongoing advertising fee.

GETTING STARTED

Unless you choose to start with a space in your home, you'll probably want about 5,000 square feet in a commercial park or building to house your Steamatic business. Company personnel will help you choose your location and implement the quality-control manual's guidelines regarding standardized uniforms, equipment, vehicles, chemicals, and procedures. The standard Steamatic franchise package includes eighteen pieces of key equipment; twenty-one cleaning compounds; miscellaneous supplies; office supplies, including an accounting system and sales manual; and newspaper and telephone-book ads and optional television and radio commercials. A typical business will employ four full-time and four part-time personnel.

For two weeks company officials in Grand Prairie, Texas, will train you using videotaped presentations, classroom techniques, and on-the-job experiences. You'll learn how to run the business, how to do the cleaning and restoration services, and how to recruit and train your crew. In addition, your training will also cover consumer advertising, telephone techniques, customer relations, and guidelines for establishing prices. You'll also learn how to help victims of fire and flood deal with the emotional and psychological aspects of entrusting their personal belongings to you. You can expect to be in business within about one month after purchasing your franchise.

MAKING IT WORK

Part of your initial franchise fee will cover telephone-book and newspaper ads. Some national media coverage is free, as are the press releases you'll give to the local media. You'll pay a cooperative fee for the television and radio commercials, mailers, brochures, signs, seasonal materials, in-house videotapes, and the public-relations manual.

Every other year Steamatic holds national and regional conferences, and seminars and citywide franchise meetings are called as needed. You'll get a monthly newsletter and periodic updates on the cleaning industry, advances in cleaning and restoration technology, and the company's activities. Company manuals for policy, management procedure, and customer service will answer many of your everyday operating questions, but you'll also have help from company personnel who will visit you regularly and serve as instant resources via the toll-free hotline. Steamatic will provide your bookkeeping and expense-analysis systems as well as forms for ordering and accounting.

The compounds and equipment needed to run your business can be purchased from any source, but they must meet the company standards and specifications. You may decide to use the company's merchandise, however, because the central purchasing system will give you the financial advantage of volume discounts, and the company's research-and-development staff continually improves products and services.

COMMENTS

Steamatic was ranked 162nd in *Entrepreneur* magazine's 1987 "Franchise 500." A member of the IFA since 1981 and an operating division of BMS Enterprises, the company wants to expand in most states and in foreign countries.

GETTING MORE INFORMATION

The franchise information packet includes a brochure about the company, a newsletter, sample story boards of television commercials, photos and listings of franchise equipment, photos of restoration work and equipment, and a confidential questionnaire. For more information, contact:

William R. Sims
Franchise Director
Steamatic, Inc.
1601 109th Street
Grand Prairie, TX   75050
(800)   527–1295 or (214)   647–1244 (call collect)

Suddenly Slender, *The* Body Wrap & Health Center

BUSINESS: body wrap inch-loss program	NO. OF UNITS		AS OF		PROJECTED BY	
			1/1/85	1/1/86	1/1/87	1/1/88
FOUNDED: 1969	OWNED BY: COMPANY		0	0	0	0
FRANCHISED: 1981		FRANCHISEES	189	242	342	500
START-UP	LOCATED:	IN U.S.	187	200	300	400
INVESTMENT:		OUTSIDE U.S.	2	42	42	100
$60,000–$80,000	TOTAL:		189	242	342	500
	NO. OF STATES W/ UNITS		11	12	18	24

THE BUSINESS

Victoria Morton has developed *The* Body Wrap, a safe, relaxing process that takes off inches and tightens the skin in only seventy minutes. It involves wrapping the body with porous elastic bandages that have been soaked in a special mineral solution. The process removes toxin-ladened fluid from between fat cells and compacts the tissues in the space created—in effect, reducing sags, wrinkles, and cellulite, but not fat. Both the solution and the wrapping process have patents pending.

    The Body Wrap offers two guarantees: a female patron will lose a total of at least six inches on the first wrap (four for men), and the lost inches will not return if the patron does not gain weight. The wrap is helpful for people who retain water and those who have disproportionately large hips, thighs, abdomen, and calves. Specialty wraps include face sculpturing—which radically tightens the skin, smooths wrinkles, highlights the cheekbones, raises eyebrows, eliminates jowls and double chins—and bust improvement. Patrons may visit a Suddenly Slender Center as often as they wish, with each visit costing $45 to $65. The centers also carry a line of beauty and health products. Suddenly Slender reports that the average center has annual sales of $300,000, with a net income of $160,000.

WHAT IT TAKES

Your franchise fee will be $20,000 for an exclusive territory with a population of 100,000 or more people. Furniture, equipment, supplies, and training will cost an additional $29,900 for a four-station center and $37,500 for a six-station center. Your total investment will be $60,000 to $80,000, all in cash. Your franchise agreement will run for a term of ten years, with a ten-year renewal. Additional franchises have the same $20,000 fee, and master franchises are available. Your royalty fee will be $350 per month or 7 percent of gross revenues, whichever is greater. Your advertising fee will be 1 percent of gross revenues. To purchase a Suddenly Slender franchise, you will need experience in business and sales, marketing, or public relations.

GETTING STARTED

The typical center is 1,200 square feet in a mall, shopping center, or freestanding building. Suddenly Slender will help you select a site and negotiate the lease or purchase. The company will help you meet its special requirements for layout and decoration, which are flexible, so you can customize your center to your taste. You'll also have the company's help purchasing equipment and supplies.

You will be able to select the uniforms for your staff, which will include eight full-time and three to four part-time people. Suddenly Slender will help you with hiring and training. You and three of your staff will study the comprehensive training manual. Then the four of you will go to the training center in Denver, Colorado, for three weeks of intensive study. With a combination of classroom instruction, videotapes, and hands-on experience, you'll learn about wrapping techniques, employee selection and training, shop procedures, sales, bookkeeping systems, and management. You'll then be certified wrappers. Suddenly Slender will help you with your grand opening, which can be as soon as two to three months after your franchise purchase.

MAKING IT WORK

An expert at promoting the company, Victoria Morton constantly gives interviews for newspapers and magazines and appears on television and radio talk shows. The changes that the process brings are immediate and readily apparent, and the company claims such celebrity patrons as Meredith MacRae, Amy Irving, Marty Allen, and the Solid Gold dancers. Your advertising royalty will supply you with newspaper and magazine ads, radio commercials, and press packets. You'll also get one-to-one advertising tools like brochures and mailers. The process sells itself, and patrons return because they want to, not because they are contractually obligated or confronted with high-pressure sales techniques. Centers do not offer series contracts. However, some centers offer memberships that give a substantial discount.

Suddenly Slender holds an annual national conference and distributes a monthly newsletter and periodic reports about the company and the wrapping industry. If you need help training a new employee or solving a problem, a specialist from Suddenly Slender headquarters will come to your center for $200 per day plus expenses. Operating your center will be simplified with the company's bookkeeping, inventory, and expense-analysis systems. There are manuals to explain management procedures and policies, as well as forms for ordering and accounting. Your insurance package will include property, liability, auto, life, major-medical, dental, and disability coverage. You can participate in the company's varied recognition programs.

Suddenly Slender Centers have done over a million wraps in sixteen years and have never had so much as an allergic reaction because of the purity of the pharmaceutical-grade minerals used in the solution. Hygienic standards in the centers are the highest in the industry. Suddenly Slender's own lab develops new techniques and products. Recent additions to the Suddenly Slender product line include vitamins and compounds for losing weight and slowing the aging process. You'll get volume discounts for Suddenly Slender products, but you can stock other brands, too, if you get company approval.

COMMENTS

Suddenly Slender was ranked 111th in *Entrepreneur* magazine's 1987 "Franchise 500" and 33d in *Venture* magazine's 1986 "Franchise 100." A unit of Victory International, Inc., and a member of the IFA since 1986, Suddenly Slender is seeking franchisees throughout the United States.

GETTING MORE INFORMATION

The franchise information packet includes fact sheets on the company and the wrapping process, photos of celebrities who endorse the process, a listing of recent articles and reprints of several, a marketing brochure, photos of face-sculpturing improvements, and Victoria Morton's biography. For more information, call or write:

Victoria M. Morton
Founder
Suddenly Slender, *The* Body Wrap & Health Center
1231 South Parker Road, Suite 105
Denver, CO   80231
(303)   753–6337

Sunshine Polishing Systems

BUSINESS: car-care service
FOUNDED: 1983
FRANCHISED: 1983
START-UP INVESTMENT: $3,000–$50,000

NO. OF UNITS		AS OF		PROJECTED BY	
		1/1/85	1/1/86	1/1/87	1/1/88
OWNED BY: COMPANY		0	0	1	3
	FRANCHISEES	140	190	270	400
LOCATED: IN U.S.		134	185	264	393
	OUTSIDE U.S.	6	5	7	10
TOTAL:		140	190	271	403
NO. OF STATES W/ UNITS		18	23	30	40

THE BUSINESS

A well-maintained car gets more efficient gas mileage and brings a higher resale price later, say car-care experts. Sunshine Polishing Centers offer total auto-appearance services for exterior and interior. The company uses exclusive polish and sealant products with Teflon for paint and fiberglass protection of cars, trucks, boats, and aircraft. All vehicle exterior work is done with a state-of-the-art orbital polisher, an exclusively designed machine that effectively ap-

plies all sealants, waxes, and preparation chemicals with no damage
to paint or fiberglass. Other services include interior cleaning and
protection for vinyl, leather, and upholstery. A new type of SPS
store, Auto Appearance Centers, have added rustproofing, sound-
proofing, engine cleaning, pinstriping, body molding and accents,
and window tinting to the standard service line. The company offers
both a mobile and a fixed-base franchise, allowing the franchisee to
start with a mobile operation and upgrade to a fixed-base location.

WHAT IT TAKES

You will need $975 for the initial mobile franchise fee, and $15,000
for the fixed-base franchise. Establishing an exclusive territory
based on population, the agreement will be valid for three to ten
years, with renewal rights. Your total investment will be $3,000 to
$50,000, depending on how much you decide to invest in supplies
and other expenses plus your working capital of approximately
$10,000. For a sample operation this total would cover the franchise
fee ($15,000), equipment ($10,000), supplies and opening inventory
($10,000), real estate lease ($5,000), leasehold improvements
($3,000), insurance ($1,000), initial advertising ($3,000), and miscel-
laneous supplies ($2,000). You must have cash for the entire amount.
Additional mobile franchises are not available, but additional fixed-
base franchises can be purchased for $10,000 each. Master fran-
chises are not available. You may be an owner-investor, but Sunshine prefers that you be active in the business. You will pay an
ongoing royalty fee of 5 percent of gross sales the first year, increasing to 7 percent in subsequent years. The graduated advertising fee
will be $100 per month or 2 percent of gross monthly sales (which-
ever is greater) the first year, increasing to $200 a month or 4 percent
of gross monthly sales. No previous experience in auto services is
required.

GETTING STARTED

Sunshine will help with site selection; lease and purchase negotiation; construction; facility layout and decoration; lease or purchase
of furniture, fixtures, and equipment; service or maintenance contracts; and acquisition of materials, supplies, and merchandise. The
typical Sunshine facility is 1,500 to 2,000 square feet, located in a
freestanding building, commercial industrial park, or auto-service
mall. Company approval is required on site selection, facility layout
and decoration, and construction design. Sunshine will sell equipment to you at below market value.

Your staff will consist of four full-time and two part-time employees. Two staff members will go to corporate headquarters for ten
days of training, covering paint-sealant application, rustproofing,
undercoating, pinstriping, auto detailing, interiors and carpets, marketing, business practices, employee relations, and hiring. The di-

rector of franchise training will come to your location to train all your employees for five days. You can be open for business within two to five months after buying your franchise. Sunshine will assist with your grand opening.

MAKING IT WORK

Sunshine offers co-op advertising funds for telephone-book ads, brochures, radio and television commercials, point-of-purchase displays, signs, banners, a lead-referral system, and a public-relations/marketing manual. You will receive periodic surveys, as well as a bimonthly newsletter to cover auto-detailing news and updates on products, service, company information and market trends. Videos are available to help train your employees. Sunshine honors franchisees for performance. Administrative backup services include headquarters resource persons; a toll-free hotline; manuals on policy, customer service, and management procedure; all types of forms; and systems for bookkeeping, inventory, expense analysis, computerized management information, and computerized billing. A company research-and-development department continually tests new products. Sunshine has a central purchasing and merchandising system offering volume discounts on company-label products, but you may sell noncompany products that meet Sunshine standards. The company sponsors insurance for property and general-liability coverage.

COMMENTS

Sunshine was ranked 143d in *Entrepreneur* magazine's 1987 "Franchise 500" and 61st in *Venture* magazine's 1986 "Franchise 100." The company wants to add new franchises throughout the world.

GETTING MORE INFORMATION

The franchise information packet contains question-and-answer brochures on the company's operations, schedules of expenses for the company in 1984 and 1985, sample price guides, a company newsletter, franchise owners' testimonials, and an application form. For details, contact:

Dennis Soto
Vice-President, Franchise Marketing
Sunshine Polishing Systems
1551 Camino Del Rio South, #218
San Diego, CA   92108
(800)   621–5640 or (619)   285–9222

Sylvan Learning Centers

BUSINESS:			AS OF		PROJECTED BY	
supplemental	NO. OF UNITS		1/1/85	1/1/86	1/1/87	1/1/88
education, preschool	OWNED BY: COMPANY		0	35	70	105
to adult	FRANCHISEES		102	212	275	335
FOUNDED: 1979	LOCATED: IN U.S.		102	245	335	420
FRANCHISED: 1979	OUTSIDE U.S.		0	2	10	20
START-UP	TOTAL:		102	247	345	440
INVESTMENT:	NO. OF STATES W/ UNITS		30	44	50	50
$45,000–$110,000						

THE BUSINESS

The Sylvan Learning Corporation is a publicly held company with little competition in the business of providing individualized supplemental education for people of all ages. The need is staggering. For example, over half the population of gifted students in the United States do not match their tested ability with comparable achievement in school. Nearly 40 percent of seventeen-year-olds do not possess the expected higher-order thinking skills. Adult illiteracy has been identified as a major national problem. The goal at Sylvan is to help such people by offering an attractive educational program.

Sylvan offers individualized programs in preschool reading readiness, elementary-school reading skills, reading comprehension, mathematics, and college-entrance preparation. The centers assess the students' needs and learning styles, then teach one-on-one with strong doses of positive reinforcement and rewards. Tokens given for performance can be exchanged for goods at the Sylvan Store.

WHAT IT TAKES

You need not be an educator to run a Sylvan Learning Center—just possess organizational ability and motivation. You can open and run your Sylvan Learning Center for ten years (renewable for subsequent ten-year periods) with an initial franchise fee of $20,000 to $30,000, depending on the area you choose. Your territory—and the size of your center—will be individually determined by company personnel. The same fee structure would apply for any additional learning centers you might purchase. Even if you won't be operating your own center, Sylvan will still expect you to participate actively.

Your total initial investment, which also will vary with the territory, could range from about $50,000 to $110,000. Small centers, usually owner operated in smaller towns, cost $50,000 to $60,000, with a minimum cash requirement of $25,000. Larger centers, located in metropolitan areas and larger towns with greater student enrollments, range from $90,000 to $110,000 and require $65,000 in cash. In addition to the franchise fee you'll pay approximately $12,800 to $14,100 for learning materials and educational equipment;

$750 to $3,000 for the lease deposit; $2,500 to $6,100 for furniture, office supplies, and teaching aids; $1,000 to $2,800 for computers; $2,000 to $8,000 for grand-opening expenses; $8,000 to $35,000 for working/operating capital; and $2,500 to $8,000 for miscellaneous expenses. Sylvan Learning Corporation does not offer any direct financial assistance, but it does make available a loan-application guide and help qualified applicants obtain financing. Your ongoing royalty fee of 8 to 10 percent of gross revenues and your advertising fee of $1,000 to $2,000 a month will also be determined by your territory.

GETTING STARTED

As a new Sylvan franchisee, you'll choose your territory using the company's computerized service. You'll also receive a step-by-step kit of licensed materials that includes information on choosing an appropriate location, which for most Sylvan Centers is in a medical/dental building or professional office park. Sylvan will help you negotiate your lease agreement. Sylvan Learning Centers typically have 800 to 1,200 square feet and include a testing room and instructional area designed to meet company specifications and maintain the unified Sylvan image. For a fee the company will supply educational material and some custom furniture, but you can buy from alternate sources as well.

You and your key personnel—the director and assistant director—will receive two weeks of classroom training at headquarters in Montgomery, Alabama. You'll learn about diagnostic testing, prescription preparation, educational program application, basic business administration, and marketing. In addition to the two full-time personnel, you'll probably need four part-time people, and the franchise kit includes information on finding and hiring key personnel. Approximately three to six months after purchasing your franchise, you will be ready to open your center. After it's been open three to six weeks, Sylvan will assist you in formally introducing your center to the community with an open house accompanied by a major advertising and public-relations campaign that will be given to you in a step-by-step plan.

MAKING IT WORK

You will pay an average of $1,000 to $2,000 a month for a complete communications and marketing program. The corporate-sponsored advertising materials—such as black-and-white magazine slicks, media packages, and point-of-purchase displays—are supplemented with professional ad kits for local advertising. The company also produces items such as mailers, brochures, and presentation books for you to distribute to potential customers. You can purchase television and radio commercials locally by participating in the cooperative advertising agreement.

You will have the support of a regional Sylvan field representative, who will inform Sylvan senior management of your progress and perform routine quality-assurance checks at your center. If you have questions that are not answered in the set of business and educational operations manuals you'll get during training, you can use the toll-free hotline. If you need further assistance, corporate personnel will troubleshoot at your center.

Sylvan produces a quarterly tabloid newspaper; holds an annual national conference, quarterly regional conferences, and periodic areawide franchise meetings; and sponsors various achievement awards. In addition to company forms for your inventory and personnel, Sylvan produces hundreds of testing materials, forms, student-record systems, literature, stationery, award certificates, and other consumables that bear the Sylvan Learning Center registered trademark. These volume-discounted consumables and the learning materials themselves—which franchisees are required to use—are constantly updated. Some of the new developments evolve from the work of a Sylvan advisory council chaired by Dr. T. H. Bell, former Secretary of Education, and comprised of leading national educators, politicians, academicians, and business people. The Sylvan company sponsors a general-liability insurance plan and accounts-receivable financing.

COMMENTS

Sylvan Learning Centers was ranked 45th in *Venture* magazine's 1986 "Franchise 100" and 80th in *Entrepreneur* magazine's 1987 "Franchise 500." A member of the IFA since 1984, the company is owned by Kinder-Care Learning Centers, Inc. The company wants to increase franchise operations throughout the United States and in Australia and Canada.

GETTING MORE INFORMATION

The franchise information packet includes a brochure describing the Sylvan Learning Corporation; several informational sheets explaining the Sylvan system, detailing the costs of opening a center, introducing the corporate management, and summarizing the contents of *A Nation at Risk,* a report of the National Commission on Excellence in Education; several magazine and newspaper reprints; and a detailed confidential qualification report. For more details, contact:

W. S. Butch Garrison
Vice-President of Franchise Sales
Sylvan Learning Corporation
2400 Presidents Drive
P.O. Box 5605
Montgomery, Alabama   36103–5605
(800)   545–5060 or (205)   277–7720 (call collect)

Taco del Sol

BUSINESS: Mexican			AS OF		PROJECTED BY	
fast-food and full-	NO. OF UNITS		1/1/85	1/1/86	1/1/87	1/1/88
service restaurant	OWNED BY: COMPANY		0	0	2	4
FOUNDED: 1975		FRANCHISEES	26	24	30	42
FRANCHISED: 1978	LOCATED: IN U.S.		26	24	32	44
START-UP		OUTSIDE U.S.	0	0	0	0
INVESTMENT:	TOTAL:		26	24	32	44
$85,000–$250,000	NO. OF STATES W/ UNITS		4	4	5	6

THE BUSINESS

Taco del Sol describes its restaurants as warm and comfortable with casual southwestern decor. Its Mexican food specialties are served on real china with silverware and glassware, making it the only Mexican fast-food franchise to do so. Children's business is an important segment not courted by most Mexican restaurants, but menus and facilities reflect Taco del Sol's desire to please the entire family. The atmosphere compares favorably with that of dinner houses and the prices with those of other fast-food restaurants. In 1985, Taco del Sol franchises grossed $3 million, with average gross sales per unit of $160,000.

WHAT IT TAKES

You will pay $15,000 for the initial franchise fee. Valid for twenty years and renewable for ten, the agreement will guarantee you an exclusive territory within a three-mile radius from your restaurant. Your total investment will range from $85,000 to $250,000, with $25,000 to $40,000 required in cash. Financial assistance is not available, but Taco del Sol will provide advice, documentation, and references to help you with your arrangements. The fee for additional units is negotiable, and master franchises are available. The company prefers that you be the onsite manager. Ongoing royalty fees are 4 percent of gross sales, and advertising fees are 2 percent. Prior restaurant experience is not required.

GETTING STARTED

Taco del Sol helps with site selection (and must give final approval), lease and purchase negotiation, construction, facility layout and decoration, service or maintenance contracts, and lease or purchase of furniture, fixtures, equipment, vehicles, supplies, and merchandise. The company can provide a turnkey operation if you desire. The typical facility is 2,000 square feet, and the company charges for construction blueprints. You will need three full-time and ten part-time employees, whom Taco del Sol will help you hire. Your training, held in Lincoln, Nebraska, for two weeks, will cover food preparation, costing, employee relations, bookkeeping, inventory control, ordering, sanitation, and management skills. Hands-on training for employees will be conducted in your restaurant. You can expect to be open within three to four months after buying your franchise, and the company will help with your grand opening.

MAKING IT WORK

For your monthly advertising fee you'll receive newspaper ads, mailers, telephone-book ads, and point-of-purchase displays. Co-op funding is available for radio commercials, signs, banners, contests, seasonal promotional materials, brochures, and presentation books. Taco del Sol holds national conventions once a year, regional conferences twice annually, and onsite training whenever requested. The company publishes a bimonthly newsletter and updates as needed. Backup systems include headquarters and regional resource persons; all types of forms; and systems for bookkeeping, inventory, personnel, and expense analysis. Research and development departments continually study menus, methods, and procedures. The company makes available not only special seasoning and spices but also printed items and proprietary items you will need and makes recommendations on sources for less specialized products. Taco del Sol sponsors insurance for property, general-liability, automobile, life, major-medical, worker's compensation, and third-party-bonding coverage.

COMMENTS

Taco del Sol is seeking to expand in seven states.

GETTING MORE INFORMATION

The franchise information packet contains a sample menu, an answer sheet on commonly asked questions, brochures on company operations, and an application form. For more details, contact:

Richard E. Drummond
President
Taco del Sol
6132 Havelock Avenue
Lincoln, NE   68507
(402)   464–9004

Taco John's

		AS OF		PROJECTED BY	
BUSINESS: Mexican	NO. OF UNITS	1/1/85	1/1/86	1/1/87	1/1/88
fast-food restaurant	OWNED BY: COMPANY	5	5	5	5
FOUNDED: 1969	FRANCHISEES	360	392	450	500
FRANCHISED: 1970	LOCATED: IN U.S.	365	397	455	505
START-UP	OUTSIDE U.S.	0	0	0	0
INVESTMENT:	TOTAL:	365	397	455	505
$50,000–$350,000	NO. OF STATES W/ UNITS	32	32	35	35
plus land					

THE BUSINESS

Taco John's ranks second in size nationally in the Mexican fast-food industry. The restaurant chain caters to the eighteen-to-thirty-five-year-old age group with a menu that includes tacos, softshell tacos, Taco Bravos, taco burgers, burritos, tostados, enchiladas, chili, taco salads, nachos, Apple Grandes, and Potato Oles. Taco John's restaurants range from simple taco-stand take-out operations to more elaborate buildings with drive-up windows and comfortable dining rooms. The company reports that a well-managed Taco John's restaurant can show a net profit of 20 to 30 percent of gross sales. In 1985, Taco John's restaurants grossed $125 million, with individual sales per unit of $255,000.

WHAT IT TAKES

You will need $16,500 for the initial franchise fee, granting you a license to operate as a Taco John's for twenty years, renewable for twenty years. In addition to the cost of land if you build a free-standing restaurant, you'll have a total investment of $50,000 to $350,000, 30 percent of which must be in cash. The company will provide materials to assist you in making the best possible bank presentation for financing. Additional units sell for the same amount; master franchises are not available. You may be an owner-investor, but the company prefers that you be an integral part of the management team. Monthly royalty fees (4%) and advertising fees (2%) are based on adjusted gross sales. Prior restaurant experience is not necessary, but the company emphasizes that the successful owner will put in hard work and long hours.

GETTING STARTED

Taco John's will help you with site selection; lease or purchase negotiation; lease or purchase of furniture, fixtures, and equipment; and acquisition of supplies and merchandise. For a fee the company offers construction, facility-layout, and decoration services. The typical restaurant is 1,600 square feet, located in a mall, shopping center, freestanding building, or commercial industrial park. You will be expected to use the company's standard logo, building design, and kitchen layout. Including yourself, your staff will consist of two full-time and sixteen part-time employees. You will attend fifteen days of training in the Cheyenne, Wyoming, facilities for classroom and hands-on instruction in management, operations, accounting, marketing, and training. Additional training will be held for all employees at regional centers and at your store. You can be open within six months after buying a Taco John's franchise. The company will help with your grand opening.

MAKING IT WORK

For part of your advertising fee you will receive newspaper ads, magazine ads, telephone-book ads, brochures, television and radio commercials, national media coverage, point-of-purchase displays, banners, and press releases. Co-op funding is available for four-color magazine ads, presentation books, billboard posters, and seasonal promotional materials. Taco John's holds a national convention once a year, regional conferences every six months, one-day seminars periodically, and regular onsite training. You'll receive a monthly company newsletter and magazine; updates on products, company information, and market trends; a customer-oriented publication; and periodic surveys. You will also be able to attend area-wide franchise meetings and participate in the company's award programs.

Administrative tasks will be simplified with headquarters and regional resource persons; a toll-free hotline; regular onsite visits, onsite troubleshooting; manuals for policy, customer service, and management procedure; all types of forms; and systems for bookkeeping, inventory, personnel, expense analysis, and computerized management information. New products and service ideas are tested by a division of the company. You will be required to sell only company products, but the company will recommend sources for the less-specialized types of food and supplies that you will need.

COMMENTS

Taco John's was ranked seventy-ninth in *Entrepreneur* magazine's 1987 "Franchise 500." A member of the IFA since 1984, the company offers joint-venture franchising. The company wants to expand operations in forty states.

GETTING MORE INFORMATION

The franchise information packet contains a detailed guide to presenting your loan proposal, details on Taco John's remodeling program, brochures on franchise operations, location evaluation data, a five-page application form, and question-and-answer sheets on the company. For details, contact:
Paul C. Wolbert
Director of Development
Taco John's International
808 West 20th
Cheyenne, WY 82001
(307) 635–0101 (call collect)

TacoTime

BUSINESS: Mexican
  fast-food restaurant
FOUNDED: 1959
FRANCHISED: 1961
START-UP
  INVESTMENT:
  $105,200–$175,200

NO. OF UNITS		AS OF		PROJECTED BY	
		1/1/85	1/1/86	1/1/87	1/1/88
OWNED BY:	COMPANY	19	17	19	21
	FRANCHISEES	210	219	254	289
LOCATED:	IN U.S.	179	179	196	213
	OUTSIDE U.S.	50	57	77	97
TOTAL:		229	236	273	310
NO. OF STATES W/ UNITS		13	13	23	33

THE BUSINESS

By emphasizing a strong policy of franchisee service and support, TacoTime has become a very successful Mexican fast-food restaurant. The TacoTime menu features a variety of low-priced items such as tacos, taco salad, six kinds of burritos, nachos, enchiladas, tostados, chips, and more. All items are prepared with high-quality fresh ingredients. The company strives to be actively and personally involved with its franchisees and is always receptive to new ideas. In 1985 the total sales for all TacoTime restaurants were $80,000,000.

WHAT IT TAKES

TacoTime has two franchising plans. You can get a single-unit franchise for an initial fee of $15,000, or an area-development agreement for $25,000. The single-unit franchises are for a smaller market and are not usually sold in large metropolitan areas. When you buy an area-development agreement, the company will schedule development of a designated number of stores in your area. The $25,000 fee covers payment for the first store and the $10,000 fee for your second store. For more stores, you will pay an additional $10,000 fee each. To qualify for a franchise you must have a net worth of $150,000, including $70,000 cash. Total costs will run from $105,200 to $165,200 for a single store, and $115,200 to $175,200 for an area-development agreement. These figures include approximately $8,000 for initial inventory, $53,000 to $110,000 for equipment and furniture, $13,000 to $16,000 for signs, $40,000 for employee training costs, $1,200 for uniforms, $7,000 for working capital, and $5,000 for miscellaneous expenses. TacoTime will help you find and apply for appropriate financing.

Your franchise agreement will apply for fifteen years, with five-year renewal periods, and will entitle you to an exclusive territory based on market and demographic studies. The company prefers that you manage your store but allows passive ownership. Each month you'll pay a royalty fee of 5 percent of gross sales based on sales for the previous month. You'll pay another 0.5 percent to the TacoTime Marketing Council for advertising costs.

GETTING STARTED

The company will give you a list of possible market areas across the country, conduct an evaluation of your proposed site, review their findings with you, and recommend potential locations. Once you've selected a site, TacoTime will help you negotiate a lease for the property and will offer you options in floor plans and decor. The average store size is 1,700 square feet, and you can choose either of two store designs. Stores can be located in malls, shopping centers, or freestanding buildings. Company representatives will help you choose equipment and furniture suppliers, suggest sources nearest you, and inform you about special prices. You may buy from other sources as long as TacoTime specifications are met.

You'll need approximately fifteen full-time and fifteen part-time employees, whom the company will help you select. Your training at the company headquarters in Eugene, Oregon, will last from three to six weeks. You'll get both classroom and hands-on training in leadership, scheduling, positioning, customer service, personnel management and relations, time management, marketing, and promotions. You'll also learn technical skills for food preparation, sanitation, and maintenance and study safety, liability, stress survival, and motivation. The company will provide you with videotapes for training employees. All of your training is paid for by the company; however, you will be responsible for food, lodging, and transportation.

One week before you open, a preopening team will come to your store to help you get ready. Ad-Mark, the company's in-house ad agency, will help you tailor an opening ad campaign. You can open your store within about six months after purchasing your franchise.

MAKING IT WORK

Your advertising fee will go to the TacoTime Marketing Council for the research and development of advertising programs. This non-profit organization is made up primarily of franchisees elected to a board of seven directors, each representing a geographic region. The council directs Ad-Mark in the production of high-quality magazine ads, radio and television commercials, billboard ads, and point-of-purchase displays. You can advertise cooperatively with other franchisees in your area using mailers, signs, banners, seasonal promotionals, and incentives. The council will provide a market manual to guide you in advertising and public relations.

You'll attend annual national conventions, and three times a year you and other franchisees in your region will meet with the Franchise Advisory Council, which serves as representative to TacoTime International. You'll receive the company newsletter three times yearly, plus company, product, and market updates. The company sponsors various awards for franchisees.

You'll have policy, procedure, and customer-service manuals and access to headquarters personnel via a toll-free hotline. TacoTime personnel will visit your store routinely to help you solve problems and offer support. You'll also have bookkeeping, inventory, expense-analysis, and personnel systems, as well as forms for accounting, ordering, inventory, and personnel. You and your employees can get special rates through the company for major-medical and life insurance coverage.

When you buy food and supplies for your store, the company will work with you to find independent area distributors. You can get volume discounts through the central purchasing program. You're not limited to selling company products but are required to use their trademarked secret spices in TacoTime's recipes. The company may supervise the quality of your products and services to assure protection of its trademark and reputation. The research-and-development department continually designs and tests new products and procedures.

COMMENTS

A member of the IFA since 1962, TacoTime was ranked 132rd in *Entrepreneur* magazine's 1987 "Franchise 500." The company participates in a wide variety of community programs for organizations like Goodwill, the Red Cross, Easter Seals, Boy Scouts, and Campfire girls. TacoTime is seeking new franchisees in every state (except Washington) and in Canada, Europe, and Japan.

GETTING MORE INFORMATION

The franchise information packet contains a brochure with numerous color photographs, three sample floor plans, and an application. For more information, contact:

Jim Thomas
Vice-President of Franchise Sales
TacoTime International, Inc.
3880 West 11th Avenue
Eugene, OR   97402
(800)   547–8907 or (503)   687–8222

Travel Pros

BUSINESS: travel
 agency
  FOUNDED: 1982
  FRANCHISED: 1982
START-UP
 INVESTMENT:
 $50,000–$70,000

		AS OF		PROJECTED BY	
NO. OF UNITS		1/1/85	1/1/86	1/1/87	1/1/88
OWNED BY:	COMPANY	0	0	1	1
	FRANCHISEES	16	20	40	60
LOCATED:	IN U.S.	16	18	36	51
	OUTSIDE U.S.	0	2	5	10
TOTAL:		16	20	41	61
NO. OF STATES W/ UNITS		8	10	15	20

THE BUSINESS

The travel industry as a whole has expanded over 800 percent during the past five years, and travel-agency franchising has exploded as well, growing from less than 700 franchise agencies in 1982 to nearly 1,000 in 1986. In 1985 Americans spent $234 billion on travel expenditures, with travel agents booking over 90 percent of all foreign air travel from the United States and 60 percent of domestic air travel. Travel agents earn approximately 10 percent in commissions from airlines and cruiselines. That 10 percent amounted to a Travel Pros companywide $15 million business for 1985, with $800,000 average gross sales per franchise and $40,000 net income.

WHAT IT TAKES

Your initial franchise fee will be $27,300 for ten years' control of an exclusive territory determined by population. You can renew your franchise for subsequent five-year periods. Your total investment will range from $50,000 to $70,000, of which $42,300 must be in cash. If you want to expand your operation, you'll pay the same franchise fee for any additional units you purchase. You may also choose to set up passive ownership of your agencies and hire someone else to run them. Your royalty payment will be a flat fee based on the volume of business your agency generates. No previous travel-agency experience is required.

GETTING STARTED

If you have a location in mind, Travel Pros personnel will evaluate that site. If not, they will assist you in finding one and negotiating its lease and/or purchase. You'll most likely choose 800 square feet in an office building or mall. Once the location has been chosen, Travel Pros will provide you with a custom floor plan and layout that meet the company's comprehensive standards. Your standardized advanced reservation system will be the best in the industry. You'll also get a year's subscription to several trade publications and trade papers, as well as a complete inventory of letterhead, envelopes, and business cards.

   Travel Pros will help you hire the travel experts you need, including a qualified agency manager with at least two years experience and two other full-time employees. You and/or your manager will complete five days of initial classroom training in Denver, Colorado, where you'll study operations, organization, accounting, cost control, budgeting, sales and promotion, staffing, credit, and collection. Your manager and/or agents will spend another five days in Miami, Florida, training on the airline automation system. You can open your agency about three months after your purchase. When you open, your company start-up supervisor will assist during your first few days of operation.

MAKING IT WORK

Your franchise fee will cover newspaper, telephone-book, and black-and-white magazine ads; mailers; brochures; and presentation books. In addition, the franchisee-controlled advertising committee buys radio commercials, national media coverage, contests, and in-house media packages for a lower price than you could get individually. Travel Pros offers periodic training seminars, holds a national conference twice a year and regional conferences three to five times annually, and mails updates on travel-industry and company developments. Some of your most important first-hand information will come from tax-deductible familiarization trips to destinations you plan to recommend to clients.

You will save substantial money and time by using the standardized Eastern Airlines Systemone automation system to make advanced reservations. The United Apollo System is also available on a preferred basis in certain areas. Travel Pros has developed an optional accounting package to be used on IBM PC hardware, so your agency can be totally automated. You'll have systems for bookkeeping, inventory, personnel, expense analysis, and computerized management information—along with all the necessary forms. Travel Pros will also provide you with manuals on operations, sales, general policy, and customer service.

COMMENTS

A member of the IFA, Travel Pros was ranked 490th in *Entrepreneur* magazine's 1987 "Franchise 500." The company wants to expand in most states and many foreign countries.

GETTING MORE INFORMATION

The franchise information packet includes a company letter and three photocopied pages describing the company's concept and objectives, five additional information sheets, several magazine reprints, and a deposit agreement and extensive confidential franchise questionnaire. For further information, contact:

Ila Bishop
President
Travel Pros
2186 South Holly, Suite 4
Denver, CO   80222
(800)   621–8385, extension 659, or (303)   753–0040

Travel ServicentreS

BUSINESS: travel
  agency
    FOUNDED: 1980
    FRANCHISED: 1980
START-UP
  INVESTMENT:
  $65,000 (Canadian)

NO. OF UNITS		AS OF		PROJECTED BY	
		1/1/85	1/1/86	1/1/87	1/1/88
OWNED BY:	COMPANY	1	1	1	1
	FRANCHISEES	28	34	44	64
LOCATED:	IN U.S.	0	0	5	10
	OUTSIDE U.S.	28	35	40	55
TOTAL:		29	35	45	65
NO. OF STATES W/ UNITS		0	0	3	4

THE BUSINESS

Even with a recession economy, travel sales have increased steadily over the past ten years. The number of travel agencies, however, has grown at the rate of only 50 percent of the number of travel sales. Almost half of all travel sales are purchased through agencies, more than 80 percent of which are small independents.

Travel ServicentreS Systems, Inc., is a Canadian-based franchise travel agency that is expanding into the United States. In addition to the standard services, the company offers exclusive travel packages and corporate services. The total dollar volume for Travel Servicentres franchises in 1985 was $50,000,000 (Canadian). The average gross sales per franchise were $1,600,000 (Canadian).

WHAT IT TAKES

Your Travel ServicentreS franchise fee will be $29,000 (Canadian), which will bring you an exclusive territory based on population density. Your agreement can be five or ten years, with a five-year renewal period. You'll have a total investment of around $62,500 (Canadian), of which $35,000 must be in cash. In addition to the franchise fee, your start-up costs will include $25,000 for operating capital, $7,500 for furniture and fixtures, and $1,000 for supplies. You can purchase additional franchises for half your original franchise fee, and master franchises are available. Your ongoing royalty will be .5 percent of sales, and you'll pay $1,000 each year for advertising. You will not need any prior experience in the travel industry to operate your Servicentre.

GETTING STARTED

Your ServicentreS office will be about 600 square feet in a shopping center, mall, office building, or other suitable location. The company will help you find the right site. The company will also help with lease or purchase negotiations for the site as well as for furniture, fixtures, and equipment. With volume purchasing power you can get the furnishings for less. As alternatives to preparing your own facility, you can either hire the company to build your ServicentreS turnkey, or you can convert an existing travel agency into a ServicentreS, phasing in the new elements over an eighteen-month period.

You'll need two full-time and two part-time employees, and you and one or two employees will have four weeks of intensive training. The initial two weeks will be spent at the Training Centre in Mississauga, Ontario, where you'll learn about marketing and operating your ServicentreS. In the final two weeks you'll concentrate on the company's reservations and accounting systems. When you're ready, the company's counselors will help you set up your computerized accounting functions, train your personnel, plan your grand opening, and manage your day-to-day operations.

MAKING IT WORK

The travel industry is tightly regulated. The company will help you understand the complex rules as well as assist you in assembling required documentation and in filing for domestic and international airline appointments such as IATA. The comprehensive sales-representative program will help you market your ServicentreS. You'll learn how to recruit representatives and how to structure commission scales, training schedules, reporting, and follow-up. You'll have access to such exclusive company packages as the corporate discount and corporate-rate hotel programs. And you can expect up to 50 percent more income as a result of the company's special agreements with a select group of travel suppliers. The co-op advertising program will make suppliers' dollars work to your benefit. You'll get exposure from the company's corporate promotion and publicity programs and have the ads, mailers, brochures, and tools to conduct your local campaign.

You can attend two national conventions each year and a regional conference each month. Headquarters staff will visit your ServicentreS on a quarterly basis. You'll get a company newsletter every three months and constant updates and information from airlines, hotels, and other suppliers. To help your ServicentreS run smoothly and efficiently, you'll be using state-of-the-art integrated reservations-accounting and word processing systems. And you'll have access to the Travel ServicentreS support team for advice on all aspects of your business, from marketing to financial control. You can continue your training and education through seminars for both management and staff. The company has recognition programs for the best franchise and best suppliers.

COMMENTS

Travel ServicentreS was ranked 382nd in *Entrepreneur* magazine's 1987 "Franchise 500." The company provides an earnings claim document available upon request. It is seeking franchisees in Alaska, Hawaii, and nine additional states and in Canada.

GETTING MORE INFORMATION

The franchise information packet includes a fact sheet about the company, costs, and the process of getting a franchise; marketing brochures; biographical information on the headquarters staff; a list

of corporate references; and a form to accompany the deposit required for a franchise reservation. For more information, call or
write:

Ash Mukherjee
President
Travel ServicentreS Systems, Inc.
175 Airway Centre
5945 Airport Road
Mississauga, Ontario, CANADA   L4V   1R9
(416)   671–4114

TriMark

BUSINESS: direct-mail			AS OF		PROJECTED BY	
marketing	NO. OF UNITS		1/1/85	1/1/86	1/1/87	1/1/88
FOUNDED: 1969	OWNED BY: COMPANY		0	0	0	0
FRANCHISED: 1978		FRANCHISEES	70	87	110	135
START-UP	LOCATED: IN U.S.		70	87	110	135
INVESTMENT:		OUTSIDE U.S.	0	0	0	0
$27,900–$34,900	TOTAL:		70	87	110	135
	NO. OF STATES W/ UNITS		24	34	38	40

THE BUSINESS

All types of businesses, retailers, and professionals benefit greatly
from reaching their potential clients directly with information about
their services. TriMark's direct-mail marketing concept involves a
cooperative advertising effort that reaches more than 60,000 homes
and businesses four times a year per franchise—a total of over 400
million ads per year. Eighty-three percent of businesses that advertise with TriMark become repeat customers. The TriMark method
gives businesses and retailers the opportunity to reach their prime
market areas for less than four cents per ad. Noncompetitive businesses advertise in a single coupon package using high-quality designs and graphics. The packages can be sent to residences, businesses, and professionals' offices. Solo direct mailings are also
offered. Clients can also have an annual ad-campaign agreement,
renewable annually.

Experts predict this co-op direct-mail method will be a leading and
growing advertising medium. The total sales for all TriMark franchises in 1985 were $11,250,000. Company volume has grown an
average of 25 percent per year over the last decade.

WHAT IT TAKES

Your initial franchise fee will be determined by the number of mailable addresses in your territory—ranging from $24,900 for up to
150,000 homes to $33,900 for 251,000 to 300,000 mailable homes.

These figures are determined by subtracting addresses considered to be low income (according to 1980 census-tract information) from a given area's population. TriMark will agree not to sell any other similar franchises in your territory for the term of your agreement, which is indefinite. You can buy additional territory for your franchise for $100 per 1,000 households. The total initial investment, including the franchise fee, can range from $27,900 to $34,900 and will cover your initial training and demographic marketing assistance. You'll pay no royalty fees. Sales-management experience is helpful but not required for potential franchisees.

GETTING STARTED

Before you buy a territory, TriMark's demographic and marketing specialists will research your preferred area extensively. Once you've agreed on a territory, the company will help you structure it into specific mailing areas based on shopping trends and the number of homes and businesses. Most TriMark offices are located in office buildings or commercial centers. You can operate your business in 700 square feet of office space, and you'll probably need three or more full-time employees.

You'll learn how to operate your business in a week-long classroom training program at the home office in New Castle, Delaware. Lectures and role playing are used to teach management, sales, recruiting, goal setting, marketing, ad design, time management, and income planning. You'll tour the plant; attend workshops; learn about art, copy and layout, bookkeeping, and mailing cycles; and see how TriMark handles printing and mailing at the home office. After your training the company will set up and distribute an initial mailing to a thousand of the retail and business customers you'll be contacting. A company representative will work with you at your office for one week after you open for business, reviewing what you learned in class, helping you get started, and going along on sales calls to offer support and feedback. The company also has a cash-flow assistance program to help you recoup some of your initial investment. You can do your first 20,000 mailers free of charge, except for postage. You'll also get all the initial office supplies needed to get started, including contracts, letterhead, business cards, statements, and forms. The company will provide you with sales kits, sample coupons, price schedules, ink and paper samples, brochures, and sales proposals for your sales and marketing tools. You should be able to get into business within three weeks after buying your territory.

MAKING IT WORK

TriMark will offer you many creative and innovative marketing tools and support services to make your business grow. With its information-exchange program the company tracks ads in over 100 categories for percentage of coupons redeemed and volume of new business generated. These data not only provide potential clients with convincing statistics about advertising in TriMark packages but also let you foresee marketing trends so you can advise clients accordingly. You'll be able to offer clients twenty-nine different types of advertising formats, including four-color ads. You'll get comprehensive distributor and sales manuals, learning materials, a national account folder, and a cassette-tape library to help improve sales and promote business. The company will supply, at no cost, newspaper ads, mailers, seasonal promotional materials, radio commercials, national media coverage, and incentive programs. They'll also provide you with up to four thousand business name-and-address labels for promotional mailings to prospects. TriMark aggressively solicits accounts from national clients whose ads can be inserted into your ad packages.

Specific company personnel work exclusively with franchisees as teachers, advisors, and problem solvers. You can reach the home office at any time on the company's toll-free hotline. Additional support comes from a variety of company publications, such as the company's bimonthly magazine and newsletter. You'll handle bookkeeping, billing, accounting, expense analysis, and graphic design on your personal computer with software customized for your office and salespeople. You can even send camera-ready art to the home office using your phone and computer. Then typesetters and proofreaders will work with you to produce the ads. Marketing personnel will handle label ordering and mailing for you from production plants on both the East and West coasts. The company sponsors an annual national convention, regional conventions twice a year, and periodic seminars and training reviews. The company also sponsors achievement awards and offers bonuses and incentive programs.

COMMENTS

TriMark was ranked 293rd in *Entrepreneur* magazine's 1987 "Franchise 500." A member of the IFA since 1981, the company makes an earnings claim document available. TriMark is seeking new franchisees throughout the United States.

GETTING MORE INFORMATION

The franchise information packet includes a brochure, an ad-format idea booklet, a company magazine, a list of references, and an application. For more information, contact:

David H. Clayton
Vice-President of Sales & Marketing
TriMark, Inc.
184 Quigley Boulevard
New Castle, DE   19720
(800)   TRI–MARK or (302)   322–2143

Tubby's Sub Shops

BUSINESS:
 submarine-sandwich
 shop
FOUNDED: 1968
FRANCHISED: 1977
START-UP
 INVESTMENT:
 $172,500–$412,500

NO. OF UNITS		AS OF		PROJECTED BY	
		1/1/85	1/1/86	1/1/87	1/1/88
OWNED BY: COMPANY		11	11	12	13
FRANCHISEES		30	35	44	55
LOCATED: IN U.S.		41	46	56	68
OUTSIDE U.S.		0	0	0	0
TOTAL:		41	46	56	68
NO. OF STATES W/ UNITS		2	2	4	5

THE BUSINESS

Even before the four Paganes brothers began to franchise their sand-wich shops, the uniform decor, signs, and menus they used gave the impression that their shops were part of a national fast-food opera-tion. By 1977 they had established a strong market identity with only twelve shops. This solid business image prompted hundreds of in-quiries about franchising. Total sales from all shops in 1985 were $15,000,000, and the average per shop was $400,000 in gross sales. The Tubby's menu features salami, ham, steak, and burger subs made with fresh lettuce, tomatoes, onions, cheese, mushrooms, and a variety of sauces and dressings. Customers can also get specialties such as gyros and Italian sausage subs, soup, fries, and desserts.

WHAT IT TAKES

The fee for a Tubby's franchise is $12,500, which will entitle you to an exclusive territory for the seven-year term of the agreement, re-newable for another seven years. Other expenses vary depending on whether you'll be leasing or buying the property. If you lease an existing building, the cost for converting it will be $160,000, of which you'll need to pay $80,000 in cash. If you build your own shop, you will need about $400,000, including an estimated $100,000 for land acquisition. Tubby's requires you to have $150,000 in cash in this case. The company can recommend acceptable means of fi-nancing, if needed. You'll pay a continuing royalty fee each month of 4 percent of gross sales. Another 3.5 percent per month is re-quired to fund the company's advertising program. The price for additional franchises is negotiable, but the company would prefer that you run your restaurants yourself. Master franchises are available.

GETTING STARTED

Tubby's Sub Shops can be found in malls, shopping centers, and freestanding buildings. You'll need a facility with about 1,800 square feet and a staff of twelve full-time and eight part-time employees. Company representatives will help you choose a site; and select and train your employees; negotiate the lease or purchase of property;

and furnish and decorate the shop; and acquire fixtures, furnishings, and food-service equipment. You'll get a complete sign package for both interior and exterior. If you are converting an existing building, you'll get site-plan drawings, construction materials, and engineering and construction services. Everything you need to operate is figured into the estimated start-up cost.

You'll attend a week of classroom training to learn about inventory control, product preparation, sanitation, maintenance, and all other topics covered in the training manual. Before you open, you and your employees will spend several weeks at a conveniently located Tubby's, where you'll get hands-on training. You'll be ready for your grand opening within two to three months after buying your shop.

MAKING IT WORK

The company's own in-house advertising agency will produce campaigns and promotional programs, and you'll get layout and format guidelines and a public-relations manual for local advertising. Tubby's advertises in newspapers, magazines, and mailers and on radio and television.

The company sponsors semiannual regional conventions, citywide meetings, and monthly Franchisee Advisory Council meetings. You'll get the company newsletter every three months and technical and industry updates periodically. Company personnel will visit your site regularly and they will be able to assist you whenever a problem arises. The policy and management-procedure manuals can answer questions and reinforce your initial training. You'll be provided with the necessary forms for personnel, accounting, inventory, and ordering. You can increase your net profits by ordering products from the company's central purchasing program, which passes volume discounts on to you. You can also buy from other suppliers, as long as the products meet Tubby's requirements. The company's purchasing director conducts an ongoing program of product research and development. The company sponsors various recognition programs; and the employee-relations department, among other things, sponsors an annual family picnic and supplies holiday decorations for the stores. Emphasizing good community relations, Tubby's sponsors events such as an annual art contest, group tours, and senior-citizen discounts.

COMMENTS

Tubby's was ranked 373rd in *Entrepreneur* magazine's 1987 "Franchise 500." The company makes an earnings claim document available; and it contributes to Easter Seals, the Muscular Dystrophy Association, and the March of Dimes. Tubby's is seeking franchisees in several southern and midwestern states.

GETTING MORE INFORMATION

The franchise information packet contains nine pages of company information on Tubby's letterhead, applications for credit and franchise, a newsletter, and a sample menu. To get more information, contact:

J. Thomas Paganes
Director, Franchising
Tubby's Sub Shops
34500 Doreka Drive
Fraser, MI   48026
(313)   296–1270

Tuff-Kote Dinol

BUSINESS:
automobile
rustproofing and
preservation
FOUNDED: 1964
FRANCHISED: 1967
START-UP
INVESTMENT:
$36,000–$43,000

		AS OF		PROJECTED BY	
NO. OF UNITS		1/1/85	1/1/86	1/1/87	1/1/88
OWNED BY: COMPANY		7	8	9	10
	FRANCHISEES	151	153	158	172
LOCATED: IN U.S.		148	151	155	168
	CANADA	10	10	12	14
TOTAL:		158	161	167	182
NO. OF STATES W/ UNITS		22	22	23	27

THE BUSINESS

Today people are keeping their cars longer than they did a few years ago. But a car must be superbly maintained to remain drivable and salable when it's older. In areas where icy roads are salted during the winter, where sea air and humidity prevail, or where industrial air pollution is high, vehicles must be protected. That's why Tuff-Kote Dinol's preservation services are so valuable to both retail and commercial customers. In 1985, Tuff-Kote Dinol's 2,400 centers worldwide totaled $22,000,000 in gross sales. The average per franchise was $156,000 gross and approximately $40,000 net. Tuff-Kote has franchisees in 53 countries.

Franchisees offer customers a unique two-step rustproofing system, available only from Tuff-Kote Dinol, which actually penetrates through existing rust down to the bare metal, neutralizing the oxidized metal. In the second step, a sealant is applied and cured to form a protective coating on surfaces prone to rust and wear. The system is so effective that cars up to three years old that have never been rustproofed can be treated and warrantied for the life of the car. Customers can also get fabric protectors, exterior glaze, a sound-deadener undercoat, pop-up sunroofs, gravel deflectors, truck-bed liners, pinstriping, side moldings, and door-edge guards. Commercial customers with garages can have the work done at their locations.

WHAT IT TAKES

The franchise fee will depend on the population of your protected territory; it can range from $4,000 to $11,000. The company can finance half of the fee (except for the low $4,000 fee) at 12 percent interest. You may buy additional centers at a 50 percent discount. Other start-up costs include approximately $8,000 for equipment and inventory, $3,000 for two months' lease of a building site, $1,000 for insurance and local fees, $5,000 for purchase and installation of signs and building identification, and $15,000 for working capital and employee wages.

A lease agreement is available at approximately $225 per month in lieu of purchasing signs and building identification for $5,000. You'll also pay an ongoing royalty fee of 8 percent of gross sales. The franchise agreement applies for ten years, with a ten-year renewal period. You can hire a manager, but the company prefers that you run the center.

GETTING STARTED

If you already have an automobile-related business with extra bays or a separate building, you may locate your Tuff-Kote Dinol center there. If not, the company's experts will help you choose the best location. Most shops are in freestanding buildings, commercial centers, or industrial parks and are about 2,500 square feet. In addition, the company will help you lay out your shop and supply you with a complete set of application tools for rustproofing. If you pay an extra fee, they'll help you decorate, furnish, and set up for your grand opening. The average shop employs one part-time and three full-time people.

The franchise fee will cover all of your training, which will include one week at the home office plus three days at your shop. At the home office you'll get both classroom and hands-on training in product applications, equipment maintenance, marketing, management, and sales. After training, the company will assist you in setting up your marketing operations. Sales advisors will even go with you to make the first sales calls. You'll be able to start up about three months after your franchise purchase.

MAKING IT WORK

For a fee of 1 percent of gross sales you'll have access to effective, professionally designed advertising. You can get newspaper and magazine ads, telephone-book ads, mailers, presentation books and catalogs, radio and television commercials, and national media coverage. For an additional payment you can also get signs, banners, seasonal promotional displays, and brochures. If you're located near other Tuff-Kote Dinol franchisees, you can share local advertising expenses, and the company will help you advertise effectively.

You'll receive technical updates, surveys, and the semiannual company magazine. Also, there are one-day seminars in which you can learn about new products and techniques. The company holds an annual national convention, and you'll meet with other franchisees in your area periodically to exchange information and how-to tips.

Tuff-Kote Dinol will visit your center regularly and offer troubleshooting expertise for both technical and management problems. Their field-service specialists will help you maintain consistently high standards of products and services. Your management manual will answer many routine questions about running your business. You'll also have a customer-service and policy manuals, order and accounting forms, and a bookkeeping system.

You can save money by buying company-brand products through a central purchasing system and by using the centralized merchandising system. You may sell noncompany products that meet Tuff-Kote's specifications for performance. Tuff-Kote Dinol sponsors an ongoing recognition program for franchisees.

COMMENTS

Tuff-Kote Dinol was ranked 170th in *Entrepreneur* magazine's 1987 "Franchise 500." A member of the IFA since 1978 and a division of Dinol International, the company is seeking franchisees in seventeen states and Canada.

GETTING MORE INFORMATION

The franchise information packet contains one large and eight small brochures, the company magazine, and a map depicting areas across the United States where rust hazards exist. There is also a qualification questionnaire for you to fill out and return. For more information, call or write:

Mr. Deane Presar
Vice-President, Marketing
Tuff-Kote Dinol, Inc.
15045 Hamilton Avenue
Highland Park, MI   48203
(313)   867–4700 (call collect)

TV Scene

BUSINESS:
publication of local
TV and cable guide
FOUNDED: 1982
FRANCHISED: 1982
START-UP
INVESTMENT:
$26,500

NO. OF UNITS		AS OF		PROJECTED BY	
		1/1/85	1/1/86	1/1/87	1/1/88
OWNED BY:	COMPANY	3	0	0	5
	FRANCHISEES	16	41	80	130
LOCATED:	IN U.S.	19	41	80	135
	OUTSIDE U.S.	0	0	0	0
TOTAL:		19	41	80	135
NO. OF STATES W/ UNITS		8	11	20	30

THE BUSINESS

The growth of cable television has created a public demand for a comprehensive, easy-to-read television magazine. While local newspapers provide a weekly television supplemental, they don't seem to meet the full needs of the reader and the advertiser. TV Scene meets those needs by offering a weekly television magazine that features accurate, up-to-date listings of network, cable, and pay-TV programs; special reader features; local community news; effective advertisements; and special promotional sections targeted toward specific advertisers. The magazines are distributed free through high-traffic retail distribution points, inserted into local newspapers, or mailed directly to cable and TV subscribers. The franchise generates revenue through local advertising sales.

WHAT IT TAKES

When you purchase a TV Scene franchise for $21,500, you'll secure the exclusive territorial rights to publish the *TV Scene* magazine in your designated market for fifteen years. You will need a minimum of $5,000 for operating costs. Before your franchise is granted, your territory will be evaluated by the company. Some larger areas have multiple franchise territories. If you wish to expand into these multiple market areas, you can purchase rights at a discount rate. You can also purchase additional franchises for $16,125 each. Passive ownership is discouraged. Your royalty fee will be based on the size of your magazine: $80 to $250 for twenty-four to fifty-six pages and an additional $15 for each four-page increment. You do not need prior sales or publishing experience to become a *TV Scene* publisher.

GETTING STARTED

You'll probably put your magazine-publishing business in an office building, a shopping center, or a commercial park, and you'll need two or three full-time employees. Both you and your sales associates and staff members will be trained at the company's Publisher's College and Sales Seminar, which is offered monthly at corporate headquarters in Fort Myers, Florida. The five-day classroom program covers everything from the history and structure of TV Scene,

Inc., to advertising composition, prospecting, sales, telemarketing, and business procedures. Afterwards, TV Scene's training director will work with you for three days in your own market, accompanying you on sales calls, supporting you on initial sales presentations, assisting you in writing advertising contracts, helping you design and prepare ads, and providing expertise in setting up your operational systems. You can open your business about two months after buying your franchise.

MAKING IT WORK   Though you'll pay no advertising fee, the company has a cooperative advertising arrangement. TV Scene will provide you with a series of radio and television commercials, and media in your area will receive press releases developed by the company's marketing director. You'll get not only a complete promotional package every month to use in your magazine but also holiday and special promotions and contests. Yearly promotions include the dining and entertainment guide, an ask-the-experts feature, business scene, the service directory, and an apartment locator. Two affiliated support companies—Graphic Scene and Print Brokers—will insure the quality of your magazine. Print Brokers secures the most cost-effective and highest-quality suppliers of composition, listings, and printing for franchisees. Graphic Scene consolidates the typesetting, artwork, and composition services using state-of-the-art equipment to lay out and design each magazine within a three- to four-day production schedule.

TV Scene holds an annual national convention and sponsors a yearly sales contest as well as various achievement awards. You'll also benefit from the work of the Franchisee Advisory Council, which is composed of five owners who meet three times a year to plan ways to increase earning power and value of the franchisees. You'll have an operations manual, with a supplemental handbook, and the marketing/promotions manual which offers several promotions for each month. Every quarter you'll get the newsletter of the *TV Scene* magazine; you'll also get periodic technical updates. The company will supply your forms for personnel and accounting as well as a life and major-medical insurance package. Your magazine will include only company-produced materials purchased at volume discounts. The marketing division constantly researches and updates company materials.

COMMENTS   TV Scene was ranked 435th in *Entrepreneur* magazine's 1987 "Fortune 500." The company makes an earnings claim document available to potential franchisees upon request prior to or during the personal interview. Anderson Communication Group, Inc., is the holding company of TV Scene, Print Brokers, Inc., and Graphic Scene, Inc. The company wants to expand in thirty-five states.

GETTING MORE INFORMATION

The franchise information packet includes professionally produced information about the company, its personnel, and projected future; a newsletter; and a sample copy of *TV Scene* in a slick folder. For more details, contact:

William W. Anderson
President
TV Scene, Inc.
11641 Marshwood Lane Southwest
Ft. Myers, FL 33908
(813) 466–8707 (call collect)

TV Tempo

BUSINESS:		AS OF		PROJECTED BY	
		1/1/85	1/1/86	1/1/87	1/1/88
publication of local TV and cable guide	NO. OF UNITS				
	OWNED BY: COMPANY	1	1	1	1
FOUNDED: 1974	FRANCHISEES	105	130	150	170
FRANCHISED: 1974	LOCATED: IN U.S.	106	131	151	171
START-UP	OUTSIDE U.S.	0	0	0	0
INVESTMENT:	TOTAL:	106	131	151	171
$21,500–$25,500	NO. OF STATES W/ UNITS	17	18	19	21

THE BUSINESS

TV Tempo creates a national format of features and articles on current television programming and offers franchisees the opportunity to tap into that system while catering to local advertisers. The result is a professionally designed publication with local appeal that generates good cash flow and investment return. Using the resources of this national publishing system, you can keep costs low and operate from your home or a small office. This franchise offers independence without the complications of numerous employees, leases, and other time-consuming activities.

WHAT IT TAKES

Your initial franchise fee will be $19,500 for an exclusive territory established by you and TV Tempo. This franchise agreement will be valid for fifteen years and renewable for five. Your total investment will range from $21,500 to $25,500, with all of that required in cash. You may purchase a franchise without being the operating manager. Additional units may be bought at 10 to 20 percent reductions, depending on the units; master franchises are available. Ongoing royalty fees start at $75 during the first 180 days and are $110 on all sixteen- to twenty-eight-page magazines and $130 on all thirty-two-page or larger magazines after the first 180 days. Prior experience in magazine publishing is not required, although sales experience is helpful.

GETTING STARTED

This is a business that can be run from your home or a small office. In preparing *TV Tempo,* you will be required to conform to the national appearance, design, and layout. Including yourself, you will need one to two full-time employees. Training will be held in Athens, Georgia, for five days in a classroom setting for you and your account executives. Covering all facets of the business, this training will continue at your offices for two days when you are ready to open the business, generally six weeks after you purchase the franchise.

MAKING IT WORK

For part of your ongoing royalty fee the company will provide black-and-white magazine ads, brochures, presentation books, radio commercials, and signs. You will continue to learn about the business through periodic regional conferences, normally about three per year; at one- to two-day seminars; and with onsite training in sales and closing techniques held two to three times a year. Refresher classroom training is also available. The company publishes a monthly newsletter and regular updates on company information and industry/market data.

Areawide franchise meetings are held approximately every three months, and surveys are conducted occasionally. The company annually honors excellence in business performance. Backup services include headquarters resource persons, onsite troubleshooting, manuals for setting policy and management procedure, accounting forms, a bookkeeping system, and presentation manuals. The company has its own research and development departments and a central purchasing program that offers volume discounts to franchisees.

COMMENTS

TV Tempo will provide an earnings claim document at a potential franchisee's first meeting with a company representative. The company wants to open franchises in forty of the fifty states.

GETTING MORE INFORMATION

To learn more about this company's publishing operation and its franchise plan, contact:

Paul M. King
President
TV Tempo, Inc.
3131 Atlanta Highway
Athens, GA   30606
(404)   546–6001

UBI Business Brokers

BUSINESS:
  multinational
  business brokerage
  network
FOUNDED: 1966
FRANCHISED: 1982
START-UP
  INVESTMENT:
  $49,000–$60,000

NO. OF UNITS	AS OF		PROJECTED BY	
	1/1/85	1/1/86	1/1/87	1/1/88
OWNED BY: COMPANY	0	0	0	0
FRANCHISEES	35	45	70	125
LOCATED: IN U.S.	35	45	70	125
OUTSIDE U.S.	0	0	0	0
TOTAL:	35	45	70	125
NO. OF STATES W/ UNITS	10	12	18	25

THE BUSINESS

Nearly 90 percent of the 10 million businesses in the United States gross less than $1 million a year. Of those 9 million businesses, one out of four changes hands every twelve months. At an average selling price of $80,000 each, a total of $180 billion in businesses is sold each year. Since the standard commission for selling a business is 10 percent, potential commissions in this field are $18 billion annually. UBI Business Brokers has sold more than $500 million worth of businesses in the past twenty years. In 1985 total sales approached $100 million.

WHAT IT TAKES

You will need previous business experience to succeed as a UBI owner. A background in communication, negotiation, finance, professional sales, accounting, law and/or management is especially helpful. Your initial franchise fee will be $27,500 cash. That buys an exclusive ten-year territory determined by demographics and business potential. Your total initial investment will be $49,000 to $60,000, and in special circumstances the company will offer direct financial assistance. UBI requires that you actively run your brokerage business. Additional franchises can be purchased for $27,500 each. You'll pay 6 percent of your gross commission to UBI as an ongoing royalty fee and another 2 percent advertising fee.

GETTING STARTED

You will need a professional office with about 1,250 to 1,400 square feet in an office or freestanding building. Company personnel will advise you on site location. Although you'll have your own choice of layout, the company will make some recommendations for effective operation.

During your initial ten-day training at corporate headquarters in Los Angeles, California, you'll view videotaped presentations on every aspect of business brokerage, including management techniques, advertising, and public relations. The topics include, among others, developing listing sources, writing the listing contract, conducting the buyer interview, presenting the purchase agreement, and conducting a sales meeting. You'll also learn about effective recruitment advertising, interviewing, qualifying potential sales associates, and training sales associates.

You'll be managing five full-time employees, including several sales associates. Once you're open, you'll have strong support from the UBI field staff, who will continue to train you and your agents. You can expect to open your UBI business within two to three months after purchasing your franchise.

MAKING IT WORK

For your advertising fee you will get a full array of advertising materials, including brochures, newspaper ads, mailers, and recruitment literature (and a polished recruitment film) to help you attract the right sales personnel. To assist in training your sales staff, you'll have a videotape machine and a library of fifteen hours of videotaped information integrated with workbooks. Three times a month, UBI will supplement your complete operations manual—which you'll get during initial training—with the company newsletter. Additional company-information updates come out periodically. UBI provides continuing education, including management seminars and field training sessions, and holds two national conferences annually, quarterly regional conferences, and one-day seminars. At the annual conferences the company recognizes outstanding UBI owners.

You'll benefit from the company's exclusive Internal Multiple Listing Service (IMLS), which routes every listing in an area through corporate headquarters and then to all offices within your area. An important adjunct to your business will be the UBI Financial Network, Inc., developed specifically to focus on the growing involvement in business transactions ranging from $350,000 to $15 million. Using Analyx, the data-processing system developed by UBI, prospective buyers and sellers can see how pricing and value are determined. This system, based on over $500 million in business sales and thousands of transactions, has a statistical base greater than that in any similar firm in the United States. UBI can supply your business forms, which are constantly updated and legally researched for your protection. The company also sponsors errors and omissions liability insurance.

COMMENTS

UBI wants to expand in twenty-seven states and in Europe and Asia.

GETTING MORE INFORMATION

The franchise information packet includes an introduction to UBI and the answers to six most-asked questions; sample newsletters, briefings, and customer brochures; information about the financial network; two brochures reviewing the computer system; and a two-page confidential questionnaire. For more details, contact:

Harold C. Lembke
Vice-President
UBI Business Brokers, Inc.
11965 Venice Boulevard
Los Angeles, CA   90066
(213)   390–8635

Uniforce Temporary Services

BUSINESS:			AS OF		PROJECTED BY	
temporary-personnel	NO. OF UNITS		1/1/85	1/1/86	1/1/87	1/1/88
services	OWNED BY: COMPANY		1	3	11	14
FOUNDED: 1962		FRANCHISEES	48	49	74	92
FRANCHISED: 1979	LOCATED: IN U.S.		49	52	85	106
START-UP		OUTSIDE U.S.	0	0	0	0
INVESTMENT:	TOTAL:		49	52	85	106
$30,000–$40,000	NO. OF STATES W/ UNITS		20	20	25	30

THE BUSINESS

The advantages of hiring temporary workers to supplement an existing staff are numerous: temporary personnel, or temps, can be used during seasonal peaks, reorganizations, or periods when new equipment is introduced, and they can be quickly added or removed as economic conditions dictate. Today's narrowing profit margins and ballooning overheads have created a permanent need for temporary personnel. Once used mainly as vacation fill-ins, modern temps now provide total staffing flexibility and significant cost reductions for more than 90 percent of our country's businesses. The Uniforce franchise program involves a true operating partnership that gives franchisees unlimited financing for temp payrolls and accounts receivable, plus 100 percent ownership and control of their business. By eliminating most administrative burdens, the company enables franchisees to focus on varied marketing strategies to accelerate expansion. This franchise does not require expensive inventory and can be operated by an individual, family, or team. In 1985, Uniforce's franchises grossed $52,267,000.

WHAT IT TAKES

You will need $15,000 in cash for the initial franchise fee, which will guarantee you an exclusive territory based on population and industry base for a perpetual term. Your total investment, including the franchise fee, will be $30,000 to $40,000. Additional units also sell for $15,000 each; you must be the operating manager of your franchise units. Your ongoing royalty fee will be 45 percent of gross profit (less temporaries' payroll and taxes). Previous industry experience is not required.

GETTING STARTED   Uniforce will assist with site selection, construction, facility layout and decoration, lease or purchase of furniture and equipment, and acquisition of materials and supplies. The typical Uniforce office is 650 to 800 square feet, located in an office building, mall, shopping center, or freestanding building. You must follow a uniform layout for all units and use the company logo on forms, supplies, and materials. Besides yourself, you'll need two employees, and the company will help with hiring. You'll receive four days of video and classroom training in New Hyde Park, New York, followed by ongoing onsite visits to train account executives, personnel coordinators, and managers. Subjects covered will be Uniforce operations, staff hiring, recruiting, legal aspects, payroll, billing, insurance, time and territory management, prospecting, sales objections and closings, credit, collections, and office setup and supplies. You can be open for business within two months after buying your franchise, and Uniforce will help with your grand opening.

MAKING IT WORK   You will pay only for your office rent, payroll for permanent staff, classified ads for temp recruiting, telephone, and miscellaneous expenses such as office supplies. Uniforce will pay for financing of your temp payroll, financing of accounts receivable, preparation of temp payroll checks, client invoicing, liability insurance and bonding for temps, printing of all internal forms, hands-on training for you and your staff, filing of unemployment and disability claims, government reporting (W2s, 941s, etc.), national advertising, public relations, development of sales and marketing material, national account sharing, temp evaluation systems, computerized reports on and analyses of your business, and ongoing operational support.

Uniforce holds national conventions once a year, supplemented by regional conferences as needed. You will receive a newsletter every six months, along with bimonthly service and market updates, and weekly company-information updates. The company conducts surveys twice a year, and sponsors various recognition programs to honor achievement. Other backup administration systems Uniforce offers include headquarters and regional resource persons; regular onsite visits and onsite troubleshooting; and manuals for policy, management procedure, and customer service. A Uniforce training and development department is dedicated to research and development of new techniques, ideas, and procedures. Group insurance for temporary employees offers general-liability, disability, worker's compensation, and third-party-bonding coverage.

COMMENTS   Ranked 259th in *Entrepreneur* magazine's 1987 "Franchise 500," Uniforce offers an earnings claim document during a potential franchisee's personal interview. Uniforce wants to add new franchises throughout the United States and in Canada.

**GETTING MORE
INFORMATION**

The franchise information packet contains the company's latest annual report, a brochure describing the Uniforce system, and copies of numerous articles published in major business publications on temporary service and its future growth. For details, contact:

Rosemary Maniscalco
Executive Vice-President
Uniforce Temporary Services
1335 Jericho Turnpike
New Hyde Park, NY   11040
(516)   437–3300

Uniglobe Travel

BUSINESS: travel
   agency
   FOUNDED: 1979
   FRANCHISED: 1980
**START-UP
   INVESTMENT:**
   $125,000–$150,000

		AS OF		PROJECTED BY	
NO. OF UNITS		1/1/85	1/1/86	1/1/87	1/1/88
OWNED BY: COMPANY		0	0	0	0
	FRANCHISEES	170	328	525	750
LOCATED: IN U.S.		100	250	400	600
	OUTSIDE U.S.	70	78	125	150
TOTAL:		170	328	525	750
NO. OF STATES W/ UNITS		12	23	50	50

THE BUSINESS

Travel is now the second-largest industry in the world and is projected to become the largest by the end of the decade as the maturing "bulge generation" reaches its maximum earning potential and finds more time and money to enjoy travel. The travel industry also affords an enjoyable lifestyle—it's a "clean" product, it's fun to sell, and it's totally people oriented. Uniglobe reported $500 million in total sales for its franchisees in 1985, with average gross sales per unit of $1.5 million. Ranked number one in retail travel franchising and one of the top four travel organizations in North America, Uniglobe is designed to benefit both new and existing independent travel agencies. The company builds its name recognition through prime-time TV advertising and has financial computer software programs specially designed for the travel industry. Uniglobe's Career Academy offers general public entry-level travel training, backed with a strong franchisor/franchisee support system ratio.

WHAT IT TAKES

Your initial franchise fee will be $39,500 for a nonexclusive franchise valid for ten years and renewable for five-year periods. Your total investment will be $125,000–$150,000, with $50,000 of that required to be in cash. The company may provide some assistance with financing, depending on your region and its contacts there. Additional units sell for $20,000; you may be an investor-owner, but Uniglobe prefers that you be the actual manager. You will pay an ongoing royalty fee based on a percentage of your gross revenues. Prior experience is not necessary.

GETTING STARTED

Uniglobe will help you set up a new agency by assisting with site selection, lease and leasehold negotiations, and custom office layout and design, and by providing initial office supplies, initial travel manuals, Uniglobe career apparel, filing system and client recall, and direct mail-outs to travel suppliers. The typical facility is 1,000 square feet, located in an office building, shopping center, freestanding building, or commercial/industrial park. You will need eight full-time employees. Your training begins at The International Management Academy in Vancouver, B.C., with four days of classroom and hands-on learning, followed by a comprehensive schedule of regional training for both you and your employees. Your agency can be open ninety days after you buy the franchise, and Uniglobe has an opening promotion to get you off to a good start.

MAKING IT WORK

As part of your advertising fee ($560 per month), Uniglobe provides newspaper ads, black-and-white and four-color magazine ads, mailers, telephone-book ads, radio and television commercials, and national media coverage. Cooperative advertising funds apply to brochures, presentation books, in-house media packages (slides, videotapes), signs, banners, a lead-referral system, incentives, press releases, and a public relations/marketing manual. You will be invited to attend a national convention once a year, regional annual conferences, and a minimum of five days per month of one- to two-day seminars in each region.

Uniglobe emphasizes new business development and use of its exclusive computer software, sales tools, and business-development systems in training. Onsite business-development training is held quarterly and as needed. The company publishes a quarterly newsletter; service, industry, and company updates as needed; a quarterly customer-oriented publication; and monthly regional bulletins. Areawide franchise meetings are held each month and surveys are conducted annually. Top performers are recognized with sales and achievement awards.

Backup services include headquarters and regional resource persons; regular onsite visits and troubleshooting; manuals for policy, management procedure, and customer service; forms for inventory, personnel, and ordering; and systems for bookkeeping, inventory, expense analysis, computerized management information, and computerized billing. The company's research-and-development departments focus on industry standards, product development, software programs, automation, sales and marketing programs, and training programs. Uniglobe's central purchasing program offers volume discounts, supplemented by a centralized merchandising system and company labels. You will be allowed to sell all travel products that meet company standards. Uniglobe offers customer accounts-receivable financing but no insurance.

COMMENTS

In *Entrepreneur*'s 1987 "Franchise 500," Uniglobe ranked first in the travel industry and number 87 overall. A member of the IFA since 1984, the company has also received the ASTA Crest Award and is active in the National Easter Seal campaign. The company wants to develop new franchises in all fifty states and Canada.

**GETTING MORE
INFORMATION**

The franchise information packet contains copies of recent articles on the travel industry and Uniglobe, biographical material and photos of top officers, question-and-answer sheets, fact sheets, charts of the company's structure, testimonials, references, a sample newsletter, and an application form. For more details, contact:
Michael Levy
Senior Vice-President
Uniglobe Travel (International) Inc.
90-10551 Shellbridge Way
Richmond, British Columbia, Canada   V6X 2W9
(604)   270–2241

United Consumers Club

BUSINESS: specialty			AS OF		PROJECTED BY	
buyer's club	NO. OF UNITS		1/1/85	1/1/86	1/1/87	1/1/88
FOUNDED: 1971	OWNED BY: COMPANY		11	7	5	3
FRANCHISED: 1971		FRANCHISEES	44	44	55	75
START-UP	LOCATED: IN U.S.		55	51	60	78
INVESTMENT:		OUTSIDE U.S.	0	0	0	0
$70,000–$85,000	TOTAL:		55	51	60	78
	NO. OF STATES W/ UNITS		19	19	22	25

THE BUSINESS

The United Consumers Club began in the early 1970s, amidst inflation and high interest rates. The company offers a unique buyer's club that increases consumer purchasing power by offering significant discounts to club members. Although United Consumers Club was organized to offer consumers a buying alternative in poor economic conditions, its business is not tied to the state of the economy, because consumers want to get the most for their money regardless of the economic climate.

United Consumers Club purchases merchandise at dealer prices and passes the savings on to club members. Members pay only the manufacturer's cost of an item; a small club charge for processing, handling, and shipping costs; and sales tax. Members can make their product selections by visiting a United showroom to view items on display and thumb through a complete line of manufacturers' catalogs with confidential price lists. In return for the $800 two-year membership fee, which can be financed through the company, the consumer can choose from thousands of name-brand products from apparel to furniture. Further benefits include special local and national discounts for various goods and services from car rentals to discounted movie passes.

WHAT IT TAKES

You can expect to invest $70,000 to $85,000 to establish your United Consumers Club franchise. Your start-up costs will include the $50,000 franchise fee, plus approximately $6,000 for office furniture, fixtures, and equipment; $6,000 for showroom furnishings for display; $4,000 for leasehold improvements; $2,500 for security deposits, lease, and utilities; and at least $15,000 for initial working capital. Approximately $50,000—the amount of your franchise fee—must be in cash. However, you may qualify for financial assistance from the company, which can finance up to $35,000 of your franchise fee. As a club franchisee, you will own your business for twenty years, with a renewal period of the same.

Owners do not have an exclusive territory, but for an additional fee you may buy a master franchise, which would achieve the same effect. You'll pay 22 percent of each membership fee in royalties to the company, plus an additional 5 percent for advertising. United Consumers Club does not encourage franchise ownership by investment groups or absentee owners; therefore, you must be willing to handle the day-to-day operations of your franchise.

GETTING STARTED

The company's planning committee reviews potential store sites before granting approval for any particular location. The United Consumers Club 4,500- to 5,500-square-foot showrooms are usually located in industrial parks, office warehouse areas, freestanding buildings, and other suburban locations. Elaborate showrooms are not needed, so you will not spend a great deal on leasehold improvements and furnishings. In fact, you will start your new franchise with complimentary ready-to-use supplies and samples to add to your facility. You'll also have the benefit of obtaining furniture, fixtures, and equipment at direct-from-the-manufacturer prices, saving you in some cases over half of the retail price.

You will need twelve full-time and two part-time employees. Training for you and one other employee will be provided at the company's Indiana headquarters for three weeks. Round-trip transportation and lodging for both of you will be provided. Major topics covered in the training include implementation of the club's business plan, operational guidelines, and the marketing program to consumers. Training is conducted in the classroom and onsite. After you've opened, you'll be able to have an additional week of classroom training at the home office. You can be in business within one month after securing your showroom location.

MAKING IT WORK
The company sponsors biannual national, regional, and local training seminars and distributes quarterly information updates. Your advertising fee will provide you with the company's latest marketing programs and operations manuals, including one on public relations. In-house media packages are also provided, and cooperative advertising is available for seasonal promotional materials and billboard posters. You'll receive continuing support in operating your business. Free onsite or telephone consultations will provide you with advice on any business concerns and regional resource personnel will make regular onsite visits. To help you make the large-ticket sales, United has a customer credit program for your customers to finance their purchases.

COMMENTS
Ranked 295th in *Entrepreneur* magazine's 1987 "Franchise 500," United Consumers Club makes an earnings claim document available prior to a potential franchisee's personal interview. An IFA member since 1981, the company wants to increase operations in eighteen states and in Canada.

GETTING MORE INFORMATION
The franchise information packet includes sample advertisements, a copy of the company's newsletter, a loose-leaf folder explaining the company's operations, and a four-page application. For more information, write or call:
Tony Foster
National Franchise Director
United Consumers Club
8450 Broadway
Merrillville, IN   46410
(219)   736–1100

U.S. Tech

BUSINESS: retail
  home electronics
  sales
FOUNDED: 1977
FRANCHISED: 1981
START-UP
  INVESTMENT:
  $140,000–$295,000

		AS OF		PROJECTED BY	
NO. OF UNITS		1/1/85	1/1/86	1/1/87	1/1/88
OWNED BY:	COMPANY	0	0	5	8
	FRANCHISEES	22	31	60	92
LOCATED:	IN U.S.	22	31	65	100
	OUTSIDE U.S.	0	0	0	0
TOTAL:		22	31	65	100
NO. OF STATES W/ UNITS		7	9	14	22

THE BUSINESS

Sales of home and car stereo systems, televisions, VCRs, computers, and software have skyrocketed from $5.1 billion in 1975 to a staggering $25.9 billion in 1984. Industry experts believe that these figures represent sales to only 10 percent of the potential market and that retail sales could go as high as $56 billion by the year 1990. Technological breakthroughs in the last decade have profoundly affected the lifestyles of the American public. Consumers can no longer depend on department or computer stores to provide them with adequate advice, service, and product knowledge. U.S. Tech has filled the gap by providing a one-stop home electronic center, where knowledgeable personnel not only advise customers on name-brand stereo, video, and computer products but also offer ongoing support and service. As a result, the company has become a national leader in the home electronics industry. U.S. Tech sales totaled $16,000,000 for 1985, with an average of $725,000 gross per franchise.

WHAT IT TAKES

The franchise fee of $25,000 will buy you a ten-year agreement, with a ten-year renewal option, and entitle you to an exclusive territory based on population. Other start-up costs will vary, depending on the population and the gross retail sales in your area. Typical ranges for the costs are as follows:

	COST	
ITEM	LOW	HIGH
Leasehold improvements	$15,000– 35,000	$ 35,000– 45,000
Furniture and fixtures	15,000– 25,000	25,000– 35,000
Opening inventory	80,000–130,000	115,000–175,000
Grand-opening inventory	5,000– 7,000	10,000– 15,000
Franchise fee	25,000	25,000
Total:	$140,000–222,000	$210,000–295,000

The figures in the "low" column are based on a population of 20,000 to 250,000 and gross area retail sales of $150 million to $900 million. The figures in the "high" column are for a population of over 250,000 and gross area retail sales of over $700 million. The size, condition, and layout of the store, as well as labor costs and geographic location, may also cause costs to vary.

You'll be expected to pay $50,000 of the total initial costs in cash, and the company will help you find financing for the remainder. You can buy additional franchises for only $10,000 each. The company allows passive ownership but prefers that franchisees personally manage their stores. You'll pay a royalty of 6 percent on products sold each week.

GETTING STARTED

U.S. Tech stores are usually located in freestanding buildings or shopping centers and require from 2,500 to 5,000 square feet. The company will help you choose the best site; negotiate the lease or purchase; and establish a schedule for the layout, construction, and furnishing phases as well as for your grand opening. You can choose from several interior decors, and the company will help you design the different areas of the store. U.S. Tech recommends that, in addition to yourself, you have four full-time employees, whom the company will help hire and train.

You'll spend three weeks at headquarters in Denver, Colorado, where you'll learn to use the company's products. You'll also learn about sales techniques, merchandising, financial planning, and overall management. Your training expenses, including airfare and lodging, will all be paid for by the company. While you're in training, the company's advertising staff will analyze your market and design a grand-opening campaign tailored to your area. You can open for business within about three months after buying your franchise.

MAKING IT WORK

The U.S. Tech advertising program will offer you continuing support through national media coverage and free, regularly updated local campaigns. The company participates in a cooperative program to get newspaper and magazine ads, brochures, mailers, seasonal promotional materials, and many other types of advertising. You also can use the lead-referral system, marketing manuals, and videotaped sales and marketing programs.

U.S. Tech will send you a monthly newsletter and periodic technical updates and surveys on products and services. The company holds an annual national convention and periodic one- to two-day seminars and meetings. Six times a year company representatives will come to your store to offer support and training as needed, and you can also get advice through a toll-free hotline and your operations manual. All the forms you'll need for accounting, inventory, personnel, and ordering will be provided by the company.

A company division that distributes merchandise and a central purchasing program will save you money on name brands like Kenwood, Fisher, and Hitachi. You'll have over 1,500 products to choose from—including IBM, Apple, and Compaq computers—all stored in the company's new 24,000-square-foot warehouse in Florida. For a lesser royalty fee you can choose to sell only company-brand products. U.S. Electronics Group sponsors various recognition programs for franchisees.

COMMENTS

An operator of U.S. Electronics group, U.S. Tech is looking for franchisees throughout the United States.

GETTING MORE INFORMATION

The franchise information packet includes a brochure, a research report from Stuart-James investment bankers, a consumer electronics report, a press release, and an application. For more information, contact:
Richard White
Vice-President of Marketing
U.S. Electronics Group
15700 East First Avenue
Aurora, CO   80011
(800)   437–1101 or (303)   367–0200 (call collect)

The Weed Man

		AS OF		PROJECTED BY	
		1/1/85	1/1/86	1/1/87	1/1/88
NO. OF UNITS					
OWNED BY: COMPANY		3	3	3	3
FRANCHISEES		75	83	100	120
LOCATED: IN U.S.		1	2	15	30
OUTSIDE U.S.		77	84	88	93
TOTAL:		78	86	103	123
NO. OF STATES W/ UNITS		1	2	4	6

BUSINESS: lawn-maintenance services
FOUNDED: 1970
FRANCHISED: 1976
START-UP INVESTMENT: $37,500

THE BUSINESS

Started in Canada, The Weed Man's lawn-care maintenance program includes regular application of high-quality, slow-release, granular fertilizer, specially formulated for The Weed Man dealers; seasonal application of liquid herbicide for weed control; and custom applications for insect and crabgrass control. In 1985, The Weed Man franchises grossed $16 million in sales, with average gross sales per unit of $200,000 and average net income of $65,000.

WHAT IT TAKES

You will need $31,000 for your initial franchise fee. The franchise agreement, valid for fifty years, will guarantee you an exclusive territory. Your total initial investment, including the franchise fee, will be $37,500. You must either pay the entire amount in cash or make a $12,000 minimum deposit, with the balance due 31 January in the year that operations are scheduled to commence. Discounts off the total price will apply if you choose the second option and pay the balance in full before the due date. Additional units may be bought for the same amount; however, the company prefers that you be an active part of the business. Ongoing royalty fees consist of a flat rate on your production units (spray trucks) adjusted to the annual published Consumer Price Index. No prior experience in lawn care is necessary. Master franchises are available.

GETTING STARTED

The Weed Man will help you with site selection, facility layout, lease or purchase of equipment and vehicles, and acquisition of supplies. In addition to videotapes, manuals, and training seminars, the launch package will provide your truck, truck license fee, paint and decals, and a security deposit. You will lease the truck with spray equipment as a single unit, usually for three years with a buy-out option at the end of the lease. The average service life of the trucks with proper maintenance is ten years. You will also receive initial office supplies and forms; advertising, including business cards and lawn gauges; a fertilizer spreader and miscellaneous parts; and uniforms. The typical The Weed Man facility is located in an office building, a freestanding building, or a commercial industrial park. Most of the company's products are privately labeled with The Weed Man logo and will be shipped directly to you from the manufacturer. You'll receive a week of training in Toronto, Ontario, with intensive classroom, video, and hands-on experience covering technical aspects, sales and marketing, customer service, and office administration. On-the-job training will be provided for your staff, the size of which will vary. You can open within a month after purchasing your The Weed Man franchise.

MAKING IT WORK

There is no advertising fee, but you will receive television and radio commercials; newspaper, magazine, and telephone book ads; mailers and brochures; billboard posters, signs, and banners; inhouse media packages and catalogues; seasonal promotional materials, contests, and incentives; and a lead-referral system, press releases, and a public relations/marketing manual. The company holds a national convention three times a year and offers one- to two-day seminars and areawide franchise meetings as requested. Head-office representatives will offer any onsite training you desire. You'll receive a company newsletter six times a year, plus periodic updates on products, service, company information, and market information. Surveys are also conducted periodically. The company recognizes excellence in service and sales with award programs.

Your administrative tasks will be simplified with headquarters resource persons; onsite troubleshooting; manuals for policy, management procedures, and customer service; forms for accounting, ordering, personnel, and inventory; and a bookkeeping system. Research and development focus on product and equipment innovation and on market research. The Weed Man has divisions that produce or distribute equipment and supplies, a central purchasing program to offer volume discounts, a centralized merchandising system, and company labels. If you use noncompany products, they must match or exceed company-supplied material quality. Company-sponsored insurance offers life, major-medical, dental, and environmental-liability coverage.

COMMENTS

A supporter of the Toronto Sick Childrens Hospital, The Weed Man wants to add new franchises in nine northern states and in Canada, Australia, and Europe.

GETTING MORE INFORMATION

The franchise information packet contains question-and-answer sheets on the company and its operations, projected earnings sheets, sample brochures, and a four-page application form. For details, contact:

Bob McCannell
National Sales and Marketing Manager
The Weed Man/Turf Management Systems, Inc.
2399 Royal Windsor Drive
Mississauga, Ontario   L5J 1K9
CANADA
(416)   823–8550

Wendy's

BUSINESS: fast-food		AS OF		PROJECTED BY	
restaurant	NO. OF UNITS	1/1/85	1/1/86	1/1/87	1/1/88
FOUNDED: 1969	OWNED BY: COMPANY	1,057	1,257	N/A	N/A
FRANCHISED: 1972	FRANCHISEES	1,935	2,185	N/A	N/A
START-UP	LOCATED: IN U.S.	2,815	3,241	N/A	N/A
INVESTMENT:	OUTSIDE U.S.	177	201	N/A	N/A
$750,000–$1.3 million	TOTAL:	2,992	3,442	N/A	N/A
	NO. OF STATES W/ UNITS	50	50	50	50

THE BUSINESS

A leader in the highly competitive fast-food hamburger field, Wendy's offers not only fresh hamburgers but also chicken, salad, baked potatoes, and an expanding array of other high-quality foods. In the past few years Wendy's has experimented with breakfast foods, hot dogs, taco salads, and multigrain buns. The company is also signing agreements to move into new types of locations, such as Days Inn motels, K-Mart stores, hospitals, college campuses, shopping malls, and zoos. In 1985, Wendy's franchises grossed $1.7 billion, with average gross sales per unit of $850,000. Wendy's recently adopted the slogan "Choose fresh, choose Wendy's."

WHAT IT TAKES

You will need $30,000 for the initial franchise fee, which covers a license to operate in a nonexclusive territory for twenty years. Your total initial investment will be $750,000 to $1.3 million, with $200,000 to $250,000 required in cash. The company does not offer financial assistance. Your investment will range from $150,000 to $450,000 for land, $190,000 to $280,000 for the building, $70,000 to $200,000 for site improvement, $147,000 to $220,000 for equipment and signs, and $100,000 to $200,000 for such costs as insurance and working capital. Additional units sell for $25,000 each; master franchises are not available. Wendy's charges an ongoing royalty fee of 4 percent of gross sales.

Restaurant experience is considered helpful, but a successful business track record is more important. You will be expected to manage your franchise, live within a fifty-mile radius of the restaurant, and devote 100 percent of your business time and effort to the development and operation of the franchise. The company recommends a personal net worth of at least $250,000 ($200,000 in cash or liquid assets excluding personal effects, residence, and automobiles) available for the business. (In California you will need $300,000 net worth and a minimum of $250,000 in liquid assets.)

GETTING STARTED

Wendy's does not charge for consulting on the layout of your restaurant and on your acquisition of supplies and merchandise. There is a fee for help with site selection, lease or purchase negotiation, construction, and facility decoration. The typical Wendy's restaurant is 2,610 square feet, located in an office building, mall, shopping center, freestanding building, commercial industrial park, airport, military base, or college campus. You must follow standards for restaurant design and use of trademarks, uniforms, and equipment. The company has purchasing agreements and arrangements with approved suppliers.

Your staff will consist of four full-time and thirty to fifty part-time employees, whom Wendy's will help you hire. You will receive at least fourteen weeks of training in the corporate office in Dublin, Ohio, using classroom, video, and hands-on experience regarding operations, business skills, and the use of a computer-based restaurant-management system. You can open your restaurant six months after buying the franchise, and the company will help with the grand opening.

MAKING IT WORK

Advertising fees are 2 percent of gross sales for national campaigns and 2 percent of gross sales for local efforts. In 1985 the company spent 2 percent of domestic sales for national advertising ($50 million, up from $20 million in 1983). The company offers brochures, in-house media packages (slides, videotapes), point-of-purchase displays, signs, seasonal promotional materials, incentives, and a public-relations/marketing manual for part of your fee. Co-op funding is also available for newspaper ads, black-and-white and four-color magazine ads, mailers, television and radio commercials, billboards, contests, and press releases. The company holds an annual national convention, one-day seminars every three months, quarterly area-wide franchise meetings, and onsite training as needed.

You'll receive a monthly magazine; a monthly newsletter; and periodic product, service, company-information, and market-information updates. Wendy's offers headquarters and regional resource persons; regular onsite visits; onsite troubleshooting; manuals for policy and management procedure; forms for inventory and personnel; systems for bookkeeping, inventory, personnel, expense analysis, and computerized management information; and various franchise award programs. Wendy's continually studies new products and service systems. The company has a centralized purchasing program offering volume discounts and company brands. You must sell company products only and purchase those—and your equipment—from independent suppliers approved by Wendy's.

COMMENTS

A member of the IFA, Wendy's was ranked third in *Entrepreneur* magazine's 1987 "Franchise 500" and sixth in *Venture* magazine's 1986 "Franchise 100." In December 1985, *Restaurants & Institutions* magazine published its sixth annual Tastes of America Survey and named Wendy's the most popular hamburger restaurant for the fifth year in a row (from a field of seventy-four chains). The company has received numerous awards and honors nationwide and was a recent national sponsor of Children's Miracle Network Telethon. The company has only a limited number of franchise opportunities open but wants to expand operations throughout the United States and in Canada.

GETTING MORE INFORMATION

The franchise information packet contains a copy of the latest annual report, a preliminary information sheet, and a questionnaire. In the second stage of the application process you'll receive an FTC information offering, authorization for release of your financial information, and an eight-page application form. For details, contact:

Franchise Application Specialist
Wendy's Old Fashioned Hamburgers
Wendy's International, Inc.
P.O. Box 256
Dublin, OH   43017
(614) 764–3100

Wicks 'N' Sticks

BUSINESS: candles
and home-accessory
retailer
FOUNDED: 1968
FRANCHISED: 1968
START-UP
INVESTMENT:
$150,000–$200,000

		AS OF		PROJECTED BY	
		1/1/85	1/1/86	1/1/87	1/1/88
NO. OF UNITS					
OWNED BY:	COMPANY	9	9	1	1
	FRANCHISEES	246	280	318	353
LOCATED:	IN U.S.	255	289	314	339
	OUTSIDE U.S.	0	0	5	15
TOTAL:		255	289	319	354
NO. OF STATES W/ UNITS		41	42	42	42

THE BUSINESS

A growing number of consumers see their homes as a retreat from their hectic work lives and the demands of the outside world. Wicks 'N' Sticks retailers capitalize on this trend by emphasizing unique, quality home decorations and the vivid, warm touch of candles. Each store offers an aromatic display of candles with brass, glass, and silk floral accessories. More than thirty shades and scents of candles are designed to appeal to the discriminating yet cost-conscious shopper. The company pleases its franchisees, too. In a recent poll more than 90 percent of Wicks 'N' Sticks owners said they would like to purchase another franchise. The total annual dollar volume of Wicks 'N' Sticks franchise operations for 1985 was over $58 million, with average gross sales per unit at $232,326.

WHAT IT TAKES

Your franchise fee will be $27,500, and the ten-year agreement, with ten-year renewal increments, will establish an exclusive territory within your specific shopping mall. Additional franchise units also cost $27,500 for each. You will pay 6 percent of the gross sales to the company as an ongoing royalty fee.

Your total start-up cost will range from $150,000 to $200,000. This total cost includes, besides the franchise fee, approximately $25,000 for display fixtures, equipment, freight, and storage; $79,500 for construction and leasehold improvements; $35,000 for merchandise and supplies; and $10,000 for working capital. The total estimated cost will vary depending on your geographic location, store size, and other considerations. The company will assist you with financing, either directly through WNS or indirectly through conventional Small Business Administration loans. Previous experience is not necessary. You may hire a manager to run your store, but Wicks 'N' Sticks would prefer that you manage it.

GETTING STARTED

The company will help you choose a site. Your Wicks 'N' Sticks shop will require about 800 to 1,000 square feet in high-traffic areas in major shopping malls. Company real estate experts will help you negotiate favorable lease rates. Construction subsidies are available, and you'll have a uniform layout and decorating scheme to follow. Your regional franchise director and new-store coordinator will assist you in stocking the original inventory and in acquiring all your Wicks 'N' Sticks logo-marked bags, boxes, and other supplies.

As the owner-manager, you'll receive one week of classroom training at the corporate headquarters. This covers merchandising, marketing, purchasing, bookkeeping, inventory, selling, and employee management. You and all your store employees—usually one full-time and five part-time people—will also receive nine days of operational and merchandising training in the first weeks of business. You can have your grand opening within two to three months after the franchise purchase.

MAKING IT WORK

There is no charge for the grand-opening materials, press materials, and the marketing manual. Other materials—such as brochures, mailers, special signs, and seasonal promotional materials—can be purchased. You'll also be able to buy newspaper and telephone-book ads. Wicks 'N' Sticks merchandising experts travel the world to find original, finely-crafted products; the company's product-development teams produce new items; and visual-merchandising experts develop eye-catching store displays. You'll benefit, too, from the company's merchandising system and volume discounts.

Wicks 'N' Sticks holds annual national conferences, biannual regional conferences, and both one-day seminars and citywide franchise meetings every other month. You receive the company newsletter four times a year, and product and company updates about that often. Monthly teleconferences are a unique additional communication link between the head office and franchisees. You will get policy, management, and customer-service manuals, as well as forms and systems for controlling inventory and expenses. Regional and headquarters resource persons will provide you with both ongoing advice and onsite troubleshooting. Wicks 'N' Sticks also sponsors a franchisee insurance package with property, general-liability, major-medical, dental, and worker's compensation coverage. The company recognizes franchisee achievement with various awards.

COMMENTS

An IFA member, Wicks 'N' Sticks was ranked 94th in *Venture* magazine's 1986 "Franchise 100" and 122nd in *Entrepreneur* magazine's 1987 "Franchise 500." The parent company, WNS, Inc., is publicly held and also franchises Deck the Walls, Prints 'N' Things and Wallpapers to Go. The company will make an earnings claim document available during a potential franchisee's personal interview. Wicks 'N' Sticks wants to expand in all states except Alaska and in Canada.

GETTING MORE INFORMATION

The franchise information packet includes two posters showing interiors of the company's shops, ten pages of information, a pre-stamped inquiry card, and a confidential personal profile form. For more information, write or call:

    Houghton B. Hutcheson
    Vice-President, Franchise Development
    WNS, Inc.
    P.O. Box 4586
    Houston, TX   77210–4586
    (800)   231–6337 or (713)   890–5900 (call collect in Texas)

The Window Man

BUSINESS: vinyl replacement windows and doors
FOUNDED: 1983
FRANCHISED: 1983
START-UP INVESTMENT: $35,000

		AS OF		PROJECTED BY	
NO. OF UNITS		1/1/85	1/1/86	1/1/87	1/1/88
OWNED BY:	COMPANY	0	0	0	0
	FRANCHISEES	20	40	60	100
LOCATED:	IN U.S.	20	40	60	100
	OUTSIDE U.S.	0	0	0	0
TOTAL:		20	40	60	100
NO. OF STATES W/ UNITS		1	3	6	9

THE BUSINESS

With 70 percent of U.S. housing at least seventeen years old, professional remodeling—a $58.4 billion business in 1986—is a growing field. Replacing windows and doors is the number one priority in this field. The total dollar volume for window and door replacements combined has increased from $5.8 billion in 1982 to $6.5 billion in 1983 to its present $7 billion.

The Window Man leads the field with affordably priced, European-designed, thermally improved, solid vinyl replacement windows and doors featuring insulated glass and a wireless security system approved by the Federal Communications Commission. Field testing in the southeastern United States proved that The Window Man products decrease utility costs up to 50 percent. If the 30-percent reduction guaranteed by the company does not occur, the customer will receive up to $500 difference in cash from the company during the first year.

After installation of ten million The Window Man windows in the past twenty-five years, the company's basic design of custom shop vinyl windows is still considered to be the tightest, toughest, best-engineered, most maintenance-free on the market. A skilled The Window Man craftsman customizes each window separately, building from the precise measurement of the opening. In 1985 the total dollar volume of The Window Man franchises was $4,876,000, with average gross sales of $243,800 for each franchise and average net income of $61,000.

WHAT IT TAKES

You'll need $25,000 to cover the initial franchise fee, which covers a renewable five-year agreement, plus another $10,000 for working capital. By using an established company relationship with Bank of America, you may be able to finance your franchise fee. Six percent of your gross sales will go to the company as an ongoing royalty fee and an additional $300 or 1 percent of your monthly gross, whichever is higher, for advertising. Your franchise territory will be based on population. Passive ownership is allowed, and master franchises are available. No previous experience in installing windows and doors is required.

GETTING STARTED

Company personnel will help you with site selection. They often recommend a small home office or a sales office of about 1,000 square feet in rental property, with the expectation that you'll eventually grow into a larger office with a showroom. At first you'll also need a storage space—such as your garage or a miniwarehouse—to house completed windows prior to installation.

For the first month you'll get continuous education and training, both at the home office and in your own territory. During five days of classroom work in Durham, North Carolina, you'll learn about The Window Man doors and windows, generating leads, the mechanics of sales presentations, and effective, efficient business procedures. After that, company personnel will come to your office to help you with sales, advertising, accounting, and the technical areas of your business. You'll need to hire three part-time employees. You can begin business within a month and a half after signing your franchise agreement.

MAKING IT WORK

Using your ongoing advertising fee, the company's vice-president for advertising directs an advertising agency to design television and radio commercials, and newspaper ads. You'll also get special-event displays and sales brochures for home shows and county and state fairs. The company advertising is targeted at North Carolina, South Carolina, and Georgia, with Virginia next on the list and Florida, Tennessee, and West Virginia in the wings.

The Window Man's lead-management program both generates and tracks leads. The company uses customer survey information to target its promotion budget. Every week you'll communicate with headquarters by telephone, and sales and field representatives will visit your business as needed. At required quarterly one-day seminars you'll get updates on industry changes, product and technical research, marketing, and performance reports and incentives. You and your key employees will attend ongoing management workshops.

You can also update your skills by taking advantage of the company's National Library of Technical Information which lists seminars being conducted by associations across the country. You'll receive a quarterly company newsletter and industry updates as well as monthly technical and company-information updates. The company makes available their books and tapes on the remodeling industry, which you can use at home. You'll receive manuals on policy, management procedure, and customer service; and the company will provide stationery, envelopes, business cards, contracts, invoices, purchase orders, and job signs—all purchased in volume to save you money.

Unless you arrange approved alternatives, you'll sell only company products through the centralized merchandising program. The company is developing plans for an assembly factory in each region to manufacture the products quickly. You can use your own installers or take advantage of company-recommended ones. Your customers' purchases can be financed through the company. The Window Man awards outstanding franchisees and sponsors a major-medical insurance package.

COMMENTS

The Window Man was ranked 411th in *Entrepreneur* magazine's 1987 "Franchise 500." A member of the IFA since 1985, the company provides an earnings claim document upon request. The Window Man contributes to the Special Olympics. The company wants to expand in selected southeastern states.

GETTING MORE INFORMATION

The franchise information packet contains a brochure describing the windows, three pages of company information, a list of current franchise owners, short biographies of several company officials, several magazine reprints, a U.S. Department of Commerce reprint of *Qualified Remodeler,* and a four-page franchisee application. For more details, write to:

Conrad L. Harris
Chairman of the Board
Windows of Opportunity
711 Rigsbee Avenue
Durham, NC 27701
(800) 672–5736 (in North Carolina)
(800) 458–5858 (in Georgia, South Carolina, Tennessee,
   Virginia, Maryland, Washington, D.C., Ohio, Delaware, and
   West Virginia)
(919) 682–5515 (call collect)

World Bazaar

		AS OF		PROJECTED BY	
BUSINESS: imported- gifts and home- furnishings store	NO. OF UNITS	1/1/85	1/1/86	1/1/87	1/1/88
	OWNED BY: COMPANY	189	189	190	200
FOUNDED: 1965	FRANCHISEES	90	121	150	180
FRANCHISED: 1968	LOCATED: IN U.S.	279	310	340	380
START-UP	OUTSIDE U.S.	0	0	0	0
INVESTMENT:	TOTAL:	279	310	340	380
$130,700–$247,800	NO. OF STATES W/ UNITS	28	29	30	32

THE BUSINESS

World Bazaar stores offer an amazing collection of gifts, furniture, decorating accessories, and housewares imported from around the world at bargain prices. The company estimates that over 20 million Americans have purchased something for their homes at World Bazaar. Recently, the parent company, Munford, Inc., established manufacturing facilities in the Far East to insure that the quality and design of their merchandise remains unsurpassed in the import retail industry.

WHAT IT TAKES

You'll need $50,000 for the initial franchise fee. You can pay $5,000 down, and the company will finance the remaining $45,000 for five years. Your franchise agreement will apply for the same length of time as the lease of your location and will be renewable on the same terms. You'll be guaranteed an exclusive territory within a one-mile radius of your store. You can buy a second franchise for a fee of $25,000 and subsequent stores for $15,000 each.

In addition to the franchise fee, the total investment requires about $75,000 for leasehold improvements in a new mall and $15,000 for those in a strip shopping center, $18,700 to $20,800 for equipment and fixtures, $4,000 for supplies, $8,000 for payroll, and $80,000 to $90,000 for merchandise and inventory. Your total initial investment will run between $130,700 and $247,800, with at least $100,000 in cash. You may pay the balance over a five-year period at the prime interest rate plus 1 percent. Munford, Inc., will finance up to $50,000 in merchandise and fixtures from its distribution center. You'll pay a royalty of 8 percent on the first $1 million in net sales and 5 percent on sales over $1 million. The company prefers that you manage your own store. Neither experience nor knowledge in the industry is required; however, retail, buying, or accounting experience is helpful.

GETTING STARTED

Your franchise fee will cover the cost of such expenses as store blueprints, lease negotiation, construction, leasehold-improvement recommendations, preopening merchandising, opening supervision, and a grand-opening advertising package. A representative of World Bazaar's real estate department will visit your chosen site, review it, and make suggestions for improvements. Your store should be in a mall or strip shopping center and have between 3,000 and 5,000 square feet of floor space. The company will help you decorate your store; lease or purchase the needed equipment, furniture, and fixtures; and lay out your merchandise in attractive displays.

World Bazaar recommends that you attend a two-day classroom training at the company headquarters in Atlanta, Georgia, and one week of hands-on training at a store already in operation. You'll learn about merchandise presentation, open-to-buy ordering techniques, item control, item promotion, and advertising techniques. You'll also be given a tour of a typical store and of the company facilities. You can open your store within three to four months after your franchise purchase. You'll need two full-time and four part-time employees.

MAKING IT WORK

World Bazaar will advertise for you, free of charge, in newspapers and magazines and on the radio. You'll also be able to get slides or videotape packages, point-of-purchase displays, seasonal promotional displays, signs, banners, presentation books, and catalogs. Representatives offer advice on merchandising, advertising, and display techniques on an as-needed basis. The company's 500,000-square-feet distribution center, located just outside Atlanta, has over 6,000 items from more than forty countries. When you order your merchandise from the distribution center, it will be quickly and efficiently dispatched by transportation coordinators at ATL, Inc., another division of Munford, Inc. The central purchasing program, as well as the company's own brand of merchandise, will save you money. You may also buy products from outside domestic sources, and the company will supply you with auxiliary domestic vendor information. World Bazaar representatives regularly visit other countries to find new and unique merchandise.

The company holds biannual national conventions as well as biannual city- or areawide franchise meetings. You'll receive the company's annual magazine, quarterly newsletter, periodic updates, and surveys once or twice a year. If problems or questions arise, headquarters and regional personnel and field representatives are available for financial counseling, operational assistance, and onsite troubleshooting. You'll be provided with a policy manual; systems for bookkeeping, inventory, and personnel; and all necessary forms. Franchisees and their employees enjoy company-sponsored insurance packages offering life, major-medical, dental, and disability coverage. World Bazaar also sponsors recognition for franchisees.

COMMENTS

World Bazaar was ranked 126th in *Entrepreneur* magazine's 1987 "Franchise 500." The parent company, Munford, Inc., was founded in 1909 and runs furniture manufacturing plants in Thailand and the Philippines. With plans to convert many company-owned stores to franchise status, the company is seeking new franchisees in most states.

GETTING MORE INFORMATION

The franchise information packet contains details on the World Bazaar system, answers to questions most often asked by franchisees, color photographs of World Bazaar shops and merchandise, an application and financial statement form, a list of stores and warehouses, and a franchise offering circular for prospective franchisees. For more information, contact:

William A. Richardson
Director of Sales—Franchise Operations
World Bazaar, A Division of Munford, Inc.
1860 Peachtree Road, Northwest
Atlanta, GA   30309
(404)   766–5300

Zack's Famous Frozen Yogurt

BUSINESS: frozen-			AS OF		PROJECTED BY	
yogurt store	NO. OF UNITS		1/1/85	1/1/86	1/1/87	1/1/88
FOUNDED: 1977	OWNED BY: COMPANY		5	3	6	9
FRANCHISED: 1977		FRANCHISEES	31	47	106	180
START-UP	LOCATED:	IN U.S.	36	50	107	179
INVESTMENT:		OUTSIDE U.S.	0	0	5	10
$100,600–$117,200	TOTAL:		36	50	112	189
	NO. OF STATES W/ UNITS		5	8	25	40

THE BUSINESS

Frozen yogurt had its beginning in the summer of 1972, when H. P. Hood, a food-marketing company in Boston, was commissioned by a fast-food outlet to develop a new and different product that would appeal to its customers—young people interested in natural foods. Hood invented Frogurt, which was quickly in high demand. The demand exploded when Bloomingdales' department store introduced the frosty treat in its 40 Carrots Restaurant in 1975. Sales of frozen yogurt jumped nearly 700 percent in 1976.

Zack's offers a full line of frozen desserts, including banana splits, sundaes, smoothies, malts, shakes, cups, and cones of yogurt with fresh fruit and a variety of nut toppings. Zack's is simply a dessert store, which means no extensive cooking, bagging, or complicated procedures. The yogurt is prepared fresh each morning in the yogurt machine and dispensed in one easy step. The total volume of business for Zack's franchises in 1985 was $11.5 million. The average gross sales per franchise were $170,000, with a net income of $35,000.

WHAT IT TAKES

Your franchise fee will be $17,000. The term of your agreement will be twenty years, with a twenty-year renewal period. You'll get an exclusive territory for a one-mile radius around your store. Your range of investment will be $100,600 to $117,200, depending on your lease or purchase price and improvements. The entire amount must be in cash. Your start-up costs beyond the franchise fee will include $40,000 to $42,000 for equipment; $32,000 to $40,500 for leasehold improvements; $2,500 to $4,000 for leases and deposits; $2,000 to $3,000 for inventory; $3,500 to $4,500 for working capital; and $3,600 to $6,200 for advertising, insurance, and training.

The fee for additional franchises is negotiable, and master franchises are available. You would not be required to operate your shop personally, but the company will recommend that you or a responsible manager spend at least forty hours per week onsite. You will pay a royalty of 5 percent of your weekly gross sales (after sales tax) and 3 percent for your advertising fee.

GETTING STARTED

Your shop will be 1,000 to 1,500 square feet in a shopping center, mall, office building, or other accessible location. The company will perform a demographic analysis to help you select a site and will send skilled personnel to handle your lease negotiation. Zack's provides prototype construction drawings and details on signs, equipment, and installation. The trademarks, distinctive signs, unusual color schemes, and efficient layout and design create the Zack's total identity program. The company's established relationships with manufacturers will enable you to save money on equipment purchases.

Training will begin with your home study of the operations manual, a complete guide to day-to-day operations, policies, and procedures. After mastering the manual, you'll begin hands-on training in an operating Zack's shop. During this period, you will become familiar with every aspect of physically operating the franchise, including customer relations, daily report forms, cleanliness standards, product preparation, and cash-register procedures. When you get back home, you'll receive help in recruiting your one full-time and five or six part-time staff. You can open your Zack's shop about three months after signing the agreement. Operations specialists will be on hand to coordinate the grand opening, help you refine the operations of your staff, assist in training new employees, place your advertising, and coordinate your promotional campaign.

MAKING IT WORK

You will get brochures, displays, signs, banners, and other marketing materials for your Zack's store. Ads, mailers, radio and television commercials, and seasonal promotional materials are available on a co-op basis. You'll be able to attend seminars twice a year, and the company plans to initiate regular national conferences. Periodically you'll receive updates about the company and frozen yogurt industry, as well as information of interest to your customers.

Zack's will provide consultation and advice, as needed, on new trends, advertising and promotional campaigns, and products and supplies. You'll receive an operations manual, which contains a complete review of all the major business functions and the valuable trade secrets of special recipes and procedures created by the company. You'll get standardized forms to help you with inventory control, accounting, and daily and weekly reporting; and you'll enjoy volume discounts on supplies and products through a central purchasing program. You'll be required to sell the company's line of frozen yogurt, but you can purchase toppings and other supplies from outside sources.

COMMENTS

A member of the IFA since 1982, Zack's was ranked 213th in *Entrepreneur* magazine's 1987 "Franchise 500." The company is seeking franchisees in all states and several foreign countries.

GETTING MORE INFORMATION

The franchise information packet contains a brochure describing the frozen-yogurt industry, the franchise system, and the advantages of a Zack's franchise; three pages of questions and answers; a cost breakdown; the IFA code of ethics; and an application. For more information, call or write:

Sam Holt
President
Zack's Famous Frozen Yogurt
P.O. Box 8522
Metairie, LA   70011–8522
(504)   836–7080

Ziebart Corporation

BUSINESS:
  automobile-
  appearance and
  -protection services
FOUNDED: 1954
FRANCHISED: 1962
START-UP INVESTMENT:
$48,000–$58,000 (plus land and building)

NO. OF UNITS		AS OF		PROJECTED BY	
		1/1/85	1/1/86	1/1/87	1/1/88
OWNED BY: COMPANY		22	23	26	30
FRANCHISEES		595	591	632	677
LOCATED: IN U.S.		364	370	384	403
CANADA		253	244	274	304
TOTAL:		617	614	658	707
NO. OF STATES W/ UNITS		35	36	39	43

THE BUSINESS

With the ever-higher cost of new cars, automobile buyers are increasingly conscious of taking care of their investment. This desire creates a strong market for companies such as Ziebart that specialize in automobile-appearance and -protection services such as rust, paint, and interior protection; radiator or air conditioning maintenance and repair; and related automotive services such as sun roofs, running boards, pickup truck bedliners, and vehicle reconditioning. The company continues to add new services to give their franchisees greater diversification. Ziebart is the largest franchisor of radiator and air-conditioning service centers in North America.

WHAT IT TAKES

You will need $15,000 for the initial franchise fee, which will cover a nonexclusive territory, valid for ten years. Your total investment will be $48,000 to $58,000, plus the cost of land and building—all of which must be in cash. Additional franchises may be bought for $6,000 each; master franchises are not available. You may be an owner-investor, but Ziebart does not recommend the practice. Your ongoing royalty fee will be 8 percent of weekly gross sales, plus 5 percent for advertising. Prior experience in the automotive field is not necessary.

GETTING STARTED

Ziebart will help you select a site; lay out and decorate the facility; lease or purchase furniture, fixtures, and equipment; and acquire supplies and merchandise, including a complete package of patented, custom-built rustproofing tools. Ziebart also offers national fleet sales assistance. The typical Ziebart location is 4,000 to 6,000 square feet, located in a shopping center or freestanding building. You will be expected to follow the company's building and showroom-decor standards and to use trademarks on office materials such as invoices. Your business will be staffed by five full-time and two part-time employees. Eighteen days of training for all employees will begin at the Troy, Michigan, headquarters with both classroom and hands-on experience covering technical subjects (all Ziebart products and services), and sales and management (general and specific sales and management techniques). This will be followed by five days of on-the-job education for you in your store and five days of training for all employees during start-up. You can be in business within three months after buying a Ziebart franchise. Company representatives will be on hand to help with your grand opening.

MAKING IT WORK

For your advertising fee you will be provided with newspaper ads, black-and-white and four-color magazine ads, telephone-book ads, presentation books, catalogs, television and radio commercials, seasonal promotional materials, press releases, and a public-relations/marketing manual. Co-op funds are available for signs. Ziebart sponsors coordinated multiregional, national advertising campaigns to boost business. The company sponsors an annual national convention, semiannual regional conferences, monthly areawide franchise meetings, periodic one-day seminars, and onsite training sessions as needed.

The company distributes a newsletter every two months and updates on products, service, company information, and market trends as needed. Ziebart conducts surveys as needed and recognizes top performance among franchisees. Administrative backup tools include headquarters and regional resource persons; regular onsite visits; onsite troubleshooting; manuals on policy, management procedure, and customer service; order forms; a toll-free order-desk telephone number; and a computerized billing system. The company maintains research and development departments to test new types of services and to conduct laboratory testing of competitive sealants. You will be required to purchase sealant and some other products from the home office. Ziebart has divisions that produce merchandise and equipment, a central purchasing program offering volume discounts, a centralized merchandising system, and company brands. The company does not offer any group insurance plans.

COMMENTS

Ziebart was ranked 107th in *Entrepreneur* magazine's 1987 "Franchise 500." A division of Ziebart International Corporation, the Ziebart Corporation has been a member of the IFA since 1964. An earnings claim document is available during a potential franchisee's personal interview.

GETTING MORE INFORMATION

The franchise information packet contains a brochure with answers to frequently asked questions, a list of advantages Ziebart dealers enjoy, steps to a Ziebart grand opening, and a four-page application form. For details, contact:

Richard C. Johnson
Director of Licensing
Ziebart Corporation
P.O. Box 1290
Troy, MI   48007–1290
(800)   521–1313 or (313)   588–4100

RESOURCES

Government Offices

FEDERAL TRADE COMMISSION

The Washington, D.C., office of the FTC keeps files on complaints and legal action against franchise companies. Call or write for information.

Mr. Neil Blickman
Federal Trade Commission
Bureau of Consumer Protection
6th Street and Pennsylvania Avenue, NW
Washington, D.C.   20580
(202)   326-3038

SMALL BUSINESS ADMINISTRATION REGIONAL OFFICES

The SBA provides a variety of assistance to small businesses. Contact your regional office for the office nearest you.

450 Golden Gate Avenue
Room 15307
San Francisco, CA   94102
(415)   556–7487

26 Federal Plaza
Room 29–118
New York, NY   10278
(212)   264–7772

1375 Peachtree Street, NE
Fifth Floor
Atlanta, GA   30367
(404)   881–4999

231 St. Asaphs Road
Suite 640
Philadelphia, PA   19004
(215)   596–5889

230 South Dearborn Street
Room 510
Chicago, IL   60604
(312)   353–0359

8625 King George Drive
Building C
Dallas, TX   75235
(214)   767–7643

60 Batterymarch Street
Tenth Floor
Boston, MA   02110
(617)   223–3204

2615 Fourth Avenue
Room 440
Seattle, WA   98121
(206)   442–5676

911 Walnut Street
Thirteenth Floor
Kansas City, MO   64106
(816)   374–5288

State Franchise Regulatory Agencies

Fifteen states require franchise companies that want to do business in their states to register and file disclosure statements. Disclosure statements must be kept on file at the agency and made available to prospective franchise buyers before the payment of money and the signing of an agreement. The state agencies are good resources.

If you live in a state that does not have a state agency specifically responsible for franchising, call the state attorney general's office to inquire which state agency can provide information about the franchise-company practices in the state.

Here is the listing of the fifteen states with agencies.

Department of Corporations
1025 P Street
Sacramento, CA   95814
(916) 445-7205

Agency of Commerce and
    Consumer Affairs
1010 Richards Street
Honolulu, HI   96813
(808) 548-5317

Assistant Attorney General
Chief, Franchise Division
Office of Attorney General
500 South Second Street
Springfield, IL   62706
(217) 782-1090

Deputy Commissioner
Franchise Division
Indiana Securities Division
Secretary of State
012 State House
Indianapolis, IN   46204
(317) 232-6681

Maryland Division of Securities
Second Floor, The Munsey
    Building
7 North Calvert Street
Baltimore, MD   21202
(301) 576-6360

Office of Franchise and Agent
    Licensing
Michigan Corporation and
    Securities Bureau
Department of Commerce
P.O. Box 30222
Lansing, MI   48909
(517) 334-6302

Securities Division
Minnesota Department of
    Commerce
500 Metro Square Building
St. Paul, MN   55101
(612) 296-2283

Special Deputy Attorney
  General
Bureau of Investor Protection
  and Securities
New York State Department of
  Law
120 Broadway
New York, NY   10005
(212) 341-2222

Franchise Examiner
Office of Securities
  Commissioner
Third Floor
Capitol Building
Bismarck, ND   58505
(701) 224-2910

Assistant Corporations
  Commissioner—Franchises
Corporation Division
Commerce Building
Salem, OR   97310
(503)   378-4387

Chief Security Examiner
Securities Section
Banking Division
100 North Main Street
Providence, RI   02903
(401)   277-2405

Franchise Administrator
Division of Securities
State Capitol
Pierre, SD   57501
(605)   773-4013

Examination Coordinator
Franchise Section
Division of Securities and
  Retail Franchising
11 South 12th Street
Richmond, VA   23219
(804)   786-7751

Registrations Attorney
Department of Licensing
Securities Division
Business and Professions
  Administration
P.O. Box 648
Olympia, WA   98504
(206)   753-6928

Franchise Investment Division
Wisconsin Securities
  Commission
P.O. Box 1768
Madison, WI   53701
(608)   266-3414

Nongovernmental Organizations

The International Franchise Association (IFA) is a trade association representing more than 500 franchise companies. Founded in 1960, it requires its members to follow a code of ethics, which is reprinted after the listing of publications.

International Franchise Association
1350 New York Avenue, NW
Suite 900
Washington, D.C.   20005
(202)   628–8000

Organized in 1977, the National Alliance of Franchisees is composed of eleven national franchise associations (such as 7-Eleven, Dairy Queen, Midas Muffler, etc.) and many individual franchise owners. It represents the rights and interests of the franchisees.

National Alliance of Franchisees
7713 Barlowe Road
Landover, MD   20785
(301)   386–4817

Publications

From the International Franchise Association:

Answers to the 21 Most Commonly Asked Questions about Franchising
14 pages; free

Investigate before Investing
By Robert E. Kishell and Carl E. Zwisler III
32 pages; $3.00

Is Franchising for You?
By Robert K. McIntosh
20 pages; $2.95

From the Superintendent of Documents, U.S. Government Printing Office, Washington, D.C.   20402

Franchising the Economy (annual edition)
Prepared by Andrew Kostecka, U.S. Department of Commerce
90+ pages; $3.50

Franchise Opportunities Handbook (annual edition)
Compiled by Andrew Kostecka, U.S. Department of Commerce
400+ pages; $15.00

From the Small Business Administration, P.O. Box 15434, Ft. Worth, TX   76119. All booklets are free.

Franchised Businesses
Thinking about Going into Business
Checklist for Going into Business
Learning about Your Market
The ABC's of Borrowing
Marketing for Small Business

From the Council of Better Business Bureaus, Inc., 1515 Wilson Boulevard, Arlington, VA   (703)   276–0100

Selecting a Franchise
12 pages; free

Code of Ethics

The International Franchise Association requires its members to abide by the following six guidelines:

Each member company pledges:

1. In the advertisement and grant of franchises or dealerships a member shall comply with all applicable laws and regulations and the member's offering circulars shall be complete, accurate and not misleading with respect to the franchisee's or dealer's investment, the obligations of the member and the franchise or dealer under the franchise or dealership and all material facts relating to the franchise or dealership.

2. All matters material to the member's franchise or dealership shall be contained in one or more written agreements, which shall clearly set forth the terms of the relationship and the respective rights and obligations of the parties.

3. A member shall select and accept only those franchisees or dealers who, upon reasonable investigation, appear to possess the basic skills, education, experience, personal characteristics and financial resources requisite to conduct the franchised business or dealership and meet the obligations of the franchise or dealer under the franchise and other agreements. There shall be no dis-

crimination in the granting of franchises based solely on race, color, religion, national origin or sex. However, this in no way prohibits a franchisor from granting franchises to prospective franchisees as part of a program to make franchises available to persons lacking the capital, training, business experience, or other qualifications ordinarily required of franchisees or any other affirmative action program adopted by the franchisor.

4. A member shall provide reasonable guidance to its franchisees or dealers in a manner consistent with its franchise agreement.

5. Fairness shall characterize all dealings between a member and its franchisees or dealers. A member shall make every good faith effort to resolve complaints by and disputes with its franchisees or dealers through direct communication and negotiation. To the extent reasonably appropriate in the circumstances, a member shall give its franchisee or dealer notice of, and a reasonable opportunity to cure, a breach of their contractual relationship.

6. No member shall engage in the pyramid system of distribution. A pyramid is a system wherein a buyer's future compensation is expected to be based primarily upon recruitment of new participants, rather than upon the sale of products or services.

DIRECTORY OF FRANCHISES BY BUSINESS TYPE

AUTOMOTIVE

American International Rent A Car
Dr. Vinyl
Endrust
Grease Monkey
Holiday-Payless Rent-A-Car
MAACO Auto Painting &
  Bodyworks
Meineke Discount Mufflers
Miracle Auto Painting & Body
  Repair

P&D/Premier Auto Parts
The Pit Pros
Precision Tune
Rent-A-Dent
Sunshine Polishing Systems
Tuff-Kote Dinol
Ziebart

BUILDING & HOUSING

Eldorado Stone
Lincoln Log Homes
Lindal Cedar Homes

Mr. Build
The Window Man

BUSINESS SERVICES

Comprehensive Accounting
  Corporation
Corporate Finance Associates
Corporate Investment Business
  Brokers
Debit One Mobile Bookkeeping
Dunhill Personnel
Foliage Design Systems
Foremost Sales Promotions
Health Force

Management Recruiters
  International
Mifax
Money Mailer
Norrell
Paul Davis Systems
ROMAC
Service Personnel
TriMark
UBI Business Brokers
Uniforce Temporary Services

CLEANING, MAINTENANCE, AND REPAIR SERVICES

Bath Genie
Chem-Dry
Dial One
Duraclean
Jani-King
Langenwalter Dye Concept
The Maids International
Merry Maids
Miracle Method

Molly Maid
Rainbow International Carpet
  Dyeing & Cleaning Company
RainSoft Water Conditioning
  Company
ServiceMaster
Servpro
Steamatic

COMPUTER	Entré Computer Centers MicroAge Computer Stores	
DIET & HEALTH	Diet Center Dwight Dental Care First Optometry Eye Care Centers Miracle-Ear	Pearle Vision Centers Slender Center Suddenly Slender, *The* Body Wrap & Health Center
EDUCATION	Gymboree	Sylvan Learning Centers

FAST FOODS	Baskin-Robbins Ice Cream
	  Company
	Blimpie
	Bojangles'
	Brownies Fried Chicken
	Dairy Queen
	Dunkin' Donuts
	Gelato Classico Italian Ice Cream
	Happy Joe's Pizza & Ice Cream
	  Parlor
	Hardee's
	I Can't Believe It's Yogurt
	Ice Cream Churn
	Island Snow Hawaii
	Jack In The Box
	Long John Silver's Seafood
	  Shoppes
		Mazzio's Pizza
		McDonald's
		Papa Aldo's Take & Bake Pizza
		  Shops
		Pizza Inn
		Rax Restaurants
		Round Table Pizza Restaurants
		Roy Rogers
		Schlotzsky's
		Taco del Sol
		Taco John's
		TacoTime
		Tubby's Sub Shops
		Wendy's
		Zack's Famous Frozen Yogurt

HAIR CARE	Command Performance Fantastic Sam's	Great Clips HairCrafters
HOTELS & MOTELS	Holiday Inn	Scottish Inns/Red Carpet Inn/ Master Hosts Inns Sheraton Inns
LAWN & LANDSCAPING SERVICES	Nitro-Green Professional Lawn and Tree Care	Spring-Green Lawn Care The Weed Man
PRINTING & COPYING	American Speedy Printing Centers Kwik-Kopy Printing PIP Postal Instant Press	PrintMasters Sir Speedy Printing Centers
PUBLISHING	Create-A-Book TV Scene	TV Tempo
REAL ESTATE	Century 21 Help-U-Sell HouseMaster of America	Realty World RE/MAX

RESTAURANTS

Boston Pizza
The Ground Round

K-Bob's

RETAIL SHOPS

Budget Tapes & Records
Coast to Coast Total Hardware
ColorTyme
Deck The Walls
Docktor Pet Centers
Flowerama
In 'N' Out Food Stores
Just Pants
Kits Cameras
Little Professor Book Centers
The Medicine Shoppe
M.G.M. Liquor Warehouse

National Video
Nation-wide General Rental
    Centers
Scandia Down Shops
7-Eleven
Sounds Easy
Spring Crest Drapery Centers
Stained Glass Overlay
United Consumers Club
U.S. Tech
Wicks 'N' Sticks
World Bazaar

SERVICE BUSINESSES

Duds 'N Suds
H&R Block
Mail Boxes Etc. USA
One Hour Moto-Photo

Packy the Shipper
P.k.g.'s
Sara Care
Security Alliance

SPORTS & RECREATION

Athletic Attic
Fleet Feet
Grand Slam USA
KOA Kampgrounds of America

Putt-Putt Golf Courses
Second Sole
Sport-About
Sport Shack

TRAVEL AGENCIES

Travel Pros
Travel ServicentreS

Uniglobe Travel

DIRECTORY OF FRANCHISES
BY INVESTMENT AMOUNT

$10,000 AND UNDER

Chem-Dry
Create-A-Book
Dial One
First Optometry Eye Care Centers
Foliage Design Systems
Help-U-Sell
H&R Block
Ice Cream Churn
Jani-King

Lincoln Log Homes
Lindal Cedar Homes
Mr. Build
Packy the Shipper
Realty World
RE/MAX
Service Personnel
Sunshine Polishing Systems

$10,001–$25,000

Bath Genie
Century 21
Debit One Mobile Bookkeeping
Dr. Vinyl
Duraclean
First Optometry Eye Care Centers
Foliage Design Systems
Help-U-Sell
Langenwalter Dye Concept
Lincoln Log Homes
Lindal Cedar Homes
Merry Maids
Mifax
Miracle-Ear

Miracle Method
Molly Maid
Money Mailer
Rainbow International Carpet
    Dyeing & Cleaning
Rainsoft Water Conditioning
    Company
Realty World
RE/MAX
ServiceMaster
Servpro
Spring-Green Lawn Care
Sunshine Polishing Systems
TV Tempo

$25,001–$50,000

American International Rent A Car
Budget Tapes & Records
ColorTyme
Command Performance
Corporate Finance Associates
Diet Center
Dunhill Personnel
Duraclean International
Eldorado Stone
Endrust
Fantastic Sam's
First Optometry Eye Care Centers
Flowerama
Grease Monkey
Gymboree

Help-U-Sell
Holiday-Payless Rent-A-Car
HouseMaster of America
Island Snow Hawaii
Lincoln Log Homes
Lindal Cedar Homes
The Maids International
Mail Boxes Etc. USA
Management Recruiters
    International
Meineke Discount Mufflers
Merry Maids
Money Mailer
National Video
Norrell

Nitro-Green Professional Lawn and Tree Care
One Hour Moto-Photo
Paul Davis Systems
P&D/Premier Auto Parts
Pearle Vision Centers
P.k.g.'s
RainSoft Water Conditioning Company
RE/MAX
ROMAC
Sara Care
7-Eleven
Slender Center
Spring Crest Drapery Centers
Spring-Green Lawn Care

Stained Glass Overlay
Steamatic
Sunshine Polishing Systems
Sylvan Learning Centers
Taco John's
Travel Pros
TriMark
Tuff-Kote Dinol
TV Scene
TV Tempo
UBI Business Brokers
Uniforce Temporary Services
The Weed Man
The Window Man
Ziebart

$50,001–$100,000

American International Rent A Car
Baskin-Robbins Ice Cream Company
Blimpie
Brownies Fried Chicken
Budget Tapes & Records
ColorTyme
Comprehensive Accounting Corporation
Corporate Investment Business Brokers
Dunhill Personnel
Eldorado Stone
Fantastic Sam's
First Optometry Eye Care Centers
Fleet Feet
Flowerama
Foremost Sales Promotions
Gelato Classico Italian Ice Cream
Grease Monkey
Great Clips
HairCrafters
Health Force
Holiday-Payless Rent-A-Car
In 'N' Out Food Stores
Island Snow Hawaii
Kits Cameras
KOA Kampgrounds of America
Kwik-Kopy Printing
Lincoln Log Homes
Lindal Cedar Homes
Little Professor Book Centers
The Maids International
Mail Boxes Etc. USA

The Medicine Shoppe
Money Mailer
Nation-wide General Rental Centers
National Video
Norrell
One Hour Moto-Photo
Papa Aldo's Take & Bake Pizza Shops
Pearle Vision Centers
PIP Postal Instant Press
The Pit Pros
Precision Tune
Printmasters
Putt-Putt Golf Courses
ROMAC
Scandia Down Shops
Second Sole
Security Alliance
Sounds Easy
Sport About
Sport Shack
Spring Crest Drapery Centers
Stained Glass Overlay
Suddenly Slender, *The* Body Wrap & Health Center
Sylvan Learning Centers
Taco del Sol
Taco John's
Travel Pros
Travel ServicentreS
UBI Business Brokers
United Consumers Club
Ziebart

$100,001–$250,000

American International Rent A Car
American Speedy Printing Centers
Athletic Attic
Baskin-Robbins Ice Cream
   Company
Blimpie
Boston Pizza
Brownies Fried Chicken
Coast to Coast Total Hardware
Deck The Walls
Docktor Pet Centers
Duds 'N Suds
Dunhill Personnel
Dunkin' Donuts
Dwight Dental Care
First Optometry Eye Care Centers
Fleet Feet
Foremost Sales Promotions
Gelato Classico Italian Ice Cream
Grand Slam USA
HairCrafters
Happy Joe's Pizza & Ice Cream
   Parlor
I Can't Believe It's Yogurt
Just Pants
Kits Cameras
Lindal Cedar Homes
MAACO Auto Painting &
   Bodyworks

M.G.M. Liquor Warehouse
Miracle Auto Painting & Body
   Repair
Money Mailer
National Video
Pearle Vision Centers
Pizza Inn
Precision Tune
Putt-Putt Golf Courses
Rent-A-Dent
Round Table Pizza
Scandia Down Shops
Schlotzsky's
Second Sole
Sir Speedy Printing Centers
Sounds Easy
Sport-About
Sport Shack
Sylvan Learning Centers
Taco del Sol
Taco John's
TacoTime
Tubby's Sub Shops
Uniglobe Travel
U.S. Tech
Wicks 'N' Sticks
World Bazaar
Zack's Famous Frozen Yogurt

$250,001–$500,000

American International Rent A Car
Boston Pizza
Coast to Coast Total Hardware
Dairy Queen
Entré Computer Centers
Happy Joe's Pizza & Ice Cream
   Parlor
K-Bob's
Long John Silver's Seafood
   Shoppes

Mazzio's Pizza
McDonald's
M.G.M. Liquor Warehouse
MicroAge Computer Stores
Pearle Vision Centers
Putt-Putt Golf Courses
Round Table Pizza
Taco John's
U.S. Tech

$500,001 +

Bojangles'
Boston Pizza
Dairy Queen
Entré Computer Centers
The Ground Round
Hardee's
Holiday Inn
Jack In The Box
K-Bob's
Long John Silver's Seafood
   Shoppes

Mazzio's Pizza
Putt-Putt Golf Courses
Rax Restaurants
Roy Rogers
Scottish Inns, Red Carpet Inn,
   Master Hosts Inns
Sheraton Inns
Wendy's

DIRECTORY OF FRANCHISES BY GEOGRAPHICAL AREA

U. S. Locations

NOTE: Franchisors that are planning to increase operations in all fifty states are listed under the heading "Throughout United States."

ALABAMA

Athletic Attic
Blimpie
Bojangles'
Comprehensive Accounting
   Corporation
Corporate Investment Business
   Brokers
Create-A-Book
Debit One Mobile Bookkeeping
Deck The Walls
Docktor Pet Centers
Dr. Vinyl
Duds 'N Suds
Eldorado Stone
Entré Computer Centers
Flowerama
Foliage Design Systems
Grand Slam USA
Gymboree
HairCrafters
Health Force
Holiday-Payless Rent-A-Car
HouseMaster of America
H&R Block
I Can't Believe It's Yogurt
Just Pants
KOA Kampgrounds of America
Langenwalter Dye Concept
Little Professor Book Centers
Long John Silver's Seafood
   Shoppes
MAACO Auto Painting &
   Bodyworks
Mail Boxes Etc. USA
Mazzio's Pizza

Meineke Discount Mufflers
Mifax
Miracle Method
Miracle-Ear
Money Mailer
Mr. Build
Packy the Shipper
P&D/Premier Auto Parts
PIP Postal Instant Press
Pearle Vision Centers
P.k.g.'s
Precision Tune
Rainbow International Carpet
   Dyeing & Cleaning Company
Rax Restaurants
ROMAC
Sara Care
Scandia Down Shops
Scottish Inns, Red Carpet Inn,
   Master Hosts Inns
Servpro
Sounds Easy
Sport Shack
Steamatic
Taco John's
TacoTime
Travel Pros
TriMark
Tubby's Sub Shops
TV Scene
TV Tempo
UBI Business Brokers
Wicks 'N' Sticks
World Bazaar
Zack's Famous Frozen Yogurt

ALASKA

Athletic Attic
Budget Tapes & Records
Corporate Finance Associates
Corporate Investment Business
   Brokers
Dairy Queen
Duds 'N' Suds
Dunkin' Donuts
Foliage Design Systems
Foremost Sales Promotions
Gymboree
Holiday-Payless Rent-A-Car
I Can't Believe It's Yogurt
Ice Cream Churn
Kits Cameras
KOA Kampgrounds of America
Mail Boxes Etc. USA
Meineke Discount Mufflers
Mifax
Miracle-Ear

Papa Aldo's Take & Bake Pizza
   Shops
P&D/Premier Auto Parts
PIP Postal Instant Press
Precision Tune
Rainbow International Carpet
   Dyeing & Cleaning Company
Rax Restaurants
Sara Care
Scottish Inns, Red Carpet Inn,
   Master Hosts Inns
Servpro
Sounds Easy
Steamatic
TacoTime
Travel Pros
Travel ServicentreS
TriMark
UBI Business Brokers
Zack's Famous Frozen Yogurt

ARIZONA

Athletic Attic
Boston Pizza
Budget Tapes & Records
Coast to Coast Total Hardware
Comprehensive Accounting
   Corporation
Corporate Finance Associates
Corporate Investment Business
   Brokers
Create-A-Book
Dairy Queen
Debit One Mobile Bookkeeping
Deck The Walls
Docktor Pet Centers
Dr. Vinyl
Duds 'N Suds
Dunkin' Donuts
Eldorado Stone
Foliage Design Systems
Foremost Sales Promotions
Grand Slam USA
Great Clips
Gymboree
HairCrafters
Health Force
Holiday-Payless Rent-A-Car
HouseMaster of America
I Can't Believe It's Yogurt
Island Snow Hawaii

Just Pants
K-Bob's
Kits Cameras
KOA Kampgrounds of America
Langenwalter Dye Concept
Little Professor Book Centers
Mail Boxes Etc. USA
Mazzio's Pizza
Meineke Discount Mufflers
M.G.M. Liquor Warehouse
Miracle Auto Painting & Body
   Repair
Miracle-Ear
Miracle Method
Mr. Build
Nitro-Green Professional Lawn and
   Tree Care
One Hour Moto-Photo
Packy the Shipper
Papa Aldo's Take & Bake Pizza
   Shops
P&D/Premier Auto Parts
Pearle Vision Centers
PIP Postal Instant Press
P.k.g.'s
PrintMasters
Rainbow International Carpet
   Dyeing & Cleaning Company
Rax Restaurants

Round Table Pizza Restaurants
Sara Care
Scandia Down Shops
Schlotzsky's
Scottish Inns, Red Carpet Inn,
   Master Hosts Inns
Servpro
7-Eleven
Sounds Easy
Sport Shack
Steamatic

Taco John's
TacoTime
Travel Pros
TriMark
TV Scene
TV Tempo
UBI Business Brokers
United Consumers Club
Wicks 'N' Sticks
Zack's Famous Frozen Yogurt

ARKANSAS

Athletic Attic
Bojangles'
Coast to Coast Total Hardware
Comprehensive Accounting
   Corporation
Corporate Finance Associates
Corporate Investment Business
   Brokers
Create-A-Book
Dairy Queen
Debit One Mobile Bookkeeping
Deck The Walls
Docktor Pet Centers
Dr. Vinyl
Duds 'N Suds
Eldorado Stone
Flowerama
Foliage Design Systems
Grand Slam USA
Health Force
Holiday-Payless Rent-A-Car
HouseMaster of America
I Can't Believe It's Yogurt
K-Bob's
KOA Kampgrounds of America
Langenwalter Dye Concept
Little Professor Book Centers
Mail Boxes Etc. USA
Mazzio's Pizza
Meineke Discount Mufflers
Miracle Method

Miracle-Ear
Money Mailer
Mr. Build
Packy the Shipper
P&D/Premier Auto Parts
PIP Postal Instant Press
P.k.g.'s
Precision Tune
Rainbow International Carpet
   Dyeing & Cleaning Company
Rax Restaurants
ROMAC
Sara Care
Scandia Down Shops
Scottish Inns, Red Carpet Inn,
   Master Hosts Inns
Servpro
Sounds Easy
Sport Shack
Spring-Green Lawn Care
Steamatic
Taco John's
TacoTime
Travel Pros
TriMark
TV Tempo
UBI Business Brokers
Wicks 'N' Sticks
World Bazaar
Zack's Famous Frozen Yogurt

CALIFORNIA

Athletic Attic
Blimpie
Boston Pizza
Budget Tapes & Records
Coast to Coast Total Hardware
ColorTyme

Comprehensive Accounting
   Corporation
Corporate Investment Business
   Brokers
Create-A-Book
Dairy Queen

Debit One Mobile Bookkeeping
Deck The Walls
Docktor Pet Centers
Dr. Vinyl
Duds 'N Suds
Dunkin' Donuts
Eldorado Stone
Entré Computer Centers
First Optometry Eye Care Centers
Fleet Feet
Foremost Sales Promotions
Grand Slam USA
Gymboree
HairCrafters
Health Force
HouseMaster of America
Island Snow Hawaii
Just Pants
K-Bob's
Kits Cameras
KOA Kampgrounds of America
Langenwalter Dye Concept
Little Professor Book Centers
Long John Silver's Seafood
    Shoppes
MAACO Auto Painting &
    Bodyworks
Mail Boxes Etc. USA
Mazzio's Pizza
Meineke Discount Mufflers
M.G.M. Liquor Warehouse
Mifax
Miracle Auto Painting & Body
    Repair

Miracle-Ear
Miracle Method
Mr. Build
Nitro-Green Professional Lawn and
    Tree Care
One Hour Moto-Photo
Packy the Shipper
Papa Aldo's Take & Bake Pizza
    Shops
P&D/Premier Auto Parts
PIP Postal Instant Press
The Pit Pros
Precision Tune
PrintMasters
Rainbow International Carpet
    Dyeing & Cleaning Company
Rax Restaurants
ROMAC
Round Table Pizza
Sara Care
Scandia Down Shops
Schlotzsky's
Servpro
7-Eleven
Sport Shack
Steamatic
Taco John's
TacoTime
Travel Pros
Travel ServicentreS
TriMark
UBI Business Brokers
Wicks 'N' Sticks
Zack's Famous Frozen Yogurt

COLORADO

Athletic Attic
Boston Pizza
Budget Tapes & Records
Coast to Coast Total Hardware
Comprehensive Accounting
    Corporation
Corporate Finance Associates
Corporate Investment Business
    Brokers
Create-A-Book
Dairy Queen
Debit One Mobile Bookkeeping
Deck The Walls
Docktor Pet Centers
Dr. Vinyl
Duds 'N Suds

Dunkin' Donuts
Eldorado Stone
Entré Computer Centers
Flowerama
Foliage Design Systems
Foremost Sales Promotions
Grand Slam USA
Great Clips
Gymboree
HairCrafters
Hardee's
Health Force
HouseMaster of America
I Can't Believe It's Yogurt
Just Pants
K-Bob's

KOA Kampgrounds of America
Little Professor Book Centers
Mail Boxes Etc. USA
Mazzio's Pizza
Meineke Discount Mufflers
Miracle Auto Painting & Body
  Repair
Miracle-Ear
Miracle Method
Mr. Build
Nitro-Green Professional Lawn and
  Tree Care
One Hour Moto-Photo
Packy the Shipper
Papa Aldo's Take & Bake Pizza
  Shops
P&D/Premier Auto Parts
Pearle Vision Centers
PIP Postal Instant Press
P.k.g.'s

Precision Tune
Rainbow International Carpet
  Dyeing & Cleaning Company
Sara Care
Scandia Down Shops
Schlotzsky's
Servpro
Sounds Easy
Steamatic
Taco del Sol
Taco John's
TacoTime
Travel Pros
TriMark
TV Scene
TV Tempo
UBI Business Brokers
Wicks 'N' Sticks
Zack's Famous Frozen Yogurt

CONNECTICUT

Athletic Attic
Blimpie
Comprehensive Accounting
  Corporation
Corporate Finance Associates
Corporate Investment Business
  Brokers
Dairy Queen
Debit One Mobile Bookkeeping
Deck The Walls
Dunkin' Donuts
Dwight Dental Care
Foliage Design Systems
Foremost Sales Promotions
Grand Slam USA
The Ground Round
Gymboree
Health Force
HouseMaster of America
I Can't Believe It's Yogurt
Just Pants
KOA Kampgrounds of America
Little Professor Book Centers
Long John Silver's Seafood
  Shoppes
Mail Boxes Etc. USA
Meineke Discount Mufflers
Miracle-Ear
Miracle Method
Mr. Build

One Hour Moto-Photo
Packy the Shipper
P&D/Premier Auto Parts
Pearle Vision Centers
PIP Postal Instant Press
P.k.g.'s
Precision Tune
Rainbow International Carpet
  Dyeing & Cleaning Company
Roy Rogers
Sara Care
Scandia Down Shops
Scottish Inns, Red Carpet Inn,
  Master Hosts Inns
Servpro
7-Eleven
Slender Center
Sounds Easy
Spring-Green Lawn Care
Stained Glass Overlay
Steamatic
TacoTime
Travel Pros
Tuff-Kote Dinol
TV Scene
UBI Business Brokers
United Consumers Club
Wicks 'N' Sticks
World Bazaar
Zack's Famous Frozen Yogurt

DELAWARE

Athletic Attic
Comprehensive Accounting
    Corporation
Corproate Finance Associates
Corporate Investment Business
    Brokers
Dairy Queen
Deck The Walls
Duds 'N Suds
Dunkin' Donuts
Eldorado Stone
Foliage Design Systems
Grand Slam USA
The Ground Round
Gymboree
HairCrafters
Health Force
Holiday-Payless Rent-A-Car
HouseMaster of America
I Can't Believe It's Yogurt
Just Pants
KOA Kampgrounds of America
Langenwalter Dye Concept
Little Professor Book Centers
Long John Silver's Seafood
    Shoppes
Mail Boxes Etc. USA
Meineke Discount Mufflers

Miracle-Ear
Miracle Method
Packy the Shipper
P&D/Premier Auto Parts
Pearle Vision Centers
PIP Postal Instant Press
Precision Tune
Rainbow International Carpet
    Dyeing & Cleaning Company
Roy Rogers
Sara Care
Scandia Down Shops
Scottish Inns, Red Carpet Inn,
    Master Hosts Inns
Servpro
7-Eleven
Sounds Easy
Spring-Green Lawn Care
Stained Glass Overlay
Steamatic
TacoTime
Travel Pros
TV Scene
United Consumers Club
Wicks 'N' Sticks
World Bazaar
Zack's Famous Frozen Yogurt

**DISTRICT OF
COLUMBIA**

Bojangles'

Dwight Dental Care

FLORIDA

Athletic Attic
Blimpie
Bojangles'
Coast to Coast Total Hardware
Comprehensive Accounting
    Corporation
Corporate Investment Business
    Brokers
Create-A-Book
Dairy Queen
Debit One Mobile Bookkeeping
Deck The Walls
Dr. Vinyl
Duds 'N Suds
Dunkin' Donuts
Dwight Dental Care
Eldorado Stone
Entré Computer Centers

First Optometry Eye Care Centers
Fleet Feet
Flowerama
Foremost Sales Promotions
Grand Slam USA
Great Clips
Gymboree
HairCrafters
Hardee's
Health Force
Holiday-Payless Rent-A-Car
HouseMaster of America
I Can't Believe It's Yogurt
Island Snow Hawaii
K-Bob's
KOA Kampgrounds of America
Langenwalter Dye Concept
Little Professor Book Centers

Long John Silver's Seafood
  Shoppes
MAACO Auto Painting &
  Bodyworks
Mail Boxes Etc. USA
Mazzio's Pizza
Meineke Discount Mufflers
M.G.M Liquor Warehouse
Miracle Auto Painting & Body
  Repair
Miracle-Ear
Miracle Method
Mr. Build
One Hour Moto-Photo
Packy the Shipper
P&D/Premier Auto Parts
Pearle Vision Centers
PIP Postal Instant Press
P.k.g.'s
Precision Tune
Rainbow International Carpet
  Dyeing & Cleaning Company
Rax Restaurants
Sara Care

Scandia Down Shops
Schlotzsky's
Scottish Inns, Red Carpet Inn,
  Master Hosts Inns
Service Personnel
Servpro
Sounds Easy
Sport Shack
Steamatic
Taco John's
TacoTime
Travel Pros
Travel ServicentreS
TriMark
Tubby's Sub Shops
Tuff-Kote Dinol
TV Scene
TV Tempo
UBI Business Brokers
United Consumers Club
Wicks 'N' Sticks
The Window Man
Zack's Famous Frozen Yogurt

GEORGIA

Athletic Attic
Blimpie
Bojangles'
Coast to Coast Total Hardware
Comprehensive Accounting
  Corporation
Corporate Investment Business
  Brokers
Create-A-Book
Dairy Queen
Debit One Mobile Bookkeeping
Deck The Walls
Dr. Vinyl
Duds 'N Suds
Dunkin' Donuts
Dwight Dental Care
Eldorado Stone
Entré Computer Centers
Flowerama
Foliage Design Systems
Foremost Sales Promotions
Grand Slam USA
Great Clips
Gymboree
HairCrafters

Health Force
H&R Block
I Can't Believe It's Yogurt
Just Pants
KOA Kampgrounds of America
Little Professor Book Centers
MAACO Auto Painting &
  Bodyworks
Mail Boxes Etc. USA
Mazzio's Pizza
Meineke Discount Mufflers
Miracle Auto Painting & Body
  Repair
Miracle-Ear
Miracle Method
Money Mailer
Mr. Build
One Hour Moto-Photo
Packy the Shipper
P&D/Premier Auto Parts
Pearle Vision Centers
PIP Postal Instant Press
The Pit Pros
P.k.g.'s
Precision Tune

Rainbow International Carpet
  Dyeing & Cleaning Company
Rax Restaurants
Sara Care
Scandia Down Shops
Schlotzsky's
Scottish Inns, Red Carpet Inn,
  Master Hosts Inns
Service Presonnel
Servpro
Sounds Easy
Sport Shack

Steamatic
Taco John's
TacoTime
Travel Pros
Tubby's Sub Shops
TV Scene
TV Tempo
UBI Business Brokers
United Consumers Club
Wicks 'N' Sticks
The Window Man
Zack's Famous Frozen Yogurt

HAWAII

Boston Pizza
Budget Tapes & Records
Coast to Coast Total Hardware
Comprehensive Accounting
  Corporation
Corporate Finance Associates
Corporate Investment Business
  Brokers
Dunkin' Donuts
Eldorado Stone
Foliage Design Systems
Gymboree
Health Force
HouseMaster of America
I Can't Believe It's Yogurt
Ice Cream Churn
Island Snow Hawaii
K-Bob's
Langenwalter Dye Concept
Long John Silver's Seafood
  Shoppes
Mail Boxes Etc. USA

Meineke Discount Mufflers
Miracle Method
Mr. Build
One Hour Moto-Photo
Papa Aldo's Take & Bake Pizza
  Shops
P&D/Premier Auto Parts
PIP Postal Instant Press
Precision Tune
Rainbow International Carpet
  Dyeing & Cleaning Company
Scottish Inns, Red Carpet Inn,
  Master Hosts Inns
Servpro
Sounds Easy
Stained Glass Overlay
Steamatic
TacoTime
Travel Pros
Travel ServicentreS
UBI Business Brokers
Zack's Famous Frozen Yogurt

IDAHO

Blimpie
Boston Pizza
Budget Tapes & Records
Coast to Coast Total Hardware
ColorTyme
Comprehensive Accounting
  Corporation
Corporate Finance Associates
Corporate Investment Business
  Brokers
Create-A-Book
Dairy Queen
Debit One Mobile Bookkeeping
Deck The Walls

Docktor Pet Center
Duds 'N Suds
Eldorado Stone
Foliage Design Systems
Gymboree
I Can't Believe It's Yogurt
Kits Cameras
KOA Kampgrounds of America
Langenwalter Dye Concept
Little Professor Book Centers
Long John Silver's Seafood
  Shoppes
Mail Boxes Etc. USA
Meineke Discount Mufflers

Miracle-Ear
Miracle Method
Mr. Build
Nitro-Green Professional Lawn and
   Tree Care
Packy the Shipper
Papa Aldo's Take & Bake Pizza
   Shops
P&D/Premier Auto Parts
Pearle Vision Centers
PIP Postal Instant Press
Precision Tune
Rainbow International Carpet
   Dyeing & Cleaning Company

Rax Restaurants
ROMAC
Sara Care
Servpro
7-Eleven
Sounds Easy
Sport Shack
Steamatic
Taco John's
TacoTime
Travel Pros
TV Tempo
Wicks 'N' Sticks
Zack's Famous Frozen Yogurt

ILLINOIS

Athletic Attic
Blimpie
Coast to Coast Total Hardware
Comprehensive Accounting
   Corporation
Corporate Finance Associates
Corporate Investment Business
   Brokers
Create-A-Book
Dairy Queen
Debit One Mobile Bookkeeping
Deck The Walls
Docktor Pet Centers
Dr. Vinyl
Duds 'N Suds
Dunkin' Donuts
Eldorado Stone
Entré Computer Centers
First Optometry Eye Care Centers
Flowerama
Foremost Sales Promotions
Grand Slam USA
The Ground Round
Gymboree Corporation
HairCrafters
Happy Joe's Pizza & Ice Cream
   Parlors
Health Force
HouseMaster of America
H&R Block
I Can't Believe It's Yogurt
Just Pants
K-Bob's
KOA Kampgrounds of America
Langenwalter Dye Concept

Little Professor Book Centers
Mail Boxes Etc. USA
Mazzio's Pizza
Meineke Discount Mufflers
Miracle Auto Painting & Body
   Repair
Miracle-Ear
Miracle Method
Mr. Build
One Hour Moto-Photo
Packy the Shipper
P&D/Premier Auto Parts
Pearle Vision Centers
PIP Postal Instant Press
The Pit Pros
P.k.g.'s
Precision Tune
Rainbow International Carpet
   Dyeing & Cleaning Company
Rax Restaurants
Sara Care
Scandia Down Shops
Schlotzsky's
Scottish Inns, Red Carpet Inn,
   Master Hosts Inns
Service Personnel
Servpro
7-Eleven
Slender Center
Sounds Easy
Sport Shack
Spring-Green Lawn Care
Stained Glass Overlay
Steamatic
Taco John's

TacoTime
Travel Pros
Travel ServicentreS
TriMark
Tuff-Kote Dinol
TV Scene

TV Tempo
UBI Business Brokers
Wicks 'N' Sticks
World Bazaar
Zack's Famous Frozen Yogurt

INDIANA

Athletic Attic
Bojangles'
Coast to Coast Total Hardware
Comprehensive Accounting
  Corporation
Corporate Finance Associates
Corporate Investment Business
  Brokers
Create-A-Book
Dairy Queen
Debit One Mobile Bookkeeping
Deck The Walls
Docktor Pet Centers
Dr. Vinyl
Duds 'N Suds
Dunkin' Donuts
Eldorado Stone
Entré Computer Centers
Flowerama
Foremost Sales Promotions
Grand Slam USA
Great Clips
The Ground Round
Gymboree
HairCrafters
Health Force
Holiday-Payless Rent-A-Car
HouseMaster of America
H&R Block
I Can't Believe It's Yogurt
Just Pants
K-Bob's
KOA Kampgrounds of America
Little Professor Book Centers
Mail Boxes Etc. USA
Mazzio's Pizza
Meineke Discount Mufflers
Mifax

Miracle-Ear
Miracle Method
Mr. Build
Nitro-Green Professional Lawn and
  Tree Care
One Hour Moto-Photo
Packy the Shipper
P&D/Premier Auto Parts
Pearle Vision Centers
PIP Postal Instant Press
The Pit Pros
P.k.g.'s
Precision Tune
Rainbow International Carpet
  Dyeing & Cleaning Company
Rax Restaurants
ROMAC
Scandia Down Shops
Schlotzsky's
Scottish Inns, Red Carpet Inn,
  Master Hosts Inns
Service Personnel
Servpro
7-Eleven
Slender Center
Sport Shack
Spring-Green Lawn Care
Stained Glass Overlay
Steamatic
Taco John's
TacoTime
Travel Pros
Tuff-Kote Dinol
TV Scene
TV Tempo
Wicks 'N' Sticks
World Bazaar
Zack's Famous Frozen Yogurt

IOWA

Athletic Attic
Bojangles'
Budget Tapes & Records
Coast to Coast Total Hardware

Comprehensive Accounting
  Corporation
Corporate Investment Business
  Brokers

Dairy Queen
Debit One Mobile Bookkeeping
Deck The Walls
Docktor Pet Centers
Dr. Vinyl
Duds 'N Suds
Eldorado Stone
Flowerama
Great Clips
The Ground Round
Gymboree
HairCrafters
Happy Joe's Pizza & Ice Cream
  Parlors
Health Force
Holiday-Payless Rent-A-Car
HouseMaster of America
H&R Block
I Can't Believe It's Yogurt
Langenwalter Dye Concept
Little Professor Book Centers
Mail Boxes Etc. USA
Mazzio's Pizza
Meineke Discount Mufflers
Miracle-Ear
Miracle Method
Money Mailer
Mr. Build
Nitro-Green Professional Lawn and
  Tree Care

Packy the Shipper
P&D/Premier Auto Parts
Pearle Vision Centers
The Pit Pros
P.k.g.'s
Precision Tune
Rainbow International Carpet
  Dyeing & Cleaning Company
ROMAC
Sara Care
Scandia Down Shops
Scottish Inns, Red Carpet Inn,
  Master Hosts Inns
Servpro
Slender Center
Sounds Easy
Sport Shack
Spring-Green Lawn Care
Steamatic
Taco del Sol
Taco John's
TacoTime
Travel Pros
TriMark
Tuff-Kote Dinol
TV Scene
TV Tempo
Wicks 'N' Sticks
World Bazaar
Zack's Famous Frozen Yogurt

KANSAS

Athletic Attic
Budget Tapes & Records
Coast to Coast Total Hardware
Comprehensive Accounting
  Corporation
Corporate Investment Business
  Brokers
Create-A-Book
Dairy Queen
Debit One Mobile Bookkeeping
Deck The Walls
Dr. Vinyl
Duds 'N Suds
Dunkin' Donuts
Eldorado Stone
Flowerama
Great Clips
Gymboree
HairCrafters

Happy Joe's Pizza & Ice Cream
  Parlors
Hardee's
Health Force
Holiday-Payless Rent-A-Car
HouseMaster of America
H&R Block
I Can't Believe It's Yogurt
K-Bob's
Little Professor Book Centers
Mail Boxes Etc. USA
Mazzio's Pizza
Meineke Discount Mufflers
Miracle-Ear
Miracle Method
Money Mailer
Nitro-Green Professional Lawn and
  Tree Care
One Hour Moto-Photo

Packy the Shipper
P&D/Premier Auto Parts
PIP Postal Instant Press
P.k.g.'s
Precision Tune
Rainbow International Carpet
  Dyeing & Cleaning Company
Rax Restaurants
ROMAC
Sara Care
Scandia Down Shops
Schlotzsky's
Scottish Inns, Red Carpet Inn,
  Master Hosts Inns

Servpro
Sounds Easy
Sport Shack
Steamatic
Taco del Sol
Taco John's
TacoTime
Travel Pros
TV Scene
TV Tempo
UBI Business Brokers
Wicks 'N' Sticks
World Bazaar
Zack's Famous Frozen Yogurt

KENTUCKY

Athletic Attic
Blimpie
Bojangles'
Coast to Coast Total Hardware
Comprehensive Accounting
  Corporation
Corporate Finance Associates
Corporate Investment Business
  Brokers
Create-A-Book
Dairy Queen
Debit One Mobile Bookkeeping
Deck The Walls
Docktor Pet Centers
Dr. Vinyl
Duds 'N Suds
Dunkin' Donuts
Eldorado Stone
Flowerama
Foliage Design Systems
Foremost Sales Promotions
Grand Slam USA
The Ground Round
Gymboree
HairCrafters
Health Force
Holiday-Payless Rent-A-Car
HouseMaster of America
H&R Block
I Can't Believe It's Yogurt
Just Pants
KOA Kampgrounds of America
Little Professor Book Centers
Mail Boxes Etc. USA
Mazzio's Pizza

Meineke Discount Mufflers
Miracle-Ear
Miracle Method
Money Mailer
One Hour Moto-Photo
Packy the Shipper
P&D/Premier Auto Parts
Pearle Vision Centers
PIP Postal Instant Press
The Pit Pros
P.k.g.'s
Precision Tune
Rainbow International Carpet
  Dyeing & Cleaning Company
Rax Restaurants
ROMAC
Sara Care
Scandia Down Shops
Schlotzsky's
Scottish Inns, Red Carpet Inn,
  Master Hosts Inns
Service Personnel
Servpro
Sounds Easy
Sport Shack
Steamatic
Taco John's
TacoTime
Travel Pros
Tubby's Sub Shops
TV Scene
TV Tempo
Wicks 'N' Sticks
World Bazaar
Zack's Famous Frozen Yogurt

LOUISIANA

Athletic Attic
Blimpie
Comprehensive Accounting
  Corporation
Corporate Finance Associates
Corporate Investment Business
  Brokers
Create-A-Book
Dairy Queen
Debit One Mobile Bookkeeping
Deck The Walls
Docktor Pet Centers
Dr. Vinyl
Duds 'N Suds
Dunkin' Donuts
Eldorado Stone
Flowerama
Foliage Design Systems
Grand Slam USA
Gymboree
HairCrafters
Hardee's
Health Force
Holiday-Payless Rent-A-Car
H&R Block
I Can't Believe It's Yogurt
Just Pants
K-Bob's
KOA Kampgrounds of America
Langenwalter Dye Concept
Little Professor Book Centers
MAACO Auto Painting &
  Bodyworks
Mail Boxes Etc. USA
Mazzio's Pizza
Meineke Discount Mufflers

Miracle-Ear
Miracle Method
Money Mailer
One Hour Moto-Photo
Packy the Shipper
P&D/Premier Auto Parts
Pearle Vision Centers
PIP Postal Instant Press
P.k.g.'s
Precision Tune
Rainbow International Carpet
  Dyeing & Cleaning Company
Rax Restaurants
ROMAC
Sara Care
Scandia Down Shops
Scottish Inns, Red Carpet Inn,
  Master Hosts Inns
Service Personnel
Servpro
Sounds Easy
Sport Shack
Spring-Green Lawn Care
Stained Glass Overlay
Steamatic
Taco John's
TacoTime
Travel Pros
TriMark
TV Scene
TV Tempo
UBI Business Brokers
United Consumers Club
Wicks 'N' Sticks
World Bazaar

MAINE

Athletic Attic
Comprehensive Accounting
  Corporation
Corporate Investment Business
  Brokers
Dairy Queen
Debit One Mobile Bookkeeping
Deck The Walls
Dunkin' Donuts
Eldorado Stone
Grand Slam USA
The Ground Round
Gymboree

Holiday-Payless Rent-A-Car
HouseMaster of America
I Can't Believe It's Yogurt
Langenwalter Dye Concept
Little Professor Book Centers
Long John Silver's Seafood
  Shoppes
Mail Boxes Etc. USA
Meineke Discount Mufflers
Mifax
Miracle-Ear
Miracle Method
Money Mailer

Mr. Build
Packy the Shipper
P&D/Premier Auto Parts
Pearle Vision Centers
PIP Postal Instant Press
Precision Tune
Rainbow International Carpet
   Dyeing & Cleaning Company
Roy Rogers
Sara Care
Scandia Down Shops
Scottish Inns, Red Carpet Inn,
   Master Hosts Inns

Servpro
Sounds Easy
Steamatic
TacoTime
Travel Pros
Tuff-Kote Dinol
TV Tempo
The Weed Man
Wicks 'N' Sticks
World Bazaar
Zack's Famous Frozen Yogurt

MARYLAND

Athletic Attic
Bojangles'
Comprehensive Accounting
   Corporation
Corporate Finance Associates
Corporate Investment Business
   Brokers
Create-A-Book
Dairy Queen
Debit One Mobile Bookkeeping
Deck The Walls
Dunkin' Donuts
Dwight Dental Care
Entré Computer Centers
Fleet Feet
Foremost Sales Promotions
Grand Slam USA
The Ground Round
Gymboree
H&R Block
I Can't Believe It's Yogurt
Just Pants
KOA Kampgrounds of America
Little Professor Book Centers
Long John Silver's Seafood
   Shoppes
Mail Boxes Etc. USA
Meineke Discount Mufflers
Miracle-Ear
Miracle Method

Mr. Build
One Hour Moto-Photo
Packy the Shipper
P&D/Premier Auto Parts
Pearle Vision Centers
PIP Postal Instant Press
P.k.g.'s
Precision Tune
Rainbow International Carpet
   Dyeing & Cleaning Company
Rax Restaurants
Roy Rogers
Scandia Down Shops
Scottish Inns, Red Carpet Inn,
   Master Hosts Inns
7-Eleven
Spring-Green Lawn Care
Steamatic
Taco John's
TacoTime
Travel Pros
TriMark
Tuff-Kote Dinol
TV Scene
TV Tempo
UBI Business Brokers
United Consumers Club
Wicks 'N' Sticks
World Bazaar
Zack's Famous Frozen Yogurt

MASSACHUSETTS

Athletic Attic
Comprehensive Accounting
   Corporation
Corporate Finance Associates
Corporate Investment Business
   Brokers

Dairy Queen
Debit One Mobile Bookkeeping
Deck The Walls
Dunkin' Donuts
Dwight Dental Care
Eldorado Stone

Entré Computer Centers
Foliage Design Systems
Foremost Sales Promotions
Grand Slam USA
The Ground Round
Gymboree
Health Force
HouseMaster of America
H&R Block
I Can't Believe It's Yogurt
Just Pants
KOA Kampgrounds of America
Langenwalter Dye Concept
Little Professor Book Centers
Long John Silver's Seafood
  Shoppes
Mail Boxes Etc. USA
Meineke Discount Mufflers
Mifax
Miracle-Ear
Miracle Method
Mr. Build
One Hour Moto-Photo
Packy the Shipper
P&D/Premier Auto Parts
Pearle Vision Centers
PIP Postal Instant Press
P.k.g.'s

Precision Tune
Rainbow International Carpet
  Dyeing & Cleaning Company
Rax Restaurants
Roy Rogers
Sara Care
Scandia Down Shops
Scottish Inns, Red Carpet Inn,
  Master Hosts Inns
Servpro
7-Eleven
Slender Center
Sounds Easy
Spring-Green Lawn Care
Stained Glass Overlay
Steamatic
TacoTime
Travel Pros
TriMark
Tuff-Kote Dinol
TV Scene
TV Tempo
United Consumers Club
The Weed Man
Wicks 'N' Sticks
World Bazaar
Zack's Famous Frozen Yogurt

MICHIGAN

Athletic Attic
Coast to Coast Total Hardware
Comprehensive Accounting
  Corporation
Corporate Finance Associates
Corporate Investment Business
  Brokers
Create-A-Book
Dairy Queen
Debit One Mobile Bookkeeping
Deck The Walls
Docktor Pet Centers
Dr. Vinyl
Duds 'N Suds
Dunkin' Donuts
Entré Computer Centers
First Optometry Eye Care Centers
Flowerama
Foremost Sales Promotions
Grand Slam USA
The Ground Round
Gymboree

Hardee's
Health Force
Holiday-Payless Rent-A-Car
HouseMaster of America
H&R Block
I Can't Believe It's Yogurt
Just Pants
Langenwalter Dye Concept
Little Professor Book Centers
Long John Silver's Seafood
  Shoppes
Mail Boxes Etc. USA
Meineke Discount Mufflers
Mifax
Miracle Auto Painting & Body
  Repair
Miracle-Ear
Miracle Method
Mr. Build
One Hour Moto-Photo
Packy the Shipper
P&D/Premier Auto Parts

Pearle Vision Centers
PIP Postal Instant Press
The Pit Pros
P.k.g.'s
Precision Tune
Rainbow International Carpet
 Dyeing & Cleaning Company
Rax Restaurants
ROMAC
Sara Care
Scandia Down Shops
Scottish Inns, Red Carpet Inn,
 Master Hosts Inns
Servpro
7-Eleven
Slender Center

Sounds Easy
Sport Shack
Spring-Green Lawn Care
Stained Glass Overlay
Steamatic
Taco John's
TacoTime
Travel Pros
Travel ServicentreS
TriMark
Tubby's Sub Shops
TV Scene
Wicks 'N' Sticks
World Bazaar
Zack's Famous Frozen Yogurt

MINNESOTA

Athletic Attic
Coast to Coast Total Hardware
Comprehensive Accounting
 Corporation
Corporate Finance Associates
Dairy Queen
Deck The Walls
Docktor Pet Centers
Dr. Vinyl
Duds 'N Suds
Dunkin' Donuts
Entré Computer Centers
Grand Slam USA
Great Clips
The Ground Round
Gymboree
Happy Joe's Pizza & Ice Cream
 Parlors
Health Force
HouseMaster of America
H&R Block
I Can't Believe It's Yogurt
Just Pants
Little Professor Book Centers
Long John Silver's Seafood
 Shoppes
Mail Boxes Etc. USA
Meineke Discount Mufflers
M.G.M. Liquor Warehouse
Miracle Method
Mr. Build

Nitro-Green Professional Lawn and
 Tree Care
One Hour Moto-Photo
Packy the Shipper
P&D/Premier Auto Parts
Pearle Vision Centers
PIP Postal Instant Press
Precision Tune
Rainbow International Carpet
 Dyeing & Cleaning Company
Scandia Down Shops
Schlotzsky's
Scottish Inns, Red Carpet Inn,
 Master Hosts Inns
Servpro
Slender Center
Sounds Easy
Sport Shack
Spring-Green Lawn Care
Steamatic
Taco John's
TacoTime
Travel Pros
TriMark
Tuff-Kote Dinol
TV Scene
TV Tempo
The Weed Man
Wicks 'N' Sticks
World Bazaar
Zack's Famous Frozen Yogurt

MISSISSIPPI

Athletic Attic
Comprehensive Accounting
  Corporation
Corporate Investment Business
  Brokers
Create-A-Book
Dairy Queen
Debit One Mobile Bookkeeping
Deck The Walls
Docktor Pet Centers
Dr. Vinyl
Duds 'N Suds
Eldorado Stone
Flowerama
Foremost Sales Promotions
Grand Slam USA
Gymboree
Health Force
Holiday-Payless Rent-A-Car
HouseMaster of America
H&R Block
I Can't Believe It's Yogurt
K-Bob's
KOA Kampgrounds of America
Langenwalter Dye Concept
Little Professor Book Centers
Long John Silver's Seafood
  Shoppes
Mail Boxes Etc. USA
Mazzio's Pizza

Meineke Discount Mufflers
Miracle-Ear
Miracle Method
Money Mailer
Packy the Shipper
P&D/Premier Auto Parts
Pearle Vision Centers
PIP Postal Instant Press
P.k.g.'s
Precision Tune
Rainbow International Carpet
  Dyeing & Cleaning Company
Rax Restaurants
ROMAC
Sara Care
Scandia Down Shops
Scottish Inns, Red Carpet Inn,
  Master Hosts Inns
Servpro
Sounds Easy
Sport Shack
Steamatic
Taco John's
TacoTime
Travel Pros
TV Scene
TV Tempo
Wicks 'N' Sticks
World Bazaar
Zack's Famous Frozen Yogurt

MISSOURI

Athletic Attic
Bojangles'
Budget Tapes & Records
Coast to Coast Total Hardware
Comprehensive Accounting
  Corporation
Corporate Finance Associates
Corporate Investment Business
  Brokers
Create-A-Book
Dairy Queen
Debit One Mobile Bookkeeping
Deck The Walls
Dr. Vinyl
Duds 'N Suds
Dunkin' Donuts
Eldorado Stone
Flowerama
Foliage Design Systems

Foremost Sales Promotions
Grand Slam USA
Great Clips
The Ground Round
Gymboree
Happy Joe's Pizza & Ice Cream
  Parlors
Health Force
Holiday-Payless Rent-A-Car
HouseMaster of America
H&R Block
I Can't Believe It's Yogurt
K-Bob's
KOA Kampgrounds of America
Little Professor Book Centers
Mail Boxes Etc. USA
Mazzio's Pizza
Meineke Discount Mufflers
Miracle-Ear

Miracle Method
One Hour Moto-Photo
Packy the Shipper
P&D/Premier Auto Parts
Pearle Vision Centers
PIP Postal Instant Press
P.k.g.'s
Precision Tune
Rainbow International Carpet
    Dyeing & Cleaning Company
Rax Restaurants
ROMAC
Sara Care
Scandia Down Shops
Schlotzsky's
Scottish Inns, Red Carpet Inn,
    Master Hosts Inns
Service Personnel

Servpro
Sounds Easy
Sport Shack
Spring-Green Lawn Care
Steamatic
Taco del Sol
Taco John's
TacoTime
Travel Pros
TriMark
Tuff-Kote Dinol
TV Scene
TV Tempo
UBI Business Brokers
Wicks 'N' Sticks
World Bazaar
Zack's Famous Frozen Yogurt

MONTANA

Boston Pizza
Budget Tapes & Records
Coast to Coast Total Hardware
ColorTyme
Comprehensive Accounting
    Corporation
Corporate Finance Associates
Corporate Investment Business
    Brokers
Debit One Mobile Bookkeeping
Deck The Walls
Dr. Vinyl
Duds 'N Suds
Eldorado Stone
Gymboree
HouseMaster of America
I Can't Believe It's Yogurt
Little Professor Book Centers
Long John Silver's Seafood
    Shoppes
Mail Boxes Etc. USA
Meineke Discount Mufflers
Mifax
Miracle-Ear

Miracle Method
Nitro-Green Professional Lawn and
    Tree Care
Packy the Shipper
Papa Aldo's Take & Bake Pizza
    Shops
P&D/Premier Auto Parts
Pearle Vision Centers
PIP Postal Instant Press
Precision Tune
Rainbow International Carpet
    Dyeing & Cleaning Company
Rax Restaurants
ROMAC
Sara Care
Servpro
Sounds Easy
Sport Shack
Steamatic
Taco John's
TacoTime
Wicks 'N' Sticks
Zack's Famous Frozen Yogurt

NEBRASKA

Athletic Attic
Bojangles'
Budget Tapes & Records
Coast to Coast Total Hardware
Comprehensive Accounting
    Corporation

Corporate Investment Business
    Brokers
Dairy Queen
Debit One Mobile Bookkeeping
Deck The Walls
Dr. Vinyl

Duds 'N Suds
Eldorado Stone
Flowerama
Grand Slam USA
Great Clips
Gymboree
HairCrafters
Health Force
HouseMaster of America
I Can't Believe It's Yogurt
K-Bob's
Little Professor Book Centers
Mail Boxes Etc. USA
Meineke Discount Mufflers
Miracle Method
Money Mailer
Nitro-Green Professional Lawn and
  Tree Care
Packy the Shipper
P&D/Premier Auto Parts
Pearle Vision Centers

PIP Postal Instant Press
Precision Tune
Rainbow International Carpet
  Dyeing & Cleaning Company
Rax Restaurants
ROMAC
Sara Care
Scandia Down Shops
Servpro
Sounds Easy
Sport Shack
Steamatic
Taco del Sol
Taco John's
TacoTime
TriMark
TV Scene
TV Tempo
Wicks 'N' Sticks
Zack's Famous Frozen Yogurt

NEVADA

Budget Tapes & Records
Comprehensive Accounting
  Corporation
Corporate Finance Associates
Dairy Queen
Debit One Mobile Bookkeeping
Deck The Walls
Dr. Vinyl
Duds 'N' Suds
Eldorado Stone
Fleet Feet
Grand Slam USA
Gymboree
HairCrafters
Health Force
HouseMaster of America
I Can't Believe It's Yogurt
Island Snow Hawaii
K-Bob's
KOA Kampgrounds of America
Little Professor Book Centers
Mail Boxes Etc. USA
Mazzio's Pizza
Meineke Discount Mufflers
M.G.M. Liquor Warehouse
Mifax
Miracle Auto Painting & Body
  Repair

Miracle-Ear
Mr. Build
Nitro-Green Professional Lawn and
  Tree Care
One Hour Moto-Photo
Packy the Shipper
Papa Aldo's Take & Bake Pizza
  Shops
P&D/Premier Auto Parts
PIP Postal Instant Press
Precision Tune
Rainbow International Carpet
  Dyeing & Cleaning Company
ROMAC
Sara Care
Scandia Down Shops
Servpro
7-Eleven
Sounds Easy
Sport Shack
Steamatic
Taco John's
TacoTime
Travel Pros
Travel ServicentreS
TriMark
Tuff-Kote Dinol
TV Tempo

UBI Business Brokers
Wicks 'N' Sticks

Zack's Famous Frozen Yogurt

NEW HAMPSHIRE

Comprehensive Accounting
    Corporation
Corporate Finance Associates
Dairy Queen
Deck The Walls
Duds 'N Suds
Dunkin' Donuts
Eldorado Stone
The Ground Round
Gymboree
HairCrafters
Health Force
Holiday-Payless Rent-A-Car
HouseMaster of America
I Can't Believe It's Yogurt
Just Pants
Little Professor Book Centers
Long John Silver's Seafood
    Shoppes
Mail Boxes Etc. USA
Mazzio's Pizza
Meineke Discount Mufflers
Miracle-Ear
Miracle Method
Money Mailer
Mr. Build
One Hour Moto-Photo

Packy the Shipper
P&D/Premier Auto Parts
Pearle Vision Centers
PIP Postal Instant Press
Precision Tune
Rainbow International Carpet
    Dyeing & Cleaning Company
Roy Rogers
Sara Care
Scandia Down Shops
Scottish Inns, Red Carpet Inn,
    Master Hosts Inns
Servpro
7-Eleven
Sounds Easy
Sport Shack
Steamatic
TacoTime
Travel Pros
Tuff-Kote Dinol
TV Scene
TV Tempo
The Weed Man
Wicks 'N' Sticks
World Bazaar
Zack's Famous Frozen Yogurt

NEW JERSEY

Athletic Attic
Blimpie
Bojangles'
Comprehensive Accounting
    Corporation
Corporate Investment Business
    Brokers
Create-A-Book
Deck The Walls
Duds 'N Suds
Dunkin' Donuts
Dwight Dental Care
Foliage Design Systems
Foremost Sales Promotions
Grand Slam USA
The Ground Round
Gymboree
HairCrafters
Health Force

I Can't Believe It's Yogurt
Just Pants
KOA Kampgrounds of America
Langenwalter Dye Concept
Little Professor Book Centers
Long John Silver's Seafood
    Shoppes
Mail Boxes Etc., USA
Mifax
Miracle-Ear
Miracle Method
One Hour Moto-Photo
Packy the Shipper
P&D/Premier Auto Parts
Pearle Vision Centers
P.k.g.'s
PIP Postal Instant Press
Precision Tune

Rainbow International Carpet
   Dyeing & Cleaning Company
Roy Rogers
Sara Care
Scandia Down Shops
Scottish Inns, Red Carpet Inn,
   Master Hosts Inns
Servpro
7-Eleven
Sounds Easy
Spring-Green Lawn Care

Stained Glass Overlay
Steamatic
Taco John's
TacoTime
Travel Pros
UBI Business Brokers
United Consumers Club
Wicks 'N' Sticks
World Bazaar
Zack's Famous Frozen Yogurt

NEW MEXICO

Athletic Attic
Budget Tapes & Records
Coast to Coast Total Hardware
Comprehensive Accounting
   Corporation
Corporate Finance Associates
Dairy Queen
Debit One Mobile Bookkeeping
Deck The Walls
Dr. Vinyl
Duds 'N Suds
Dunkin' Donuts
Eldorado Stone
Flowerama
Foremost Sales Promotions
Gymboree
HairCrafters
Health Force
HouseMaster of America
I Can't Believe It's Yogurt
Just Pants
KOA Kampgrounds of America
Little Professor Book Centers
Mail Boxes Etc. USA
Mazzio's Pizza
Meineke Discount Mufflers
Miracle Auto Painting & Body
   Repair
Miracle-Ear
Miracle Method
Nitro-Green Professional Lawn and
   Tree Care

One Hour Moto-Photo
Packy the Shipper
Papa Aldo's Take & Bake Pizza
   Shops
P&D/Premier Auto Parts
Pearle Vision Centers
PIP Postal Instant Press
Precision Tune
Rainbow International Carpet
   Dyeing & Cleaning Company
Rax Restaurants
ROMAC
Sara Care
Scandia Down Shops
Schlotzsky's
Scottish Inns, Red Carpet Inn,
   Master Hosts Inns
Servpro
Sounds Easy
Sport Shack
Steamatic
Taco John's
TacoTime
Travel Pros
TriMark
TV Tempo
UBI Business Brokers
Wicks 'N' Sticks
Zack's Famous Frozen Yogurt

NEW YORK

Athletic Attic
Blimpie
Bojangles'
Comprehensive Accounting
   Corporation

Corporate Finance Associates
Dairy Queen
Deck The Walls
Duds 'N Suds
Dunkin' Donuts

Dwight Dental Care
Eldorado Stone
Entré Computer Centers
Foremost Sales Promotions
Grand Slam USA
The Ground Round
Gymboree
HairCrafters
Hardee's
Health Force
HouseMaster of America
Just Pants
K-Bob's
KOA Kampgrounds of America
Langenwalter Dye Concept
Long John Silver's Seafood
   Shoppes
Mail Boxes Etc., USA
Miracle-Ear
Miracle Method
Mr. Build
One Hour Moto-Photo
Packy the Shipper
P&D/Premier Auto Parts

Pearle Vision Centers
PIP Postal Instant Press
Precision Tune
Rainbow International Carpet
   Dyeing & Cleaning Company
ROMAC
Roy Rogers
Scandia Down Shops
Scottish Inns, Red Carpet Inn,
   Master Hosts Inns
Servpro
7-Eleven
Spring-Green Lawn Care
Stained Glass Overlay
TacoTime
Travel Pros
Travel ServicentreS
TriMark
Tuff-Kote Dinol
TV Scene
The Weed Man
Wicks 'N' Sticks
World Bazaar
Zack's Famous Frozen Yogurt

NORTH CAROLINA

Athletic Attic
Blimpie
Bojangles'
Coast to Coast Total Hardware
Comprehensive Accounting
   Corporation
Corporate Finance Associates
Corporate Investment Business
   Brokers
Dairy Queen
Debit One Mobile Bookkeeping
Deck The Walls
Dr. Vinyl
Duds 'N Suds
Dunkin' Donuts
Eldorado Stone
Flowerama
Foliage Design Systems
Grand Slam USA
The Ground Round
Gymboree
HairCrafters
Health Force
Holiday-Payless Rent-A-Car
HouseMaster of America

I Can't Believe It's Yogurt
Just Pants
KOA Kampgrounds of America
Little Professor Book Centers
Long John Silver's Seafood
   Shoppes
Mail Boxes Etc. USA
Mazzio's Pizza
Meineke Discount Mufflers
Miracle-Ear
Miracle Method
Mr. Build
One Hour Moto-Photo
Packy the Shipper
P&D/Premier Auto Parts
Pearle Vision Centers
P.k.g.'s
PIP Postal Instant Press
Precision Tune
Rainbow International Carpet
   Dyeing & Cleaning Company
Rax Restaurants
ROMAC
Sara Care
Scandia Down Shops

Scottish Inns, Red Carpet Inn,
   Master Hosts Inns
Service Personnel
Servpro
Sounds Easy
Sport Shack
Steamatic
Taco John's
TacoTime
Travel Pros

TriMark
Tubby's Sub Shops
TV Scene
TV Tempo
UBI Business Brokers
United Consumers Club
Wicks 'N' Sticks
The Window Man
World Bazaar
Zack's Famous Frozen Yogurt

NORTH DAKOTA

Boston Pizza
Budget Tapes and Records
Coast to Coast Total Hardware
ColorTyme
Comprehensive Accounting
   Corporation
Corporate Finance Associates
Create-A-Book
Deck The Walls
Duds 'N Suds
Eldorado Stone
The Ground Round
Happy Joe's Pizza & Ice Cream
   Parlors
HouseMaster of America
I Can't Believe It's Yogurt
Little Professor Book Centers
Long John Silver's Seafood
   Shoppes
Mail Boxes Etc. USA
Meineke Discount Mufflers
M.G.M. Liquor Warehouse

Miracle-Ear
Nitro-Green Professional Lawn and
   Tree Care
Packy the Shipper
P&D/Premier Auto Parts
Pearle Vision Centers
PIP Postal Instant Press
Precision Tune
Rainbow International Carpet
   Dyeing & Cleaning Company
Rax Restaurants
ROMAC
Scandia Down Shops
Servpro
Sounds Easy
Steamatic
Taco John's
TacoTime
TV Tempo
Wicks 'N' Sticks
Zack's Famous Frozen Yogurt

OHIO

Athletic Attic
Blimpie
Bojangles'
Coast to Coast Total Hardware
Comprehensive Accounting
   Corporation
Corporate Finance Associates
Corporate Investment Business
   Brokers
Create-A-Book
Dairy Queen
Debit One Mobile Bookkeeping
Deck The Walls
Dr. Vinyl
Duds 'N Suds
Dunkin' Donuts

Dwight Dental Care
Entré Computer Centers
First Optometry Eye Care Centers
Flowerama
Foliage Design Systems
Foremost Sales Promotions
Grand Slam USA
The Ground Round
Gymboree
HairCrafters
Hardee's
Health Force
Holiday-Payless Rent-A-Car
HouseMaster of America
H&R Block
I Can't Believe It's Yogurt

Just Pants
KOA Kampgrounds of America
Langenwalter Dye Concept
Little Professor Book Centers
Mail Boxes Etc., USA
Meineke Discount Mufflers
Mifax
Miracle-Ear
Miracle Method
Money Mailer
Mr. Build
One Hour Moto-Photo
Packy the Shipper
P&D/Premier Auto Parts
Pearle Vision Centers
P.k.g.'s
PIP Postal Instant Press
The Pit Pros
Precision Tune
Rainbow International Carpet
    Dyeing & Cleaning Company
Rax Restaurants

Sara Care
Scandia Down Shops
Scottish Inns, Red Carpet Inn,
    Master Hosts Inns
Servpro
7-Eleven
Slender Center
Sounds Easy
Sport Shack
Stained Glass Overlay
Steamatic
Taco John's
TacoTime
Travel Pros
Travel ServicentreS
TriMark
Tubby's Sub Shops
TV Scene
TV Tempo
Wicks 'N' Sticks
World Bazaar
Zack's Famous Frozen Yogurt

OKLAHOMA

Athletic Attic
Budget Tapes & Records
Coast to Coast Total Hardware
Comprehensive Accounting
    Corporation
Corporate Finance Associates
Corporate Investment Business
    Brokers
Dairy Queen
Debit One Mobile Bookkeeping
Deck The Walls
Dr. Vinyl
Duds 'N Suds
Dunkin' Donuts
Eldorado Stone
Flowerama
Foliage Design Systems
Great Clips
Gymboree
Health Force
Holiday-Payless Rent-A-Car
HouseMaster of America
I Can't Believe It's Yogurt
Just Pants
K-Bob's
KOA Kampgrounds of America
Little Professor Book Centers

Mail Boxes Etc. USA
Meineke Discount Mufflers
Miracle-Ear
Miracle Method
Money Mailer
Nitro-Green Professional Lawn and
    Tree Care
One Hour Moto-Photo
Packy the Shipper
P&D/Premier Auto Parts
P.k.g.'s
PIP Postal Instant Press
Precision Tune
Rainbow International Carpet
    Dyeing & Cleaning Company
ROMAC
Sara Care
Scandia Down Shops
Schlotzsky's
Scottish Inns, Red Carpet Inn,
    Master Hosts Inns
Service Personnel
Servpro
Sounds Easy
Spring-Green Lawn Care
Steamatic
Taco John's

TacoTime
Travel Pros
TV Scene
TV Tempo
UBI Business Brokers

United Consumers Club
Wicks 'N' Sticks
World Bazaar
Zack's Famous Frozen Yogurt

OREGON

Boston Pizza
Budget Tapes & Records
Coast to Coast Total Hardware
Comprehensive Accounting
   Corporation
Corporate Finance Associates
Corporate Investment Business
   Brokers
Create-A-Book
Deck The Walls
Docktor Pet Centers
Duds 'N Suds
Dunkin' Donuts
Eldorado Stone
Foliage Design Systems
Gymboree
HairCrafters
Happy Joe's Pizza & Ice Cream
   Parlors
HouseMaster of America
I Can't Believe It's Yogurt
Kits Cameras
KOA Kampgrounds of America
Little Professor Book Centers
Mail Boxes Etc. USA
Meineke Discount Mufflers
Mifax
Miracle Auto Painting & Body
   Repair
Miracle-Ear
Miracle Method
Money Mailer

Mr. Build
Nitro-Green Professional Lawn and
   Tree Care
One Hour Moto-Photo
Packy the Shipper
Papa Aldo's Take & Bake Pizza
   Shops
P&D/Premier Auto Parts
Pearle Vision Centers
PIP Postal Instant Press
P.k.g.'s
Precision Tune
Rainbow International Carpet
   Dyeing & Cleaning Company
Rax Restaurants
ROMAC
Sara Care
Servpro
7-Eleven
Sounds Easy
Sport Shack
Stained Glass Overlay
Steamatic
Taco John's
TacoTime
Travel Pros
TriMark
TV Tempo
UBI Business Brokers
United Consumers Club
Wicks 'N' Sticks
Zack's Famous Frozen Yogurt

PENNSYLVANIA

Athletic Attic
Blimpie
Bojangles'
Comprehensive Accounting
   Corporation
Corporate Investment Business
   Brokers
Create-A-Book
Dairy Queen
Debit One Mobile Bookkeeping
Deck The Walls

Docktor Pet Centers
Dr. Vinyl
Duds 'N Suds
Dunkin' Donuts
Dwight Dental Care
Entré Computer Centers
Flowerama
Foliage Design Systems
Grand Slam USA
The Ground Round
Gymboree

HairCrafters
Hardee's
Health Force
Holiday-Payless Rent-A-Car
HouseMaster of America
H&R Block
I Can't Believe It's Yogurt
Just Pants
KOA Kampgrounds of America
Langenwalter Dye Concept
Little Professor Book Centers
Long John Silver's Seafood
  Shoppes
Mail Boxes Etc. USA
Meineke Discount Mufflers
Mifax
Miracle-Ear
Miracle Method
Money Mailer
One Hour Moto-Photo
Packy the Shipper
P&D/Premier Auto Parts
Pearle Vision Centers
P.k.g.'s
PIP Postal Instant Press
The Pit Pros

Precision Tune
Rainbow International Carpet
  Dyeing & Cleaning Company
Rax Restaurants
Roy Rogers
Sara Care
Scandia Down Shops
Scottish Inns, Red Carpet Inn,
  Master Hosts Inns
Servpro
7-Eleven
Sounds Easy
Sport Shack
Spring-Green Lawn Care
Stained Glass Overlay
Steamatic
TacoTime
Travel Pros
Tuff-Kote Dinol
TV Scene
TV Tempo
United Consumers Club
The Weed Man
Wicks 'N' Sticks
World Bazaar
Zack's Famous Frozen Yogurt

RHODE ISLAND

Comprehensive Accounting
  Corporation
Corporate Finance Associates
Corporate Investment Business
  Brokers
Deck The Walls
Dunkin' Donuts
Eldorado Stone
Entré Computer Centers
First Optometry Eye Care Centers
Foliage Design Systems
Grand Slam USA.
The Ground Round
Gymboree
Holiday-Payless Rent-A-Car
HouseMaster of America
I Can't Believe It's Yogurt
Just Pants
Little Professor Book Centers
Long John Silver's Seafood
  Shoppes
Mail Boxes Etc. USA
Meineke Discount Mufflers

Miracle-Ear
Miracle Method
Money Mailer
Mr. Build
One Hour Moto-Photo
Packy the Shipper
P&D/Premier Auto Parts
Pearle Vision Centers
PIP Postal Instant Press
Precision Tune
Rainbow International Carpet
  Dyeing & Cleaning Company
Scandia Down Shops
Scottish Inns, Red Carpet Inn,
  Master Hosts Inns
Servpro
7-Eleven
Slender Center
Sounds Easy
Spring-Green Lawn Care
Steamatic
TacoTime
Travel Pros

TriMark
TV Scene
TV Tempo
United Consumers Club

The Weed Man
Wicks 'N' Sticks
World Bazaar
Zack's Famous Frozen Yogurt

SOUTH CAROLINA

Athletic Attic
Blimpie
Bojangles'
Coast to Coast Total Hardware
Comprehensive Accounting
    Corporation
Corporate Finance Associates
Corporate Investment Business
    Brokers
Create-A-Book
Dairy Queen
Debit One Mobile Bookkeeping
Deck The Walls
Docktor Pet Centers
Dr. Vinyl
Dunkin' Donuts
Eldorado Stone
Entré Computer Centers
Flowerama
Foremost Sales Promotions
Grand Slam USA
Gymboree
HairCrafters
Health Force
Holiday-Payless Rent-A-Car
HouseMaster of America
I Can't Believe It's Yogurt
Just Pants
KOA Kampgrounds of America
Little Professor Book Centers
Long John Silver's Seafood
    Shoppes
Mail Boxes Etc. USA
Meineke Discount Mufflers
Miracle-Ear

Miracle Method
Money Mailer
Mr. Build
One Hour Moto-Photo
Packy the Shipper
P&D/Premier Auto Parts
Pearle Vision Centers
P.k.g.'s
PIP Postal Instant Press
Precision Tune
Rainbow International Carpet
    Dyeing & Cleaning Company
Rax Restaurants
ROMAC
Sara Care
Scandia Down Shops
Scottish Inns, Red Carpet Inn,
    Master Hosts Inns
Service Personnel
Servpro
Sounds Easy
Sport Shack
Steamatic
Taco John's
TacoTime
Travel Pros
Tubby's Sub Shops
TV Scene
TV Tempo
UBI Business Brokers
United Consumers Club
Wicks 'N' Sticks
The Window Man
World Bazaar
Zack's Famous Frozen Yogurt

SOUTH DAKOTA

Budget Tapes & Records
Coast to Coast Total Hardware
ColorTyme
Comprehensive Accounting
    Corporation
Corporate Finance Associates
Corporate Investment Business
    Brokers
Create-A-Book

Deck The Walls
Eldorado Stone
Entré Computer Centers
The Ground Round
Happy Joe's Pizza & Ice Cream
    Parlors
HouseMaster of America
I Can't Believe It's Yogurt
KOA Kampgrounds of America

Langenwalter Dye Concept
Little Professor Book Centers
Long John Silver's Seafood
  Shoppes
Meineke Discount Mufflers
M.G.M. Liquor Warehouse
Miracle-Ear
Miracle Method
Nitro-Green Professional Lawn and
  Tree Care
Packy the Shipper
P&D/Premier Auto Parts
Pearle Vision Centers
PIP Postal Instant Press

Precision Tune
Rainbow International Carpet
  Dyeing & Cleaning Company
ROMAC
Servpro
Sounds Easy
Sport Shack
Steamatic
Taco del Sol
Taco John's
TacoTime
TV Tempo
Wicks 'N' Sticks
Zack's Famous Frozen Yogurt

TENNESSEE

Athletic Attic
Blimpie
Bojangles'
Coast to Coast Total Hardware
Comprehensive Accounting
  Corporation
Corporate Finance Associates
Corporate Investment Business
  Brokers
Create-A-Book
Dairy Queen
Debit One Mobile Bookkeeping
Deck The Walls
Dr. Vinyl
Duds 'N Suds
Dunkin' Donuts
Eldorado Stone
Entré Computer Centers
Flowerama
Foliage Design Systems
Foremost Sales Promotions
Grand Slam USA
Gymboree
Health Force
Holiday-Payless Rent-A-Car
HouseMaster of America
I Can't Believe It's Yogurt
Just Pants
KOA Kampgrounds of America
Langenwalter Dye Concept
Little Professor Book Centers
Mail Boxes Etc. USA
Mazzio's Pizza
Meineke Discount Mufflers
Mifax

Miracle Method
Money Mailer
One Hour Moto-Photo
Packy the Shipper
P&D/Premier Auto Parts
Pearle Vision Centers
PIP Postal Instant Press
P.k.g.'s
Precision Tune
Rainbow International Carpet
  Dyeing & Cleaning Company
Rax Restaurants
Sara Care
Scandia Down Shops
Scottish Inns, Red Carpet Inn,
  Master Hosts Inns
Service Personnel
Servpro
Sounds Easy
Sport Shack
Stained Glass Overlay
Steamatic
Taco John's
TacoTime
Travel Pros
TriMark
Tubby's Sub Shops
TV Scene
TV Tempo
UBI Business Brokers
Wicks 'N' Sticks
The Window Man
World Bazaar
Zack's Famous Frozen Yogurt

TEXAS

Athletic Attic
Blimpie
Budget Tapes & Records
Coast to Coast Total Hardware
Comprehensive Accounting
  Corporation
Corporate Investment Business
  Brokers
Create-A-Book
Dairy Queen
Debit One Mobile Bookkeeping
Deck The Walls
Dr. Vinyl
Duds 'N Suds
Dunkin' Donuts
Eldorado Stone
Entré Computer Centers
Flowerama
Foliage Design Systems
Grand Slam USA
Great Clips
Gymboree
HairCrafters
Hardee's
Health Force
HouseMaster of America
I Can't Believe It's Yogurt
Island Snow Hawaii
Just Pants
K-Bob's
KOA Kampgrounds of America
Little Professor Book Centers
MAACO Auto Painting &
  Bodyworks
Mail Boxes Etc. USA
Mazzio's Pizza
Meineke Discount Mufflers
M.G.M. Liquor Warehouse
Miracle Auto Painting & Body
  Repair

Miracle-Ear
Miracle Method
Mr. Build
Nitro-Green Professional Lawn and
  Tree Care
One Hour Moto-Photo
Papa Aldo's Take & Bake Pizza
  Shops
P&D/Premier Auto Parts
Pearle Vision Centers
PIP Postal Instant Press
The Pit Pros
P.k.g.'s
Precision Tune
PrintMasters
Rax Restaurants
ROMAC
Sara Care
Scandia Down Shops
Schlotzsky's
Scottish Inns, Red Carpet Inn,
  Master Hosts Inns
Service Personnel
Servpro
Sounds Easy
Sport Shack
Spring-Green Lawn Care
Steamatic
Taco John's
TacoTime
Travel Pros
Travel ServicentreS
TriMark
TV Scene
TV Tempo
UBI Business Brokers
United Consumers Club
Wicks 'N' Sticks
World Bazaar
Zack's Famous Frozen Yogurt

UTAH

Athletic Attic
Blimpie
Budget Tapes & Records
Coast to Coast Total Hardware
ColorTyme
Comprehensive Accounting
  Corporation
Corporate Investment Business
  Brokers

Debit One Mobile Bookkeeping
Deck The Walls
Duds 'N Suds
Eldorado Stone
Foliage Design Systems
Grand Slam USA
Gymboree
HouseMaster of America
I Can't Believe It's Yogurt

K-Bob's
KOA Kampgrounds of America
Little Professor Book Centers
Mail Boxes Etc. USA
Meineke Discount Mufflers
Miracle Auto Painting & Body
  Repair
Miracle-Ear
Miracle Method
Money Mailer
Mr. Build
Nitro-Green Professional Lawn and
  Tree Care
One Hour Moto-Photo
Packy the Shipper
Papa Aldo's Take & Bake Pizza
  Shops
P&D/Premier Auto Parts
Pearle Vision Centers
PIP Postal Instant Press

Precision Tune
Rainbow International Carpet
  Dyeing & Cleaning Company
Rax Restaurants
ROMAC
Sara Care
Scandia Down Shops
Servpro
Sounds Easy
Steamatic
Taco John's
TacoTime
Travel Pros
TriMark
TV Tempo
UBI Business Brokers
Wicks 'N' Sticks
World Bazaar
Zack's Famous Frozen Yogurt

VERMONT

Athletic Attic
Comprehensive Accounting
  Corporation
Corporate Finance Associates
Corporate Investment Business
  Brokers
Dairy Queen
Deck The Walls
Duds 'N Suds
Eldorado Stone
Grand Slam USA
The Ground Round
Gymboree
HouseMaster of America
I Can't Believe It's Yogurt
KOA Kampgrounds of America
Little Professor Book Centers
Long John Silver's Seafood
  Shoppes
Mail Boxes Etc. USA
Meineke Discount Mufflers
Miracle-Ear
Miracle Method
Mr. Build
One Hour Moto-Photo
Packy the Shipper

P&D/Premier Auto Parts
Pearle Vision Centers
PIP Postal Instant Press
Rainbow International Carpet
  Dyeing & Cleaning Company
Rax Restaurants
Roy Rogers
Sara Care
Scandia Down Shops
Scottish Inns, Red Carpet Inns,
  Master Hosts Inns
Servpro
Sounds Easy
Stained Glass Overlay
Steamatic
TacoTime
Travel Pros
Travel ServicenterS
Tuff-Kote Dinol
TV Scene
TV Tempo
The Weed Man
Wicks 'N' Sticks
World Bazaar
Zack's Famous Frozen Yogurt

VIRGINIA

Athletic Attic
Bojangles'

Coast to Coast Total Hardware

Comprehensive Accounting
  Corporation
Corporate Finance Associates
Corporate Investment Business
  Brokers
Create-A-Book
Debit One Mobile Bookkeeping
Deck The Walls
Dr. Vinyl
Dunkin' Donuts
Eldorado Stone
Flowerama
Grand Slam USA
The Ground Round
Gymboree
HairCrafters
Health Force
Holiday-Payless Rent-A-Car
HouseMaster of America
I Can't Believe It's Yogurt
KOA Kampgrounds of America
Little Professor Book Centers
Mail Boxes Etc. USA
Meineke Discount Mufflers
Mifax
Miracle-Ear
Miracle Method
Mr. Build
One Hour Moto-Photo

Packy the Shipper
Pearle Vision Centers
PIP Postal Instant Press
Precision Tune
Rainbow International Carpet
  Dyeing & Cleaning Company
Rax Restaurants
Roy Rogers
Scandia Down Shops
Schlotzsky's
Scottish Inns, Red Carpet Inns,
  Master Hosts Inns
Servpro
7-Eleven
Slender Care
Sounds Easy
Stained Glass Overlay
Steamatic
Taco John's
TacoTime
Travel Pros
TriMark
TV Scene
TV Tempo
UBI Business Brokers
Wicks 'N' Sticks
The Window Man
World Bazaar
Zack's Famous Frozen Yogurt

WASHINGTON

Athletic Attic
Boston Pizza
Budget Tapes & Records
Coast to Coast Total Hardware
Comprehensive Accounting
  Corporation
Corporate Finance Associates
Corporate Investment Business
  Brokers
Create-A-Book
Deck The Walls
Dunkin' Donuts
Eldorado Stone
Fleet Feet
Foliage Design Systems
Grand Slam USA
Gymboree
HairCrafters
HouseMaster of America
I Can't Believe It's Yogurt

Kits Cameras
KOA Kampgrounds of America
Little Professor Book Centers
MAACO Auto Painting &
  Bodyworks
Mail Boxes Etc. USA
Meineke Discount Mufflers
Mifax
Miracle Auto Painting & Body
  Repair
Miracle-Ear
Miracle Method
Money Mailer
Mr. Build
Nitro-Green Professional Lawn and
  Tree Care
One Hour Moto-Photo
Packy the Shipper
Papa Aldo's Take & Bake Pizza
  Shops

P&D/Premier Auto Parts
Pearle Vision Centers
PIP Postal Instant Press
Precision Tune
Rainbow International Carpet
    Dyeing & Cleaning Company
Rax Restaurants
ROMAC
Schlotzsky's
Scottish Inns, Red Carpet Inn,
    Master Hosts Inns
Servpro
7-Eleven

Sounds Easy
Sport Shack
Stained Glass Overlay
Steamatic
Taco John's
Travel Pros
TriMark
TV Tempo
UBI Business Brokers
United Consumer Club
The Weed Man
Wicks 'N' Sticks
Zack's Famous Frozen Yogurt

WEST VIRGINIA

Athletic Attic
Coast to Coast Total Hardware
Comprehensive Accounting
    Corporation
Corporate Finance Associates
Corporate Investment Business
    Brokers
Dairy Queen
Debit One Mobile Bookkeeping
Deck The Walls
Dr. Vinyl
Duds 'N Suds
Dunkin' Donuts
Eldorado Stone
Flowerama
Grand Slam USA
The Ground Round
Gymboree
HairCrafters
HouseMaster of America
I Can't Believe It's Yogurt
KOA Kampgrounds of America
Little Professor Book Centers
Mail Boxes Etc. USA
Mazzio's Pizza
Meineke Discount Mufflers
Miracle-Ear
Miracle Method
Money Mailer

Mr. Build
One Hour Moto-Photo
Packy the Shipper
P&D/Premier Auto Parts
Pearle Vision Centers
PIP Postal Instant Press
P.k.g.'s
Precision Tune
Rainbow International Carpet
    Dyeing & Cleaning Company
Rax Restaurants
Sara Care
Scandia Down Shops
Scottish Inns, Red Carpet Inn,
    Master Hosts Inns
Servpro
Sounds Easy
Stained Glass Overlay
Steamatic
Taco John's
TacoTime
Travel Pros
TriMark
TV Scene
TV Tempo
Wicks 'N' Sticks
World Bazaar
Zack's Famous Frozen Yogurt

WISCONSIN

Athletic Attic
Coast to Coast Total Hardware
Comprehensive Accounting
    Corporation
Corporate Finance Associates

Dairy Queen
Debit One Mobile Bookkeeping
Deck The Walls
Docktor Pet Centers
Dr. Vinyl

Duds 'N Suds
Dunkin' Donuts
Flowerama
Foliage Design Systems
Foremost Sales Promotions
Grand Slam USA
Great Clips
The Ground Round
HairCrafters
Happy Joe's Pizza & Ice Cream
   Parlors
H&R Block
I Can't Believe It's Yogurt
Just Pants
Little Professor Book Centers
Long John Silver's Seafood
   Shoppes
Meineke Discount Mufflers
M.G.M. Liquor Warehouse
Miracle-Ear
Miracle Method
Money Mailer
One Hour Moto-Photo
Packy the Shipper
Pearle Vision Centers
PIP Postal Instant Press
The Pit Pros

P.k.g.'s
Precision Tune
Rainbow International Carpet
   Dyeing & Cleaning Company
Rax Restaurants
Sara Care
Scandia Down Shops
Schlotzsky's
Scottish Inns, Red Carpet Inn,
   Master Hosts Inns
Servpro
Slender Care
Sounds Easy
Sport Shack
Spring-Green Lawn Care
Stained Glass Overlay
Steamatic
Taco John's
TacoTime
Travel Pros
TriMark
Tuff-Kote Dinol
TV Scene
Wicks 'N' Sticks
World Bazaar
Zack's Famous Frozen Yogurt

WYOMING

Budget Tapes & Records
Coast to Coast Total Hardware
ColorTyme
Comprehensive Accounting
   Corporation
Corporate Finance Associates
Corporate Investment Business
   Brokers
Dairy Queen
Debit One Mobile Bookkeeping
Deck The Walls
Dr. Vinyl
Duds 'N Suds
Dunkin' Donuts
Eldorado Stone
Flowerama
Foliage Design Systems
Foremost Sales Promotions
HouseMaster of America
I Can't Believe It's Yogurt
K-Bob's

Little Professor Book Centers
Long John silver's Seafood
   Shoppes
Mail Boxes Etc. USA
Meineke Discount Mufflers
Miracle-Ear
Miracle Method
Nitro-Green Professional Lawn and
   Tree Care
One Hour Moto-Photo
Packy the Shipper
Papa Aldo's Take & Bake Pizza
   Shops
P&D/Premier Auto Parts
Pearle Vision Centers
PIP Postal Instant Press
Precision Tune
Rainbow International Carpet
   Dyeing & Cleaning Company
ROMAC
Sara Care

Scandia Down Shops
Servpro
Sounds Easy
Steamatic
Taco del Sol

Taco John's
TacoTime
TV Tempo
Wicks 'N' Sticks
Zack's Famous Frozen Yogurt

THROUGHOUT UNITED STATES

American International Rent A Car
American Speedy Printing Centers
Baskin-Robbins Ice Cream
   Company
Bath Genie
Brownies Fried Chicken
Century 21
Chem-Dry
Command Performance
Dial One
Diet Center
Dunhill Personnel
Duraclean
Endrust
Fantastic Sam's
Gelato Classico Italian Ice Cream
Grease Monkey
Help-U-Sell
Holiday Inn
In 'N' Out Food Stores
Jani-King
Kwik-Kopy Printing
Lincoln Log Homes
Lindal Cedar Homes
McDonald's
The Maids International
Management Recruiters
   International
The Medicine Shoppe
Merry Maids

MicroAge Computer Stores
Molly Maid
Nation-wide General Rental
   Centers
National Video
Norrell
Paul Davis Systems
Pizza Inn
Putt-Putt Golf Courses
RainSoft Water Conditioning
   Company
Realty World
RE/MAX
Rent-A-Dent
Second Sole
Security Alliance
ServiceMaster
Sheraton Inns
Sir Speedy Printing Centers
Sport-About
Spring Crest Drapery Centers
Suddenly Slender, *The* Body Wrap
   & Health Center
Sunshine Polishing Systems
Sylvan Learning Centers
U.S. Tech
Uniforce Temporary Services
Uniglobe Travel
Wendy's
Ziebart

Areas Outside the United States

AFRICA

Bath Genie
Brownies Fried Chicken
Century 21
Chem-Dry
Corporate Investment Business
   Brokers
Diet Center
Duraclean
Eldorado Stone
Endrust

Fantastic Sam's
Grease Monkey
Holiday Inn
Ice Cream Churn
In 'N' Out Food Stores
Kwik-Kopy Printing
Lincoln Log Homes
Lindal Cedar Homes
Management Recruiters
   International

Molly Maid
Pizza Inn
Putt-Putt Golf Courses
RainSoft Water Conditioning
   Company
Realty World
Security Alliance
Servpro

Sheraton Inns
Spring Crest Drapery Centers
Suddenly Slender
Sunshine Polishing Systems
Travel Pros
Zack's Famous Frozen Yogurt
Ziebart

ASIA

Baskin-Robbins Ice Cream
   Company
Bath Genie
Brownies Fried Chicken
Century 21
Chem-Dry
Corporate Finance Associates
Corporate Investment Business
   Brokers
Diet Center
Dunkin' Donuts
Duraclean
Eldorado Stone
Endrust
Fantastic Sam's
Grease Monkey
Holiday Inn
Ice Cream Churn
In 'N' Out Food Stores
Lincoln Log Homes
Lindal Cedar Homes

McDonald's
Management Recruiters
   International
Miracle Method
Molly Maid
Pizza Inn
Putt-Putt Golf Courses
RainSoft Water Conditioning
   Company
Realty World
Security Alliance Corporation
Servpro
Sheraton Inns
Sir Speedy Printing Centers
Suddenly Slender
Sunshine Polishing Systems
Travel Pros
UBI Business Brokers
Zack's Famous Frozen Yogurt
Ziebart

AUSTRALIA

Baskin-Robbins Ice Cream
   Company
Bath Genie
Brownies Fried Chicken
Boston Pizza
Century 21
Chem-Dry
Corporate Finance Associates
Corporate Investment Business
   Brokers
Dial One
Diet Center
Duds 'N Suds
Dunkin' Donuts
Duraclean
Eldorado Stone
Endrust
Entré Computer Centers
Fantastic Sam's
Foliage Design Systems
Gelato Classico Italian Ice Cream

Grease Monkey
Help-U-Sell
Holiday Inn
HouseMaster of America
Ice Cream Churn
In 'N' Out Food Stores
Island Snow Hawaii
Jani-King
Kwik-Kopy Printing
Lincoln Log Homes
Lindal Cedar Homes
McDonald's
The Maids International
Management Recruiters
   International
Miracle Method
Molly Maid
Money Mailer
PIP Postal Instant Press
Pizza Inn
Putt-Putt Golf Courses

RainSoft Water Conditioning
   Company
Realty World
Sara Care
Security Alliance Corporation
ServiceMaster
Servpro
Sheraton Inns
Sir Speedy Printing Centers

Spring Crest Drapery Centers
Steamatic
Suddenly Slender
Sunshine Polishing Systems
Sylvan Learning Center
Travel Pros
The Weed Man
Zack's Famous Frozen Yogurt
Ziebart

CANADA

American International Rent A Car
American Speedy Printing Centers
Baskin-Robbins Ice Cream
   Company
Bath Genie
Blimpie
Boston Pizza
Century 21
Chem-Dry
Corporate Investment Business
   Brokers
Create-A-Book
Dial One
Diet Center
Duds 'N Suds
Dunhill Personnel
Dunkin' Donuts
Duraclean
Eldorado Stone
Endrust
Entré Computer Centers
Fantastic Sam's
Foliage Design Systems
Gelato Classico Italian Ice Cream
Grease Monkey
The Ground Round
Gymboree
HairCrafters
Help-U-Sell
Holiday Inn
Holiday-Payless Rent-A-Car
HouseMaster of America
I Can't Believe It's Yogurt
Ice Cream Churn
In 'N' Out Food Stores
Island Snow Hawaii
Jani-King
Kwik-Kopy Printing
Langenwalter Dye Concept
Lincoln Log Homes

Lindal Cedar Homes
Long John Silver's Seafood
   Shoppes
McDonald's
The Maids International
Management Recruiters
   International
Meineke Discount Mufflers
Merry Maids
MicroAge Computer Stores
Miracle Method
Molly Maid
Money Mailer
National Video
Norrell
Papa Aldo's Take & Bake Pizza
   Shops
Paul Davis Systems
Pearle Vision Centers
PIP Postal Instant Press
Pizza Inn
Precision Tune
Putt-Putt Golf Courses
Rainbow International Carpet
   Dyeing & Cleaning Company
RainSoft Water Conditioning
   Company
RE/MAX
Realty World
Sara Care
Security Alliance Corporation
ServiceMaster
Sheraton Inns
Sir Speedy Printing Centers
Spring Crest Drapery Centers
Steamatic
Suddenly Slender
Sunshine Polishing Systems
Sylvan Learning Center
TacoTime

Travel Pros
Tuff-Kote Dinol
Uniforce Temporary Services
Uniglobe Travel
United Consumers Club

The Weed Man
Wendy's
Wicks 'N' Sticks
Zack's Famous Frozen Yogurt
Ziebart

CARIBBEAN

American International Rent A Car

EGYPT

Happy Joe's Pizza & Ice Cream
    Parlors

EUROPE

Baskin-Robbins Ice Cream
    Company
Bath Genie
Blimpie
Boston Pizza
Century 21
Chem-Dry
Command Performance
Corporate Finance Associates
Corporate Investment Business
    Brokers
Dial One
Diet Center
Duds 'N Suds
Duraclean
Eldorado Stone
Endrust
Entré Computer Centers
Fantastic Sam's
Gelato Classico Italian Ice Cream
Grease Monkey
Gymboree
Holiday Inn
Ice Cream Churn
In 'N' Out Food Stores
Island Snow Hawaii
Jani-King
Lincoln Log Homes
Lindal Cedar Homes

McDonald's
Management Recruiters
MicroAge Computer Stores
Miracle Method
Molly Maid
One Hour Moto-Photo
Pearle Vision Centers
PIP Postal Instant Press
Pizza Inn
Precision Tune
Putt-Putt Golf Courses
Rainbow International Carpet
    Dyeing & Cleaning Company
RainSoft Water Conditioning
    Company
Realty World
Security Alliance
ServiceMaster
Sheraton Inns
Spring Crest Drapery Centers
Steamatic
Suddenly Slender
Sunshine Polishing Systems
TacoTime
Travel Pros
UBI Business Brokers
The Weed Man
Zack's Famous Frozen Yogurt
Ziebart

INDIA

Duds 'N Suds

JAPAN

Athletic Attic
Baskin-Robbins Ice Cream
    Company
Bath Genie
Boston Pizza
Century 21

Chem-Dry
Command Performance
Corporate Finance Associates
Corporate Investment Business
    Brokers
Dial One

Diet Center
Duds 'N Suds
Dunkin' Donuts
Duraclean
Eldorado Stone
Endrust
Fantastic Sam's
Gelato Classico Italian Ice Cream
Grease Monkey
Gymboree
Holiday Inn
Ice Cream Churn
In 'N' Out Food Stores
Island Snow Hawaii
Jani-King
Lincoln Log Homes
Lindal Cedar Homes
McDonald's
Management Recruiters
  International
Merry Maids
Molly Maid
Money Mailer

Mr. Build
Pearle Vision Centers
PIP Postal Instant Press
Pizza Inn
Precision Tune
Putt-Putt Golf Courses
Rainbow International Carpet
  Dyeing & Cleaning Company
RainSoft Water Conditioning
  Company
Realty World
Sara Care
Security Alliance
ServiceMaster
Sheraton Inns
Sir Speedy Printing Centers
Steamatic
Suddenly Slender
Sunshine Polishing Systems
TacoTime
Travel Pros
Zack's Famous Frozen Yogurt
Ziebart

MALAYSIA   Chem-Dry

MEXICO

Bath Genie
Brownies Fried Chicken
Century 21
Chem-Dry
Corporate Finance Associates
Corporate Investment Business
  Brokers
Diet Center
Duraclean
Eldorado Stone
Endrust
Fantastic Sam's
Grease Monkey
Holiday Inn
Ice Cream Churn
In 'N' Out Food Stores
Lincoln Log Homes
Lindal Cedar Homes
McDonald's

Management Recruiters
  International
Miracle Method
Molly Maid
PIP Postal Instant Press
Pizza Inn
Putt-Putt Golf Courses
RainSoft Water Conditioning
  Company
Realty World
Security Alliance
Sheraton Inns
Sir Speedy Printing Centers
Steamatic
Suddenly Slender
Sunshine Polishing Systems
Zack's Famous Frozen Yogurt
Ziebart

NEW ZEALAND   Athletic Attic   Chem-Dry

PUERTO RICO   Comprehensive Accounting
                    Corporation

SOUTH AMERICA

Bath Genie
Brownies Fried Chicken
Century 21
Chem-Dry
Corporate Finance Associates
Corporate Investment Business
　Brokers
Diet Center
Dunkin' Donuts
Duraclean
Eldorado Stone
Endrust
Fantastic Sam's
Grease Monkey
Holiday Inn
Ice Cream Churn
In 'N' Out Food Store
Lincoln Log Homes

Lindal Cedar Homes
McDonald's
Management Recruiters
　International
Miracle Method
Molly Maid
Pizza Inn
Putt-Putt Golf Courses
RainSoft Water Conditioning
　Company
Realty World
Security Alliance Corp.
Sheraton Inns
Steamatic
Suddenly Slender
Sunshine Polishing Systems
Zack's Famous Frozen Yogurt
Ziebart

SOUTH PACIFIC

Ziebart

TAIWAN

Fantastic Sam's